ROBERT LOUIS STEVENSON

COLLECTED POEMS

ROBERT LOUIS STEVENSON

COLLECTED POEMS

SECOND EDITION

Edited, with an Introduction and Notes, by
JANET ADAM SMITH

NEW YORK   THE VIKING PRESS

First published in England by Rupert Hart-Davis Ltd. 1950

Second edition Copyright © 1971 by Janet Adam Smith

All rights reserved
Published in 1971 by The Viking Press, Inc.
625 Madison Avenue, New York, N.Y. 10022

SBN 670–22909–1
Library of Congress catalog card number: 79–144343

Printed and bound in Great Britain

CONTENTS

POEMS 1869–1879

[5]

91884

CONTENTS

CONTENTS

PIECES IN LALLAN

UNDERWOODS

BOOK I: IN ENGLISH

[7]

CONTENTS

[8]

CONTENTS

[9]

CONTENTS

CONTENTS

[11]

POEMS 1880–1894

CONTENTS

[13]

CONTENTS

CONTENTS

LIGHT VERSE

[15]

CONTENTS

POEMS FOR CHILDREN

A CHILD'S GARDEN OF VERSES

CONTENTS

CONTENTS

CONTENTS

CONTENTS

[20]

CONTENTS

INTRODUCTION

I

WE enjoy Stevenson's poetry when we are young and full of emotion about situations that we have not yet experienced in real life. Some of his lyrics perfectly catch the gestures and moods of youth—the actual moods and the wished-for gestures. The verses of 'Youth and Love' chime in with our romantic longings for adventure and noble renunciation. 'Blows the wind today' moves us to tears for a lost home and a lost youth when our own childhood is only just round the corner. 'Under the wide and starry sky' satisfies our aspirations for beautiful and heroic death. The witty, the conversational, the narrative pieces are slid over in our search for lines that crystallise our own airy, turbulent moods.

To readers whose taste in poetry does not develop after adolescence, these lyrics of Stevenson's remain entirely satisfying: he has expressed some moods perfectly, and it is these moods that such readers associate in their minds with poetry. But the readers who are constantly enlarging their field tend to leave Stevenson behind with their own adolescence. The poems may be remembered with the deprecatory affection we give to outgrown enthusiasms, but they have ceased to be relevant. And, along with the poems that once expressed our deepest yearnings, are dismissed all the other poems that a youthful taste passed over. Stevenson, as a poet, is written off by many a sensitive and intelligent reader because the sentiment and language of his most familiar poems are out of tune with contemporary moods.

[23]

A generation that knows too much about death and killing may be forgiven for finding a ring of smugness about

> Glad did I live and gladly die,
> And I laid me down with a will

and for suspecting that the author of the lines was a cheerful nineteenth-century progressive who brushed aside real suffering in order to strike a heroic note. (The poem, in fact, was written when Stevenson was miserably ill and poor in San Francisco.) When a critic reproached him for his 'voluntary aversion from the painful sides of life,' Stevenson admitted the limitation; but said it was deliberate. 'The sufferings of life,' he answered, 'may be handled by the very greatest in their hours of insight; it is of its pleasures that our common poems should be formed.'

In his verse, as in his prose, Stevenson has sometimes been unlucky in his admirers. The passionate Stevensonian is not always discriminating, and the implicit attitude of the editors of his posthumously published poems was that every scrap of Stevenson's verse was valuable. When a writer has become the object of a cult, as Burns and Stevenson have, a resistance is set up in readers outside the circle. They suspect, often rightly, that the devotees accept their favourite without reservation, and tend to judge him by special standards, instead of applying the same standards to him and to his contemporaries. In reaction, other readers refuse to treat the object of the cult as a serious writer at all. Criticism of Burns and Stevenson is always in danger of becoming an affair of patriotism (Scotland v. England), of local patriotism (Edinburgh v. Glasgow, or Edinburgh v. Ayrshire), or of personal feelings about the writer.

This new collection of Stevenson's poems will, I hope, stimulate some real criticism, and encourage readers to take Stevenson's poetry seriously—not solemnly. To do this, it is important to find out what kind of poems he was trying to write, what sort of a poet he wanted to be. To make a start, we might look at some of the poets he admired. For his earliest poems he had many models:

> *Cain*, an epic, was (save the mark!) an imitation of *Sordello*: *Robin Hood*, a tale in verse, took an eclectic middle course among the fields of Keats, Chaucer and Morris: in *Monmouth*, a tragedy, I reclined on the bosom of Mr Swinburne; in my innumerable gouty-footed lyrics I followed many masters; in the first draft of *The King's Pardon*, a tragedy, I was on the trail of no lesser man than John Webster; in the second draft of the same piece, with staggering versatility, I had shifted my allegiance to Congreve.*

He tried his hand at versions of Heine and Baudelaire; he wrote essays on Charles d'Orléans, Béranger and Villon. At twenty-two he discovered Whitman, and pressed his enthusiasm on his friends.

But the poets to whom he came back most often in his letters, and with most affection, were Horace, Martial and Herrick—all masters of occasional verse. And Stevenson's aim in much of his poetry is to find the right words for an occasion—a birthday, a parting, a gift, a death, a letter, a rejoicing. The situation already exists: the poet finds the happiest words for it. 'It is not so much the thing they say, as the way they say it,' Stevenson wrote, in an early letter,† of Horace and Pope: 'The dicta are often trivial and commonplace, or so undeniably true as to become part of orthodox boredom; but when you find an idea put in either of them, *it is put in its optimum form.*' The occasion

---

* *A College Magazine: Memories and Portraits*, 1887.

† Letter to R. A. M. Stevenson, September 1868, printed in the Catalogue of the sale of Stevenson Letters at Christie's, 11 July, 1922.

fully matched, the commonplace said as well as it could be: this was certainly one of his aims in writing poetry.

Stevenson certainly did not lack the qualities of creative imagination; but they went mainly into his prose. It was stories, not poems, that rushed up from his subconscious mind and possessed him till he gave them form. *Olalla* came to him in a dream, as did *Jekyll and Hyde*; a landscape, a situation, a mood could set up reverberations in his imagination that harried him to produce a story to express their essence. Stevenson had a poet's imagination, a poet's capacity for creating myths and images to correspond to experiences below the level of conscious feeling; but it worked in his stories. 'A person with a poetic character and no poetic talent' he described himself at twenty-three; 'just as my prose muse has all the ways of a poetic one.' *The Merry Men, The Beach of Falesá, Weir of Hermiston* were conceived with imagination at white heat: the poetry, by contrast, was conceived on a wholly conscious level, with the reason—and the ear—in complete control. Certainly, after his twenty-fifth year, the stories had first claim on his nervous energy: it was usually when he was not fit for sustained work—for the imaginative effort, or the physical effort of writing—that he turned to verse. Many of the rhymes for *A Child's Garden of Verses* were composed when he was on his back in a dark room at Hyères, with a hæmorrhage; and his step-daughter Isobel Strong noted at Vailima that 'he generally fills in his convalescence with poetry.' It was while illness kept him from work on *Weir* that he produced the series of verses on the Vailima household. His close friends, wrote Sir Edmund Gosse,* always associated his poetry with his illness, and so found something 'sorrowful and patient' even in the most cheerful of the songs.

Stevenson himself made no great claims for his poetry:

* Pentland Edition of Stevenson's Works, Vol. XIII.

'a kind of prose Herrick, divested of the gift of verse, and you behold the Bard.' Writing about his poems, his tone was hesitant. 'I am a weak brother in verse,' he wrote to Henley in 1879 about 'Our Lady of the Snows': 'you ask me to re-write things that I have already managed just to write with the skin of my teeth. If I don't re-write them, it's because I don't see how to write them better, not because I don't think they should be.' And returning proofs to Scribner's for a proposed volume of poems, in 1890, he was full of doubts.

> The deuce is in this volume. It has cost me more botheration and dubiety than any other I ever took in hand. On one thing my mind is made up: the verses at the end have no business there, and throw them down. Many of them are bad, many of the rest want nine years keeping, and the remainder are not relevant—throw them down; some I never want to hear of more, others will grow in time towards decent items in a second *Underwoods*—and in the meanwhile, down with them! At the same time, I have a sneaking idea the ballads are not altogether without merit—I don't know if they're poetry, but they're good narrative, or I'm deceived.

There is no need to let Stevenson's self-depreciation blind us to what he did achieve. He was a master of the occasional poem—and his range of occasions was far wider than for most of those who have excelled in the genre. The lyric that pins down a mood, the epistle that conveys the quality of friendship, the lines that are a charming gesture of welcome or good-bye, the squibs that exactly bring back a shared joke or escapade—Stevenson can do them all with grace and vitality. On more solemn occasions his touch may not always be so sure, and contemporary taste is likely to prefer his epistles to K. de M. and to Henry

James (in *Underwoods*) to the blank-verse lyrics to W. E. Henley and R. A. M. Stevenson, with their *thees* and *thous*, their uncomfortably heightened, consciously noble, language—conversation conducted in decently solemn voices, sentiments dressed in Sunday-best. He is more successful when he celebrates a solemn occasion with a more formal structure, as in the verses 'In Memoriam F. A. S.,' where the decent blacks have been exchanged for full mourning robes, a formal stanza is used, and there is no pretence at the personal rhythm of conversation.

The circumstances of Stevenson's life were rich in opportunities for his particular talent. There were island kings and princesses to be greeted in verse, as well as members of the Savile Club; long separations to be bridged over with the intimacies of doggerel or the rhyming epistle. This range of occasion was matched by a range of technique. We know from Stevenson's essays how passionately interested he was in the mechanics of writing—in the variety and subtlety of language, in the possibilities of sounds and rhythms. In his verse there is a strong element of experiment and virtuosity: he is testing what it feels like to write as Whitman, as Arnold (the poet of *The Strayed Reveller*); he is exploring the possibilities of English, and seeing if it can produce equivalents for Horatian alcaics, for French rondeaux. There is more than virtuosity in this; surely part of Stevenson's pleasure in writing poetry was in the element of play, in the dance of words and measures. Discussing the elements of style,* he noted that the prose-writer juggles with two oranges: he has to satisfy the demands of logic, he has to please the supersensual ear. The verse-writer has another orange to play with in his chosen pattern of prosody. 'All that we have a right to ask of any prosody,' he observed, 'is, that it shall lay down a pattern

* 'On Some Technical Elements of Style in Literature.' Edinburgh Edition, 1895. Vol. XI.

for the writer, and that what it lays down shall be neither too easy nor too hard.' Three oranges to juggle with instead of two; 'added difficulty, added beauty; and the pattern, with every fresh element, becoming more interesting in itself.'

What fascinated him above all in verse was the possibility of variation and counterpoint: variation within a rhythm, counterpoint where the poet now contrasts, and now combines, the double pattern of the texture of the sense, and of the verse; the line ending, but not the sentence; the sentence, but not the line; the two combining 'to reach their solution on the same ringing syllable.' This counterpoint can be greatly enjoyed in Stevenson's own octosyllabics, such as the poems to Henry James, Will Low and H. F. Brown in *Underwoods*, or the sequence on the Family in his later poems. 'Octosyllabics' is hardly correct; many of the poems have seven-syllable lines, the others have seven- and nine-syllable lines varying the regular eight; all, however, have four beats to a line. But the rhythm never clatters; there is no regular clop-clop as in Scott's octosyllabics. The line goes easy and lively; the rhymes do not mercilessly thump down; the form can be used for the conversational intimacy of the poem to Henry James, the descriptions of 'The Woodman' or 'The House of Tembinoka' (in *Songs of Travel*), for the argument of 'Our Lady of the Snows' or the statement of 'The Celestial Surgeon.' Though Stevenson only mentions him once or twice* it is very likely that the suppleness of his four-beat line was learnt in part from Marvell.

The play element comes out strongly in the verses in classical metres written at Davos, one result of the hours

* The line from Marvell's 'Bermudas,'

   Thus sang they in the English boat

appears on the title page of *An Inland Voyage*.

of smoky discussion with J. A. Symonds and Horatio Brown, when his interest in technique flared up again. It is particularly marked too in the poems in Scots. It was a very old game that Stevenson was playing in these poems, written in what we now call the Burns stanza: a game that started long before Burns, with Sir John Sempill's 'Elegy on Habbie Simpson, Piper of Kilbarchan' in the seventeenth century, with Allan Ramsay and James Beattie and Robert Fergusson. 'It is all a game of language,' W. P. Ker described it;* '"crambo-clink" with rules and patterns of its own, used for fun by men who wrote their serious business letters in English.' Stevenson wrote with conscious pleasure in the tradition: 'Robert Ramsay Fergusson Stevenson' he signed himself to Henry James, in a letter telling him about *Underwoods*, 'much of which will be cast in my native speech, that very dark oracular medium.' It was a medium admirably suited to the friendly or teasing epistle, to homely satire and pastoral. We get the satire in 'A Lowden Sabbath Morn,' the pastoral in 'When aince Aprile'; once or twice a pure lyric note, more like Fergusson than Burns, slips into the cheerful or humorous stanzas:

> The wind blaws clean about the cairn
> Wi' caller air;
> The muircock an' the barefit bairn
> Are happy there.

Stevenson shares more than the classic Scots stanza with Burns; he had something too of Burns's preoccupation with tunes. An air haunted him—a Scots tune, like 'Wandering Willie,' a melody of Schubert, a Gælic air—and he must find words for it. In a prefatory note to an edition of *Underwoods* published after his death, his wife described some of the verses she had found in his library, written out with the music: 'The Stormy Evening' ('Air after Oldfield'), 'We have Lived and Loved' ('Air after Diabelli,'

* 'The Politics of Burns': *Collected Essays of W. P. Ker*, Vol. I.

op. 168, No. 1), 'Over the Sea to Skye.' Mrs Stevenson
also printed an old Scots air, sent her by a correspondent,
that exactly matched 'The Spaewife.'

Yet for all the fun in them, I think it was in one or two
of the Scots poems that Stevenson came nearest to tapping
that intense dramatic imagination that is his power as a
novelist. In 'Sing me a Song of a Lad that is gone' he
wrote directly of lost youth : a commonplace idea, which he
tried to express 'in optimum form.' 'A Mile and a Bit-
tock' could also be said to be about lost youth; but instead
of stating the theme directly, Stevenson created one of his
clear-cut unforgettable scenes—three men walking back
and forth along a country road in the moonlight. The
picture is the emotional equivalent of the idea, and I find
the pathos and poetry inherent in the idea far more appar-
ent in the poem that creates the scene than in the more
direct lament of the song.

If we are looking for poetry that has mature passion and
mystery, that explores sensibility, that drills down into the
subconscious, we shall not come to Stevenson. But if we
care for the dance of sounds and meanings, for the verse
that, elegantly or humorously, can always rise to the re-
quired occasion, for the great commonplace made memorable
by style—then Stevenson has a great deal to offer. His
best-known poems may often have been in the mouths and
on the pens of the wrong people; that should not blind us
to the fact that they are extremely well written. Stevenson
is a minor poet; but with a range and technique that make
him far more interesting than other minor poets who were
his contemporaries, Henley, Dowson, Lionel Johnson.
The poet he can most easily be compared with is Hous-
man, whose own work is so full of echoes from Stevenson.
And it is interesting to speculate whether, if Stevenson's
poetry had been as rigorously selected as Housman's, he
might not have enjoyed the same order of reputation.

II

The poems published in Stevenson's lifetime presented no textual difficulties: I have followed the text of the first edition of *Underwoods*, *Ballads*, *A Child's Garden of Verses* and the hand-printed pamphlets later collected as *Moral Emblems*. For the *Songs of Travel*, collected by Stevenson shortly before his death, and prepared for the press by Sidney Colvin with some help from Edmund Gosse, I have followed the text of the first editions with one or two minor emendations (specified in the Notes) suggested by Gosse's set of proofs. But with the other posthumously published poems, the situation was clearly very different. Uneasy memories of a *hounded kebbock* that *mat* the *mud*, and of Johnie Adam aye *unsicken* on his feet, suggested that a collation with original manuscripts or facsimiles was essential. So I embarked on an attempt to round them all up.

The first few months of search produced very disappointing results. Extensive enquiries of libraries, salerooms and private collectors, both in this country and in the United States, yielded a scanty harvest of some half-dozen facsimiles of original manuscripts, and an almost total lack of information about the recent ownership of the manuscripts on which the three volumes published by the Bibliophile Society of Boston were based. Promising trails were followed from Boston to New York, Minneapolis, California, Texas and Berkeley Square, but they all petered out without any whiff of a manuscript. Then, in the spring of 1949, came the news that an important collection of Stevenson manuscripts was to be sold at Sotheby's. This collection, which had passed through several hands, contained the bulk of the manuscripts I was looking for; and thanks to the courtesy and consideration of Messrs Sotheby,

I was able to check the text of the poems before the two sales of the collection, in May and November 1949.

My scrutiny of these manuscripts led me to make a very careful examination of the volumes published by the Bibliophile Society of Boston in 1916 and 1921, and the volume of *New Poems* published by Chatto and Windus in 1918, in which the poems were first presented to English readers. Study of these involved me in the history of the Stevenson manuscripts not published in his lifetime, and a study of the various editions of these poems. I summarise the story below: because it is a demonstration of what can happen to a decent writer who has the misfortune to attract the less discriminating type of collector, and because the treatment of the poems, in manuscript and in print, perhaps explains in part the neglect of Stevenson's poetry today.

Stevenson died at Vailima in 1894, and in his will bequeathed his books, royalties and manuscripts, along with other effects and property, 'in life rent to my wife Fanny van de Grift or Osbourne or Stevenson, and in fee to her son Lloyd Osbourne.' Among these manuscripts were a number of note-books full of poems, most of them unpublished, and some manuscript poems on loose sheets. When Mrs Stevenson finally left Vailima in 1899 the manuscripts went with her to California: and on her death, in 1914, they passed to her daughter Isobel Strong,* who had lived with them at Vailima and to whom Stevenson had dictated much of his work. She decided to sell: and in the autumn of that year the Anderson Galleries, New York, announced a sale of autograph letters, original manuscripts, books, portraits and South Sea curios from the library of the late Robert Louis Stevenson—'consigned for unrestricted public sale by the present owner, Mrs Isobel Strong, of

---

* In view of the provisions of the will, I do not understand why the manuscripts did not go to Lloyd Osbourne on his mother's death.

Santa Barbara, California, who inherited it from her mother, Mrs R. L. Stevenson.' There were three sales of this material: on Nov. 23, 24 and 25, 1914; on Jan. 25, 26 and 27, 1915; on Feb. 16 and 17, 1916. A separate catalogue was issued for each sale. The words 'original manuscripts' appeared on the front cover of each catalogue, the introductory descriptions were, even by saleroom standards, quite enthusiastic—'by far the largest and most important collection of material relating to the late Robert Louis Stevenson that has ever come on the market'— attention was drawn to the note-books containing manuscript essays and verses, and the catalogues gave fairly full descriptions of individual items. No. 348 in the second sale, for instance, was described as—'Manuscript poems written on nine sheets of folio size and containing 16 pages in the handwriting of the author. All of the poems appear to be unpublished and all were written in his early manhood, probably in 1870. Many of them show the influence of Walt Whitman and are written in the same rugged, uneven form in which he wrote.'

At this point enter the collectors; and what happened at the sale is not quite clear. In a foreword to the two volumes of Stevenson poems published by the Bibliophile Society, Boston, in 1916,* Mr Henry H. Harper, treasurer of the Society, spoke of the members' debt to Mr George S. Hellman, the editor, 'who "unearthed" the major portion of these poems'—'unearthing' seems an odd word to use in connection with manuscripts that had been so fully catalogued—and to 'our generous fellow-member Mr Francis S. Peabody, who took up the option held on them by The Bibliophile Society, with the understanding that full permission be granted to print them for the members.' (Three

* *Poems by Robert Louis Stevenson: hitherto unpublished*, with Introduction and Notes by George S. Hellman. The Bibliophile Society. Printed for Members Only. 2 vols. Boston, 1916.

[34]

other collectors, Mr William Harris Arnold, Mr Edmund D. Brooks and Dr Roderick Terry were also thanked for providing, 'for the purpose of the present edition many extremely valuable manuscripts never before printed.') Mr Peabody, according to this account, comes in at a later stage than the actual sale. But in his note on the Stevenson manuscripts printed in the third Bibliophile Society volume,* Mr Harper assigns to Mr Peabody a more active role. 'There was, however, one vigilant Stevenson collector, in the person of Mr Francis S. Peabody, who bought a large part of the unpublished manuscript at the sale, and has since acquired most of the remainder.' It is Mr Harper himself who appears as the prime mover in the Report of the Council of the Bibliophile Society for 1923.

In 1915 Mr Harper, our Treasurer, bought a collection of about 120 unpublished holograph poems by Stevenson for a cash consideration of eighteen thousand dollars, including copyright privileges. These poems had previously been sold by the heirs of Robert Louis Stevenson, who in parting with them conveyed the rights of publication. These rights passed from Stevenson to his heirs by inheritance, and as no reservation was made, under the existing law they were conveyed to the purchaser with the title to the manuscripts. Shortly after purchasing these MSS. Mr Harper transferred them to his friend the late F. S. Peabody at the purchase price, reserving the publication rights for The Bibliophile Society.

Finally there is Mr Hellman's own version in *The True*

---

* *Poems by Robert Louis Stevenson, hitherto unpublished*, with Introduction and Notes by George S. Hellman and William P. Trent. The Bibliophile Society. Printed for Members Only. Boston, 1921.

*Stevenson.** He describes his astonishment, in examining the manuscripts, at discovering the 'very considerable number of unpublished poems that revealed Stevenson's youth in a manner left undescribed by any biographer and practically uncommented upon by any editor. Imagine, for instance, over one hundred pages of autobiographical verse, accompanied, as was item No. 304, by less than two inches of description, while so important an item as a blank book (No. 366) with its first drafts of a large group of poems published in *Underwoods,* showing variant forms of considerable significance in the study of Stevenson as a stylist, was, with its altogether unpublished verses, passed over with an inch of description. And so I might go on through the catalogue, pointing out how rich material in verse, letters, essays and fiction was offered with inadequate understanding of its importance.' (It might be retorted that the function of a sale catalogue is to describe what is actually there, and that it should be left to others to assess the significance of the items; by this standard the Anderson Galleries catalogue seems quite adequate. But one gets the impression that Mr Hellman, with his emphasis on inches, would have been satisfied with nothing less than bold capitals announcing STEVENSON: STARTLING REVELATIONS.) Horrified by this state of affairs, Mr Hellman proceeded to action. On the first day of the sale he bought one 'minor manuscript': next morning he went round to various 'confrères in the rare book business' and offered to buy manuscripts to be selected by him from those that they had purchased, at 50 per cent more than the sale price. They at once accepted, the same procedure was followed the next day, and though a few items were kept back for private collectors, Mr Hellman managed to get together almost all of Stevenson's unpublished poems.

Some time later Professor W. P. Trent of Columbia sent

* Boston, 1925.

Mr Hellman a list of Stevenson manuscripts belonging to
Mr F. S. Peabody of Chicago; and 'after I had reported to
Professor Trent that some of these items were unpublished
poems and that others were portions of manuscripts which
I had in their entirety, I was asked by the Bibliophile
Society of Boston to undertake the editing of Mr Pea-
body's manuscripts and my own, jointly.' And so over one
hundred new Stevenson poems were published in the two
volumes issued by the Bibliophile Society in 1916.

Thus the manuscripts were sold and published. Soon
after publication (again I quote from the Council's Report
for 1923) the Bibliophile Society 'received a peremptory
demand from one of the Stevenson heirs for the assignment
of our copyright to him; but when it was discovered that
we could not be "bluffed" into surrendering our legal rights
the demand was softened into a polite request that we per-
mit the poems to be republished in the interest of litera-
ture.'

Mr Hellman in his narrative records a visit to him from
Mr Charles Scribner (of the firm which published Steven-
son in America) questioning the ethics of a Stevenson
publication without prior consent of the heirs, and this was
followed up by an interview with Lloyd Osbourne. He,
too, felt he should have been consulted in the matter of
publication: but the interview was concluded on a friendly
note, and when, in 1918, Chatto and Windus published
New Poems, an edition for the English reader of the poems
that had appeared in the two volumes of the limited
Bibliophile Society edition in 1916, Lloyd Osbourne con-
tributed an appreciative foreword.*

The difficulties with Scribner were not over. At some
stage in the conversations—the dates are not given—the

---

* There were two impressions in 1918 of this edition: the one
catalogued first in the British Museum, printed on thin paper,
has no foreword by Lloyd Osbourne.

Bibliophile Society acceded to Scribner's request to publish a general edition of the poems in the two 1916 volumes, due acknowledgment to be made to the Society. The permission did not extend to the third volume of Stevenson poems published by the Society in 1921, which carried a note by Mr Harper explaining that the policy of the limited edition was 'not inspired by selfish motives, but purely as a matter of necessity in preserving the organisation' of the Society.

· In 1922 Scribner's, in New York, and Heinemann, in London (in association with Chatto and Windus, Cassell, and Longmans Green), published the Vailima Edition of Stevenson's complete works—a handsome and expensive production in twenty-six volumes, limited to 1000 sets for sale in the States, and 1000 in Britain. Volume VIII was devoted to the poetry and—still under the heading 'New Poems'—included all the poems that had appeared in the Bibliophile Society volumes of 1916 and 1921, as well as some of the 'Additional Poems' of the Pentland Edition (1907), and a further group of hitherto unpublished poems. No editor's name appears in this volume, but there is an Editorial Note in the final volume, XXVI, dated May, 1923, in which Lloyd Osbourne expresses thanks to Will D. Howe, 'who has been associated with me in the editorship,' and to a number of other persons 'for loan of manuscripts or photographs and for information.' Among these names are The Bibliophile Society of America (*sic*), and W. Harris Arnold and Francis S. Peabody, who had been associated with the production of the Bibliophile Society's volumes. It appears therefore that the limited Vailima Edition was produced with the goodwill of the Society; but the publication by Scribner's of a general edition of the poems alone in the autumn of 1923 evoked a very different response.

This *Complete Poems of Robert Louis Stevenson* contained, in the 'New Poems' section, not only the poems published in the two 1916 volumes, for which permission had been given, but also those from the 1921 volume, for which no permission had been given—and all without a word of acknowledgment to the Bibliophile Society. The Council naturally were greatly disturbed, and drew up a statement of the position in their Report for 1923.* The arrangement of the 'New Poems' section in this Scribner edition is, with minor variations, the same as the arrangement in the Vailima Edition, though it added to the main body a further handful of poems that had been published in Vol. XXVI of that edition (*Miscellanea*). When in 1923–4 Heinemann (again in association with Chatto and Windus, Cassell, and Longmans Green) published the unlimited Tusitala Edition of Stevenson, the 'New Poems' section in Vol. XXIII followed the text and, with minor variations, the arrangement of the Vailima Edition —adding as the Scribner 1923 volume had done, the poems from Vol. XXVI of the Vailima Edition.†

This was the way the manuscripts reached publication: their subsequent history as manuscripts is not altogether clear. Those owned by the collectors mentioned by Mr Harper in the 1916 volume, Mr W. H. Arnold, Mr E. D. Brooks and Dr Roderick Terry, were sold: the Peabody collection passed, on his death, to his wife, and then to her second husband, Mr C. Glidden Osborne, who sold it at Sotheby's in 1949.

---

* This section of the Report was privately printed for Members in 1924.

† The same mistakes occur in the Vailima Edition and the first impression of the Tusitala Edition, *e.g.*, in the Dedication to *Weir of Hermiston, indefensible* for *indefeasible*, and 'rainbow *dawn*' for *drawn*; a footnote to *The Family* explaining that 'The Adorner of the Uncomely' was 'the daughter of Mrs Strong, Mrs Stevenson's grand-daughter'—whereas Mrs Strong had no daughter and the poem referred to herself. These errors were corrected in the third impression.

The next point of interest is how the manuscripts were handled and edited. And to appreciate what happened to them it will be helpful, I think, to have an idea of some of the preoccupations of the chief persons involved.

Mr Hellman (I take this information from his published reminiscences*) was engaged in the 'book and picture business,' devoting himself largely 'to the acquisition of rarities for a few private collectors, notably J. Pierpont Morgan and W. K. Bixby.' He had considerable experience of handling the private papers of distinguished men, and had been involved in deciding whether to publish the love letters of Hawthorne and the letters written by President Cleveland to his mistress: as a result of such labours he concluded that 'the sex theme is, in one way or another, at the bottom of the majority of editorial suppressions or changes.' Mr Peabody was the head of a Chicago coal company, and well known as a collector. In the note in the 1921 volume, Mr Harper speaks of Mr Peabody's generous offer 'to share the enjoyment of his Stevenson treasures with his fellow bibliophiles, and we are indebted to him for the privilege of issuing the first printed edition of many precious items, without which no collection of Stevensoniana can ever be regarded as being complete.' The officers of the Bibliophile Society were actuated by a strong sense of responsibility towards their own members: and justified their policy of a limited edition by an appeal to 'certain fundamental rules, without which no cohesive body of booklovers can long exist.'

Thus Mr Hellman had a nose for rarities and personal revelations: Mr Peabody was concerned with adding to a store of treasures: the officers of the Bibliophile Society felt responsible for giving their members good value for money. All had an interest in enhancing the value of the literary property they had acquired. These preoccupations could

* *Lanes of Memory.* New York, 1927.

go with a trained interest in poetry, and with a concern for Stevenson the writer: I have not come across evidence to show that in fact they did.

Mr Hellman and Mr Harper made clear their attitudes in their contributions to the 1916 volume. Mr Harper put it strongly: that so many unpublished Stevenson poems should now be revealed was, he considered, so remarkable an event, as to test the credulity of the literary world. 'Far from being "rejected" poems,' he went on, 'they are among the most intimate, the most self-revealing utterances that ever fell from Stevenson's pen.' After referring to the possible reasons why the poems had escaped publication, Mr Harper added that 'not, however, in the instance of even so much as a single poem need this be attributed to any lack of literary quality.' Mr Hellman admitted that among the manuscripts were some of 'manifestly poor verse' but these had not been printed, and those that had been included 'are poems which Stevenson himself would doubtless have been entirely willing to have printed.' Familiarity with Stevenson's intentions is much in evidence in both Mr Hellman and Mr Harper. After arguing that the reception of *Ballads* (1890) may have led Stevenson to delay issuing a further volume, Mr Hellman went on to demonstrate that the existence of a dedicatory poem in manuscript* proved the intention to produce another book of poems, and, skating lightly from surmise to

---

* He does not specify which: perhaps it is the lines on p. 187 of Vol. II of the Tusitala *Poems* to which there is a footnote: 'doubtless expressing Stevenson's intention of putting together his verses in a volume.'

> To friends at home, the lone, the admired, the lost,
> The gracious old, the lovely young, to May
>   The fair, December the beloved,
> These from my blue horizon and green isles,
> These from this pinnacle of distance, I
>   The unforgetful, dedicate.

certainty, finished up by declaring that 'to include these beautiful poems of the Samoan period is therefore but to fulfil the plan of the poet himself.'

Mr Hellman, of course, had been hot on the biographical trail. Many of the poems placed and dated by Stevenson himself in his manuscript books were clearly love poems of his early Edinburgh days. Revelations! Startling revelations! But revelations imply concealment: and the arch-concealer was at once shown to be Mrs Stevenson, 'determined to hide from the public the intense sex side of Stevenson's nature': she had, he alleged, destroyed 'a novel on the sex theme,'* and she had kept 'from the reading public, as indeed from the eyes of her own children, many love poems of his youth.' She was credited with not destroying the manuscripts outright 'partially, it may be, because of their considerable market value as Stevenson manuscripts, and partially, we like to believe and do believe, because their destruction would have been an act very nearly of sacrilege.'

Mr Hellman clearly regarded himself as a fearless stripper of whitewash, revealer of truth. When he came to edit the volumes for the Bibliophile Society, these preoccupations were evident in his discursive notes which say very little about the state of the manuscript—whether a draft or fair copy, ink or pencil—and a great deal about Stevenson's moods and feelings without, however, much cross-reference to other sources of evidence, such as his published letters. In dating the poems, good use is made of the word 'presumably,' already so well-worked in the discussions of Stevenson's intentions regarding the poems. One poem ('All Night Through, Raves or Brood') is said to have been 'presumably written on the same day' as the short poem entitled 'Soon our Friends Perish,' on the

* 'Sex is, of course, not the only theme,' Mr Hellman reassures us a few paragraphs later.

[42]

evidence that both manuscripts mention a high wind. In one, it is 'the damned wind,' in the other 'the fitful wind'—'the same wind, presumably, as raved on that same night' concludes Mr Hellman, leaving us to presume that a windy night is a rare occurrence in Edinburgh, and that a poet can only write of a windy night on a windy night. No emotion recollected in tranquillity for Mr Hellman.

The notes did, however, help to place the poems, by giving some indications of the circumstances of composition. When the poems in the two 1916 volumes of the Bibliophile Society were reprinted in the English edition issued by Chatto and Windus in 1918,* without the notes, the reader was left completely in the dark. He was confronted with four-and-a-half pages of fragmentary and repetitive verse headed 'Air of Diabelli's' with no word to explain that these were the roughest drafts and re-writings of the poem whose final form had been published in *Songs of Travel* ('Berried brake and reedy island'). He passed to a number of poems with Latin titles, without a word to tell him that these were a series of translations from Martial. A series of numbered sonnets (of early date) merged—with never a heading to separate them—into a series of short descriptive poems which, though there was no note to say so, related to the household at Vailima.

The obvious misprints of the Bibliophile Society volume, perpetuated in the Chatto volume, betrayed a sometimes sketchy knowledge of Stevenson's background and occasionally even of his other writings. The Epistle to Charles Baxter 'on the death of . . . John Adam, Clerk of Court,' speaks of the '*winter* lads'—any book of reference about the Scottish legal system would have made it clear that certain Scottish solicitors are *Writers* to the Signet.

* No editor's name is given. The volume follows the order of the two 1916 volumes but omits a number of variations, and unpublished portions of previously printed poems.

Mrs MacMorland, a Davos friend of Stevenson's, appeared
as MacMarland, and the poem addressed to her began 'In
Schnee der Alpen.' Perhaps the strangest alteration in the
text of a poem came in the 1921 volume. Here is the
poem, as printed on the page:

> The moon is sinking—the tempestuous weather
>   Grows worse, the squalls disputing our advance;
> And as the feet fall well and true together
>   In the last moonlight, see! the standards glance!
>
> One hour, one moment, and that light for ever.
>   Quite so.
>   Jes' so.

I have seen the manuscript of this poem: the first five lines
are in ink (and crossed out in pencil); 'Quite so' and 'Jes'
so' are in pencil—satirical comments made by the author on
looking over his early stuff, in the spirit in which he added
'*Bon*,' '*Pas mal*,' '*Bien mal*', or '*Tout à fait intolérable*' to the
manuscript of other early poems.

The note opposite the poem in the Bibliophile Edition
remarks that, 'The lines have little in themselves to re-
commend them, and Stevenson after having laid aside his
mediocre beginning comes back to it later just long enough
to add the amusing comments of the last four words of his
manuscript.' Quite so; just so; but does one print an
author's comment on a poem as if it were an integral part
of that poem, with nothing to distinguish one from the
other on the page? If one does, then observe what may
happen. The Scribner 1923 Edition, and the Vailima
Edition, had no notes: and the fragment appears in both of
them, with the pencilled comment printed as part of the
poem, and never a footnote to explain the monstrosity. It
is a pity that we cannot have Stevenson's further comments
in seeing these scraps and gobbets in print.

Yet many of these aberrations of the printed text cease
to be quite so startling once the manuscripts have been

examined, not because of the state of the manuscripts as Stevenson left them, but because of the things that were subsequently done to them. Most of the poems, as the Anderson Galleries sale catalogue made clear, and as Mr Hellman's account confirmed, were contained in note-books and copy-books. Some of these note-books, which were bought by other collectors, were preserved intact, and kept in cases specially made for them. The manuscript poems from the Peabody collection, which I saw at the Sotheby sales in 1949, were in very different trim. They were encased in volumes of 'red levant morocco gilt' (or blue or green or grey or lilac), 'gilt lettering on side and back, silk end leaves.' Each volume consisted of manuscript poems, transcripts in typescript, a portrait of Stevenson, a picture of 'association interest' such as Swanston, or Vailima—and a great many blank pages. Some of the volumes contained only two or three poems: and examination soon showed that many of the original copy-books had been simply torn apart and their pages distributed to make two, three or more of these pretentious volumes. Thus, it was possible to deduce that the poems scattered through three of these volumes (Nos. 60, 71 and 79 in Sotheby's first sale) had come from one note-book. There was a sequence of poems, headed 'Pieces in Lallan' and numbered. Nos. I and II ('To The Commissioners of Northern Lights' and 'To Mesdames Zassetsky and Garschine') were in one Peabody volume. Nos. IV and V (Two Epistles to Charles Baxter, 'Noo lyart leaves' and 'On Johnie Adam') were in another, and No. VII ('When aince Aprile'—published in *Underwoods*) in yet another. A handful of poems written in one note-book in Stevenson's Bournemouth days were split into three of the Peabody volumes. The series of poems written on his South Sea cruises in 1887–1891 and published in *Songs of Travel* had been split into two Peabody volumes.

The person responsible for this dismemberment, this pretentious dolling up, is—I might almost say *presumably*—likely to have been either Mr Peabody himself, or Mr Hellman, whose pencil notes appear on the fly-leaf of each volume.*
The disadvantages of this mutilation are all too obvious: it makes the dating and grouping of the poems very much more difficult. Mr Hellman, who was so outraged by Mrs Stevenson's 'concealment' of the copy-books, does not seem to have been at all disturbed by their mutilation. If the treatment of the manuscripts is disturbing, so is the transcription. To take one instance: a line in the fifth verse of the Epistle to Charles Baxter on the death of Johnie Adam reads quite plainly in the manuscript as:

> Wi' a kind o' Gospel look ower a'—

but the accompanying typescript omits *look*—and so does the Bibliophile Society volume, and the Chatto *New Poems*, and the Vailima Edition—making hay with the rhythm, and nonsense of the meaning. Again, the poem which in manuscript begins quite clearly with 'The old world moans and *tosses*' is transcribed as *topes* (Stevenson had used a long S) though the rhythm demands a feminine ending.

Subsequent editions of Stevenson's poetry repeated most of the errors of the Bibliophile volumes (though *topes* had been corrected back to *tosses* by the Scribner Edition and in later impressions of the Tusitala Edition). But 'edition' is perhaps not the word: no editor's name is given for the Chatto *New Poems* or the Scribner 1923 collection, no name beyond Lloyd Osbourne's general editorship with

* With most unfortunate results as far as the Sotheby sales were concerned. The Sotheby catalogue followed Mr Hellman's notes and listed the majority of poems as 'unpublished'—a description true enough when the note was originally pencilled, but which a glance at, for instance, the Tusitala edition of the poems would have quickly shown to be quite out of date.

the help of Will D. Howe for the Vailima Edition, and the publishers of the Tusitala Edition have been unable to find any record even of what person saw the volumes through the press. Nor did the volumes carry any editorial note to say whether the Bibliophile text was being followed, whether any attempt had been made to check the printed text with the originals, or to indicate on what principle the poems had been arranged.

Here the editions subsequent to the Bibliophile Society's introduced new disorder. In the Society's 1916 volumes the poems were printed, as far as possible, in chronological order, from 1869 to 1894, followed by a group of 'poems of uncertain date,' and the Martial translations. Again, in the Society's 1921 volume the poems followed a chronological order, ranging from 1868 to 1894. In the Vailima Edition, poems from the 1921 Bibliophile volume were put beside poems of roughly the same date from the 1916 volume: but there was not much attempt to keep a strict chronological order, and the earliest poems of 1868 and 1869 were placed after nine poems dating from the early 1870s. The group of 'poems of uncertain date' from the 1916 volume appeared, still grouped together, after some datable poems of the 1880s and just before some poems of the Vailima years. Nine of the 'Additional Poems' (mainly from Stevenson's published Letters) that Edmund Gosse had printed in Volume XIII of the Pentland Edition of Stevenson's works in 1907, were sprinkled in (along with some more Samoan verses that had appeared in Isobel Strong's *R.L.S. Teuila*, 1899) and a further number of occasional verses from letters, dedications in books and a group of early poems, showing the strong influence of Walt Whitman and Matthew Arnold.* These, though plainly early work, appear at the end of the 'New Poems' section: and there are no dates to help the reader recon-

* No. 348 in the second sale at the Anderson Galleries.

[47]

struct the order for himself. On the rare occasion where there is a footnote, it may add to confusion. Thus, a footnote to the lines beginning 'The indefeasible impulse of my blood' runs: 'These lines are found in the manuscript of *Weir of Hermiston*. They suggest a projected dedication of the book to Mrs Stevenson'; in fact, a slightly different version of these lines had been printed as a dedication to *Weir of Hermiston* since its first publication in 1896.

It is impossible to trace any sort of plan in the final lack of arrangement.* Nothing but a fine higgledy-piggledy: drafts jostling finished poems, early printed after late, a poem called 'Apologetic Postscript of a Year Later,' separated by five poems from the poem to which it is a postscript (and which it had accompanied in the manuscript), with never a cross-reference.† It is impossible from the Scribner or the Vailima editions to form any picture of Stevenson's growth and development as a poet, impossible to read the poems in their right categories and contexts.

Serious as this is, perhaps the greatest disservice these editors, known and unknown, rendered to Stevenson's poetry was to put his posthumously published poems in a wrong focus.

On the issues raised by Mr Hellman, Mr Harper and others, a great deal could be said. They believed that Stevenson intended all the poems to be published. Lloyd Osbourne, in the note to the Chatto *New Poems*, put it strongly: 'That Stevenson should have preserved these poems through all the vicissitudes of his wandering life shows how dearly he must have valued them; and shows too, I think, beyond any contradiction, that he meant they

* The trouble Stevenson took in arranging his work is reflected in an unpublished letter to Colvin (now at Yale, Beinecke 2999). Referring to 'Notes on the Movements of Young Children', he writes: 'I never knew anything cost me so much actual *pain* as this morsel of rearrangement.'

† There had been a note in the Bibliophile Edition.

should be ultimately published.'* And Mr Hellman, because Lloyd Osbourne had expressed surprise at the existence of the manuscript books from Vailima, assumed a deliberate suppression on Mrs Stevenson's part.

These allegations and assumptions strike one as showing a lack of familiarity with the goings-on of a literary household. From some acquaintance with poets, I should say that a poet might very well carry round with him, and affectionately cherish, poems which he did not think worth publishing. Like old letters, old photographs or books he once enjoyed, they had become part of his possessions, even though his opinion of their literary merit might be low. Some he might keep in the hope that further work on them might some day turn them into real poems. And against Mr Hellman's and Lloyd Osbourne's assurances of Stevenson's intentions, we can set his own comments on some of the poems—*Bien mal, Tout à fait intolérable*—and his outburst to Colvin, when he was seeking juvenilia for the Edinburgh Edition, against 'hawking unripe fruit.' If Stevenson had wished to publish his early poems, the Edinburgh Edition offered an excellent opportunity: even if personal considerations would have kept back the love poems, there were plenty more available which could have caused no embarrassment to his family or friends. Many early poems, which he did think well of, had already been published in *Underwoods*, which contains one poem dated 1869 and several from the early seventies.

Nor need Mrs Stevenson's action strike us as particularly impious or discreditable if, when faced with the stack of copy-books containing poems which she knew her

* The point was put rather less strongly in his note to the 'New Poems' section in the Vailima Edition, which also contains the sentence beginning, 'That Stevenson should have preserved these poems' but omits the phrase 'I think, beyond any contradiction.' Various other phrases in this Vailima note are echoed in the blurb to the Scribner Edition a year later.

husband had not considered good enough to print, she did nothing about them. There *may* have been concealment, as in a locked cupboard, under a loose floor-board or up a chimney: but on the known evidence, it is just as likely that the copy-books sat in a pile among Stevenson's books and multitudinous other papers, first at Vailima and then at her home in California. If she had been bent on suppression at all costs, it is difficult to understand why she did not destroy the early love poems out of hand. If blame is going, it should attach not to Mrs Stevenson, who at least left the poems as Stevenson wrote them, but to those responsible for dismembering the note-books, binding them with hideous vulgarity and ostentation, transcribing them incorrectly and turning them into 'collectors' items' and manufactured rarities.

If we are at all concerned with Stevenson as a writer, the real issue raised by the so-called 'New Poems' is not the personal one: the amount of autobiographical revelation, the motives of Mrs Stevenson. The real issue is, are they good poems or are there good poems among them? Do they add to our understanding of Stevenson's poetry, or of his aims as a poet?

Once we begin to look at them as poems, and not as biographical documents, one fact stands out. Of the early poems—written before Stevenson's marriage in 1880—the love poems may have remained unpublished for reasons of tact or prudence, but the rest are rejects in the sense that they were passed over when Stevenson made the selection for *Underwoods*. He took for that book a poem of 1869 ('To Minnie, with a hand-glass'), but rejected a poem written out immediately before it in the manuscript book ('The Gloomy Northern Day'). For *Underwoods* he chose a poem written at San Francisco, 'In the States': in *New Poems* there is another poem about the States, 'I look across the Ocean,' in much the same key and written at much the same time. I find it hard to believe that he chose the one for *Underwoods*, and rejected the other, for any other reason but that he considered the second not good enough. The same with the note-book full of 'Pieces in Lallan,' of which four were rejected from *Underwoods*.

I do not wish to go to the opposite extreme from Mr Hellman and Mr Harper and say that because Stevenson did not choose a poem for publication, it never should be published. But when these poems are published, it should be made clear, where possible, what was his own valuation of the salvaged poems; what kind of poems he was writing and for what occasion, so that the reader will not look for lyrical intensity in a light set of verses tossed off in a letter. For a fastidious writer who was as particular about the presentation of his work as about the writing of it, there could be no more painful purgatory than to see his remains jumbled up in a formless hotchpotch like the 'New Poems' section of the Vailima, Scribner or Tusitala editions.

Stevenson's friends in this country felt very strongly about it. Gosse, reviewing the Chatto *New Poems* in *The Times Literary Supplement*, 5 December, 1918 (an unsigned review, but the present Editor confirms the authorship), spoke of 'the atrocious neglect with which the contents of this volume are huddled together' and asserted that 'careless editors who do not distinguish between [authors'] juvenile efforts and their masterpieces ought to be made ashamed of themselves.' Four years later, commenting in *The Times* (21 June, 1922) on the Stevenson items in a recent sale, he stated that 'the whole question of emptying the nursery waste-paper basket of eminent authors into the public Press is one which more and more loudly calls for a decision. The dead should be protected against their own carelessness.' On the following day Sir Sidney Colvin came in with a letter regretting 'the posthumous publication of a volume of Stevenson's stray leavings in verse. . . . In the case of an artist so scrupulous as he was as to style and finish, I hold such publication to be especially ill-judged.' These letters moved Lloyd Osbourne, then in London, to reply (on 24 June). He maintained that: 'This unpublished work of Stevenson's is of extraordinary value, and so revealing of the man and so felicitous in its varied expression that I am sincerely glad to give it to the world.'

III

My arrangement of the posthumously published poems has been made with a view to sharpening our picture of Stevenson as a poet. I have selected rigorously: but in choosing the early poems I have tried to keep enough of them to show the range of forms and subject. On the whole I have followed a chronological order, though some poems of different dates—for instance, the Lallan group—called to be grouped together. I have segregated the light verse, the trivial occasional piece which has some grace to recommend it, and given the circumstance of composition in the Notes, so that such verse may be read in an appropriate spirit.

So these poems fall into three sections. The first, *Poems 1869–1879*, which covers the years up to Stevenson's journey to California to marry Fanny Osbourne, contains the poems he wrote as a very young man, intent on being a writer, but not yet mainly dedicated to prose. Here are some of the early poems to Claire and the other loves of his Edinburgh days*; the poems that recall his personal pre-

---

* We now know that 'Claire' was a poetic name for Mrs Sitwell. The Edinburgh girl postulated by Mr G. S. Hellman has been shown to be non-existent by J. C. Furnas in his *Voyage to Windward*, London, 1952, pp. 394–399. J.A.S. 1970.

dicaments and hopes; the early experiments in metrical forms. The second section, *Poems 1880–1894*, includes the experiments in classical metre, the translations from Martial, and the sequence on the household at Vailima. I have been uneasily haunted, in preparing this edition, by the knowledge that Stevenson was such a rigorous selector of his own work, and by his warning against 'hawking unripe fruit.' I have hoped, by firmly segregating the jokes and doggerel, in a third section, to make a gesture of reassurance towards their dead and critical author that they are not being presented as important poems at all.

I do not wish to make extravagant claims for this edition, and I am not so naïve as to suppose it entirely free from error. On particular points—Stevenson's Scots, the poems in classical metres—I have gone for advice to authorities who know far more than myself. My aim has been to get a clearer idea myself of Stevenson as a poet, and to present his poems in such a way that others can form their own view. Those concerned with the first publication of the new poems had an obsession with biography and a sense of responsibility towards collectors and bibliophiles, but little sense of responsibility towards Stevenson as a serious writer, or towards poetry. Collectors' values predominated; the value of a manuscript as a rarity or relic was confused with its value as a poem, and inflating the value of the poem might enhance its value as a rarity and as a piece of marketable property. For thirty-four years these collectors' values have distorted our estimate of Stevenson as a poet. It is the aim of the present edition to correct the picture.

JANET ADAM SMITH, 1950

NOTE TO SECOND EDITION

'SHALL any pious hand re-edit us?', Stevenson asks Andrew Lang in a poem printed on p. 310 of the present volume. Twenty years after the publication of this collection of his poems it is time for pious hands to get to work again. Since 1950 much has been added to our knowledge of Stevenson and many more manuscripts have come to light. There has been the admirable biography of Mr J. C. Furnas, *Voyage to Windward*, and the publication of Stevenson's *Letters to Charles Baxter*, 1956. There has been the growth of the Beinecke Collection at Yale, which now contains most of the material sold at Sothebys in 1949, and where poems originally written in one notebook, then scattered, have been brought together again. There has been the production of the six volumes of the Beinecke Catalogue, 1951–1964. There has been the accession to the National Library of Scotland of much Stevenson material from the papers of Graham Balfour. So for this edition of the *Collected Poems* it has been possible to print two new poems, *The Gods are Dead* and *Lord Nelson and the Tar* (p. 358 and p. 449), to check poems with manuscripts not available in 1950*, to correct some errors in the first edition (including a few errors in transcription discovered from a second look at difficult manuscripts), to supply dates of composition, and to add information— here the Beinecke Catalogue was particularly useful— about rare and privately printed editions not mentioned in the Prideaux-Livingston bibliography.

J. A. S. 1970

* A few of the Beinecke manuscripts now available for checking poems unpublished in Stevenson's lifetime are very rough drafts. Where it looks as if the earliest printed text had been taken from a fair copy that cannot now be traced, I have used my judgment as to how far to correct the printed text by the draft.

ACKNOWLEDGMENTS

I WISH to make grateful acknowledgments to the authorities of the following institutions, who have supplied facsimiles of Stevenson's manuscripts from their collections: the Robert Louis Stevenson Club, Edinburgh; the National Library of Scotland; the Henry W. and Albert A. Berg Collection of the New York Public Library; the Harry Widener Collection of the Library of Harvard University; the Henry E. Huntington Library and Art Gallery, California; the Princeton University Library; also to the Rt. Hon. Isaac Foot who has allowed me to print two unpublished poems from manuscripts in his collection.

Acknowledgments are due to the Society of Authors for permission to publish the poems not printed in Stevenson's lifetime.

Permission to include A. E. Housman's lines on Stevenson has been granted by the Society of Authors as the Literary Representatives of the Trustees of the Estate of the late A. E. Housman, and Messrs Jonathan Cape, Ltd., publishers of A. E. Housman's *Collected Poems*.

In tracking down Stevenson manuscripts, and in checking the text of the poems, I have been greatly helped by Mr W. Park, of the National Library of Scotland; Mr J. H. Pafford, of the Library of London University; Mr Russell A. Scully of the Boston Public Library, Mr J. C. Furnas; Mr Graham Greene; Mr and Mrs Dods Hogg; Mrs Mirylees and Miss M. E. Murray. Messrs Sotheby allowed me to examine the Stevenson manuscripts from the Glidden Osborne Collection at the sales in May and November 1949. Professor H. W. Garrod answered my queries on classical metres, and Mr W. Park read the proofs and the notes of the Scots poems. I wish to thank them all most warmly; and I should also like to acknowledge the great help I got, in writing the Notes, from the Bibliography of Stevenson's works originally compiled by Colonel W. F. Prideaux and revised by Mrs Luther S. Livingston.

Finally, very special thanks are due to Mr E. J. Beinecke and Mr E. J. Mehew. Mr Beinecke supplied me with facsimiles and transcripts of a number of poems, allowed me to study his set of proofs of *Songs of Travel* with Colvin's and Gosse's correspondence about them, gave permission to print hitherto unpublished work, and even sent over from the United States some of his Stevenson manuscript note-books. In his treatment of the manuscripts and his understanding of them, Mr Beinecke stands out in contrast to some earlier collectors of Stevenson's manuscript poems. Mr Mehew placed at my disposal his excellent Stevenson library and his thorough knowledge of Stevenson. He drew my attention to various passages in the prose works that enlightened the poems, he found some fresh echoes of Stevenson in Henley's poems, he tracked down the 'E. H.' of *Songs of Travel* XXXIII, and he pointed out the material in *The Times* quoted in the Introduction. Without his help the Notes would have been less full, and less accurate; though I take full responsibility for any errors that remain.

J. A. S. 1950

My principal acknowledgments must again go to Mr E. J. Beinecke and to Mr E. J. Mehew. The latter has put his unrivalled knowledge of Stevenson's life and writings at my disposal, and to him I owe many of the textual corrections and most of the new material in the Notes. I must also warmly thank Miss Marjorie Wynne of the Beinecke Rare Book and Manuscript Library at Yale.

For the two poems published for the first time, *The Gods are Dead* and *Lord Nelson and the Tar*, I thank the National Library of Scotland for supplying copies of the manuscripts.

J. A. S. 1970

POEMS 1869–1879

POEMS 1869–1879

I

Dedication

My first gift and my last, to you
I dedicate this fascicle of songs—
The only wealth I have:
Just as they are, to you.

I speak the truth in soberness, and say
I had rather bring a light to your clear eyes,
Had rather hear you praise
This bosomful of trifles,

Than that the whole, hard world with one
      consent,
In one continuous chorus of applause
Poured forth for me and mine
The homage of due praise.

I write the *finis* here against my love,
This is my love's last epitaph and tomb.
Here the road forks, and I
Go my way, far from yours.

II

Last night, I lingered long without
　　My last of loves to see.
Alas! the moon-white window-panes
　　Stared blindly back at me.

To-day, I hold her very hand,
　　Her very waist embrace—
Like clouds across a pool, I read
　　Her thoughts upon her face.

And yet, as now, through her clear eyes
　　I seek the inner shrine—
I stoop to read her virgin heart,
　　In doubt if it be mine—

O looking long and fondly thus,
　　What vision should I see?
No vision, but my own white face
　　That grins and mimics me.

III

After Reading
'Antony and Cleopatra'

As when the hunt by holt and field
　　Drives on with horn and strife,
Hunger of hopeless things pursues
　　Our spirits throughout life.

The sea-roar fills us aching full
　　Of objectless desire—
The sea-roar, and the white moon-shine,
　　And the reddening of the fire.

Who talks to me of reason now?
   It would be more delight
To have died in Cleopatra's arms
   Than be alive to-night.

IV

Spring-Song

THE air was full of sun and birds,
   The fresh air sparkled clearly.
Remembrance wakened in my heart
   And I knew I loved her dearly.

The fallows and the leafless trees
   And all my spirit tingled.
My earliest thought of love, and spring's
   First puff of perfume mingled.

In my still heart, the thoughts awoke
   Came bone by bone together—
Say, birds and sun and spring, is love
   A mere affair of weather?

V

As Love and Hope together
   Walk by me for a while,
Link-armed the ways they travel
   For many a pleasant mile—
Link-armed and dumb they travel—
   They sing not, but they smile.

[61]

Hope leaving, Love commences
    To practise on the lute;
And as he sings and travels
    With lingering, laggard foot,
Despair plays *obligato*
    The sentimental flute.

Until, in singing garments,
    Comes royally, at call—
Comes limber-hipped Indiff'rence
    Free-stepping, straight and tall—
Comes singing and lamenting—
    The sweetest pipe of all.

VI

Duddingston

I

WITH caws and chirrupings, the woods
    In this thin sun rejoice,
The Psalm seems but the little kirk
    That sings with its own voice.

The cloud-rifts share their amber light
    With the surface of the mere—
I think the very stones are glad
    To feel each other near.

Once more my whole heart leaps and swells
    And gushes o'er with glee:
The fingers of the sun and shade
    Touch music stops in me.

[62]

II

Now fancy paints that bygone day
   When you were here, my fair—
The whole lake rang with rapid skates
   In the windless, winter air.

You leaned to me, I leaned to you,
   Our course was smooth as flight—
We steered—a heel-touch to the left,
   A heel-touch to the right.

We swung our way through flying men,
   Your hand lay fast in mine,
We saw the shifting crowd dispart,
   The level ice-reach shine.

I swear by yon swan-travelled lake,
   By yon calm hill above,
I swear had we been drowned that day
   We had been drowned in love.

VII

THE relic taken, what avails the shrine?
The locket, pictureless?　O heart of mine,
   Art thou not less than that,
Still warm, a vacant nest where love once sat.

Her image nestled closer at my heart
Than cherished memories, healed every smart,
   And warmed it more than wine
Or the full summer sun in noon-day shine.

[63]

This was the little weather-gleam that lit
The cloudy promontories. The real charm was it
   That gilded hills and woods
And walked beside me through the solitudes.

That sun is set. My heart is widowed now
Of that companion-thought. Alone I plough
   The seas of life, and trace
A separate furrow far from her and grace.

VIII

   ALL things on earth and sea,
   All that the white stars see,
   Turns about you and me.

   And where we two are not,
   Is darkness like a blot
   And life and love forgot.

   But when we pass that way,
   The night breaks into day,
   The year breaks into May,

   The earth through all her bowers
   Carols and breathes and flowers
   About this love of ours.

IX

   I SIT up here at midnight,
     The wind is in the street,
   The rain besieges the windows
     Like the sound of many feet.

[64]

I see the street lamps flicker,
    I see them wink and fail,
The streets are wet and empty,
    It blows an easterly gale.

Some think of the fisher skipper
    Beyond the Inchcape stone;
But I of the fisher woman
    That lies at home alone.

She raises herself on her elbow
    And watches the firelit floor;
Her eyes are bright with terror,
    Her heart beats fast and sore.

Between the roar of the flurries,
    When the tempest holds his breath
She holds her breathing also—
    It is all as still as death.

She can hear the cinders dropping,
    The cat that purrs in its sleep—
The foolish fisher woman!
    Her heart is on the deep.

X

I AM a hunchback, yellow faced,
    A hateful sight to see,
'Tis all that other men can do
    To pass and let me be.

I am a woman, my hair is white,
    I was a darkhaired lass;
The gin dances in my head,
    I stumble as I pass.

C

I am a man that God made at first,
　And teachers tried to harm,.
Here! hunchback take my friendly hand,
　Good woman, take my arm.

XI

Death

WE are as maidens one and all,
　In some shut convent place,
Pleased with the flowers, the service bells,
　The cloister's shady grace,

That whiles, with fearful, fluttering hearts,
　Look outward thro' the grate
And down the long, white road, up which,
　Some morning, soon or late,

Shall canter on his great, gray horse
　That splendid acred Lord
Who comes to lead us forth—his wife,
　But half with our accord.

With fearful fluttered hearts, we wait—
　We meet him, bathed in tears,
We are so loath to leave behind
　Those tranquil Convent years,

So loath to meet the pang, to take
　(On some poor chance of bliss)
Life's labour on the windy sea
　For a bower as still as this.

[66]

Weeping we mount the crowded aisle,
   And weeping after us
The Bridesmaids follow—Come to me!
   I will not meet you thus,

Pale rider to the Convent gate,
   Come, O rough bridegroom, Death,
Where, bashful bride, I wait you veiled,
   Flush-faced, with shaken breath.

I do not fear your kiss. I dream
   New days, secure from strife,
And, bride-like, in the future hope
   A quiet household life.

XII

A LITTLE before me, and hark!
The dogs in the village bark.
And see, in the blank of the dark,
   The eye of a window shine!

There stands the inn, the small and rude,
In this earth's vast robber-wood
The inn with the beds and the food,
   The inn of the shining wine.

We do but bait on life's bare plain,
And through the new day's joy and pain
Reach to the baiting place again.
   O rest, for the night, be mine!

Rest for the night! For to love and rest,
To clasp the hands, to keep the nest,
Are only human at the best:
   To move and to suffer divine.

XIII

Epistle to Charles Baxter

REAPED grain should fill the reaper's grange,
My fate for thine I would not change.
Thy pathway would to me be strange,
  And strange to thee
The limits of the daily range
  That pleases me.

For me, I do but ask such grace
As Icarus. Bright breathing space—
One glorious moment—face to face,
  The sun and he!
The next, fit grave for all his race,
  The splendid sea.

The father, rich in forty years
Of poor experience culled in tears,
Meanly restrained by sordid fears
  Went limping home
And hung his pinions by the spears,
  No more to roam.

O more to me a thousand fold
The son's brief triumph, wisely bold
To separate from the common fold,
  The general curse,
The accustomed way of growing old
  And growing worse.

[68]

O happy lot! A heart of fire,
In the full flush of young desire,
Not custom-taught to shun the mire
    And hold the wall,
His sole experience to aspire,
      To soar and fall.

His golden hap it was to go
Straight from the best of life below
To life above. Not his to know,
    O greatly blest,
How deadly weary life can grow
      To e'en the best.

Sad life, whose highest lore, in vain
The nobler summits to attain,
Still bids me draw the kindly strain
    Of love more tight,
And ease my individual pain
      In your delight.

For I, that would be blythe and merry,
Prefer to call Marsala sherry,
When duty-bound to cross the ferry
    Believe it smooth,
And under pleasant fictions bury
      Distasteful truth.

And hence I banish wisdom, set
The sole imperial coronet
On cheerful Folly, at regret
    Pull many a mouth,
Drown care in jovial bouts—and yet
      Sigh for the South!

[69]

O South, South, South! O happy land!
Thou beckon'st me with phantom hand.
Sweet Memories at my bedside stand
    All night in tears.
The roar upon thy nightly strand
    Yet fills mine ears.

The young grass sparkles in the breeze,
The pleasant sunshine warms my knees,
The buds are thick upon the trees,
    The clouds float high.
We sit out here in perfect ease—
    My pipe and I.

Fain would I be, where (winter done)
By dusty roads and noontide sun,
The soldiers, straggling one by one,
    Marched disarrayed
And spoiled the hedge, till every gun
    A Rose displayed.

Or, O flower-land, I would be where
(The trivial, well-beloved affair!)
The bird-watch drew with gentle care
    From up his sleeve
And gave me, fluttering from the snare,
    A *Mange-Olive*.

Aye, dear to me the slightest tie
That binds my heart to thee, O high
And sovereign land for whom I sigh
    In pain to see
The Springtime come again, and I
    So far from thee! ·

[70]

But hush! the clear-throat blackbird sings
From haugh and hill the Season brings
Great armfuls of delightful things
        To stop my mouth
Though still (caged-bird) I beat my wings
        Toward the South.

XIV

Consolation

THOUGH he, that ever kind and true,
Kept stoutly step by step with you
Your whole long gusty lifetime through,
        Be gone a while before,
Be now a moment gone before,
Yet, doubt not, soon the seasons shall restore
        Your friend to you.

He has but turned a corner—still
He pushes on with right good will,
Through mire and marsh, by heugh and hill,
        That self-same arduous way—
That self-same upland, hopeful way,
That you and he through many a doubtful day
        Attempted still.

He is not dead, this friend—not dead,
But in the path we mortals tread
Got some few, trifling steps ahead
        And nearer to the end;
So that you too, once past the bend,
Shall meet again, as face to face, this friend
        You fancy dead.

[71]

Push gaily on, strong heart! The while
You travel forward mile by mile,
He loiters with a backward smile
    Till you can overtake,
And strains his eyes to search his wake,
Or whistling, as he sees you through the brake,
    Waits on a stile.

XV

To Sydney

Not thine where marble-still and white
Old statues share the tempered light
And mock the uneven modern flight,
    But in the stream
Of daily sorrow and delight
    To seek a theme.

I too, O friend, have steeled my heart
Boldly to choose the better part,
To leave the beaten ways of art
    And wholly free
To dare, beyond the scanty chart,
    The deeper sea.

All vain restrictions left behind,
Frail bark! I loose my anchored mind
And large, before the prosperous wind
    Desert the strand—
A new Columbus sworn to find
    The morning land.

[72]

Nor too ambitious, friend. To thee
I own my weakness. Not for me
To sing the enfranchised nations' glee,
  Or count the cost
Of warships foundered far at sea
  And battles lost.

High on the far-seen, sunny hills,
Morning-content my bosom fills;
Well-pleased, I trace the wandering rills
  And learn their birth.
Far off, the clash of sovereign wills
  May shake the earth.

The nimble circuit of the wheel,
The uncertain poise of merchant weal,
Horror of famine, fire and steel
  When nations fall;
These, heedful, from afar I feel—
  I mark them all.

But not, my friend, not these I sing,
My voice shall fill a narrower ring.
Tired souls, that flag upon the wing,
  I seek to cheer:
Brave wines to strengthen hope I bring,
  Life's cantineer!

Some song that shall be suppling oil
To weary muscles strained with toil,
Shall hearten for the daily moil,
  Or widely read
Make sweet for him that tills the soil
  His daily bread—

[73]

Such songs in my flushed hours I dream
(High thought), instead of armour gleam
Or warrior cantos ream by ream
    To load the shelves—
Songs with a lilt of words, that seem
    To sing themselves.

XVI

O DULL, cold northern sky,
  O brawling sabbath bells,
  O feebly twittering Autumn bird that tells
The year is like to die!

O still, spoiled trees, O city ways,
  O sun desired in vain,
  O dread presentiment of coming rain
That clogs the sullen days!

Thee, heart of mine, I greet.
  In what hard mountain pass
  Striv'st thou ?   In what importunate morass
Sink now thy weary feet ?

Thou run'st a hopeless race
  To win despair. No crown
  Awaits success; but leaden gods look down
On thee, with evil face.

And those that would befriend
  And cherish thy defeat,
  With angry welcome shall turn sour the sweet
Home-coming of the end.

[74]

Yea, those that offer praise
  To idleness, shall yet
  Insult thee, coming glorious in the sweat
Of honourable ways.

XVII

Swallows travel to and fro,
And the great winds come and go,
And the steady breezes blow,
  Bearing perfume, bearing love.
Breezes hasten, swallows fly,
Towered clouds forever ply,
And at noonday you and I
  See the same sun shine above.

Dew and rain fall everywhere,
Harvests ripen, flowers are fair,
And the whole round earth is bare
  To the moonshine and the sun;
And the live air, fanned with wings,
Bright with breeze and sunshine, brings
Into contact distant things,
  And makes all the countries one.

Let us wander where we will,
Something kindred greets us still;
Something seen on vale or hill
  Falls familiar on the heart;
So, at scent or sound or sight,
Severed souls by day and night
Tremble with the same delight—
  Tremble, half the world apart.

XVIII

Let Love go, if go she will.
Seek not, O fool, her wanton flight to stay.
 Of all she gives and takes away
The best remains behind her still.

The best remains behind: in vain
Joy may she give and take again,
Joy she may take and leave us pain,
 If yet she leave behind
 The constant mind
To meet all fortunes nobly, to endure
All things with a good heart, and still be pure.
Still to be foremost in the foremost cause,
And still be worthy of the love that was.

Love coming is omnipotent indeed,
But not Love going. Let her go. The seed
Springs in the favouring Summer air, and grows,
And waxes strong; and when the Summer goes
 Remains, a perfect tree.

Joy she may give and take again,
Joy she may take and leave us pain.
 O Love, and what care we?
For one thing thou hast given O Love, one thing
 Is ours that nothing can remove;
And as the King discrowned is still a King,
 The unhappy lover still preserves his love.

XIX

I AM like one that for long days had sate,
  With seaward eyes set keen against the gale,
  On some long foreland, watching, sail by sail,
The portbound ships for one ship that was late;
And sail by sail, his heart burned up with joy,
  And cruelly was quenched, until at last
  One ship, the looked-for pennant at its mast,
Bore gaily, and dropt safely past the buoy;
And lo! the loved one was not there, was dead.
Then would he watch no more; no more the sea
  With myriad vessels, sail by sail, perplex
His eyes and mock his longing. Weary head,
Take now thy rest; eyes, close; for no more me
  Shall hope untried elate, or ruined vex.

For thus on love I waited; thus for love
  Strained all my senses eagerly and long;
  Thus for her coming ever trimmed my song;
Till in the far skies coloured as a dove,
A bird gold-coloured flickered far and fled
  Over the pathless water waste for me;
  And with spread hands I watched the bright bird
    flee
And waited, till before me she dropped dead.
O golden bird in these dove-coloured skies
How long I sought, how long with wearied eyes
  I sought, O bird, the promise of thy flight!
And now the morn has dawned, the morn has died,
  The day has come and gone; and once more night
About my lone life settles, wild and wide.

[77]

XX

THE roadside lined with ragweed, the sharp hills
   Standing against the glow of eve, the patch
      Of rough white oats mongst darkling granite knolls,
   The ferny coverts where the adders hatch,
The hollow that the northern sea upfills,
      The seagull wheeling by with strange, sad calls,
All these, this evening, weary me. Full fain
   Would I turn up the little elm tree way
And under the last elm tree, once again
      Stretch myself with my head among the grass;
   So lying, tyne the memories of day
      And let my loosed, insatiate being pass
Into the blackbird's song of summer ease,
Or, with the white moon, rise in spirit from the trees.

XXI

   NOT undelightful, friend, our rustic ease
   To grateful hearts; for by especial hap
   Deep nested in the hill's enormous lap
   With its own ring of walls and grove of trees
   Sits, in deep shelter, our small cottage; nor
   Far-off is seen, rose carpeted and hung
   With Clematis, the quarry whence she sprung.
   O matre pulchra filia pulchrior.
   Thither in early spring, unharnessed folk,
   We join the pairing swallows, glad to stay
   Where, bosomed in high hills, remote, unseen,
   From its tall trees, it breathes a slender smoke
   To heaven, and in the noon of sultry day
   Stands, coolly buried, to the neck in green.

XXII

As Daniel, burd-alone, in that far land,
Kneeling in fervent prayer with heart-sick eyes
Turned thro' the casement toward the westering skies;
Or as untamed Elijah, that red brand
Among the starry prophets; or that band
And company of Faithful sanctities,
Who, in all times, when persecutions rise,
Cherish forgotten creeds with fostering hand;
Such do ye seem to me, light-hearted crew,
O turned to friendly arts with all your will,
That keep a little chapel sacred still,
One rood of Holy-land in this bleak earth
Sequestered still (our homage surely due!)
To the twin Gods of mirthful wine and mirth.

XXIII

The Light-Keeper

I

THE brilliant kernel of the night,
The flaming lightroom circles me:
I sit within a blaze of light
Held high above the dusky sea.
Far off the surf doth break and roar
Along bleak miles of moonlit shore,
Where through the tides the tumbling wave
Falls in an avalanche of foam
And drives its churned waters home
Up many an undercliff and cave.

[79]

The clear bell chimes: the clockworks strain,
The turning lenses flash and pass,
Frame turning within glittering frame
With frosty gleam of moving glass:
Unseen by me, each dusky hour
The sea-waves welter up the tower
Or in the ebb subside again;
And ever and anon all night,
Drawn from afar by charm of light,
A sea bird beats against the pane.

And lastly when dawn ends the night
And belts the semi-orb of sea,
The tall, pale pharos in the light
Looks white and spectral as may be.
The early ebb is out: the green
Straight belt of seaweed now is seen,
That round the basement of the tower
Marks out the interspace of tide;
And watching men are heavy-eyed,
And sleepless lips are dry and sour.

The night is over like a dream:
The sea-birds cry and dip themselves:
And in the early sunlight, steam
The newly bared and dripping shelves,
Around whose verge the glassy wave
With lisping wash is heard to lave;
While, on the white tower lifted high,
The circling lenses flash and pass
With yellow light in faded glass
And sickly shine against the sky.

II

As the steady lenses circle
With a frosty gleam of glass;
And the clear bell chimes,
And the oil brims over the lip of the burner,
Quiet and still at his desk,
The lonely Light-Keeper
Holds his vigil.

Lured from far,
The bewildered seagull beats
Dully against the lantern;
Yet he stirs not, lifts not his head
From the desk where he reads,
Lifts not his eyes to see
The chill blind circle of night
Watching him through the panes.
This is his country's guardian,
The outmost sentry of peace.
This is the man
Who gives up that is lovely in living
For the means to live.

Poetry cunningly gilds
The life of the Light-Keeper,
Held on high in the blackness
In the burning kernel of night,
The seaman sees and blesses him,
The Poet, deep in a sonnet,
Numbers his inky fingers
Fitly to praise him.
Only we behold him,
Sitting, patient and stolid,
Martyr to a salary.

[81]

XXIV

My brain swims empty and light
Like a nut on a sea of oil;
And an atmosphere of quiet
Wraps me about from the turmoil and clamour of
   life.

I stand apart from living,
Apart and holy I stand,
In my new-gained growth of idleness, I stand,
As stood the Shekinah of yore in the holy of holies.

I walk the streets smoking my pipe
And I love the dallying shop-girl
That leans with rounded stern to look at the
   fashions;
And I hate the bustling citizen,
The eager and hurrying man of affairs I hate,
Because he bears his intolerance writ on his face
And every movement and word of him tells me how
   much he hates me.

I love night in the city,
The lighted streets and the swinging gait of harlots.
I love cool pale morning,
In the empty bye-streets,
With only here and there a female figure,
A slavey with lifted dress and the key in her hand,
A girl or two at play in a corner of waste-land
Tumbling and showing their legs and crying out to me
   loosely.

XXV

The Cruel Mistress

HERE let me rest, here nurse the uneasy qualm
That yearns within me;
And to the heaped-up sea,
Sun-spangled in the quiet afternoon,
Sing my devotions.

In the sun, at the edge of the down,
The whin-pods crackle
In desultory volleys;
And the bank breathes in my face
Its hot sweet breath—
Breath that stirs and kindles,
Lights that suggest, not satisfy—
Is there never in life or nature
An opiate for desire?
Has everything here a voice,
Saying '*I am not the goal;*
Nature is not to be looked at alone;
Her breath, like the breath of a mistress,
Her breath also,
Parches the spirit with longing
Sick and enervating longing.'

Well, let the matter rest.
I rise and brush the windle-straws
Off my clothes; and lighting another pipe
Stretch myself over the down.
Get thee behind me, Nature!
I turn my back on the sun
And face from the grey new town at the foot of
        the bay.

[83]

I know an amber lady
Who has her abode
   At the lips of the street
In prisons of coloured glass.
I had rather die of her love
Than sicken for you, O Nature!
Better be drunk and merry
Than dreaming awake!
Better be Falstaff than Obermann!

XXVI

Storm

THE narrow lanes are vacant and wet;
The rough wind bullies and blusters about the
       township.
And spins the vane on the tower
And chases the scurrying leaves,
And the straw in the damp innyard.
See—a girl passes
Tripping gingerly over the pools,
And under her lifted dress
I catch the gleam of a comely, stockinged leg.
Pah! the room stifles me,
Reeking of stale tobacco—
With the four black mealy horrible prints
After Landseer's pictures.
I will go out.

Here the free wind comes with a fuller circle,
Sings, like an angry wasp, in the straining grass,
Sings and whistles;
And the hurried flow of rain
Scourges my face and passes.

Behind me, clustered together, the rain-wet roofs
    of the town
Shine, and the light vane shines as it veers
In the long pale finger of sun that hurries across
    them to me.
The fresh salt air is keen in my nostrils,
And far down the shining sand
Foam and thunder
And take the shape of the bay in eager mirth
The white-head hungry billows.
The earth shakes
As the semicircle of waters
Stoops and casts itself down;
And far outside in the open,
Wandering gleams of sunshine
Show us the ordered horde that hurries to follow.

Ei! merry companions,
Your madness infects me.
My whole soul rises and falls and leaps and tumbles
    with you!
I shout aloud and incite you, O white-headed merry
    companions.
The sight of you alone is better than drinking.
The brazen band is loosened from off my forehead;
My breast and my brain are moistened and cool;
And still I yell in answer
To your hoarse inarticulate voices,
O big, strong, bullying, boisterous waves,
That are of all things in nature the nearest thoughts
    to human,
Because you are wicked and foolish,
Mad and destructive.

XXVII

Stormy Nights

I CRY out war to those who spend their utmost,
Trying to substitute a vain regret
For childhood's vanished moods,
Instead of a full manly satisfaction
In new development.
Their words are vain as the lost shouts,
The wasted breath of solitary hunters
That are far buried in primeval woods—
Clamour that dies in silence,
Cries that bring back no answer
But the great voice of the wind-shaken forest,
Mocking despair.

No—they will get no answer;
For I too recollect,
I recollect and love my perished childhood,
Perfectly love and keenly recollect;
I too remember; and if it could be
Would not recall it.

Do I not know, how, nightly, on my bed
The palpable close darkness shutting round me,
How my small heart went forth to evil things,
How all the possibilities of sin
That were yet present to my innocence
Bound me too narrowly,
And how my spirit beat
The cage of its compulsive purity;
How—my eyes fixed,
My shot lip tremulous between my fingers

[86]

I fashioned for myself new modes of crime,
Created for myself with pain and labour
The evil that the cobwebs of society,
The comely secrecies of education,
Had made an itching mystery to meward.

Do I not know again,
When the great winds broke loose and went abroad
At night in the lighted town—
Ah! then it was different—
Then, when I seemed to hear
The storm go by me like a cloak-wrapt horseman
Stooping over the saddle—
Go by, and come again and yet again,
Like some one riding with a pardon,
And ever baffled, ever shut from passage:
Then when the house shook and a horde of noises
Came out and clattered over me all night,
Then, would my heart stand still,
My hair creep fearfully upon my head
And, with my tear-wet face
Buried among the bed-clothes,
Long and bitterly would I pray and wrestle
Till gentle sleep
Threw her great mantle over me,
And my hard breathing gradually ceased.

I was then the Indian,
Well and happy and full of glee and pleasure,
Both hands full of life.
And not without divine impulses
Shot into me by the untried non-ego;
But, like the Indian, too,
Not yet exempt from feverish questionings,
And on my bed of leaves,

[87]

Writhing terribly in grasp of terror,
As when the still stars and the great white moon
Watch me athwart black foliage,
Trembling before the interminable vista,
The widening wells of space
In which my thought flags like a wearied bird
In the mid ocean of his autumn flight—
Prostrate before the indefinite great spirit
That the external warder
Plunged like a dagger
Into my bosom.
Now, I am a Greek
White-robed among the sunshine and the statues
And the fair porticos of carven marble—
Fond of olives and dry sherry,
Good tobacco and clever talk with my fellows,
Free from inordinate cravings.
Why would you hurry me, O evangelist,
You with the bands and the shilling packet of
        tracts
Greatly reduced when taken for distribution?
Why do you taunt my progress,
O green-spectacled Wordsworth! in beautiful
        verses,
You, the elderly poet?
So I shall travel forward
Step by step with the rest of my race,
In time, if death should spare me,
I shall come on to a farther stage,
And show you St Francis of Assisi.

XXVIII

Song at Dawn

I SEE the dawn creep round the world,
Here damm'd a moment backward by great hills,
There racing o'er the sea.
Down at the round equator,
It leaps forth straight and rapid,
Driving with firm sharp edge the night before it.
Here gradually it floods
The wooded valleys and the weeds
And the still smokeless cities.
The cocks crow up at the farms;
The sick man's spirit is glad;
The watch treads brisker about the dew-wet deck ;
The light-keeper locks his desk,
As the lenses turn,
Faded and yellow.

The girl with the embroidered shift
Rises and leans on the sill,
And her full bosom heaves
Drinking deep of the silentness.
I too rise and watch
The healing fingers of dawn—
I too drink from its eyes
The unaccountable peace—
I too drink and am satisfied as with food.
Fain would I go
Down by the winding crossroad by the trees,
Where at the corner of wet wood
The blackbird in the early grey and stillness
Wakes his first song.

Peace, who can make verses clink,
Find ictus following surely after ictus,
At such an hour as this, the heart
Lies steeped and silent.
O dreaming, leaning girl,
Already are the sovereign hill-tops ruddy,
Already the grey passes, the white streak
Brightens above dark woodlands, Day begins.

XXIX

Nous n'irons plus aux bois

WE'LL walk the woods no more
But stay beside the fire,
To weep for old desire
And things that are no more.

  The woods are spoiled and hoar,
The ways are full of mire;
We'll walk the woods no more
But stay beside the fire.

  We loved, in days of yore
Love, laughter, and the lyre.
Ah God, but death is dire
And death is at the door—
We'll walk the woods no more.

XXX

IN Autumn when the woods are red
And skies are grey and clear,
The sportsmen seek the wild fowls' bed
Or follow down the deer;

And Cupid hunts by haugh and head,
By riverside and mere,
I walk, not seeing where I tread
And keep my heart with fear,
Sir, have an eye, on where you tread,
And keep your heart with fear,
For something lingers here;
A touch of April not yet dead,
In Autumn when the woods are red
And skies are grey and clear.

XXXI

Love is the very heart of Spring;
    Flocks fall to loving on the lea
And wildfowl love upon the wing,
    When Spring first enters like a sea.
When Spring first enters like a sea
    Into the heart of everything;
Bestir yourselves religiously,
    Incense before love's altar bring.
Incense before love's altar bring,
    Flowers from the flowering hawthorn tree,
Flowers from the margin of the spring,
    For all the flowers are sweet to see.
Love is the very heart of Spring;
    When Spring first enters like a sea
Incense before love's altar bring,
    And flowers while flowers are sweet to see.
Bring flowers while flowers are sweet to see.
    Love is almighty, love's a King,
Incense before love's altar bring,
    Incense before love's altar bring.

Love's gifts are generous and free
　When Spring first enters like a sea;
When Spring first enters like a sea,
　The birds are all inspired to sing.
Love is the very heart of Spring,
　The birds are all inspired to sing,
Love's gifts are generous and free,
　Love is almighty, love's a King.

XXXII

I who all the winter through,
　Cherished other loves than you,
And kept hands with hoary policy in marriage bed and
　　pew;
　Now I know the false and true,
　For the earnest sun looks through,
And my old love comes to meet me in the dawning and
　　the dew.

　Now the hedged meads renew
　Rustic odour, smiling hue,
And the clean air shines and twinkles as the world
　　goes wheeling through;
　And my heart springs up anew,
　Bright and confident and true,
And my old love comes to meet me in the dawning and
　　the dew.

XXXIII

Here you rest among the vallies, maiden known to but
　a few;
　Here you sleep unsighing, but how oft of yore you
　　sighed!
And how oft your feet elastic trod a measure in the dew
　On a green beside the river ere you died!

[92]

Where are now the country lovers whom you trembled
     to be near—
  Who, with shy advances, in the falling eventide,
Grasped the tightlier at your fingers, whispered lowlier
     in your ear,
  On a green beside the river ere you died?

All the sweet old country dancers who went round with
     you in tune,
  Dancing, flushed and silent, in the silent eventide,
All departed by enchantment at the rising of the moon
  From the green beside the river when you died.

XXXIV

  Grown about by fragrant bushes,
  Sunken in a winding valley,
    Where the clear winds blow
    And the shadows come and go,
    And the cattle stand and low
  And the sheep bells and the linnets
    Sing and tinkle musically.
  Between the past and the future,
    Those two black infinities
    Between which our brief life
    Flashes a moment and goes out.

XXXV

Love—what is love? A great and aching heart
Wrung hands; and silence; and a long despair.
Life—what is life? Upon a moorland bare
To see love coming and see love depart.

[93]

XXXVI

DEATH, to the dead for evermore
A King, a God, the last, the best of friends—
Whene'er this mortal journey ends
Death, like a host, comes smiling to the door;
Smiling, he greets us, on that tranquil shore
Where neither piping bird nor peeping dawn
Disturbs the eternal sleep,
But in the stillness far withdrawn
Our dreamless rest for evermore we keep.

For as from open windows forth we peep
Upon the night-time star beset
And with dews for ever wet;
So from this garish life the spirit peers;
And lo! as a sleeping city, death outspread,
Where breathe the sleepers evenly; and lo!
After the loud wars, triumphs, trumpets, tears
And clamour of man's passion, Death appears
And we must rise and go.

Soon are eyes tired with sunshine, soon the ears
Weary of utterance, seeing all is said;
Soon, racked by hopes and fears,
The all-pondering, all-contriving head,
Weary with all things, wearies of the years;
And our sad spirits turn toward the dead;
And the tired child, the body, longs for bed.

XXXVII

I saw red evening through the rain,
Lower above the steaming plain;
I heard the hour strike small and still,
From the black belfry on the hill.

Thought is driven out of doors to-night
By bitter memory of delight;
The sharp constraint of finger tips,
Or the shuddering touch of lips.

I heard the hour strike small and still,
From the black belfry on the hill.
Behind me I could still look down
On the outspread monstrous town.

The sharp constraint of finger tips
Or the shuddering touch of lips,
And all old memories of delight
Crowd upon my soul to-night.

Behind me I could still look down
On the outspread feverish town;
But before me still and grey
And lonely was the forward way.

XXXVIII

The Daughter of Herodias

THREE yellow slaves were set to swing
    The doorway curtain to and fro,
With rustle of light folds and ring
    Of little bells that hung below;
    The still, hot night was tempered so.

[95]

And ever, from the carven bed,
  She watched the labour of the men;
And saw the band of moonlight spread,
  Leap up upon her feet and then
  Leap down upon the floor again;

And ever, vexed with heat and doubt,
  Below the burthen of their shawls,
The still grey olives saw without
  And glimmer of white garden walls,
  Between the alternate curtain falls.

What ailed the dainty lady then,
  The dainty lady, fair and sweet?
Unseen of these three silent men,
  A something lay upon her feet,
  Not comely for such eyes to meet.

She saw a golden salver there
  And, laid upon it, on the bed,
The white teeth showing keen and bare
  Between the sundered lips, a head
  Sallow and horrible and dead.

She saw upon the sallow cheek
  Rust-coloured blood-stains; and the eye
Her frightened glances seemed to seek
  Half-lifting its blue lid on high,
  Watching her, horrible and sly.

Thus spake she: '*Once again that head!*
  I ate too much pilau to-night,
  My mother and the eunuchs said.
  Well, I can take a hint aright—
  To-morrow's supper shall be light.'

XXXIX

As one who having wandered all night long
In a perplexed forest, comes at length,
In the first hours, about the matin song,
And when the sun uprises in his strength,
To the fringed margin of the wood, and sees,
Gazing afar before him, many a mile
Of falling country, many fields and trees,
And cities and bright streams and far-off Ocean's
    smile:

I, O Melampus, halting, stand at gaze;
I, liberated, look abroad on life,
Love, and distress, and dusty travelling ways,
The steersman's helm, the surgeon's helpful knife,
Or the lone ploughman's earth-upturning share,
The revelry of cities and the sound
Of seas, and mountain-tops aloof in air,
And of the circling earth the unsupported round:

I, looking, wonder: I, intent, adore;
And, O Melampus, reaching forth my hands
In adoration, cry aloud and soar
In spirit, high above the supine lands
And the low cares of mortal things, and flee
To the last fields of the universe untrod,
Where is nor man, nor any earth, nor sea,
And the contented soul is all alone with God.

XL

Praise and Prayer

I HAVE been well, I have been ill,
    I have been rich and poor;
I have set my back against the wall
    And fought it by the hour;

I have been false, I have been true;
    And thoro' grief and mirth,
I have done all that man can do
    To be a man of worth;

And now, when from an unknown shore,
    I dare an unknown wave,
God, who has helped me heretofore,
    O help me wi' the lave!

XLI

John Cavalier

THESE are your hills, John Cavalier.
Your father's kids you tended here,
And grew, among these mountains wild,
A humble and religious child.
Fate turned the wheel; you grew and grew;
Bold Marshals doffed the hat to you;
God whispered counsels in your ear
To guide your sallies, Cavalier.

[98]

You shook the earth with martial tread;
The ensigns fluttered by your head;
In Spain or France, Velay or Kent,
The music sounded as you went.
Much would I give if I might spy
Your brave battalions marching by;
Or, on the wind, if I might hear
Your drums and bugles, Cavalier.

In vain. O'er all the windy hill,
The ways are void, the air is still,
Alone, below the echoing rock,
The shepherd calls upon his flock.
The wars of Spain and of Cevennes,
The bugles and the marching men,
The horse you rode for many a year—
Where are they now, John Cavalier?

All armies march the selfsame way
Far from the cheerful eye of day;
And you and yours marched down below
About two hundred years ago.
Over the hills, into the shade,
Journeys each mortal cavalcade;
Out of the sound, out of the sun,
They go when their day's work is done;
And all shall doff the bandoleer
To sleep with dead John Cavalier.

XLII

The Iron Steed

In our black stable by the sea,
Five and twenty stalls you see—
Five and twenty strong are we:
The lanterns tossed the shadows round,
Live coals were scattered on the ground,
The swarthy ostlers echoing stept,
But silent all night long we slept.
Inactive we, steeds of the day,
The shakers of the mountains, lay.
Earth's oldest veins our dam and sire,
Iron chimeras fed with fire.
All we, the unweary, lay at rest;
The sleepless lamp burned on our crest;
And in the darkness far and nigh,
We heard our iron compeers cry:

Soon as the day began to spring . . .

XLIII

Of where or how, I nothing know,
      And why I do not care.
      Enough if even so,
My travelling eyes, my travelling mind can go
By flood and field and hill, by wood and meadow fair,
Beside the Susquehanna and along the Delaware.

I think, I hope, I dream no more
      The dreams of otherwhere,
      The cherished thoughts of yore;
I have been changed from what I was before;
Or breathed perchance too deep the lotus of the air
Beside the Susquehanna and along the Delaware.

Though westward steers the train, my soul
   Shall for the East declare;
   Shall take the East for goal,
Outward and upward bound; and still shall roll,
And still unconquered live, as now she spurns despair
Beside the Susquehanna and along the Delaware.

Unweary God me yet shall bring
   To lands of brighter air,
   Where I, now half a king,
Shall with superior spirit loudlier sing,
And wear a bolder front than that which now I wear
Beside the Susquehanna and along the Delaware.

PIECES IN LALLAN

I

To The Commissioners of Northern Lights, with a Paper

I SEND to you, commissioners,
A paper that may please ye, sirs,
(For troth they say it micht be worse
   An' I believ't)
And on your business lay my curse
   Before I leav't.

I thocht I'd serve wi' you, sirs, yince,
But I've thocht better of it since;
The maitter I will nowise mince,
   But tell ye true:
I'll service wi' some ither prince,
   An' no' wi' you.

I've no' been very deep, ye'll think,
Cam' delicately to the brink
An' when the water gart me shrink
    Straucht took the rue,
An' didna stoop my fill to drink—
    I own it true.

I kent on cape and isle, a light
Burnt fair an' clearly ilka night;
But at the service I took fright,
    As sune's I saw,
An' being still a neophite
    Gaed straucht awa'.

Anither course I now begin,
The weeg I'll cairry for my sin,
The court my voice sall echo in,
    An'—wha can tell?—
Some ither day I may be yin
    O' you mysel'.

II

To Mesdames Zassetsky and Garschine

THE wind may blaw the lee-lang way
And aye the lift be mirk an' gray,
An' deep the moss and steigh the brae
    Where a' maun gang—
There's still an hoor in ilka day
    For luve and sang.

And canty hearts are strangly steeled.
By some dikeside they'll find a bield,
Some couthy neuk by muir or field
    They're sure to hit,
Where, frae the blatherin' wind concealed,
    They'll rest a bit.

An' weel for them if kindly fate
Send ower the hills to them a mate;
They'll crack a while o' kirk an' State,
    O' yowes an' rain:
And when it's time to tak' the gate,
    Tak' ilk his ain.

—Sic neuk beside the southern sea
I soucht—sic place o' quiet lee
Frae a' the winds o' life. To me,
    Fate, rarely fair,
Had set a freendly company
    To meet me there.

Kindly by them they gart me sit,
An' blythe was I to bide a bit.
Licht as o' some hame fireside lit
    My life for me.
—Ower early maun I rise an' quit
    This happy lee.

III

To Charles Baxter

Noo lyart leaves blaw ower the green,
Reid are the bonny woods o' Dean,
An' here we're back in Embro, frien',
    To pass the winter.
Whilk noo, wi' frosts afore, draws in,
    An' snaws ahint her.

I've seen 's hae days to fricht us a',
The Pentlands poothered weel wi' snaw,
The ways half smoored wi' liquid thaw
    An' half congealin',
The snell an' scowtherin' norther blaw
    Frae blae Brunteelan'.

I've seen 's been unco sweir to sally
And at the door-cheeks daff an' dally—
Seen 's daidle thus an' shilly-shally
    For near a minute—
Sae cauld the wind blew up the valley,
    The deil was in it!—

Syne spread the silk an' tak the gate,
In blast an' blaudin' rain, deil hae 't!
The hale toon glintin', stane an' slate,
    Wi' cauld an' weet,
An' to the Court, gin we 'se be late,
    Bicker oor feet.

And at the Court, tae, aft I saw
Whaur Advocates by twa an' twa

Gang gesterin' end to end the ha'
    In weeg an' goon,
To crack o' what ye wull but Law
    The hale forenoon.

That muckle ha', maist like a kirk,
I've kent at braid mid-day sae mirk
Ye'd seen white weegs an' faces lurk
    Like ghaists frae Hell,
But whether Christian ghaists or Turk
    Deil ane could tell.

The three fires lunted in the gloom,
The wind blew like the blast o' doom,
The rain upo' the roof abune
    Played Peter Dick—
Ye wad nae'd licht enough i' the room
    Your teeth to pick!

But, freend, ye ken how me an' you,
The ling-lang lanely winter through,
Keep'd a guid speerit up, an' true
    To lore Horatian,
We aye the ither bottle drew—
    To inclination.

Sae let us in the comin' days
Stand sicker on oor auncient ways—
The strauchtest road in a' the maze
    Since Eve ate apples;
An' let the winter weet oor cla'es—
    We'll weet oor thrapples.

IV

To the Same

On the death of their common friend, Mr John Adam,
Clerk of Court

An' Johnie's deid. The mair's the pity!
He's deid, an' deid o' Aqua-vitae.
O Embro', you're a shrunken city,
    Noo Johnie's deid!
Tak hands, an' sing a burial ditty
    Ower Johnie's heid.

To see him was baith drink an' meat,
Gaun linkin' glegly up the street.
He but to rin or tak a seat,
    The wee bit body!
Bein' aye unsicker on his feet
    Wi' whusky toddy.

To be aye tosh was Johnie's whim.
There's nane was better tent than him,
Though whiles his gravit-knot wad clim'
    Ahint his ear,
An' whiles he'd buttons oot or in
    The less or mair.

His hair a' lank aboot his bree,
His tap-lip lang by inches three—
A slockened sort o' mou', to pree
    A' sensuality—
A drouthy glint was in his e'e
    An' personality.

An' day an' nicht, frae daw to daw,
Dink an' perjink an' doucely braw,
Wi' a kind o' Gospel look ower a',
    May or October,
Like Peden, followin' the Law
    An' no that sober.

An' wow! but John was unco sport.
Whiles he wad smile aboot the Court
Malvolio-like—whiles snore an' snort,
    Was heard afar.
The idle writer lads' resort
    Was aye John's bar.

Whusky an' he were pack thegether.
Whate'er the hour, whate'er the weather,
John kept himsel' wi' mistened leather
    An' kindled spunk.
Wi' him, there was nae askin' whether—
    John was aye drunk.

The auncient heroes gash an' bauld
In the uncanny days of Auld,
The task ance found to which th'were called,
    Stack stenchly to it.
His life sic noble lives recalled,
    Little's he knew it.

Single an' straucht, he went his way.
He kept the faith an' played the play.
Whusky an' he were man an' may
    Whate'er betided.
Bonny in life—in death, thir twae
    Were no' divided.

What's merely humourous or bonny
The warl' regairds wi' cauld astony.
Drunk men tak' aye mair place than ony;
    An' sae, ye see,
The gate was aye ower thrang for Johnie—
    Or you an' me.

John micht hae jingled cap an' bells,
Been a braw fule in silks an' fells.
In ane o' the auld warl's canty hells,
    Paris or Sodom.
I wadnae had him naething else
    But Johnie Adam.

He suffered—as have a' that wan
Eternal memory frae man,
Sin' e'er the weary warl' began—
    Mister or Madam,
Keats or Scots Burns, the Spanish Dan
    Or Johnie Adam.

We leuch, an' Johnie deid. An', fegs!
Hoo he had keept his stoiterin' legs
Sae lang's he did, 's a fact that begs
    An explanation.
He stachers fifty years—syne flegs
    To's destination.

UNDERWOODS

Of all my verse, like not a single line;
But like my title, for it is not mine.
That title from a better man I stole:
Ah, how much better, had I stol'n the whole!

BOOK I: IN ENGLISH

I

Envoy

Go, little book, and wish to all
Flowers in the garden, meat in the hall,
A bin of wine, a spice of wit,
A house with lawns enclosing it,
A living river by the door,
A nightingale in the sycamore!

II

A Song of the Road

THE gauger walked with willing foot,
And aye the gauger played the flute;
And what should Master Gauger play
But *Over the hills and far away?*

When'er I buckle on my pack
And foot it gaily in the track,
O pleasant gauger, long since dead,
I hear you fluting on ahead.

You go with me the self-same way—
The self-same air for me you play;
For I do think and so do you
It is the tune to travel to.

For who would gravely set his face
To go to this or t'other place?
There's nothing under Heav'n so blue
That's fairly worth the travelling to.

On every hand the roads begin,
And people walk with zeal therein;
But wheresoe'er the highways tend,
Be sure there's nothing at the end.

Then follow you, wherever hie
The travelling mountains of the sky.
Or let the streams in civil mode
Direct your choice upon a road;

For one and all, or high or low,
Will lead you where you wish to go;
And one and all go night and day
Over the hills and far away!

III

The Canoe Speaks

On the great streams the ships may go
About men's business to and fro.
But I, the egg-shell pinnace, sleep
On crystal waters ankle-deep:
I, whose diminutive design,
Of sweeter cedar, pithier pine,
Is fashioned on so frail a mould,
A hand may launch, a hand withhold:
I, rather, with the leaping trout
Wind, among lilies, in and out;

I, the unnamed, inviolate,
Green, rustic rivers, navigate;
My dipping paddle scarcely shakes
The berry in the bramble-brakes;
Still forth on my green way I wend
Beside the cottage garden-end;
And by the nested angler fare,
And take the lovers unaware.
By willow wood and water-wheel
Speedily fleets my touching keel;
By all retired and shady spots
Where prosper dim forget-me-nots;
By meadows where at afternoon
The growing maidens troop in June
To loose their girdles on the grass.
Ah! speedier than before the glass
The backward toilet goes; and swift
As swallows quiver, robe and shift
And the rough country stockings lie
Around each young divinity.
When, following the recondite brook,
Sudden upon this scene I look,
And light with unfamiliar face
On chaste Diana's bathing-place,
Loud ring the hills about and all
The shallows are abandoned. . . .

IV

IT is the season now to go
About the country high and low,
Among the lilacs hand in hand,
And two by two in fairy land.

The brooding boy, the sighing maid,
Wholly fain and half afraid,
Now meet along the hazel'd brook
To pass and linger, pause and look.

A year ago, and blithely paired,
Their rough-and-tumble play they shared;
They kissed and quarrelled, laughed and cried,
A year ago at Eastertide.

With bursting heart, with fiery face,
She strove against him in the race;
He unabashed her garter saw,
That now would touch her skirts with awe.

Now by the stile ablaze she stops,
And his demurer eyes he drops;
Now they exchange averted sighs
Or stand and marry silent eyes.

And he to her a hero is.
And sweeter she than primroses;
Their common silence dearer far
Than nightingale and mavis are.

Now when they sever wedded hands,
Joy trembles in their bosom-strands,
And lovely laughter leaps and falls
Upon their lips in madrigals.

V

The House Beautiful

A naked house, a naked moor,
A shivering pool before the door,
A garden bare of flowers and fruit
And poplars at the garden foot:
Such is the place that I live in,
Bleak without and bare within.

Yet shall your ragged moor receive
The incomparable pomp of eve,
And the cold glories of the dawn
Behind your shivering trees be drawn;
And when the wind from place to place
Doth the unmoored cloud-galleons chase,
Your garden gloom and gleam again,
With leaping sun, with glancing rain.
Here shall the wizard moon ascend
The heavens, in the crimson end
Of day's declining splendour; here
The army of the stars appear.
The neighbour hollows dry or wet,
Spring shall with tender flowers beset;
And oft the morning muser see
Larks rising from the broomy lea,
And every fairy wheel and thread
Of cobweb dew-bediamonded.
When daisies go, shall winter time
Silver the simple grass with rime;
Autumnal frosts enchant the pool
And make the cart-ruts beautiful;
And when snow-bright the moor expands,
How shall your children clap their hands!

To make this earth, our hermitage,
A cheerful and a changeful page,
God's bright and intricate device
Of days and seasons doth suffice.

VI

A Visit from the Sea

Far from the loud sea beaches
    Where he goes fishing and crying,
Here in the inland garden
    Why is the sea-gull flying?

Here are no fish to dive for;
    Here is the corn and lea;
Here are the green trees rustling.
    Hie away home to sea!

Fresh is the river water
    And quiet among the rushes;
This is no home for the sea-gull
    But for the rooks and thrushes.

Pity the bird that has wandered!
    Pity the sailor ashore!
Hurry him home to the ocean,
    Let him come here no more!

High on the sea-cliff ledges
    The white gulls are trooping and crying,
Here among rooks and roses,
    Why is the sea-gull flying?

VII

To a Gardener

Friend, in my mountain-side demesne,
My plain-beholding, rosy, green
And linnet-haunted garden-ground,
Let still the esculents abound.
Let first the onion flourish there,
Rose among roots, the maiden-fair,
Wine-scented and poetic soul
Of the capacious salad bowl.
Let thyme the mountaineer (to dress
The tinier birds) and wading cress,
The lover of the shallow brook,
From all my plots and borders look.
Nor crisp and ruddy radish, nor
Pease-cods for the child's pinafore
Be lacking; nor of salad clan
The last and least that ever ran
About great nature's garden-beds.
Nor thence be missed the speary heads
Of artichoke; nor thence the bean
That gathered innocent and green
Outsavours the belauded pea.

These tend, I prithee; and for me,
Thy most long-suffering master, bring
In April, when the linnets sing
And the days lengthen more and more,
At sundown to the garden door.
And I, being provided thus,
Shall, with superb asparagus,
A book, a taper, and a cup
Of country wine, divinely sup.

[117]

VIII

To Minnie

With a hand-glass

A PICTURE-FRAME for you to fill,
   A paltry setting for your face,
A thing that has no worth until
   You lend it something of your grace,

I send (unhappy I that sing
   Laid by awhile upon the shelf)
Because I would not send a thing
   Less charming than you are yourself.

And happier than I, alas!
   (Dumb thing, I envy its delight)
'Twill wish you well, the looking-glass,
   And look you in the face to-night.

IX

To K. de M.

A LOVER of the moorland bare
And honest country winds, you were;
The silver-skimming rain you took;
And loved the floodings of the brook,
Dew, frost and mountains, fire and seas,
Tumultuary silences,
Winds that in darkness fifed a tune,
And the high-riding, virgin moon.

And as the berry, pale and sharp,
Springs on some ditch's counterscarp
In our ungenial, native north—
You put your frosted wildings forth,
And on the heath, afar from man,
A strong and bitter virgin ran.

The berry ripened keeps the rude
And racy flavour of the wood.
And you that loved the empty plain
All redolent of wind and rain,
Around you still the curlew sings—
The freshness of the weather clings—
The maiden jewels of the rain
Sit in your dabbled locks again.

X

To N. V. de G. S.

THE unfathomable sea, and time, and tears,
The deeds of heroes and the crimes of kings
Dispart us; and the river of events
Has, for an age of years, to east and west
More widely borne our cradles. Thou to me
Art foreign, as when seamen at the dawn
Descry a land far off and know not which.
So I approach uncertain; so I cruise
Round thy mysterious islet, and behold
Surf and great mountains and loud river-bars,
And from the shore hear inland voices call.
Strange is the seaman's heart; he hopes, he fears;
Draws closer and sweeps wider from that coast;
Last, his rent sail refits, and to the deep
His shattered prow uncomforted puts back.

[119]

Yet as he goes he ponders at the helm
Of that bright island; where he feared to touch,
His spirit rëadventures; and for years,
Where by his wife he slumbers safe at home,
Thoughts of that land revisit him; he sees
The eternal mountains beckon, and awakes
Yearning for that far home that might have been.

XI

To Will H. Low

YOUTH now flees on feathered foot,
Faint and fainter sounds the flute,
Rarer songs of gods; and still
Somewhere on the sunny hill,
Or along the winding stream,
Through the willows, flits a dream;
Flits but shows a smiling face,
Flees but with so quaint a grace,
None can choose to stay at home,
All must follow, all must roam.

This is unborn beauty: she
Now in air floats high and free,
Takes the sun and breaks the blue;—
Late with stooping pinion flew
Raking hedgerow trees, and wet
Her wing in silver streams, and set
Shining foot on temple roof:
Now again she flies aloof,
Coasting mountain clouds and kiss't
By the evening's amethyst.

In wet wood and miry lane,
Still we pant and pound in vain;
Still with leaden foot we chase
Waning pinion, fainting face;
Still with gray hair we stumble on,
Till, behold, the vision gone!
Where hath fleeting beauty led?
To the doorway of the dead.
Life is over, life was gay:
We have come the primrose way.

XII

To Mrs Will H. Low

EVEN in the bluest noonday of July,
There could not run the smallest breath of wind
But all the quarter sounded like a wood;
And in the chequered silence and above
The hum of city cabs that sought the Bois,
Suburban ashes shivered into song.
A patter and a chatter and a chirp
And a long dying hiss—it was as though
Starched old brocaded dames through all the house
Had trailed a strident skirt, or the whole sky
Even in a wink had over-brimmed in rain.
Hark, in these shady parlours, how it talks
Of the near Autumn, how the smitten ash
Trembles and augurs floods! O not too long
In these inconstant latitudes delay,
O not too late from the unbeloved north
Trim your escape! For soon shall this low roof
Resound indeed with rain, soon shall your eyes
Search the foul garden, search the darkened rooms,
Nor find one jewel but the blazing log.

XIII

To H. F. Brown

Written during a dangerous sickness

I SIT and wait a pair of oars
On cis-Elysian river-shores.
Where the immortal dead have sate,
'Tis mine to sit and meditate;
To re-ascend life's rivulet,
Without remorse, without regret;
And sing my *Alma Genetrix*
Among the willows of the Styx.

And lo, as my serener soul
Did these unhappy shores patrol,
And wait with an attentive ear
The coming of the gondolier,
Your fire-surviving roll I took,
Your spirited and happy book;
Whereon, despite my frowning fate,
It did my soul so recreate
That all my fancies fled away
On a Venetian holiday.

Now, thanks to your triumphant care,
Your pages clear as April air,
The sails, the bells, the birds, I know,
And the far-off Friulan snow;
The land and sea, the sun and shade,
And the blue even lamp-inlaid.

For this, for these, for all, O friend,
For your whole book from end to end—
For Paron Piero's mutton-ham—
I your defaulting debtor am.

Perchance, reviving, yet may I
To your sea-paven city hie,
And in a *felze*, some day yet
Light at your pipe my cigarette.

XIV

To Andrew Lang

DEAR Andrew, with the brindled hair,
Who glory to have thrown in air,
High over arm, the trembling reed,
By Ale and Kail, by Till and Tweed:
An equal craft of hand you show
The pen to guide, the fly to throw:
I count you happy starred; for God,
When He with inkpot and with rod
Endowed you, bade your fortune lead
Forever by the crooks of Tweed,
Forever by the woods of song
And lands that to the Muse belong;
Or if in peopled streets, or in
The abhorred pedantic sanhedrin,
It should be yours to wander, still
Airs of the morn, airs of the hill,
The plovery Forest and the seas
That break about the Hebrides,
Should follow over field and plain
And find you at the window pane;

And you again see hill and peel,
And the bright springs gush at your heel.
So went the fiat forth, and so
Garrulous like a brook you go,
With sound of happy mirth and sheen
Of daylight—whether by the green
You fare that moment, or the gray;
Whether you dwell in March or May;
Or whether treat of reels and rods
Or of the old unhappy gods:
Still like a brook your page has shone,
And your ink sings of Helicon.

XV

Et Tu in Arcadia Vixisti

To R. A. M. S.

In ancient tales, O friend, thy spirit dwelt;
There, from of old, thy childhood passed; and there
High expectation, high delights and deeds,
Thy fluttering heart with hope and terror moved.
And thou hast heard of yore the Blatant Beast,
And Roland's horn, and that war-scattering shout
Of all-unarmed Achilles, ægis-crowned.
And perilous lands thou sawest, sounding shores
And seas and forests drear, island and dale
And mountain dark. For thou with Tristram rod'st
Or Bedevere, in farthest Lyonesse.
Thou hadst a booth in Samarcand, whereat
Side-looking Magians trafficked; thence, by night,
An Afreet snatched thee, and with wings upbore
Beyond the Aral mount; or, hoping gain,
Thou, with a jar of money, didst embark,
For Balsorah, by sea. But chiefly thou

In that clear air took'st life; in Arcady
The haunted, land of song; and by the wells
Where most the gods frequent. There Chiron old,
In the Pelethronian antre, taught thee lore:
The plants, he taught, and by the shining stars
In forests dim to steer. There hast thou seen
Immortal Pan dance secret in a glade,
And, dancing, roll his eyes; these, where they fell,
Shed glee, and through the congregated oaks
A flying horror winged; while all the earth
To the god's pregnant footing thrilled within.
Or whiles, beside the sobbing stream, he breathed,
In his clutched pipe, unformed and wizard strains.
Divine yet brutal; which the forest heard,
And thou, with awe; and far upon the plain
The unthinking ploughman started and gave ear.

Now things there are that, upon him who sees,
A strong vocation lay; and strains there are
That whoso hears shall hear for evermore.
For evermore thou hear'st immortal Pan
And those melodious godheads, ever young
And ever quiring, on the mountains old.

What was this earth, child of the gods, to thee?
Forth from thy dreamland thou, a dreamer, cam'st,
And in thine ears the olden music rang,
And in thy mind the doings of the dead,
And those heroic ages long forgot.
To a so fallen earth, alas! too late,
Alas! in evil days, thy steps return,
To list at noon for nightingales, to grow
A dweller on the beach till Argo come
That came long since, a lingerer by the pool
Where that desirèd angel bathes no more.

As when the Indian to Dakota comes,
Or farthest Idaho, and where he dwelt,
He with his clan, a humming city finds;
Thereon awhile, amazed, he stares, and then
To right and leftward, like a questing dog,
Seeks first the ancestral altars, then the hearth
Long cold with rains, and where old terror lodged,
And where the dead. So thee undying Hope,
With all her pack, hunts screaming through the years:
Here, there, thou fleeëst; but nor here nor there
The pleasant gods abide, the glory dwells.

That, that was not Apollo, not the god.
This was not Venus, though she Venus seemed
A moment. And though fair yon river move,
She, all the way, from disenchanted fount
To seas unhallowed runs; the gods forsook
Long since her trembling rushes; from her plains
Disconsolate, long since adventure fled;
And now although the inviting river flows,
And every poplared cape, and every bend
Or willowy islet, win upon thy soul
And to thy hopeful shallop whisper speed;
Yet hope not thou at all; hope is no more;
And O, long since the golden groves are dead,
The faery cities vanished from the land!

XVI

To W. E. Henley

THE year runs through her phases; rain and sun,
Springtime and summer pass; winter succeeds;
But one pale season rules the house of death.

Cold falls the imprisoned daylight; fell disease
By each lean pallet squats, and pain and sleep
Toss gaping on the pillows.

                       But O thou!
Uprise and take thy pipe. Bid music flow,
Strains by good thoughts attended, like the spring
The swallows follow over land and sea.
Pain sleeps at once; at once, with open eyes,
Dozing despair awakes. The shepherd sees
His flock come bleating home; the seaman hears
Once more the cordage rattle. Airs of home!
Youth, love and roses blossom; the gaunt ward
Dislimns and disappears, and, opening out,
Shows brooks and forests, and the blue beyond
Of mountains.

                Small the pipe; but O! do thou,
Peak-faced and suffering piper, blow therein
The dirge of heroes dead; and to these sick,
These dying, sound the triumph over death.
Behold! each greatly breathes; each tastes a joy
Unknown before, in dying; for each knows
A hero dies with him—though unfulfilled,
Yet conquering truly—and not dies in vain.

So is pain cheered, death comforted; the house
Of sorrow smiles to listen. Once again—
O thou, Orpheus and Heracles, the bard
And the deliverer, touch the stops again!

XVII

Henry James

WHO comes to-night? We ope the doors in vain.
Who comes? My bursting walls, can you contain
The presences that now together throng
Your narrow entry, as with flowers and song,
As with the air of life, the breath of talk?
Lo, how these fair immaculate women walk
Behind their jocund maker; and we see
Slighted *De Mauves*, and that far different she,
Gressie, the trivial sphynx; and to our feast
Daisy and *Barb* and *Chancellor* (she not least!)
With all their silken, all their airy kin,
Do like unbidden angels enter in.
But he, attended by these shining names,
Comes (best of all) himself—our welcome James.

XVIII

The Mirror Speaks

WHERE the bells peal far at sea
Cunning fingers fashioned me.
There on palace walls I hung
While that Consuelo sung;
But I heard, though I listened well,
Never a note, never a trill,
Never a beat of the chiming bell.
There I hung and looked, and there
In my gray face, faces fair
Shone from under shining hair.

Well I saw the poising head,
But the lips moved and nothing said;
And when lights were in the hall,
Silent moved the dancers all.

So awhile I glowed, and then
Fell on dusty days and men;
Long I slumbered packed in straw,
Long I none but dealers saw;
Till before my silent eye
One that sees came passing by.

Now with an outlandish grace,
To the sparkling fire I face
In the blue room at Skerryvore;
Where I wait until the door
Open, and the Prince of Men,
Henry James, shall come again.

XIX

Katharine

WE see you as we see a face
That trembles in a forest place
Upon the mirror of a pool
Forever quiet, clear and cool;
And in the wayward glass, appears
To hover between smiles and tears,
Elfin and human, airy and true,
And backed by the reflected blue.

XX

To F. J. S.

I READ, dear friend, in your dear face
Your life's tale told with perfect grace;
The river of your life, I trace
Up the sun-chequered, devious bed
To the far-distant fountain-head.

Not one quick beat of your warm heart,
Nor thought that came to you apart,
Pleasure nor pity, love nor pain
Nor sorrow, has gone by in vain;

But as some lone, wood-wandering child
Brings home with him at evening mild
The thorns and flowers of all the wild,
From your whole life, O fair and true
Your flowers and thorns you bring with you!

XXI

Requiem

UNDER the wide and starry sky,
Dig the grave and let me lie.
Glad did I live and gladly die,
    And I laid me down with a will.

This be the verse you grave for me:
Here he lies where he longed to be;
Home is the sailor, home from sea,
    And the hunter home from the hill.

XXII

The Celestial Surgeon

IF I have faltered more or less
In my great task of happiness;
If I have moved among my race
And shown no glorious morning face;
If beams from happy human eyes
Have moved me not; if morning skies,
Books, and my food, and summer rain
Knocked on my sullen heart in vain:
Lord, thy most pointed pleasure take
And stab my spirit broad awake;
Or, Lord, if too obdurate I,
Choose thou, before that spirit die,
A piercing pain, a killing sin,
And to my dead heart run them in!

XXIII

Our Lady of the Snows

OUT of the sun, out of the blast,
Out of the world, alone I passed
Across the moor and through the wood
To where the monastery stood.
There neither lute nor breathing fife,
Nor rumour of the world of life,
Nor confidences low and dear,
Shall strike the meditative ear.
Aloof, unhelpful, and unkind,
The prisoners of the iron mind,
Where nothing speaks except the bell
The unfraternal brothers dwell.

[131]

Poor passionate men, still clothed afresh
With agonising folds of flesh;
Whom the clear eyes solicit still
To some bold output of the will,
While fairy Fancy far before
And musing Memory-Hold-the-door
Now to heroic death invite
And now uncurtain fresh delight:
O, little boots it thus to dwell
On the remote unneighboured hill!

O to be up and doing, O
Unfearing and unshamed to go
In all the uproar and the press
About my human business!
My undissuaded heart I hear
Whisper courage in my ear.
With voiceless calls, the ancient earth
Summons me to a daily birth.
Thou, O my love, ye, O my friends—
The gist of life, the end of ends—
To laugh, to love, to live, to die,
Ye call me by the ear and eye!

Forth from the casemate, on the plain
Where honour has the world to gain,
Pour forth and bravely do your part,
O knights of the unshielded heart!
Forth and forever forward!—out
From prudent turret and redoubt,
And in the mellay charge amain,
To fall but yet to rise again!
Captive? ah, still, to honour bright,
A captive soldier of the right!
Or free and fighting, good with ill?
Unconquering but unconquered still!

And ye, O brethren, what if God,
When from Heav'n's top he spies abroad,
And sees on this tormented stage
The noble war of mankind rage:
What if his vivifying eye,
O monks, should pass your corner by?
For still the Lord is Lord of might;
In deeds, in deeds, he takes delight;
The plough, the spear, the laden barks,
The field, the founded city, marks;
He marks the smiler of the streets,
The singer upon garden seats;
He sees the climber in the rocks:
To him, the shepherd folds his flocks.
For those he loves that underprop
With daily virtues Heaven's top,
And bear the falling sky with ease,
Unfrowning caryatides.
Those he approves that ply the trade,
That rock the child, that wed the maid,
That with weak virtues, weaker hands,
Sow gladness on the peopled lands,
And still with laughter, song and shout,
Spin the great wheel of earth about.

But ye?—O ye who linger still
Here in your fortress on the hill,
With placid face, with tranquil breath,
The unsought volunteers of death,
Our cheerful General on high
With careless looks may pass you by.

XXIV

Not yet, my soul, these friendly fields desert,
Where thou with grass, and rivers, and the breeze,
And the bright face of day, thy dalliance hadst;
Where to thine ear first sang the enraptured birds;
Where love and thou that lasting bargain made.
The ship rides trimmed, and from the eternal shore
Thou hearest airy voices; but not yet
Depart, my soul, not yet awhile depart.

Freedom is far, rest far. Thou art with life
Too closely woven, nerve with nerve intwined;
Service still craving service, love for love,
Love for dear love, still suppliant with tears.
Alas, not yet thy human task is done!
A bond at birth is forged; a debt doth lie
Immortal on mortality. It grows—
By vast rebound it grows, unceasing growth;
Gift upon gift, alms upon alms, upreared,
From man, from God, from nature, till the soul
At that so huge indulgence stands amazed.

Leave not, my soul, the unfoughten field, nor leave
Thy debts dishonoured, nor thy place desert
Without due service rendered. For thy life,
Up, spirit, and defend that fort of clay,
Thy body, now beleaguered; whether soon
Or late she fall; whether today thy friends
Bewail thee dead, or, after years, a man
Grown old in honour and the friend of peace.
Contend, my soul, for moments and for hours;
Each is with service pregnant; each reclaimed
Is as a kingdom conquered, where to reign.

As when a captain rallies to the fight
His scattered legions, and beats ruin back,
He, on the field, encamps, well pleased in mind.
Yet surely him shall fortune overtake,
Him smite in turn, headlong his ensigns drive;
And that dear land, now safe, to-morrow fall.
But he, unthinking, in the present good
Solely delights, and all the camps rejoice.

XXV

It is not yours, O mother, to complain,
Not, mother, yours to weep,
Though nevermore your son again
Shall to your bosom creep,
Though nevermore again you watch your baby sleep.

Though in the greener paths of earth,
Mother and child, no more
We wander; and no more the birth
Of me whom once you bore,
Seems still the brave reward that once it seemed of yore;

Though as all passes, day and night,
The seasons and the years,
From you, O mother, this delight,
This also disappears—
Some profit yet survives of all your pangs and tears.

The child, the seed, the grain of corn,
The acorn on the hill,
Each for some separate end is born
In season fit, and still
Each must in strength arise to work the almighty will.

So from the hearth the children flee,
By that almighty hand
Austerely led; so one by sea
Goes forth, and one by land;
Nor aught of all man's sons escapes from that
    command.

So from the sally each obeys
The unseen almighty nod;
So till the ending all their ways
Blindfolded loth have trod:
Nor knew their task at all, but were the tools of
    God.

And as the fervent smith of yore
Beat out the glowing blade,
Nor wielded in the front of war
The weapons that he made,
But in the tower at home still plied his ringing
    trade;

So like a sword the son shall roam
On nobler missions sent;
And as the smith remained at home
In peaceful turret pent,
So sits the while at home the mother well content.

XXVI

The Sick Child

Child. O MOTHER, lay your hand on my brow!
        O mother, mother, where am I now?
        Why is the room so gaunt and great?
        Why am I lying awake so late?

Mother. Fear not at all: the night is still.
Nothing is here that means you ill—
Nothing but lamps the whole town through,
And never a child awake but you.

Child. Mother, mother, speak low in my ear,
Some of the things are so great and near,
Some are so small and far away,
I have a fear that I cannot say.
What have I done, and what do I fear,
And why are you crying, mother dear?

Mother. Out in the city, sounds begin.
Thank the kind God, the carts come in!
An hour or two more, and God is so kind,
The day shall be blue in the window-blind,
Then shall my child go sweetly asleep,
And dream of the birds and the hills of sheep.

XXVII

In Memoriam F. A. S.

YET, O stricken heart, remember, O remember
How of human days he lived the better part.
April came to bloom and never dim December
Breathed its killing chills upon the head or heart.

Doomed to know not Winter, only Spring, a being
Trod the flowery April blithely for a while,
Took his fill of music, joy of thought and seeing,
Came and stayed and went, nor ever ceased to smile.

[137]

Came and stayed and went, and now when all is finished,
 You alone have crossed the melancholy stream,
Yours the pang, but his, O his, the undiminished
 Undecaying gladness, undeparted dream.

All that life contains of torture, toil, and treason,
 Shame, dishonour, death, to him were but a name.
Here, a boy, he dwelt through all the singing season
 And ere the day of sorrow departed as he came.

XXVIII

To My Father

Peace and her huge invasion to these shores
Puts daily home; innumerable sails
Dawn on the far horizon and draw near;
Innumerable loves, uncounted hopes
To our wild coasts, not darkling now, approach:
Not now obscure, since thou and thine are there,
And bright on the lone isle, the foundered reef,
The long, resounding foreland, Pharos stands.

These are thy works, O father, these thy crown;
Whether on high the air be pure, they shine
Along the yellowing sunset, and all night
Among the unnumbered stars of God they shine;
Or whether fogs arise and far and wide
The low sea-level drown—each finds a tongue
And all night long the tolling bell resounds:
So shine, so toll, till night be overpast,
Till the stars vanish, till the sun return,
And in the haven rides the fleet secure.

[138]

In the first hour, the seaman in his skiff
Moves through the unmoving bay, to where the town
Its earliest smoke into the air upbreathes
And the rough hazels climb along the beach.
To the tugg'd oar the distant echo speaks.
The ship lies resting, where by reef and roost
Thou and thy lights have led her like a child.

This hast thou done, and I—can I be base?
I must arise, O father, and to port
Some lost, complaining seaman pilot home.

XXIX

In the States

Wɪᴛʜ half a heart I wander here
    As from an age gone by
A brother—yet though young in years,
    An elder brother, I.

You speak another tongue than mine,
    Though both were English born.
I towards the night of time decline,
    You mount into the morn.

Youth shall grow great and strong and free,
    But age must still decay:
To-morrow for the States—for me,
    England and Yesterday.

XXX

A Portrait

I AM a kind of farthing dip,
  Unfriendly to the nose and eyes;
A blue-behinded ape, I skip
  Upon the trees of Paradise.

At mankind's feast, I take my place
  In solemn, sanctimonious state,
And have the air of saying grace
  While I defile the dinner plate.

I am 'the smiler with the knife,'
  The battener upon garbage, I—
Dear Heaven, with such a rancid life,
  Were it not better far to die?

Yet still, about the human pale,
  I love to scamper, love to race,
To swing by my irreverent tail
  All over the most holy place;

And when at length, some golden day,
  The unfailing sportsman, aiming at,
Shall bag, me—all the world shall say:
  Thank God, and there's an end of that!

XXXI

Sing clearlier, Muse, or evermore be still,
Sing truer or no longer sing!
No more the voice of melancholy Jacques
To wake a weeping echo in the hill;
But as the boy, the pirate of the spring,
From the green elm a living linnet takes,
One natural verse recapture—then be still.

XXXII

A Camp

The bed was made, the room was fit,
By punctual eve the stars were lit;
The air was still, the water ran,
No need was there for maid or man,
When we put up, my ass and I,
At God's green caravanserai.

XXXIII

The Country of the Camisards

We travelled in the print of olden wars,
　　Yet all the land was green,
　　And love we found, and peace,
　　Where fire and war had been.

They pass and smile, the children of the sword—
　　No more the sword they wield;
　　And O, how deep the corn
　　Along the battlefield!

XXXIV

Skerryvore

For love of lovely words, and for the sake
Of those, my kinsmen and my countrymen,
Who early and late in the windy ocean toiled
To plant a star for seamen, where was then
The surfy haunt of seals and cormorants:
I, on the lintel of this cot, inscribe
The name of a strong tower.

XXXV

Skerryvore: The Parallel

Here all is sunny, and when the truant gull
Skims the green level of the lawn, his wing
Dispetals roses; here the house is framed
Of kneaded brick and the plumed mountain pine,
Such clay as artists fashion and such wood
As the tree-climbing urchin breaks. But there
Eternal granite hewn from the living isle
And dowelled with brute iron, rears a tower
That from its wet foundation to its crown
Of glittering glass, stands, in the sweep of winds,
Immovable, immortal, eminent.

XXXVI

My house, I say. But hark to the sunny doves
That make my roof the arena of their loves,
That gyre about the gable all day long
And fill the chimneys with their murmurous song:

Our house, they say; and *mine*, the cat declares
And spreads his golden fleece upon the chairs;
And *mine* the dog, and rises stiff with wrath
If any alien foot profane the path.
So too the buck that trimmed my terraces,
Our whilome gardener, called the garden his;
Who now, deposed, surveys my plain abode
And his late kingdom, only from the road.

XXXVII

My body which my dungeon is,
And yet my parks and palaces:
   Which is so great that there I go
All the day long to and fro,
And when the night begins to fall
Throw down my bed and sleep, while all
The building hums and wakefulness—
Even as a child of savages
When evening takes her on her way,
(She having roamed a summer's day
Along the mountain-sides and scalp)
Sleeps in an antre of that alp:
   Which is so broad and high that there,
As in the topless fields of air,
My fancy soars like to a kite
And faints in the blue infinite:
   Which is so strong, my strongest throes
And the rough world's besieging blows
Not break it, and so weak withal,
Death ebbs and flows in its loose wall
As the green sea in fishers' nets,
And tops its topmost parapets:
   Which is so wholly mine that I

Can wield its whole artillery,
And mine so little, that my soul
Dwells in perpetual control,
And I but think and speak and do
As my dead fathers move me to:
   If this born body of my bones
The beggared soul so barely owns,
What money passed from hand to hand,
What creeping custom of the land,
What deed of author or assign,
Can make a house a thing of mine?

XXXVIII

SAY not of me that weakly I declined
The labours of my sires, and fled the sea,
The towers we founded and the lamps we lit,
To play at home with paper like a child.
But rather say: *In the afternoon of time
A strenuous family dusted from its hands
The sand of granite, and beholding far
Along the sounding coast its pyramids
And tall memorials catch the dying sun,
Smiled well content, and to this childish task
Around the fire addressed its evening hours.*

BOOK II: IN SCOTS

I

The Maker to Posterity

FAR 'yont amang the years to be
When a' we think, an' a' we see,
An' a' we luve, 's been dung ajee
　　　By time's rouch shouther,
An' what was richt and wrang for me
　　　Lies mangled throu'ther,

It's possible—it's hardly mair—
That some ane, ripin' after lear—
Some auld professor or young heir,
　　　If still there's either—
May find an' read me, an' be sair
　　　Perplexed, puir brither!

'*What tongue does your auld bookie speak?*'
He'll spier; an' I, his mou to steik:
'*No bein' fit to write in Greek,*
　　　I wrote in Lallan,
Dear to my heart as the peat reek,
　　　Auld as Tantallon.

'*Few spak it than, an' noo there's nane.*
My puir auld sangs lie a' their lane,
Their sense, that aince was braw an' plain,
　　　Tint a'thegether,
Like runes upon a standin' stane
　　　Amang the heather.

'*But think not you the brae to speel;*
You, tae, maun chow the bitter peel;
For a' your lear, for a' your skeel,
        Ye're nane sae lucky;
An' things are mebbe waur than weel
        For you, my buckie.

'*The hale concern (baith hens an' eggs,*
Baith books an' writers, stars an' clegs)
Noo stachers upon lowsent legs
        An' wears awa';
The tack o' mankind, near the dregs,
        Rins unco' law.

'*Your book, that in some braw new tongue,*
Ye wrote or prentit, preached or sung,
Will still be just a bairn, an' young
        In fame an' years,
Whan the hale planet's guts are dung
        About your ears;

'*An' you, sair gruppin' to a spar*
Or whammled wi' some bleezin' star,
Cryin' to ken whaur deil ye are,
        Hame, France, or Flanders—
Whang sindry like a railway car
        An' flie in danders.'

II

Ille Terrarum

FRAE nirly, nippin', Eas'lan' breeze,
Frae Norlan' snaw, an' haar o' seas,
Weel happit in your gairden trees,
    A bonny bit,
Atween the muckle Pentland's knees,
    Secure ye sit.

Beeches an' aiks entwine their theek,
An' firs, a stench, auld-farrant clique.
A' simmer day, your chimleys reek,
    Couthy and bien;
An' here an'·there your windies keek
    Amang the green.

A pickle plats an' paths an' posies,
A wheen auld gillyflowers an' roses:
A ring o' wa's the hale encloses
    Frae sheep or men;
An' there the auld housie beeks an' dozes,
    A' by her lane.

The gairdner crooks his weary back
A' day in the pitaty-track,
Or mebbe stops awhile to crack
    Wi' Jane the cook,
Or at some buss, worm-eaten-black,
    To gie a look.

Frae the high hills the curlew ca's;
The sheep gang baaing by the wa's;

Or whiles a clan o' roosty craws
    Cangle thegether;
The wild bees seek the gairden raws,
    Weariet wi' heather.

Or in the gloamin' douce an' gray
The sweet-throat mavis tunes her lay;
The herd comes linkin' doun the brae;
    An' by degrees
The muckle siller müne maks way
    Amang the trees.

Here aft hae I, wi' sober heart,
For meditation sat apairt,
When orra loves or kittle art
    Perplexed my mind;
Here socht a balm for ilka smart
    O' humankind.

Here aft, weel neukit by my lane,
Wi' Horace, or perhaps Montaigne,
The mornin' hours hae come an' gane
    Abüne my heid—
I wadnae gi'en a chucky-stane
    For a' I'd read.

But noo the auld city, street by street,
An' winter fu' o' snaw an' sleet,
Awhile shut in my gangrel feet
    An' goavin' mettle;
Noo is the soopit ingle sweet,
    An' liltin' kettle.

An' noo the winter winds complain;
Cauld lies the glaur in ilka lane;

On draigled hizzie, tautit wean
  An' drucken lads,
In the mirk nicht, the winter rain
  Dribbles an' blads.

Whan bugles frae the Castle rock,
An' beaten drums wi' dowie shock,
Wauken, at cauld-rife sax o'clock,
  My chitterin' frame,
I mind me on the kintry cock,
  The kintry hame.

I mind me on yon bonny bield;
An' Fancy traivels far afield
To gaither a' that gairdens yield
  O' sun an' Simmer:
To hearten up a dowie chield,
  Fancy's the limmer!

III

WHEN aince Aprile has fairly come,
An' birds may bigg in winter's lum,
An' pleisure's spreid for a' and some
  O' whatna state,
Love, wi' her auld recruitin' drum,
  Than taks the gate.

The heart plays dunt wi' main an' micht;
The lasses' een are a' sae bricht,
Their dresses are sae braw an' ticht,
  The bonny birdies!—
Puir winter virtue at the sicht
  Gangs heels ower hurdies.

[149]

An' aye as love frae land to land
Tirls the drum wi' eident hand,
A' men collect at her command,
       Toun-bred or land'art,
An' follow in a denty band
       Her gaucy standart.

An' I, wha sang o' rain an' snaw,
An' weary winter weel awa',
Noo busk me in a jacket braw,
       An' tak my place
I' the ram-stam, harum-scarum raw,
       Wi' smilin' face.

IV

A Mile an' a Bittock

A MILE an' a bittock, a mile or twa,
Abüne the burn, ayont the law,
Davie an' Donal' an' Cherlie an' a',
    An' the müne was shinin' clearly!

Ane went hame wi' the ither, an' then
The ither went hame wi' the ither twa men,
An' baith wad return him the service again,
    An' the müne was shinin' clearly!

The clocks were chappin' in house an' ha',
Eleeven, twal an' ane an' twa;
An' the guidman's face was turnt to the wa',
    An' the müne was shinin' clearly!

A wind got up frae affa the sea,
It blew the stars as clear's could be,
It blew in the een of a' o' the three,
    An' the müne was shinin' clearly!

Noo, Davie was first to get sleep in his head,
'The best o' frien's maun twine,' he said;
'I'm weariet, an' here I'm awa' to my bed.'
    An' the müne was shinin' clearly!

Twa o' them walkin' an' crackin' their lane,
The mornin' licht cam gray an' plain,
An' the birds they yammert on stick an' stane,
    An' the müne was shinin' clearly!

O years ayont, O years awa',
My lads, ye'll mind whate'er befa'—
My lads, ye'll mind on the bield o' the law,
    When the müne was shinin' clearly.

V

A Lowden Sabbath Morn

THE clinkum-clank o' Sabbath bells
Noo to the hoastin' rookery swells,
Noo faintin' laigh in shady dells,
    Sounds far an' near,
An' through the simmer kintry tells
    Its tale o' cheer.

An' noo, to that melodious play,
A' deidly awn the quiet sway—
A' ken their solemn holiday,
    Bestial an' human,
The singin' lintie on the brae,
    The restin' plou'man.

He, mair than a' the lave o' men,
His week completit joys to ken;
Half-dressed, he daunders out an' in,
    Perplext wi' leisure;
An' his raxt limbs he'll rax again
    Wi' painfü' pleesure.

The steerin' mither strange afit
Noo shoos the bairnies but a bit;
Noo cries them ben, their Sinday shüit
    To scart upon them,
Or sweeties in their pouch to pit,
    Wi' blessin's on them.

The lasses, clean frae tap to taes,
Are busked in crunklin' underclaes;
The gartened hose, the weel-filled stays,
    The nakit shift,
A' bleached on bonny greens for days,
    An' white's the drift.

An' noo to face the kirkward mile:
The guidman's hat o' dacent style,
The blackit shoon, we noo maun fyle
    As white's the miller:
A waefü' peety tae, to spile
    The warth o' siller.

Our Marg'et, aye sae keen to crack,
Douce-stappin' in the stoury track,
Her emeralt goun a' kiltit back
    Frae snawy coats,
White-ankled, leads the kirkward pack
    Wi' Dauvit Groats.

A thocht ahint, in runkled breeks,
A' spiled wi' lyin' by for weeks,
The guidman follows closs, an' cleiks
    The sonsie missis;
His sarious face at aince bespeaks
    The day that this is.

And aye an' while we nearer draw
To whaur the kirkton lies alaw,
Mair neebours, comin' saft an' slaw
    Frae here an' there,
The thicker thrang the gate an' caw
    The stour in air.

But hark! the bells frae nearer clang;
To rowst the slaw, their sides they bang;
An' see! black coats a'ready thrang
    The green kirkyaird;
And at the yett, the chestnuts spang
    That brocht the laird.

The solemn elders at the plate
Stand drinkin' deep the pride o' state:
The practised hands as gash an' great
    As Lords o' Session;
The later named, a wee thing blate
    In their expression.

[153]

The prentit stanes that mark the deid,
Wi' lengthened lip, the sarious read;
Syne wag a moraleesin' heid,
     An' then an' there
Their hirplin' practice an' their creed
     Try hard to square.

It's here our Merren lang has lain,
A wee bewast the table-stane;
An' yon's the grave o' Sandy Blane;
     An' further ower,
The mither's brithers, dacent men!
     Lie a' the fower.

Here the guidman sall bide awee
To dwall amang the deid; to see
Auld faces clear in fancy's e'e;
     Belike to hear
Auld voices fa'in saft an' slee
     On fancy's ear.

Thus, on the day o' solemn things,
The bell that in the steeple swings
To fauld a scaittered faim'ly rings
     Its walcome screed;
An' just a wee thing nearer brings
     The quick an' deid.

But noo the bell is ringin' in;
To tak their places, folk begin;
The minister himsel' will shüne
     Be up the gate,
Filled fu' wi' clavers about sin
     An' man's estate.

The tünes are up—*French*, to be shüre,
The faithfü' *French*, an' twa-three mair;
The auld prezentor, hoastin' sair,
    Wales out the portions,
An' yirks the tüne into the air
    Wi' queer contortions.

Follows the prayer, the readin' next,
An' than the fisslin' for the text—
The twa-three last to find it, vext
    But kind o' proud;
An' than the peppermints are raxed,
    An' southernwood.

For noo's the time whan pows are seen
Nid noddin' like a mandareen;
When tenty mithers stap a preen
    In sleepin' weans;
An' nearly half the parochine
    Forget their pains.

There's just a waukrif' twa or three:
Thrawn commentautors sweet to 'gree,
Weans glowrin' at the bumlin' bee
    On windie-glasses,
Or lads that tak a keek a-glee
    At sonsie lasses.

Himsel', meanwhile, frae whaur he cocks
An' bobs belaw the soundin'-box,
The treesures of his words unlocks
    Wi' prodigality,
An' deals some unco dingin' knocks
    To infidality.

Wi' sappy unction, hoo he burkes
The hopes o' men that trust in works,
Expounds the fau'ts o' ither kirks,
    An' shaws the best o' them
No muckle better than mere Turks,
    When a's confessed o' them.

Bethankit! what a bonny creed!
What mair would ony Christian need?—
The braw words rumm'le ower his heid,
    Nor steer the sleeper;
And in their restin' graves, the deid
    Sleep aye the deeper.

VI

The Spaewife

O, I wad like to ken—to the beggar-wife says I—
Why chops are guid to brander and nane sae guid to fry.
An' siller, that's sae braw to keep, is brawer still to gi'e.
—*It's gey an' easy spierin'*, says the beggar-wife to me.

O, I wad like to ken—to the beggar-wife says I—
Hoo a' things come to be whaur we find them when we
    try,
The lasses in their claes an' the fishes in the sea.
—*It's gey an' easy spierin'*, says the beggar-wife to me.

O, I wad like to ken—to the beggar-wife says I—
Why lads are a' to sell an' lasses a' to buy;
An' naebody for dacency but barely twa or three.
—*It's gey an' easy spierin'*, says the beggar-wife to me.

O, I wad like to ken—to the beggar-wife says I—
Gin death's as shüre to men as killin' is to kye,
Why God has filled the yearth sae fu' o' tasty things to pree.
—*It's gey an' easy spierin'*, says the beggar-wife to me.

O, I wad like to ken—to the beggar wife says I—
The reason o' the cause an' the wherefore o' the why,
Wi' mony anither riddle brings the tears into my e'e.
—*It's gey an' easy spierin'*, says the beggar-wife to me.

VII

The Blast—1875

IT's rainin'. · Weet's the gairden sod,
Weet the lang roads whaur gangrels plod—
A maist unceevil thing o' God
       In mid July—
If ye'll just curse the sneckdraw, dod!
       An' sae wull I!

He's a braw place in Heev'n, ye ken,
An' lea's us puir, forjaskit men
Clamjamfried in the but and ben
       He ca's the earth—
A wee bit inconvenient den
       No muckle worth;

An' whiles, at orra times, keeks out,
Sees what puir mankind are about;
An' if He can, I've little doubt,
       Upsets their plans;
He hates a' mankind, brainch and root,
       An' a' that's man's.

[157]

An' whiles, whan they tak heart again,
An' life i' the sun looks braw an' plain,
Doun comes a jaw o' droukin' rain
          Upon their honours—
God sends a spate outower the plain,
          Or mebbe thun'ers.

Lord safe us, life's an unco thing!
Simmer an' Winter, Yule an' Spring,
The damned, dour-heartit seasons bring
          A feck o' trouble.
I wadnae try't to be a king—
          No, nor for double.

But since we're in it, willy-nilly,
We maun be watchfü,' wise an' skilly,
An' no mind ony ither billy,
          Lassie nor God.
But drink—that's my best counsel till 'e:
          Sae tak the nod.

VIII

The Counterblast—1886

My bonny man, the warld, it's true,
Was made for neither me nor you;
It's just a place to warstle through,
          As Job confessed o't;
And aye the best that we'll can do
          Is mak the best o't.

There's rowth o' wrang, I'm free to say;
The simmer brunt, the winter blae,
The face of earth a' fyled wi' clay
      An' dour wi' chuckies,
An' life a rough an' land'art play
      For country buckies.

An' food's anither name for clart;
An' beasts an' brambles bite an' scart;
An' what would WE be like, my heart!
      If bared o' claethin'?
—Aweel, I cannae mend your cart:
      It's that or naethin'.

A feck o' folk frae first to last
Have through this queer experience passed;
Twa-three, I ken, just damn an' blast
      The hale transaction;
But twa-three ithers, east an' wast,
      Fand satisfaction.

Whaur braid the briery muirs expand,
A waefü' an' a weary land,
A bumblebees, a gowden band,
      Are blithely hingin';
An' there the canty wanderer fand
      The laverock singin'.

Trout in the burn grow great as herr'n';
The simple sheep can find their fair'n';
The wind blaws clean about the cairn
      Wi' caller air;
The muircock an' the barefit bairn
      Are happy there.

[159]

Sic-like the howes o' life to some:
Green loans whaur they ne'er fash their thumb,
But mark the muckle winds that come,
    Soopin' an' cool,
Or hear the powrin' burnie drum
    In the shilfa's pool.

The evil wi' the guid they tak;
They ca' a gray thing gray, no black;
To a steigh brae, a stubborn back
    Addressin' daily;
An' up the rude, unbieldy track
    O' life, gang gaily.

What you would like's a palace ha',
Or Sinday parlour dink an' braw
Wi' a' things ordered in a raw
    By denty leddies.
Weel, then, ye cannae hae't: that's a'
    That to be said is.

An' since at life ye've taen the grue,
An' winnae blithely hirsle through,
Ye've fund the very thing to do—
    That's to drink speerit;
An' shüne we'll hear the last o' you—
    An' blithe to hear it!

The shoon ye coft, the life ye lead,
Ithers will heir when aince ye're deid;
They'll heir your tasteless bite o' breid,
    An' find it sappy;
They'll to your dulefü' house succeed,
    An' there be happy.

As whan a glum an' fractious wean
Has sat an' sullened by his lane
Till, wi' a rowstin' skelp, he's taen
    An' shoo'd to bed—
The ither bairns a' fa' to play'n',
    As gleg's a gled.

IX

The Counterblast Ironical

IT's strange that God should fash to frame
    The yearth and lift sae hie,
An' clean forget to explain the same
    To a gentleman like me.

They gutsy, donnered ither folk,
    Their weird they weel may dree;
But why present a pig in a poke
    To a gentleman like me?

They ither folk their parritch eat
    An' sup their sugared tea;
But the mind is no to be wyled wi' meat
    Wi' a gentleman like me.

They ither folk, they court their joes
    At gloamin' on the lea;
But they're made of a commoner clay, I suppose,
    Than a gentleman like me.

They ither folk, for richt or wrang,
    They suffer, bleed, or dee;
But a' thir things are an emp'y sang
    To a gentleman like me.

It's a different thing that I demand,
　　Tho' humble as can be—
A statement fair in my Maker's hand
　　To a gentleman like me:

A clear account writ fair an' broad,
　　An' a plain apologie;
Or the deevil a ceevil word to God
　　From a gentleman like me.

X

Their Laureate to an Academy Class Dinner Club

Dear Thamson class, whaure'er I gang
It aye comes ower me wi' a spang:
'*Lordsake! they Thamson lads—(deil hang*
　　Or else Lord mend them!)—
An' that wanchancy annual sang
　　I ne'er can send them!'

Straucht, at the name a trusty tyke,
My conscience girrs ahint the dyke;
Straucht on my hinderlands I fyke
　　To find a rhyme t' ye;
Pleased—although mebbe no pleased-like—
　　To gie my time t'ye.

'*Weel*,' an' says you, wi' heavin' breist,
'*Sae far, sae guid, but what's the neist?*
Yearly we gaither to the feast,
　　A' hopefu' men—
Yearly we skelloch "Hang the beast—
　　Nae sang again!" '

My lads, an' what am I to say?
Ye shüurely ken the Muse's way:
Yestreen, as gleg's a tyke—the day,
      Thrawn like a cuddy:
Her conduc', that to her's a play,
      Deith to a body.

Aft whan I sat an' made my mane,
Aft whan I laboured burd-alane
Fishin' for rhymes an' findin' nane,
      Or nane were fit for ye—
Ye judged me cauld's a chucky stane—
      No car'n' a bit for ye!

But saw ye ne'er some pingein' bairn
As weak as a pitaty-par'n'—
Less üsed wi' guidin' horse-shoe airn
      Than steerin' crowdie—
Packed aff his lane, by moss an' cairn,
      To ca' the howdie.

Wae's me, for the puir callant than!
He wambles like a poke o' bran,
An' the lowse rein, as hard's he can,
      Pu's, trem'lin' handit;
Till, blaff! upon his hinderlan'
      Behauld him landit.

Sic-like—I awn the weary fac'—
Whan on my Muse the gate I tak,
An' see her gleed e'e raxin' back
      To keek ahint her;—
To me, the brig o' Heev'n gangs black
      As blackest winter.

[163]

'*Lordsake! we're aff,*' thinks I, '*but whaur?*
On what abhorred an' whinny scaur,
Or whammled in what sea o' glaur,
　　Will she desert me?
An' will she just disgrace? or waur—
　　Will she no hurt me?'

Kittle the quaere! But at least
The day I've backed the fashious beast,
While she, wi' mony a spang an' reist,
　　Flang heels ower bonnet;
An' a' triumphant—for your feast,
　　Hae! there's your sonnet!

XI

Embro Hie Kirk

THE Lord Himsel' in former days
Waled out the proper tünes for praise
An' named the proper kind o' claes
　　For folk to preach in:
Preceese and in the chief o' ways
　　Important teachin'.

He ordered a' things late and air';
He ordered folk to stand at prayer.
(Although I cannae just mind where
　　He gave the warnin'.)
An' pit pomatum on their hair
　　On Sabbath mornin'.

The hale o' life by His commands
Was ordered to a body's hands;
But see! this *corpus juris* stands
      By a' forgotten;
An' God's religion in a' lands
      Is deid an' rotten.

While thus the lave o' mankind's lost,
O' Scotland still God maks His boast—
Puir Scotland, on whase barren coast
      A score or twa
Auld wives wi' mutches an' a hoast
      Still keep His law.

In Scotland, a wheen canty, plain,
Douce, kintry-leevin' folk retain
The Truth—or did so aince—alane
      Of a' men leevin';
An' noo just twa o' them remain—
      Just Begg an' Niven.

For noo, unfaithfü', to the Lord
Auld Scotland joins the rebel horde;
Her human hymn-books on the board
      She noo displays:
An' Embro Hie kirk's been restored
      In popish ways.

O *punctum temporis* for action
To a' o' the reformin' faction,
If yet, by ony act or paction,
      Thocht, word, or sermon,
This dark an' damnable transaction
      Micht yet determine!

[165]

For see—as Doctor Begg explains—
Hoo easy 't's düne! a pickle weans,
Wha in the Hie Street gaither stanes
      By his instruction,
The uncovenantit, pentit panes
      Ding to destruction.

Up, Niven, or ower late—an' dash
Laigh in the glaur that carnal hash;
Let spires and pews wi' gran' stramash
      Thegether fa';
The rumlin' kist o' whustles smash
      In pieces sma'.

Noo choose ye out a walie hammer;
About the knottit buttress clam'er;
Alang the steep roof stoyt an' stammer,
      A gate mis-chancy;
On the aul' spire, the bells' hie cha'mer,
      Dance your bit dancie.

Ding, devel, dunt, destroy, an' ruin,
Wi' carnal stanes the square bestrewin',
Till your loud chaps frae Kyle to Fruin,
      Frae Hell to Heeven,
Tell the guid wark that baith are doin'—
      Baith Begg an' Niven.

XII

The Scotsman's Return from Abroad

In a letter from Mr Thomson to Mr Johnstone

IN mony a foreign pairt I've been,
An' mony an unco ferlie seen,
Since, Mr Johnstone, you and I
Last walkit upon Cocklerye.
Wi' gleg, observant een, I pass't
By sea an' land, through East an' Wast,
And still in ilka age an' station
Saw naething but abomination.
In thir uncovenantit lands
The gangrel Scot uplifts his hands
At lack of a' sectarian füsh'n,
An' cauld religious destitütion.
He rins, puir man, frae place to place,
Tries a' their graceless means o' grace,
Preacher on preacher, kirk on kirk—
This yin a stot an' thon a stirk—
A bletherin' clan, no warth a preen,
As bad as Smith of Aiberdeen!

At last, across the weary faem,
Frae far, outlandish pairts I came.
On ilka side o' me I fand
Fresh tokens o' my native land.
Wi' whatna joy I hailed them a'—
The hilltaps standin' raw by raw,
The public house, the Hielan' birks,
And a' the bonny U.P. kirks!

But maistly thee, the bluid o' Scots,
Frae Maidenkirk to John o' Grots,
The king o' drinks, as I conceive it,
Talisker, Isla, or Glenlivet!

For after years wi' a pockmantie
Frae Zanzibar to Alicante,
In mony a fash and sair affliction
I gie't as my sincere conviction—
Of a' their foreign tricks an' pliskies,
I maist abominate their whiskies.
Nae doot, themsel's, they ken it weel,
An' wi' a hash o' leemon peel,
And ice an' siccan filth, they ettle
The stawsome kind o' goo to settle;
Sic wersh apothecary's broos wi'
As Scotsmen scorn to fyle their moo's wi'.

An' man, I was a blithe hame-comer
Whan first I syndit out my rummer.
Ye should hae seen me then, wi' care
The less important pairts prepare;
Syne, weel contentit wi' it a',
Pour in the speerits wi' a jaw!
I didnae drink, I didnae speak—
I only snowkit up the reek.
I was sae pleased therein to paidle,
I sat an' plowtered wi' my ladle.

An' blithe was I, the morrow's morn,
To daunder through the stookit corn,
And after a' my strange mishanters,
Sit doun amang my ain dissenters.
An', man, it was a joy to me
The pu'pit an' the pews to see,

The pennies dirlin' in the plate,
The elders lookin' on in state;
An' 'mang the first, as it befell,
Wha should I see, sir, but yoursel'!

I was, and I will no deny it,
At the first gliff a hantle tryit.
To see yoursel' in sic a station—
It seemed a doubtfü' dispensation.
The feelin' was a mere digression;
For shüne I understood the session,
An' mindin' Aiken an' M'Neil,
I wondered they had düne sae weel.
I saw I had mysel' to blame;
For had I but remained at hame,
Aiblins—though no ava' deservin' 't—
They micht hae named your humble servant.

The kirk was filled, the door was steeked;
Up to the pu'pit ance I keeked;
I was mair pleased than I can tell—
It was the minister himsel'!
Proud, proud was I to see his face,
After sae lang awa' frae grace.
Pleased as I was, I'm no denyin'
Some maitters were not edifyin';
For first I fand—an' here was news!—
Mere hymn-books cockin' in the pews—
A humanised abomination,
Unfit for ony congregation.
Syne, while I still was on the tenter,
I scunnered at the new prezentor;
I thocht him gesterin' an' cauld—
A sair declension frae the auld.

Syne, as though a' the faith was wreckit,
The prayer was not what I'd exspeckit.
Himsel', as it appeared to me,
Was no the man he üsed to be.
But just as I was growin' vext
He waled a maist judeecious text,
An', launchin' into his prelections,
Swoopt, wi' a skirl, on a' defections.

O what a gale was on my speerit
To hear the p'ints o' doctrine clearit,
And a' the horrors o' damnation
Set furth wi' faithfü' ministration!
Nae shauchlin' testimony here—
We were a' damned, an' that was clear.
I owned, wi' gratitude an' wonder,
He was a pleisure to sit under.

XIII

LATE in the nicht in bed I lay,
The winds were at their weary play,
An' tirlin' wa's an' skirlin' wae
      Through Heev'n they battered;
On-ding o' hail, on-blaff o' spray,
      The tempest blattered.

The masoned house it dinled through;
It dung the ship, it cowped the coo';
The rankit aiks it overthrew,
      Had braved a' weathers;
The strang sea-gleds it took an' blew
      Awa' like feathers.

The thrawes o' fear on a' were shed,
An' the hair rose, an' slumber fled,
An' lichts were lit an' prayers were said
    Through a' the kintry;
An' the cauld terror clum in bed
      Wi' a' an' sindry.

To hear in the pit-mirk on hie
The brangled collieshangie flie,
The warl', they thocht, wi' land an' sea,
    Itsel' wad cowpit;
An' for auld airn, the smashed debris
      By God be rowpit.

Meanwhile frae far Aldeboran
To folks wi' talescopes in han',
O' ships that cowpit, winds that ran,
    Nae sign was seen,
But the wee warl' in sunshine span
      As bricht's a preen.

I, tae, by God's especial grace,
Dwall denty in a bieldy place,
Wi' hosened feet, wi' shaven face,
    Wi' dacent mainners:
A grand example to the race
      O' tautit sinners!

The wind may blaw, the heathen rage,
The deil may start on the rampage;
The sick in bed, the thief in cage—
    What's a' to me?
Cosh in my house, a sober sage,
      I sit an' see.

An' whiles the bluid spangs to my bree,
To lie sae saft, to live sae free,
While better men maun do an' die
      In unco places.
'Whaur's God?' I cry, an' *'Whae is me*
      To hae sic graces?'

I mind the fecht the sailors keep,
But fire or can'le, rest or sleep,
In darkness an' the muckle deep;
      An' mind beside
The herd that on the hills o' sheep
      Has wandered wide.

I mind me on the hoastin' weans—
The penny joes on causey stanes—
The auld folk wi' the crazy banes,
      Baith auld an' puir,
That aye maun thole the winds an' rains
      An' labour sair.

An' whiles I'm kind o' pleased a blink
An' kind o' fleyed forby, to think,
For a' my rowth o' meat an' drink
      An' waste o' crumb,
I'll mebbe have to thole wi' skink
      In Kingdom Come.

For God whan jowes the Judgment bell,
Wi' His ain Hand, His Leevin' Sel',
Sall ryve the guid (as Prophets tell)
      Frae them that had it;
And in the reamin' pat o' Hell,
      The rich be scaddit.

O Lord, if this indeed be sae,
Let daw that sair an' happy day!
Again' the warl', grawn auld an' gray,
      Up wi' your aixe!
An' let the puir enjoy their play—
      I'll thole my paiks.

XIV

My Conscience!

OF a' the ills that flesh can fear,
The loss o' frien's, the lack o' gear,
A yowlin' tyke, a glandered mear,
      A lassie's nonsense—
There's just ae thing I cannae bear,
      An' that's my conscience.

Whan day (an' a' excüse) has gane,
An' wark is düne, and duty's plain,
An' to my chalmer a' my lane
      I creep apairt,
My conscience! hoo the yammerin' pain
      Stends to my heart!

A' day wi' various ends in view
The hairsts o' time I had to pu',
An' made a hash wad staw a soo,
      Let be a man!—
My conscience! whan my han's were fu',
      Whaur were ye than?

[173]

An' there were a' the lures o' life,
There pleesure skirlin' on the fife,
There anger, wi' the hotchin' knife
    Ground shairp in Hell—
My conscience!—you that's like a wife!—
    Whaur was yoursel'?

I ken it fine: just waitin' here,
To gar the evil waur appear,
To clart the guid, confüse the clear,
    Mis-ca' the great,
My conscience! an' to raise a steer
    Whan a's ower late.

Sic-like, some tyke grawn auld and blind,
Whan thieves brok' through the gear to p'ind,
Has lain his dozened length an' grinned
    At the disaster;
An' the morn's mornin', wud's the wind,
    Yokes on his master.

XV

To Doctor John Brown

(Whan the dear doctor, dear to a',
Was still amang us here belaw,
I set my pipes his praise to blaw
*   Wi' a' my speerit;*
But noo, Dear Doctor! he's awa`,
*   An' ne'er can hear it.)*

[174]

BOOK II: IN SCOTS

By Lyne and Tyne, by Thames and Tees,
By a' the various river-Dee's,
In Mars and Manors 'yont the seas
　　　Or here at hame,
Whaure'er there's kindly folk to please,
　　　They ken your name.

They ken your name, they ken your tyke
They ken the honey from your byke;
But mebbe after a' your fyke,
　　　(The trüth to tell)
It's just your honest Rab they like,
　　　An' no yoursel'.

As at the gowff, some canny play'r
Should tee a common ba' wi' care—
Should flourish and deleever fair
　　　His souple shintie—
An' the ba' rise into the air,
　　　A leevin' lintie:

Sae in the game we writers play,
There comes to some a bonny day,
When a dear ferlie shall repay
　　　Their years o' strife,
An' like your Rab, their things o' clay,
　　　Spreid wings o' life.

Ye scarce deserved it, I'm afraid—
You that had never learned the trade,
But just some idle mornin' strayed
　　　Into the schüle,
An' picked the fiddle up an' played
　　　Like Neil himsel'.

Your`e'e was gleg, your fingers dink;
Ye didnae fash yoursel' to think,
But wove, as fast as puss can link,
     Your denty wab:
Ye stapped your pen into the ink,
      An' there was Rab!

Sinsyne, whaure'er your fortune lay
By dowie den, by canty brae,
Simmer an' winter, nicht an' day,
     Rab was aye wi' ye;
An' a' the folk on a' the way
      Were blithe to see ye.

O sir, the gods are kind indeed,
An' hauld ye for an honoured heid,
That for a wee bit clarkit screed
     Sae weel reward ye,
An' lend—puir Rabbie bein' deid—
      His ghaist to guard ye.

For though, whaure'er yoursel' may be,
We've just to turn an' glisk a wee,
An' Rab at heel we're shüre to see
     Wi' gladsome caper:
The bogle of a bogle, he—
      A ghaist o' paper!

And as the auld-farrand hero sees
In Hell a bogle Hercules,
Pit there the lesser deid to please,
     While he himsel'
Dwalls wi' the muckle gods at ease
      Far raised frae hell:

Sae the true Rabbie far has gane
On kindlier business o' his ain
Wi' aulder frien's; an' his breist-bane
    An' stumpie tailie,
He birstles at a new hearth stane
    By James and Ailie.

XVI

It's an owercome sooth for age an' youth
    And it brooks wi' nae denial,
That the dearest friends are the auldest friends
    And the young are just on trial.

There's a rival bauld wi' young an' auld
    And it's him that has bereft me;
For the sürest friends are the auldest friends
    And the maist o' mines hae left me.

There are kind hearts still, for friends to fill
    And fools to take and break them;
But the nearest friends are the auldest friends
    And the grave's the place to seek them.

BALLADS

BALLADS

The Song of Rahéro
A Legend of Tahiti

TO ORI A ORI

ORI, my brother in the island mode,
In every tongue and meaning much my friend,
This story of your country and your clan,
In your loved house, your too much honoured guest,
I made in English. Take it, being done;
And let me sign it with the name you gave.
TERIITERA

I. THE SLAYING OF TÁMATÉA

IT fell in the days of old, as the men of Taiárapu tell,
A youth went forth to the fishing, and fortune favoured
       him well.
Támatéa his name: gullible, simple, and kind,
Comely of countenance, nimble of body, empty of mind,
His mother ruled him and loved him beyond the wont of a
       wife,
Serving the lad for eyes and living herself in his life.
Alone from the sea and the fishing came Támatéa the
       fair,
Urging his boat to the beach, and the mother awaited him
       there,

—'Long may you live!' said she. 'Your fishing has sped
    to a wish.
And now let us choose for the king the fairest of all your
    fish.
For fear inhabits the palace and grudging grows in the land,
Marked is the sluggardly foot and marked the niggardly
    hand,
The hours and the miles are counted, the tributes num-
    bered and weighed,
And woe to him that comes short, and woe to him that
    delayed!'

So spoke on the beach the mother, and counselled the
    wiser thing.
For Rahéro stirred in the country and secretly mined the
    king.
Nor were the signals wanting of how the leaven wrought,
In the cords of obedience loosed and the tributes grudgingly
    brought.

And when last to the temple of Oro the boat with the
    victim sped,
And the priest uncovered the basket and looked on the
    face of the dead,
Trembling fell upon all at sight of an ominous thing,
For there was the aito dead, and he of the house of the
    king.

So spake on the beach the mother, matter worthy of note,
And wattled a basket well, and chose a fish from the
    boat;
And Támatéa the pliable shouldered the basket and went,
And travelled, and sang as he travelled, a lad that was well
    content.

Still the way of his going was round by the roaring coast,
Where the ring of the reef is broke and the trades run riot
  the most.
On his left, with smoke as of battle, the billows battered the
  land;
Unscalable, turreted mountains rose on the inner hand.
And cape, and village, and river, and vale, and mountain
  above,
Each had a name in the land for men to remember and
  love;
And never the name of a place, but lo! a song in its
  praise:
Ancient and unforgotten, songs of the earlier days,
That the elders taught to the young, and at night, in the
  full of the moon,
Garlanded boys and maidens sang together in tune.
Támatéa the placable went with a lingering foot;
He sang as loud as a bird, he whistled hoarse as a flute;
He broiled in the sun, he breathed in the grateful shadow
  of trees,
In the icy stream of the rivers he waded over the knees;
And still in his empty mind crowded, a thousand-fold,
The deeds of the strong and the songs of the cunning heroes
  of old.

And now was he come to a place Taiárapu honoured the
  most,
Where a silent valley of woods debouched on the noisy
  coast,
Spewing a level river. There was a haunt of Pai.
There, in his potent youth, when his parents drove him to
  die,
Honoura lived like a beast, lacking the lamp and the fire,
Washed by the rains of the trade and clotting his hair in
  the mire;

And there, so mighty his hands, he bent the tree to his
    foot—
So keen the spur of his hunger, he plucked it naked of
    fruit.
There, as she pondered the clouds for the shadow of coming
    ills,
Ahupu, the woman of song, walked on high on the hills.

Of these was Rahéro sprung, a man of a godly race;
And inherited cunning of spirit and beauty of body and
    face.
Of yore in his youth, as an aito, Rahéro wandered the land,
Delighting maids with his tongue, smiting men with his
    hand.
Famous he was in his youth; but before the midst of his
    life
Paused, and fashioned a song of farewell to glory and strife.

> *House of mine (it went), house upon the sea,*
> *Belov'd of all my fathers, more belov'd by me!*
> *Vale of the strong Honoura, deep ravine of Pai,*
> *Again in your woody summits I hear the trade-wind cry.*

> *House of mine, in your walls, strong sounds the sea,*
> *Of all sounds on earth, dearest sound to me.*
> *I have heard the applause of men, I have heard it arise*
>   *and die:*
> *Sweeter now in my house I hear the trade-wind cry.*

These were the words of his singing, other the thought of
    his heart;
For secret desire of glory vexed him, dwelling apart.
Lazy and crafty he was, and loved to lie in the sun,
And loved the cackle of talk and the true word uttered in
    fun;

Lazy he was, his roof was ragged, his table was lean,
And the fish swam safe in his sea, and he gathered the near
and the green.
He sat in his house and laughed, but he loathed the king
of the land,
And he uttered the grudging word under the covering
hand.
Treason spread from his door; and he looked for a day to
come,
A day of the crowding people, a day of the summoning
drum,
When the vote should be taken, the king be driven forth in
disgrace,
And Rahéro, the laughing and lazy, sit and rule in his
place.

Here Támatéa came, and beheld the house on the brook;
And Rahéro was there by the way and covered an oven to
cook.
Naked he was to the loins, but the tattoo covered the lack,
And the sun and the shadow of palms dappled his muscular
back.
Swiftly he lifted his head at the fall of the coming feet,
And the water sprang in his mouth with a sudden desire of
meat;
For he marked the basket carried, covered from flies and
the sun;
And Rahéro buried his fire, but the meat in his house was
done.

Forth he stepped; and took, and delayed the boy, by the
hand;
And vaunted the joys of meat and the ancient ways of the
land:

—'Our sires of old in Taiárapu, they that created the race,

Ate ever with eager hand, nor regarded season or place,

Ate in the boat at the oar, on the way afoot; and at night

Arose in the midst of dreams to rummage the house for a bite.

It is good for the youth in his turn to follow the way of the sire;

And behold how fitting the time! for here do I cover my fire.'

—'I see the fire for the cooking but never the meat to cook,'

Said Támatéa.—'Tut!' said Rahéro. 'Here in the brook

And there in the tumbling sea, the fishes are thick as flies,

Hungry like healthy men, and like pigs for savour and size:

Crayfish crowding the river, sea-fish thronging the sea.'

—'Well it may be,' says the other, 'and yet be nothing to me.

Fain would I eat, but alas! I have needful matter in hand,

Since I carry my tribute of fish to the jealous king of the land.'

Now at the word a light sprang in Rahéro's eyes.

'I will gain me a dinner,' thought he, 'and lend the king a surprise.'

And he took the lad by the arm, as they stood by the side of the track,

And smiled, and rallied, and flattered, and pushed him forward and back.

It was 'You that sing like a bird, I never have heard you sing,'

And 'The lads when I was a lad were none so feared of a king.

And of what account is an hour, when the heart is empty of
    guile?
But come, and sit in the house and laugh with the women
    awhile;
And I will but drop my hook, and behold! the dinner
    made.'

So Támatéa the pliable hung up his fish in the shade
On a tree by the side of the way; and Rahéro carried him
    in,
Smiling as smiles the fowler when flutters the bird to the
    gin,
And chose him a shining hook, and viewed it with
    sedulous eye,
And breathed and burnished it well on the brawn of his
    naked thigh,
And set a mat for the gull, and bade him be merry and
    bide,
Like a man concerned for his guest, and the fishing, and
    nothing beside.

Now when Rahéro was forth, he paused and hearkened,
    and heard
The gull jest in the house and the women laugh at his
    word;
And stealthily crossed to the side of the way, to the shady
    place
Where the basket hung on a mango; and craft transfigured
    his face.
Deftly he opened the basket, and took of the fat of the
    fish,
The cut of kings and chieftains, enough for a goodly dish.
This he wrapped in a leaf, set on the fire to cook
And buried; and next the marred remains of the tribute he
    took,

And doubled and packed them well, and covered the basket
close
—'There is a buffet, my king,' quoth he, 'and a nauseous
dose!'—
And hung the basket again in the shade, in a cloud of
flies
—'And there is a sauce to your dinner, king of the crafty
eyes!'

Soon as the oven was open, the fish smelt excellent good.
In the shade, by the house of Rahéro, down they sat to their
food,
And cleared the leaves in silence, or uttered a jest and
laughed,
And raising the cocoanut bowls, buried their faces and
quaffed.
But chiefly in silence they ate; and soon as the meal was
done,
Rahéro feigned to remember and measured the hour by the
sun,
And 'Támatéa,' quoth he, 'it is time to be jogging, my
lad.'

So Támatéa arose, doing ever the thing he was bade,
And carelessly shouldered the basket, and kindly saluted
his host;
And again the way of his going was round by the roaring
coast.
Long he went; and at length was aware of a pleasant green,
And the stems and shadows of palms, and roofs of lodges
between
There sate, in the door of his palace, the king on a kingly
seat,
And aitos stood armed around, and the yottowas sat at his
feet.

But fear was a worm in his heart: fear darted his eyes;
And he probed men's faces for treasons and pondered their
    speech for lies.
To him came Támatéa, the basket slung in his hand,
And paid him the due obeisance standing as vassals stand.
In silence hearkened the king, and closed the eyes in his
    face,
Harbouring odious thoughts and the baseless fears of the
    base;
In silence accepted the gift and sent the giver away.
So Támatéa departed, turning his back on the day.

And lo! as the king sat brooding, a rumour rose in the
    crowd;
The yottowas nudged and whispered, the commons mur-
    mured aloud;
Tittering fell upon all at sight of the impudent thing,
At the sight of a gift unroyal flung in the face of a king.
And the face of the king turned white and red with anger
    and shame
In their midst; and the heart in his body was water and
    then was flame;
Till of a sudden, turning, he gripped an aito hard,
A youth that stood with his ómare, one of the daily
    guard,
And spat in his ear a command, and pointed and uttered a
    name,
And hid in the shade of the house his impotent anger and
    shame.

Now Támatéa the fool was far on the homeward way,
The rising night in his face, behind him the dying day.
Rahéro saw him go by, and the heart of Rahéro was
    glad,
Devising shame to the king and nowise harm to the lad;

And all that dwelt by the way saw and saluted him well,
For he had the face of a friend and the news of the town to
    tell;
And pleased with the notice of folk, and pleased that his
    journey was done,
Támatéa drew homeward, turning his back to the sun.

And now was the hour of the bath in Taiárapu: far and
    near
The lovely laughter of bathers rose and delighted his ear.
Night massed in the valleys; the sun on the mountain coast
Struck, end-long; and above the clouds embattled their
    host,
And glowed and gloomed on the heights; and the heads of
    the palms were gems,
And far to the rising eve extended the shade of their stems;
And the shadow of Támatéa hovered already at home.

And sudden the sound of one coming and running light as
    the foam
Struck on his ear; and he turned, and lo! a man on his
    track,
Girded and armed with an ómare, following hard at his
    back.
At a bound the man was upon him;—and, or ever a word
    was said,
The loaded end of the ómare fell and laid him dead.

II. THE VENGING OF TÁMATÉA

Thus was Rahéro's treason; thus and no further it sped.
The king sat safe in his place and a kindly fool was dead.

But the mother of Támatéa arose with death in her eyes.
All night long, and the next, Taiárapu rang with her cries.

As when a babe in the wood turns with a chill of doubt

And perceives nor home, nor friends, for the trees have
    closed her about,

The mountain rings and her breast is torn with the voice
    of despair:

So the lion-like woman idly wearied the air

For awhile, and pierced men's hearing in vain, and
    wounded their hearts.

But as when the weather changes at sea, in dangerous parts,

And sudden the hurricane wrack unrolls up the front of the
    sky,

At once the ship lies idle, the sails hang silent on high,

The breath of the wind that blew is blown out like the
    flame of a lamp,

And the silent armies of death draw near with inaudible
    tramp:

So sudden, the voice of her weeping ceased; in silence she
    rose

And passed from the house of her sorrow, a woman clothed
    with repose,

Carrying death in her breast and sharpening death with her
    hand.

Hither she went and thither in all the coasts of the land.

They tell that she feared not to slumber alone, in the
    dead of night,

In accursed places; beheld, unblenched, the ribbon of light

Spin from temple to temple; guided the perilous skiff,

Abhorred not the paths of the mountain and trod the verge
    of the cliff;

From end to end of the island, thought not the distance
    long,

But forth from king to king carried the tale of her wrong.

To king after king, as they sat in the palace door, she came,

Claiming kinship, declaiming verses, naming her name

And the names of all of her fathers; and still, with a heart
    on the rack,
Jested to capture a hearing and laughed when they jested
    back:
So would deceive them awhile, and change and return in a
    breath,
And on all the men of Vaiau imprecate instant death;
And tempt her kings—for Vaiau was a rich and prosperous
    land,
And flatter—for who would attempt it but warriors mighty
    of hand?
And change in a breath again and rise in a strain of song,
Invoking the beaten drums, beholding the fall of the
    strong,
Calling the fowls of the air to come and feast on the dead.
And they held the chin in silence, and heard her, and shook
    the head;
For they knew the men of Taiárapu famous in battle and
    feast,
Marvellous eaters and smiters: the men of Vaiau not least.

To the land of the Námunu-úra, to Paea, at length she
    came,
To men who were foes to the Tevas and hated their race
    and name.
There was she well received, and spoke with Hiopa the
    king.
And Hiopa listened, and weighed, and wisely considered
    the thing.
'Here in the back of the isle we dwell in a sheltered place,'
Quoth he to the woman, 'in quiet, a weak and peaceable
    race.
But far in the teeth of the wind lofty Taiárapu lies;
Strong blows the wind of the trade on its seaward face, and
    cries

Aloud in the top of arduous mountains, and utters its
    song
In green continuous forests. Strong is the wind, and
    strong
And fruitful and hardy the race, famous in battle and
    feast,
Marvellous eaters and smiters: the men of Vaiau not least.
Now hearken to me, my daughter, and hear a word of the
    wise:
How a strength goes linked with a weakness, two by two,
    like the eyes.
They can wield the ómare well and cast the javelin far;
Yet are they greedy and weak as the swine and the children
    are.
Plant we, then, here at Paea, a garden of excellent fruits;
Plant we bananas and kava and taro, the king of roots;
Let the pigs in Paea be tapu and no man fish for a year;
And of all the meat in Tahiti gather we threefold here.
So shall the fame of our plenty fill the island, and so,
At last, on the tongue of rumour, go where we wish it to go.
Then shall the pigs of Taiárapu raise their snouts in the
    air;
But we sit quiet and wait, as the fowler sits by the snare,
And tranquilly fold our hands, till the pigs come nosing the
    food:
But meanwhile build us a house of Trotéa, the stubborn
    wood,
Bind it with incombustible thongs, set a roof to the room,
Too strong for the hands of a man to dissever or fire to
    consume;
And there, when the pigs come trotting, there shall the
    feast be spread,
There shall the eye of the morn enlighten the feasters dead.
So be it done; for I have a heart that pities your state,
And Nateva and Námunu-úra are fire and water for hate.'

G   [193]

All was done as he said, and the gardens prospered; and
    now
The fame of their plenty went out, and word of it came to
    Vaiau.
For the men of Námunu-úra sailed, to the windward far,
Lay in the offing by south where the towns of the Tevas
    are,
And cast overboard of their plenty; and lo! at the Tevas'
    feet
The surf on all of the beaches tumbled treasures of meat.
In the salt of the sea, a harvest tossed with the refluent
    foam;
And the children gleaned it in playing, and ate and carried
    it home;
And the elders stared and debated, and wondered and
    passed the jest,
But whenever a guest came by eagerly questioned the
    guest;
And little by little, from one to another, the word went
    round:
'In all the borders of Paea the victual rots on the ground,
And swine are plenty as rats.   And now, when they fare to
    the sea,
The men of the Námunu-úra glean from under the tree
And load the canoe to the gunwale with all that is tooth-
    some to eat;
And all day long on the sea the jaws are crushing the
    meat,
The steersman eats at the helm, the rowers munch at the
    oar,
And at length, when their bellies are full, overboard with
    the store!'
Now was the word made true, and soon as the bait was
    bare,
All the pigs of Taiárapu raised their snouts in the air.

Songs were recited, and kinship was counted, and tales
    were told
How war had severed of late but peace had cemented of
    old
The clans of the island. 'To war,' said they, 'now set we
    an end,
And hie to the Námunu-úra even as a friend to a friend.'

So judged, and a day was named; and soon as the morning
    broke,
Canoes were thrust in the sea and the houses emptied of
    folk.
Strong blew the wind of the south, the wind that gathers
    the clan;
Along all the line of the reef the clamorous surges ran;
And the clouds were piled on the top of the island moun-
    tain-high,
A mountain throned on a mountain. The fleet of canoes
    swept by
In the midst, on the green lagoon, with a crew released
    from care,
Sailing an even water, breathing a summer air,
Cheered by a cloudless sun; and ever to left and right,
Bursting surge on the reef, drenching storms on the
    height.
So the folk of Vaiau sailed and were glad all day,
Coasting the palm-tree cape and crossing the populous bay
By all the towns of the Tevas; and still as they bowled
    along,
Boat would answer to boat with jest and laughter and
    song,
And the people of all the towns trooped to the sides of the
    sea
And gazed from under the hand or sprang aloft on the
    tree,

[195]

Hailing and cheering. Time failed them for more to
    do;

The holiday village careened to the wind, and was gone
    from view

Swift as a passing bird; and ever as onward it bore,

Like the cry of the passing bird, bequeathed its song to the
    shore—

Desirable laughter of maids and the cry of delight of the
    child.

And the gazer, left behind, stared at the wake and smiled.

By all the towns of the Tevas they went, and Pápara
    last,

The home of the chief, the place of muster in war; and
    passed

The march of the lands of the clan, to the lands of an alien
    folk.

And there, from the dusk of the shoreside palms, a column
    of smoke

Mounted and wavered and died in the gold of the setting
    sun,

'Paea!' they cried. 'It is Paea.' And so was the voyage
    done.

In the early fall of the night, Hiopa came to the shore,

And beheld and counted the comers, and lo, they were
    forty score:

The pelting feet of the babes that ran already and played,

The clean-lipped smile of the boy, the slender breasts of the
    maid,

And mighty limbs of women, stalwart mothers of men.

The sires stood forth unabashed; but a little back from his
    ken

Clustered the scarcely nubile, the lads and maids, in a
    ring,

Fain of each other, afraid of themselves, aware of the king

And aping behaviour, but clinging together with hands and
  eyes,
With looks that were kind like kisses, and laughter tender
  as sighs.
There, too, the grandsire stood, raising his silver crest,
And the impotent hands of a suckling groped in his barren
  breast.
The childhood of love, the pair well married, the innocent
  brood,
The tale of the generations repeated and ever renewed—
Hiopa beheld them together, all the ages of man,
And a moment shook in his purpose.

                    But these were the foes of his clan,
And he trod upon pity, and came, and civilly greeted the
  king,
And gravely entreated Rahéro; and for all that could fight
  or sing,
And claimed a name in the land, had fitting phrases of
  praise;
But with all who were well-descended he spoke of the
  ancient days.
And ' 'Tis true,' said he, 'that in Paea the victual rots on
  the ground;
But, friends, your number is many; and pigs must be
  hunted and found,
And the lads troop to the mountains to bring the féis
  down,
And around the bowls of the kava cluster the maids of the
  town.
So, for to-night, sleep here; but king, common, and priest
To-morrow, in order due, shall sit with me in the feast.'
Sleepless the live-long night, Hiopa's followers toiled.
The pigs screamed and were slaughtered; the spars of the
  guest-house oiled,

The leaves spread on the floor. In many a mountain
    glen
The moon drew shadows of trees on the naked bodies of
    men
Plucking and bearing fruits; and in all the bounds of the
    town
Red glowed the cocoanut fires, and were buried and trod-
    den down.
Thus did seven of the yottowas toil with their tale of the
    clan,
But the eighth wrought with his lads, hid from the sight of
    man.
In the deeps of the woods they laboured, piling the fuel
    high
In faggots, the load of a man, fuel seasoned and dry,
Thirsty to seize upon fire and apt to blurt into flame.

And now was the day of the feast. The forests, as morning
    came,
Tossed in the wind, and the peaks quaked in the blaze of
    the day
And the cocoanuts showered on the ground, rebounding
    and rolling away:
A glorious morn for a feast, a famous wind for a fire.
To the hall of feasting Hiopa led them, mother and
    sire
And maid and babe in a tale, the whole of the holiday
    throng.
Smiling they came, garlanded green, not dreaming of
    wrong;
And for every three, a pig, tenderly cooked in the ground,
Waited; and féi, the staff of life, heaped in a mound
For each where he sat;—for each, bananas roasted and
    raw
Piled with a bountiful hand, as for horses hay and straw

Are stacked in a stable; and fish, the food of desire,
And plentiful vessels of sauce, and breadfruit gilt in the fire;
And kava was common as water. Feasts have there been
    ere now,
And many, but never a feast like that of the folk of Vaiau.
All day long they ate with the resolute greed of brutes,
And turned from the pigs to the fish, and again from the
    fish to the fruits,
And emptied the vessels of sauce, and drank of the kava
    deep;
Till the young lay stupid as stones, and the strongest
    nodded to sleep.
Sleep that was mighty as death and blind as a moonless
    night
Tethered them hand and foot; and their souls were
    drowned, and the light
Was cloaked from their eyes. Senseless together, the old
    and the young,
The fighter deadly to smite and the prater cunning of
    tongue,
The woman wedded and fruitful, inured to the pangs of
    birth,
And the maid that knew not of kisses, blindly sprawled on
    the earth.
From the hall Hiopa the king and his chiefs came stealthily
    forth.
Already the sun hung low and enlightened the peaks of the
    north;
But the wind was stubborn to die and blew as it blows at
    morn,
Showering the nuts in the dusk, and e'en as a banner is
    torn,
High on the peaks of the island, shattered the mountain
    cloud.
And now at once, at a signal, a silent, emulous crowd

Set hands to the work of death, hurrying to and fro,

Like ants, to furnish the faggots, building them broad and low,

And piling them high and higher around the walls of the hall.

Silence persisted within, for sleep lay heavy on all;

But the mother of Támatéa stood at Hiopa's side,

And shook for terror and joy like a girl that is a bride.

Night fell on the toilers, and first Hiopa the wise

Made the round of the house, visiting all with his eyes;

And all was piled to the eaves, and fuel blockaded the door;

And within, in the house beleaguered, slumbered the forty score.

Then was an aito dispatched and came with fire in his hand,

And Hiopa took it.—'Within,' said he, 'is the life of a land;

And behold! I breathe on the coal, I breathe on the dales of the east,

And silence falls on forest and shore; the voice of the feast

Is quenched, and the smoke of cooking; the rooftree decays and falls

On the empty lodge, and the winds subvert deserted walls.'

Therewithal, to the fuel, he laid the glowing coal;

And the redness ran in the mass and burrowed within like a mole,

And copious smoke was conceived. But, as when a dam is to burst,

The water lips it and crosses in silver trickles at first,

And then, of a sudden, whelms and bears it away forth-right:

So now, in a moment, the flame sprang and towered in the night,

[200]

And wrestled and roared in the wind, and high over house
and tree,
Stood, like a streaming torch, enlightening land and sea.

But the mother of Támatéa threw her arms abroad,
'Pyre of my son,' she shouted, 'debited vengeance of God,
Late, late, I behold you, yet I behold you at last,
And glory, beholding! For now are the days of my agony
past,
The lust that famished my soul now eats and drinks its
desire,
And they that encompassed my son shrivel alive in the
fire.
Tenfold precious the vengeance that comes after lingering
years!
Ye quenched the voice of my singer?—hark, in your dying
ears,
The song of the conflagration! Ye left me a widow alone?
—Behold, the whole of your race consumes, sinew and
bone
And torturing flesh together: man, mother, and maid
Heaped in a common shambles; and already, borne by the
trade,
The smoke of your dissolution darkens the stars of night.'

Thus she spoke, and her stature grew in the people's sight.

III. RAHÉRO

RAHÉRO was there in the hall asleep: beside him his wife,
Comely, a mirthful woman, one that delighted in life;
And a girl that was ripe for marriage, shy and sly as a
mouse;
And a boy, a climber of trees: all the hopes of his house.

Unwary, with open hands, he slept in the midst of his
  folk,
And dreamed that he heard a voice crying without, and
  awoke,
Leaping blindly afoot like one from a dream that he fears.
A hellish glow and clouds were about him;—it roared in
  his ears
Like the sound of the cataract fall that plunges sudden and
  steep;
And Rahéro swayed as he stood, and his reason was still
  asleep.
Now the flame struck hard on the house, wind-wielded, a
  fracturing blow,
And the end of the roof was burst and fell on the sleepers
  below;
And the lofty hall, and the feast, and the prostrate bodies of
  folk,
Shone red in his eyes a moment, and then were swallowed
  of smoke.
In the mind of Rahéro clearness came; and he opened his
  throat;
And as when a squall comes sudden, the straining sail of a
  boat
Thunders aloud and bursts, so thundered the voice of the
  man.
—'The wind and the rain!' he shouted, the mustering
  word of the clan,
And 'up!' and 'to arms, men of Vaiau!' But silence
  replied,
Or only the voice of the gusts of the fire, and nothing
  beside.

Rahéro stooped and groped. He handled his womankind,
But the fumes of the fire and the kava had quenched the
  life of their mind,

And they lay like pillars prone; and his hand encountered
    the boy,
And there sprang in the gloom of his soul a sudden lightning
    of joy.
'Him can I save!' he thought, 'if I were speedy enough.'
And he loosened the cloth from his loins, and swaddled the
    child in the stuff;
And about the strength of his neck he knotted the burden
    well.

There where the roof had fallen, it roared like the mouth of
    hell.
Thither Rahéro went, stumbling on senseless folk,
And grappled a post of the house, and began to climb in the
    smoke:
The last alive of Vaiau; and the son borne by the sire.
The post glowed in the grain with ulcers of eating fire,
And the fire bit to the blood and mangled his hands and
    thighs;
And the fumes sang in his head like wine and stung in his
    eyes;
And still he climbed, and came to the top, the place of proof,
And thrust a hand through the flame, and clambered alive
    on the roof.
But even as he did so, the wind, in a garment of flames and
    pain,
Wrapped him from head to heel; and the waistcloth parted
    in twain;
And the living fruit of his loins dropped in the fire below.

About the blazing feast-house clustered the eyes of the foe,
Watching, hand upon weapon, lest ever a soul should
    flee,
Shading the brow from the glare, straining the neck to
    see.

Only, to leeward, the flames in the wind swept far and
wide,
And the forest sputtered on fire; and there might no man
abide.
Thither Rahéro crept, and dropped from the burning
eaves,
And crouching low to the ground, in a treble covert of
leaves
And fire and volleying smoke, ran for the life of his soul
Unseen; and behind him under a furnace of ardent coal,
Cairned with a wonder of flame, and blotting the night
with smoke,
Blazed and were smelted together the bones of all his folk.

He fled unguided at first; but hearing the breakers roar,
Thitherward shaped his way, and came at length to the
shore.
Sound-limbed he was: dry-eyed; but smarted in every
part;
And the mighty cage of his ribs heaved on his straining
heart
With sorrow and rage. And 'Fools!' he cried, 'fools of
Vaiau,
Heads of swine—gluttons—Alas! and where are they
now?
Those that I played with, those that nursed me, those that
I nursed?
God, and I outliving them! I, the least and the worst—
I, that thought myself crafty, snared by this herd of swine,
In the tortures of hell and desolate, stripped of all that was
mine:
All!—my friends and my fathers—the silver heads of
yore
That trooped to the council, the children that ran to the
open door

Crying with innocent voices and clasping a father's knees!
And mine, my wife—my daughter—my sturdy climber of
    trees,
Ah, never to climb again!'
                    Thus in the dusk of the night,
(For clouds rolled in the sky and the moon was swallowed
    from sight),
Pacing and gnawing his fists, Rahéro raged by the shore.
Vengeance: that must be his. But much was to do before;
And first a single life to be snatched from a deadly place,
A life, the root of revenge, surviving plant of the race:
And next the race to be raised anew, and the lands of the
    clan
Repeopled. So Rahéro designed, a prudent man
Even in wrath, and turned for the means of revenge and
    escape:
A boat to be seized by stealth, a wife to be taken by rape.

Still was the dark lagoon; beyond on the coral wall,
He saw the breakers shine, he heard them bellow and fall.
Alone, on the top of the reef, a man with a flaming brand
Walked, gazing and pausing, a fish-spear poised in his hand.
The foam boiled to his calf when the mightier breakers
    came,
And the torch shed in the wind scattering tufts of flame.
Afar on the dark lagoon a canoe lay idly at wait:
A figure dimly guiding it: surely the fisherman's mate.
Rahéro saw and he smiled. He straightened his mighty
    thews:
Naked, with never a weapon, and covered with scorch and
    bruise,
He straightened his arms, he filled the void of his body with
    breath,
And, strong as the wind in his manhood, doomed the fisher
    to death.

Silent he entered the water, and silently swam, and came
There where the fisher walked, holding on high the flame.
Loud on the pier of the reef volleyed the breach of the sea;
And hard at the back of the man, Rahéro crept to his
knee
On the coral, and suddenly sprang and seized him, the
elder hand
Clutching the joint of his throat, the other snatching the
brand
Ere it had time to fall, and holding it steady and high.
Strong was the fisher, brave, and swift of mind and of eye—
Strongly he threw in the clutch; but Rahéro resisted the
strain,
And jerked, and the spine of life snapped with a crack in
twain,
And the man came slack in his hands and tumbled a lump
at his feet.

One moment: and there, on the reef, where the breakers
whitened and beat,
Rahéro was standing alone, glowing and scorched and bare,
A victor unknown of any, raising the torch in the air.
But once he drank of his breath, and instantly set him to
fish
Like a man intent upon supper at home and a savoury dish.
For what should the woman have seen? A man with a
torch—and then
A moment's blur of the eyes—and a man with a torch
again.
And the torch had scarcely been shaken. 'Ah, surely,'
Rahéro said,
'She will deem it a trick of the eyes, a fancy born in the
head;
But time must be given the fool to nourish a fool's belief.'
So for a while, a sedulous fisher, he walked the reef,

Pausing at times and gazing, striking at times with the
  spear:
—Lastly, uttered the call; and even as the boat drew near,
Like a man that was done with its use, tossed the torch in
  the sea.

Lightly he leaped on the boat beside the woman; and she
Lightly addressed him, and yielded the paddle and place to
  sit;
For now the torch was extinguished the night was black as
  the pit.
Rahéro set him to row, never a word he spoke,
And the boat sang in the water urged by his vigorous
  stroke.
—'What ails you?' the woman asked, 'and why did you
  drop the brand?
We have only to kindle another as soon as we come to
  land.'
Never a word Rahéro replied, but urged the canoe.
And a chill fell on the woman.—'Atta! speak! is it you?
Speak! Why are you silent? Why do you bend aside?
Wherefore steer to the seaward?' thus she panted and
  cried.
Never a word from the oarsman, toiling there in the dark;
But right for a gate of the reef he silently headed the
  bark,
And wielding the single paddle with passionate sweep on
  sweep,
Drove her, the little fitted, forth on the open deep.
And fear, there where she sat, froze the woman to stone:
Not fear of the crazy boat and the weltering deep alone;
But a keener fear of the night, the dark, and the ghostly
  hour,
And the thing that drove the canoe with more than a
  mortal's power

And more than a mortal's boldness. For much she knew
of the dead

That haunt and fish upon reefs, toiling, like men, for
bread,

And traffic with human fishers, or slay them and take their
ware,

Till the hour when the star of the dead goes down, and
the morning air

Blows, and the cocks are singing on shore. And surely she
knew

The speechless thing at her side belonged to the grave.

It blew

All night from the south; all night, Rahéro contended and
kept

The prow to the cresting sea; and, silent as though she
slept,

The woman huddled and quaked. And now was the peep
of day.

High and long on their left the mountainous island lay;

And over the peaks of Taiárapu arrows of sunlight
struck.

On shore the birds were beginning to sing: the ghostly
ruck

Of the buried had long ago returned to the covered
grave;

And here on the sea, the woman, waxing suddenly
brave,

Turned her swiftly about and looked in the face of the
man.

And sure he was none that she knew, none of her country
or clan:

A stranger, mother-naked, and marred with the marks of
fire,

But comely and great of stature, a man to obey and
admire.

And Rahéro regarded her also, fixed, with a frowning face,
Judging the woman's fitness to mother a warlike race.
Broad of shoulder, ample of girdle, long in the thigh,
Deep of bosom she was, and bravely supported his eye.

'Woman,' said he, 'last night the men of your folk—
Man, woman, and maid, smothered my race in smoke.
It was done like cowards; and I, a mighty man of my
       hands,
Escaped, a single life; and now to the empty lands
And smokeless hearths of my people, sail, with yourself,
       alone.
Before your mother was born, the die of to-day was thrown
And you selected:—your husband, vainly striving, to fall
Broken between these hands:—yourself to be severed from
       all,
The places, the people, you love—home, kindred, and
       clan—
And to dwell in a desert and bear the babes of a kinless
       man.'

The Feast of Famine

Marquesan Manners

I. THE PRIEST'S VIGIL

IN all the land of the tribe was neither fish nor fruit,
And the deepest pit of popoi stood empty to the foot.
The clans upon the left and the clans upon the right
Now oiled their carven maces and scoured their daggers
       bright;
They gat them to the thicket, to the deepest of the shade,
And lay with sleepless eyes in the deadly ambuscade.

And oft in the starry even the song of morning rose,
What time the oven smoked in the country of their foes;
For oft to loving hearts, and waiting ears and sight,
The lads that went to forage returned not with the night.
Now first the children sickened, and then the women
  paled,
And the great arms of the warrior no more for war
  availed.
Hushed was the deep drum, discarded was the dance;
And those that met the priest now glanced at him askance.
The priest was a man of years, his eyes were ruby-red,
He neither feared the dark nor the terrors of the dead,
He knew the songs of races, the names of ancient date;
And the beard upon his bosom would have bought the
  chief's estate.
He dwelt in a high-built lodge, hard by the roaring shore,
Raised on a noble terrace and with tikis at the door.
Within it was full of riches, for he served his nation
  well,
And full of the sound of breakers, like the hollow of a
  shell.
For weeks he let them perish, gave never a helping sign,
But sat on his oiled platform to commune with the divine,
But sat on his high terrace, with the tikis by his side,
And stared on the blue ocean, like a parrot, ruby-eyed.
Dawn as yellow as sulphur leaped on the mountain height:
Out on the round of the sea the gems of the morning
  light,
Up from the round of the sea the streamers of the sun;
But down in the depths of the valley the day was not
  begun.
In the blue of the woody twilight burned red the cocoa-
  husk,
And the women and men of the clan went forth to bathe in
  the dusk,

A word that began to go round, a word, a whisper, a
start:
Hope that leaped in the bosom, fear that knocked on the
heart:
'See, the priest is not risen—look, for his door is fast!
He is going to name the victims; he is going to help us
at last.'

Thrice rose the sun to noon; and ever, like one of the
dead,
The priest lay still in his house with the roar of the sea in
his head;
There was never a foot on the floor, there was never a
whisper of speech;
Only the leering tikis stared on the blinding beach.
Again were the mountains fired, again the morning broke;
And all the houses lay still, but the house of the priest
awoke.
Close in their covering roofs lay and trembled the clan,
But the agèd, red-eyed priest ran forth like a lunatic man;
And the village panted to see him in the jewels of death
again,
In the silver beards of the old and the hair of women
slain.
Frenzy shook in his limbs, frenzy shone in his eyes,
And still and again as he ran, the valley rang with his cries.
All day long in the land, by cliff and thicket and den,
He ran his lunatic rounds, and howled for the flesh of men;
All day long he ate not, nor ever drank of the brook;
And all day long in their houses the people listened and
shook—
All day long in their houses they listened with bated
breath,
And never a soul went forth, for the sight of the priest was
death.

Three were the days of his running, as the gods appointed
    of yore,
Two the nights of his sleeping alone in the place of gore:
The drunken slumber of frenzy twice he drank to the lees,
On the sacred stones of the High-place under the sacred
    trees;
With a lamp at his ashen head he lay in the place of the
    feast,
And the sacred leaves of the banyan rustled around the
    priest.
Last, when the stated even fell upon terrace and tree,
And the shade of the lofty island lay leagues away to sea,
And all the valleys of verdure were heavy with manna
    and musk,
The wreck of the red-eyed priest came gasping home in the
    dusk.
He reeled across the village, he staggered along the shore,
And between the leering tikis crept groping through his
    door.

There went a stir through the lodges, the voice of speech
    awoke;
Once more from the builded platforms arose the evening
    smoke.
And those who were mighty in war, and those renowned
    for an art
Sat in their stated seats and talked of the morrow apart.

II.   THE LOVERS

HARK! away in the woods—for the ears of love are sharp—
Stealthily, quietly touched, the note of the one-stringed
    harp.
In the lighted house of her father, why should Taheia start?
Taheia heavy of hair, Taheia tender of heart,

Taheia the well-descended, a bountiful dealer in love,
Nimble of foot like the deer, and kind of eye like the dove?
Sly and shy as a cat, with never a change of face,
Taheia slips to the door, like one that would breathe a
    space;
Saunters and pauses, and looks at the stars, and lists to the
    seas;
Then sudden and swift as a cat, she plunges under the
    trees.
Swift as a cat she runs, with her garment gathered high,
Leaping, nimble of foot, running, certain of eye;
And ever to guide her way over the smooth and the sharp,
Ever nearer and nearer the note of the one-stringed harp;
Till at length, in a glade of the wood, with a naked moun-
    tain above,
The sound of the harp thrown down, and she in the arms
    of her love. ˙
'Rua,'—'Taheia,' they cry—'my heart, my soul, and my
    eyes,'
And clasp and sunder and kiss, with lovely laughter and
    sighs,
'Rua!'—'Taheia, my love,'—'Rua, star of my night,
Clasp me, hold me, and love me, single spring of delight.'

And Rua folded her close, he folded her near and long,
The living knit to the living, and sang the lover's song:

> *Night, night it is, night upon the palms.*
> *Night, night it is, the land wind has blown.*
> *Starry, starry night, over deep and height;*
> *Love, love in the valley, love all alone.*

'Taheia, heavy of hair, a foolish thing have we done,
To bind what gods have sundered unkindly into one.
Why should a lowly lover have touched Taheia's skirt,
Taheia the well-descended, and Rua child of the dirt?'

[213]

'—On high with the haka-ikis my father sits in state,
Ten times fifty kinsmen salute him in the gate;
Round all his martial body, and in bands across his face,
The marks of the tattooer proclaim his lofty place.
I too, in the hands of the cunning, in the sacred cabin of
    palm,
Have shrunk like the mimosa, and bleated like the lamb;
Round half my tender body, that none shall clasp but you,
For a crest and a fair adornment go dainty lines of blue.
Love, love, beloved Rua, love levels all degrees,
And the well-tattooed Taheia clings panting to your knees.'

'—Taheia, song of the morning, how long is the longest
    love?
A cry, a clasp of the hands, a star that falls from above!
Ever at morn in the blue, and at night when all is black,
Ever it skulks and trembles with the hunter, Death, on its
    track.
Hear me, Taheia, death! For to-morrow the priest shall
    awake,
And the names be named of the victims to bleed for the
    nation's sake;
And first of the numbered many that shall be slain ere
    noon,
Rua the child of the dirt, Rua the kinless loon.
For him shall the drum be beat, for him be raised the
    song,
For him to the sacred High-place the chaunting people
    throng,
For him the oven smoke as for a speechless beast,
And the sire of my Taheia come greedy to the feast.'
'Rua, be silent, spare me. Taheia closes her ears.
Pity my yearning heart, pity my girlish years!
Flee from the cruel hands, flee from the knife and coal,
Lie hid in the deeps of the woods, Rua, sire of my soul!'

[214]

'Whither to flee, Taheia, whither in all of the land?
The fires of the bloody kitchen are kindled on every hand;
On every hand in the isle a hungry whetting of teeth,
Eyes in the trees above, arms in the brush beneath.
Patience to lie in wait, cunning to follow the sleuth,
Abroad the foes I have fought, and at home the friends of
　　my youth.'

'Love, love, beloved Rua, love has a clearer eye,
Hence from the arms of love you go not forth to die.
There, where the broken mountain drops sheer into the
　　glen.
There shall you find a hold from the boldest hunter of
　　men;
There, in the deep recess, where the sun falls only at noon,
And only once in the night enters the light of the moon,
Nor ever a sound but of birds, or the rain when it falls with
　　a shout;
For death and the fear of death beleaguer the valley about.
Tapu it is, but the gods will surely pardon despair;
Tapu, but what of that? If Rua can only dare.
Tapu and tapu and tapu, I know they are every one right;
But the god of every tapu is not always quick to smite.
Lie secret there, my Rua, in the arms of awful gods,
Sleep in the shade of the trees on the couch of the kindly
　　sods,
Sleep and dream of Taheia, Taheia will wake for you;
And whenever the land wind blows and the woods are
　　heavy with dew,
Alone through the horror of night, with food for the soul
　　of her love,
Taheia the undissuaded will hurry true as the dove.'

'Taheia, the pit of the night crawls with treacherous things,
Spirits of ultimate air and the evil souls of things;

The souls of the dead, the stranglers, that perch in the trees
     of the wood,
Waiters for all things human, haters of evil and good.'

'Rua, behold me, kiss me, look in my eyes and read;
Are these the eyes of a maid that would leave her lover in
     need?
Brave in the eye of day, my father ruled in the fight;
The child of his loins, Taheia, will play the man in the
     night.'

So it was spoken, and so agreed, and Taheia arose
And smiled in the stars and was gone, swift as the swallow
     goes;
And Rua stood on the hill, and sighed, and followed her
     flight,
And there were the lodges below, each with its door alight;
From folk that sat on the terrace and drew out the even
     long
Sudden crowings of laughter, monotonous drone of song;
The quiet passage of souls over his head in the trees;
And from all around the haven the crumbling thunder of
     seas.
'Farewell, my home,' said Rua. 'Farewell, O quiet seat!
To-morrow in all your valleys the drum of death shall
     beat.'

III.   THE FEAST

Dawn as yellow as sulphur leaped on the naked peak,
And all the village was stirring, for now was the priest to
     speak.
Forth on his terrace he came, and sat with the chief in talk;
His lips were blackened with fever, his cheeks were whiter
     than chalk;

Fever clutched at his hands, fever nodded his head,
But, quiet and steady and cruel, his eyes shone ruby-red.
In the earliest rays of the sun the chief rose up content;
Braves were summoned, and drummers; messengers came
    and went;
Braves ran to their lodges, weapons were snatched from the
    wall;
The commons herded together, and fear was over them all.
Festival dresses they wore, but the tongue was dry in their
    mouth,
And the blinking eyes in their faces skirted from north to
    south.

Now to the sacred enclosure gathered the greatest and
    least,
And from under the shade of the banyan arose the voice of
    the feast,
The frenzied roll of the drum, and a swift, monotonous
    song.
Higher the sun swam up; the trade wind level and strong
Awoke in the tops of the palms and rattled the fans aloud,
And over the garlanded heads and shining robes of the crowd
Tossed the spiders of shadow, scattered the jewels of sun.
Forty the tale of the drums, and the forty throbbed like one;
A thousand hearts in the crowd, and the even chorus of
    song,
Swift as the feet of a runner, trampled a thousand strong.
And the old men leered at the ovens and licked their lips
    for the food;
And the women stared at the lads, and laughed and looked
    to the wood.
As when the sweltering baker, at night, when the city is
    dead,
Alone in the trough of labour treads and fashions the
    bread;

So in the heat, and the reek, and the touch of woman and
     man,
The naked spirit of evil kneaded the hearts of the clan.

Now cold was at many a heart, and shaking in many a
     seat;
For there were the empty baskets, but who was to furnish
     the meat?
For here was the nation assembled, and there were the
     ovens anigh,
And out of a thousand singers nine were numbered to die.
Till, of a sudden, a shock, a mace in the air, a yell,
And, struck in the edge of the crowd, the first of the
     victims fell.
Terror and horrible glee divided the shrinking clan,
Terror of what was to follow, glee for a diet of man.
Frenzy hurried the chaunt, frenzy rattled the drums;
The nobles, high on the terrace, greedily mouthed their
     thumbs;
And once and again and again, in the ignorant crowd
     below,
Once and again and again descended the murderous blow.
Now smoked the oven, and now, with the cutting lip of a
     shell,
A butcher of ninety winters jointed the bodies well.
Unto the carven lodge, silent, in order due,
The grandees of the nation one after one withdrew;
And a line of laden bearers brought to the terrace foot,
On poles across their shoulders, the last reserve of fruit.
The victims bled for the nobles in the old appointed way;
The fruit was spread for the commons, for all should eat
     today.
And now was the kava brewed, and now the cocoa ran,
Now was the hour of the dance for child and woman and
     man;

And mirth was in every heart, and a garland on every
    head,
And all was well with the living and well with the eight
    who were dead.
Only the chiefs and the priest talked and consulted awhile:
'To-morrow,' they said, and 'To-morrow,' and nodded
    and seemed to smile:
'Rua the child of dirt, the creature of common clay,
Rua must die to-morrow, since Rua is gone today.'

Out of the groves of the valley, where clear the blackbirds
    sang,
Sheer from the trees of the valley the face of the mountain
    sprang;
Sheer and bare it rose, unscalable barricade,
Beaten and blown against by the generous draught of the
    trade.

Dawn on its fluted brow painted rainbow light,
Close on its pinnacled crown trembled the stars at night.
Here and there in a cleft clustered contorted trees,
Or the silver beard of a stream hung and swung in the
    breeze.
High overhead, with a cry, the torrents leaped for the
    main,
And silently sprinkled below in thin perennial rain.
Dark in the staring noon, dark was Rua's ravine,
Damp and cold was the air, and the face of the cliffs was
    green.
Here, in the rocky pit, accursed already of old,
On a stone in the midst of a river, Rua sat and was cold.

'Valley of mid-day shadows, valley of silent falls.'
Rua sang, and his voice went hollow about the walls,

[219]

'Valley of shadow and rock, a doleful prison to me,
What is the life you can give to a child of the sun and the
    sea?'
And Rua arose and came to the open mouth of the glen,
Whence he beheld the woods, and the sea, and houses
    of men.
Wide blew the riotous trade, and smelt in his nostrils
    good;
It bowed the boats on the bay, and tore and divided the
    wood;
It smote and sundered the groves as Moses smote with the
    rod,
And the streamers of all the trees blew like banners abroad;
And ever and on, in a lull, the trade wind brought him
    along
A far-off patter of drums and a far-off whisper of song.

Swift as the swallow's wings, the diligent hands on the
    drum
Fluttered and hurried and throbbed. 'Ah, woe that I hear
    you come,'
Rua cried in his grief, 'a sorrowful sound to me,
Mounting far and faint from the resonant shore of the
    sea!
Woe in the song! for the grave breathes in the singers'
    breath,
And I hear in the tramp of the drums the beat of the heart
    of death.
Home of my youth! no more, through all the length of the
    years,
No more to the place of the echoes of early laughter and
    tears,
No more shall Rua return; no more as the evening ends,
To crowded eyes of welcome, to the reaching hands of
    friends.'

All day long from the High-place the drums and the singing
    came,
And the even fell, and the sun went down, a wheel of
    flame;
And night came gleaning the shadows and hushing the
    sounds of the wood;
And silence slept on all, where Rua sorrowed and stood.
But still from the shore of the bay the sound of the festival
    rang,
And still the crowd in the High-place danced and shouted
    and sang.

Now over all the isle terror was breathed abroad
Of shadowy hands from the trees and shadowy snares in the
    sod;
And before the nostrils of night, the shuddering hunter of
    men
Hurried, with beard on shoulder, back to his lighted
    den.
'Taheia, here to my side!'—'Rua, my Rua, you!'
And cold from the clutch of terror, cold with the damp of
    the dew,
Taheia, heavy of hair, leaped through the dark to his arms;
Taheia leaped to his clasp, and was folded in from alarms.

'Rua, beloved, here, see what your love has brought;
Coming—alas! returning—swift as the shuttle of thought;
Returning, alas! for tonight, with the beaten drum and the
    voice,
In the shine of many torches must the sleepless clan rejoice;
And Taheia the well-descended, the daughter of chief and
    priest,
Taheia must sit in her place in the crowded bench of the
    feast.'

So it was spoken; and she, girding her garment high,
Fled and was swallowed of woods, swift as the sight of an
 eye.

Night over isle and sea rolled her curtain of stars,
Then a trouble awoke in the air, the east was banded with
 bars;
Dawn as yellow as sulphur leaped on the mountain height;
Dawn, in the deepest glen, fell a wonder of light;
High and clear stood the palms in the eye of the brighten-
 ing east,
And lo! from the sides of the sea the broken sound of the
 feast!
As, when in days of summer, through open windows, the fly
Swift as a breeze and loud as a trump goes by,
But when frosts in the field have pinched the wintering
 mouse,
Blindly noses and buzzes and hums in the firelit house:
So the sound of the feast gallantly trampled at night,
So it staggered and drooped, and droned in the morning
 light.

IV. THE RAID

It chanced that as Rua sat in the valley of silent falls,
He heard a calling of doves from high on the cliffy walls.
Fire had fashioned of yore, and time had broken, the rocks;
There were rooting crannies for trees and nesting-places for
 flocks;
And he saw on the top of the cliffs, looking up from the pit
 of the shade,
A flicker of wings and sunshine, and trees that swung in the
 trade.
'The trees swing in the trade,' quoth Rua, doubtful of words,
'And the sun stares from the sky, but what should trouble
 the birds?'

Up from the shade he gazed, where high the parapet shone,
And he was aware of a ledge and of things that moved
 thereon.
'What manner of things are these? Are they spirits
 abroad by day?
Or the foes of my clan that are come, bringing death by a
 perilous way?'

The valley was gouged like a vessel, and round like the
 vessel's lip,
With a cape of the side of the hill thrust forth like the bows
 of a ship.
On the top of the face of the cape a volley of sun struck
 fair,
And the cape overhung like a chin a gulph of sunless air.
'Silence, heart! What is that?—that, that flickered and
 shone,
Into the sun for an instant, and in an instant gone?
Was it a warrior's plume, a warrior's girdle of hair?
Swung in the loop of a rope, is he making a bridge of the
 air?'

Once and again Rua saw, in the trenchant edge of the sky,
The giddy conjuring done. And then, in the blink of an
 eye,
A scream caught in with the breath, a whirling packet of
 limbs,
A lump that dived in the gulph, more swift than a dolphin
 swims;
And there was the lump at his feet, and eyes were alive in
 the lump.
Sick was the soul of Rua, ambushed close in a clump;
Sick of soul he drew near, making his courage stout;
And he looked in the face of the thing, and the life of the
 thing went out.

[223]

And he gazed on the tattoed limbs, and, behold, he knew
    the man:
Hoka, a chief of the Vais, the truculent foe of his clan:
Hoka a moment since that stepped in the loop of the rope,
Filled with the lust of war, and alive with courage and hope.

Again to the giddy cornice Rua lifted his eyes,
And again beheld men passing in the armpit of the skies.
'Foes of my race!' cried Rua, 'the mouth of Rua is true:
Never a shark in the deep is nobler of soul than you.
There was never a nobler foray, never a bolder plan;
Never a dizzier path was trod by the children of man;
And Rua, your evil-dealer through all the days of his years,

'Counts it honour to hate you, honour to fall by your spears.'
And Rua straightened his back. 'O Vais, a scheme for a
    scheme!'
Cried Rua and turned and descended the turbulent stair of
    the stream,
Leaping from rock to rock as the water-wagtail at home
Flits through resonant valleys and skims by boulder and
    foam.
And Rua burst from the glen and leaped on the shore of the
    brook,
And straight for the roofs of the clan his vigorous way he
    took.
Swift were the heels of his flight, and loud behind as he
    went
Rattled the leaping stones on the line of his long descent.
And ever he thought as he ran, and caught at his gasping
    breath,
'O the fool of a Rua, Rua that runs to his death!
But the right is the right,' thought Rua, and ran like the
    wind on the foam,
'The right is the right for ever, and home for ever home.

[224]

For what though the oven smoke? And what though I die
    ere morn?

There was I nourished and tended, and there was Taheia
    born.'

Noon was high on the High-place, the second noon of the
    feast;

And heat and shameful slumber weighed on people and
    priest;

And the heart drudged slow in bodies heavy with monstrous
    meals;

And the senseless limbs were scattered abroad like spokes
    of wheels;

And crapulous women sat and stared at the stones anigh

With bestial droop of the lip and a swinish rheum in the
    eye.

As about the dome of the bees in the time for the drones to
    fall,

The dead and the maimed are scattered, and lie, and stagger,
    and crawl;

So on the grades of the terrace, in the ardent eye of the day,

The half-awake and the sleepers clustered and crawled and
    lay;

And loud as the dome of the bees, in the time of a swarming
    horde,

A horror of many insects hung in the air and roared.

Rua looked and wondered; he said to himself in his heart:

'Poor are the pleasures of life, and death is the better part.'

But lo! on the higher benches a cluster of tranquil folk

Sat by themselves, nor raised their serious eyes, nor
    spoke:

Women with robes unruffled and garlands duly arranged,

Gazing far from the feast with faces of people estranged;

And quiet amongst the quiet, and fairer than all the
    fair,

Taheia, the well-descended, Taheia, heavy of hair.

H   [225]

And the soul of Rua awoke, courage enlightened his eyes,
And he uttered a summoning shout and called on the clan
  to rise.
Over against him at once, in the spotted shade of the trees,
Owlish and blinking creatures scrambled to hands and
  knees;
On the grades of the sacred terrace, the driveller woke to
  fear,
And the hand of the ham-drooped warrior brandished a
  wavering spear.
And Rua folded his arms, and scorn discovered his teeth;
Above the war-crowd gibbered, and Rua stood smiling
  beneath.
Thick, like leaves in the autumn, faint, like April sleet,
Missiles from tremulous hands quivered around his feet;
And Taheia leaped from her place; and the priest, the ruby-
  eyed,
Ran to the front of the terrace, and brandished his arms,
  and cried:
'Hold, O fools, he brings tidings!' and 'Hold, 'tis the love
  of my heart!'
Till lo! in front of the terrace, Rua pierced with a dart.

Taheia cherished his head, and the aged priest stood by,
And gazed with eyes of ruby at Rua's darkening eye.
'Taheia, here is the end, I die a death for a man.
I have given the life of my soul to save an unsavable
  clan.
See them, the drooping of hams! behold me the blinking
  crew:
Fifty spears they cast, and one of fifty true!
And you, O priest, the foreteller, foretell for yourself if you
  can,
Foretell the hour of the day when the Vais shall burst on
  your clan!

By the head of the tapu cleft, with death and fire in their
    hand,
Thick and silent like ants, the warriors swarm in the land.'

And they tell that when next the sun had climbed to the
    noonday skies
It shone on the smoke of feasting in the country of the Vais.

Ticonderoga

A Legend of the West Highlands

THIS is the tale of the man
    Who heard a word in the night
In the land of the heathery hills,
    In the days of the feud and the fight.
By the sides of the rainy sea,
    Where never a stranger came,
On the awful lips of the dead,
    He heard the outlandish name.
It sang in his sleeping ears,
    It hummed in his waking head:
The name—Ticonderoga,
    The utterance of the dead.

I. THE SAYING OF THE NAME

ON the loch-sides of Appin,
    When the mist blew from the sea,
A Stewart stood with a Cameron:
    An angry man was he.
The blood beat in his ears,
    The blood ran hot to his head,
The mist blew from the sea,
    And there was the Cameron dead.

[227]

'O, what have I done to my friend,
   O, what have I done to mysel',
That he should be cold and dead,
   And I in the danger of all?
Nothing but danger about me.
   Danger behind and before,
Death at wait in the heather
   In Appin and Mamore,
Hate at all of the ferries
   And death at each of the fords,
Camerons priming gunlocks
   And Camerons sharpening swords.'

But this was a man of counsel,
   This was a man of a score,
There dwelt no pawkier Stewart
   In Appin or Mamore.
He looked on the blowing mist,
   He looked on the awful dead,
And there came a smile on his face
   And there slipped a thought in his head.

Out over cairn and moss,
   Out over scrog and scaur,
He ran as runs the clansman
   That bears the cross of war.
His heart beat in his body,
   His hair clove to his face,
When he came at last in the gloaming
   To the dead man's brother's place.
The east was white with the moon,
   The west with the sun was red,
And there, in the house-doorway,
   Stood the brother of the dead.

'I have slain a man to my danger,
    I have slain a man to my death.
I put my soul in your hands,'
    The panting Stewart saith.
'I lay it bare in your hands,
    For I know your hands are leal;
And be you my targe and bulwark
    From the bullet and the steel.'
Then up and spoke the Cameron,
    And gave him his hand again:
'There shall never a man in Scotland
    Set faith in me in vain;
And whatever man you have slaughtered,
    Of whatever name or line,
By my sword and yonder mountain,
    I make your quarrel mine.
I bid you in to my fireside,
    I share with you house and hall;
It stands upon my honour
    To see you safe from all.'

It fell in the time of midnight,
    When the fox barked in the den
And the plaids were over the faces
    In all the houses of men,
That as the living Cameron
    Lay sleepless on his bed,
Out of the night and the other world,
    Came in to him the dead.

'My blood is on the heather,
    My bones are on the hill;
There is joy in the home of ravens
    That the young shall eat their fill.

My blood is poured in the dust,
   My soul is spilled in the air;
And the man that has undone me
   Sleeps in my brother's care.'

'I'm wae for your death, my brother,
   But if all of my house were dead,
I couldnae withdraw the plighted hand,
   Nor break the word once said.'

'O, what shall I say to our father,
   In the place to which I fare?
O, what shall I say to our mother,
   Who greets to see me there?
And to all the kindly Camerons
   That have lived and died long-syne—
Is this the word you send them,
   Fause-hearted brother mine?'

'It's neither fear nor duty,
   It's neither quick nor dead
Shall gar me withdraw the plighted hand,
   Or break the word once said.'

Thrice in the time of midnight,
   When the fox barked in the den,
And the plaids were over the faces
   In all the houses of men,
Thrice as the living Cameron
   Lay sleepless on his bed,
Out of the night and the other world
   Came in to him the dead,
And cried to him for vengeance
   On the man that laid him low;
And thrice the living Cameron
   Told the dead Cameron, no.

[230]

'Thrice have you seen me, brother,
  But now shall see me no more,
Till you meet your angry fathers
  Upon the farther shore.
Thrice have I spoken, and now,
  Before the cock be heard,
I take my leave for ever
  With the naming of a word.
It shall sing in your sleeping ears,
  It shall hum in your waking head,
The name—Ticonderoga,
  And the warning of the dead.'

Now when the night was over
  And the time of people's fears,
The Cameron walked abroad,
  And the word was in his ears.
'Many a name I know,
  But never a name like this;
O, where shall I find a skilly man
  Shall tell me what it is?'
With many a man he counselled
  Of high and low degree,
With the herdsmen on the mountains
  And the fishers of the sea.
And he came and went unweary,
  And read the books of yore,
And the runes that were written of old
  On stones upon the moor.
And many a name he was told,
  But never the name of his fears—
Never, in east or west,
  The name that rang in his ears:
Names of men and of clans;
  Names for the grass and the tree,

For the smallest tarn in the mountains,
　　The smallest reef in the sea:
Names for the high and low,
　　The names of the craig and the flat;
But in all the land of Scotland,
　　Never a name like that.

II.　THE SEEKING OF THE NAME

AND now there was speech in the south,
　　And a man of the south that was wise,
A periwig'd lord of London,
　　Called on the clans to rise.
And the riders rode, and the summons
　　Came to the western shore,
To the land of the sea and the heather,
　　To Appin and Mamore.
It called on all to gather
　　From every scrog and scaur,
That loved their fathers' tartan
　　And the ancient game of war.

And down the watery valley
　　And up the windy hill,
Once more, as in the olden,
　　The pipes were sounding shrill;
Again in highland sunshine
　　The naked steel was bright;
And the lads, once more in tartan,
　　Went forth again to fight.

'O, why should I dwell here
　　With a weird upon my life,
When the clansmen shout for battle
　　And the war-swords clash in strife?

I cannae joy at feast,
   I cannae sleep in bed,
For the wonder of the word
   And the warning of the dead.
It sings in my sleeping ears,
   It hums in my waking head,
The name—Ticonderoga,
   The utterance of the dead.
Then up, and with the fighting men
   To march away from here,
Till the cry of the great war-pipe
   Shall drown it in my ear!'

Where flew King George's ensign
   The plaided soldiers went:
They drew the sword in Germany,
   In Flanders pitched the tent.
The bells of foreign cities
   Rang far across the plain:
They passed the happy Rhine,
   They drank the rapid Main.
Through Asiatic jungles
   The Tartans filed their way,
And the neighing of the warpipes
   Struck terror in Cathay.

'Many a name have I heard,' he thought,
   'In all the tongues of men,
Full many a name both here and there,
   Full many both now and then.
When I was at home in my father's house
   In the land of the naked knee,
Between the eagles that fly in the lift
   And the herrings that swim in the sea,

[233]

And now that I am a captain-man
  With a braw cockade in my hat—
Many a name have I heard,' he thought,
  'But never a name like that.'

III.   THE PLACE OF THE NAME

THERE fell a war in a woody place,
  Lay far across the sea,
A war of the march in the mirk midnight
  And the shot from behind the tree,
The shaven head and the painted face,
  The silent foot in the wood,
In a land of a strange, outlandish tongue
  That was hard to be understood.

It fell about the gloaming
  The general stood with his staff,
He stood and he looked east and west
  With little mind to laugh.
'Far have I been and much have I seen,
  And kent both gain and loss,
But here we have woods on every hand
  And a kittle water to cross.
Far have I been and much have I seen,
  But never the beat of this;
And there's one must go down to that waterside
  To see how deep it is.'

It fell in the dusk of the night
  When unco things betide,
The skilly captain, the Cameron,
  Went down to that waterside.
Canny and soft the captain went;
  And a man of the woody land,

[234]

With the shaven head and the painted face,
    Went down at his right hand.
It fell in the quiet night,
    There was never a sound to ken;
But all of the woods to the right and the left
    Lay filled with the painted men.

'Far have I been and much have I seen,
    Both as a man and boy,
But never have I set forth a foot
    On so perilous an employ.'
It fell in the dusk of the night
    When unco things betide,
That he was aware of a captain-man
    Drew near to the waterside.
He was aware of his coming
    Down in the gloaming alone;
And he looked in the face of the man
    And lo! the face was his own.
'This is my weird,' he said,
    'And now I ken the worst;
For many shall fall the morn,
    But I shall fall with the first.
O, you of the outland tongue,
    You of the painted face,
This is the place of my death;
    Can you tell me the name of the place?'
'Since the Frenchmen have been here
    They have called it Sault-Marie;
But that is a name for priests,
    And not for you and me.
It went by another word,'
    Quoth he of the shaven head:
'It was called Ticonderoga
    In the days of the great dead.'

[235]

And it fell on the morrow's morning,
  In the fiercest of the fight,
That the Cameron bit the dust
  As he foretold at night;
And far from the hills of heather,
  Far from the isles of the sea,
He sleeps in the place of the name
  As it was doomed to be.

Heather Ale

A Galloway Legend

From the bonny bells of heather
  They brewed a drink long-syne,
Was sweeter far than honey,
  Was stronger far than wine.
They brewed it and they drank it,
  And lay in a blessed swound
For days and days together
  In their dwellings underground.

There rose a king in Scotland,
  A fell man to his foes,
He smote the Picts in battle,
  He hunted them like roes.
Over miles of the red mountain
  He hunted as they fled,
And strewed the dwarfish bodies
  Of the dying and the dead.

Summer came in the country,
  Red was the heather bell;
But the manner of the brewing
  Was none alive to tell.

[236]

In graves that were like children's
    On many a mountain head,
The Brewsters of the Heather
    Lay numbered with the dead.

The king in the red moorland
    Rode on a summer's day;
And the bees hummed, and the curlews
    Cried beside the way.
The king rode, and was angry,
    Black was his brow and pale,
To rule in a land of heather
    And lack the Heather Ale.

It fortuned that his vassals,
    Riding free on the heath,
Came on a stone that was fallen
    And vermin hid beneath.
Rudely plucked from their hiding,
    Never a word they spoke:
A son and his aged father—
    Last of the dwarfish folk.

The king sat high on his charger,
    He looked on the little men;
And the dwarfish and swarthy couple
    Looked at the king again.
Down by the shore he had them;
    And there on the giddy brink—
'I will give you life, ye vermin,
    For the secret of the drink.'

There stood the son and father
    And they looked high and low;
The heather was red around them,
    The sea rumbled below.

And up and spoke the father,
　　Shrill was his voice to hear:
'I have a word in private,
　　A word for the royal ear.

'Life is dear to the aged,
　　And honour a little thing;
I would gladly sell the secret,'
　　Quoth the Pict to the King.
His voice was small as a sparrow's,
　　And shrill and wonderful clear:
'I would gladly sell my secret,
　　Only my son I fear.

'For life is a little matter,
　　And death is nought to the young;
And I dare not sell my honour
　　Under the eye of my son.
Take *him*, O king, and bind him,
　　And cast him far in the deep;
And it's I will tell the secret
　　That I have sworn to keep.'

They took the son and bound him,
　　Neck and heels in a thong,
And a lad took him and swung him,
　　And flung him far and strong,
And the sea swallowed his body,
　　Like that of a child of ten;
And there on the cliff stood the father,
　　Last of the dwarfish men.

'True was the word I told you:
　　Only my son I feared;
For I doubt the sapling courage
　　That goes without the beard.

[238]

But now in vain is the torture,
    Fire shall never avail:
Here dies in my bosom
    The secret of Heather Ale.'

Christmas at Sea

THE sheets were frozen hard, and they cut the naked hand;
The decks were like a slide, where a seaman scarce could
    stand;
The wind was a nor'wester, blowing squally off the sea;
And cliffs and spouting breakers were the only things a-lee.

They heard the surf a-roaring before the break of day;
But 'twas only with the peep of light we saw how ill we lay.
We tumbled every hand on deck instanter, with a shout,
And we gave her the maintops'l, and stood by to go
    about.
All day we tacked and tacked between the South Head and
    the North;
All day we hauled the frozen sheets, and got no further
    forth;
All day as cold as charity, in bitter pain and dread,
For very life and nature we tacked from head to head.

We gave the South a wider berth, for there the tide-race
    roared;
But every tack we made we brought the North Head close
    aboard:
So 's we saw the cliffs and houses, and the breakers running
    high,
And the coastguard in his garden, with his glass against his
    eye.

The frost was on the village roofs as white as ocean foam;
The good red fires were burning bright in every 'longshore
    home;
The windows sparkled clear, and the chimneys volleyed
    out;
And I vow we sniffed the victuals as the vessel went about.

The bells upon the church were rung with a mighty jovial
    cheer;
For it 's just that I should tell you how (of all days in the
    year)
This day of our adversity was blessèd Christmas morn,
And the house above the coastguard's was the house where
    I was born.

O well I saw the pleasant room, the pleasant faces there,
My mother's silver spectacles, my father's silver hair;
And well I saw the firelight, like a flight of homely elves,
Go dancing round the china-plates that stand upon the
    shelves.

And well I knew the talk they had, the talk that was of me,
Of the shadow on the household and the son that went to
    sea;
And O the wicked fool I seemed, in every kind of way,
To be here and hauling frozen ropes on blessèd Christmas
    Day.

They lit the high sea-light, and the dark began to fall.
'All hands to loose topgallant sails,' I heard the captain call.
'By the Lord, she'll never stand it,' our first mate, Jackson,
    cried.
... 'It's the one way or the other, Mr Jackson,' he replied.

She staggered to her bearings, but the sails were new and
      good,
And the ship smelt up to windward just as though she
      understood.
As the winter's day was ending, in the entry of the night,
We cleared the weary headland, and passed below the light.

And they heaved a mighty breath, every soul on board but
      me,
As they saw her nose again pointing handsome out to sea;
But all that I could think of, in the darkness and the cold,
Was just that I was leaving home and my folks were
      growing old.

SONGS OF TRAVEL

SONGS OF TRAVEL

I

The Vagabond

To an air of Schubert

GIVE to me the life I love,
   Let the lave go by me,
Give the jolly heaven above
   And the byway nigh me.
Bed in the bush with stars to see,
   Bread I dip in the river—
There's the life for a man like me,
   There's the life for ever.

Let the blow fall soon or late,
   Let what will be o'er me;
Give the face of earth around
   And the road before me.
Wealth I seek not, hope nor love,
   Nor a friend to know me;
All I seek, the heaven above
   And the road below me.

Or let autumn fall on me
   Where afield I linger,
Silencing the bird on tree,
   Biting the blue finger.

White as meal the frosty field—
    Warm the fireside haven—
Not to autumn will I yield,
    Not to winter even!

Let the blow fall soon or late,
    Let what will be o'er me;
Give the face of earth around,
    And the road before me.
Wealth I ask not, hope nor love,
    Nor a friend to know me;
All I ask the heaven above,
    And the road below me.

II

Youth and Love—1

Once only by the garden gate
    Our lips we joined and parted.
I must fulfil an empty fate
    And travel the uncharted.

Hail and farewell! I must arise,
    Leave here the fatted cattle,
And paint on foreign lands and skies
    My Odyssey of battle.

The untented Kosmos my abode,
    I pass, a wilful stranger:
My mistress still the open road
    And the bright eyes of danger.

Come ill or well, the cross, the crown,
    The rainbow or the thunder,
I fling my soul and body down
    For God to plough them under.

III

Youth and Love—II

To the heart of youth the world is a highwayside.
Passing for ever, he fares; and on either hand,
Deep in the gardens golden pavilions hide,
Nestle in orchard bloom, and far on the level land
Call him with lighted lamp in the eventide.

Thick as the stars at night when the moon is down,
Pleasures assail him. He to his nobler fate
Fares; and but waves a hand as he passes on,
Cries but a wayside word to her at the garden gate,
Sings but a boyish stave and his face is gone.

IV

In dreams, unhappy, I behold you stand
    As heretofore:
The unremembered tokens in your hand
    Avail no more.

No more the morning glow, no more the grace,
    Enshrines, endears.
Cold beats the light of time upon your face
    And shows your tears.

He came and went. Perchance you wept a while
    And then forgot.
Ah me! but he that left you with a smile
    Forgets you not.

V

SHE rested by the Broken Brook
  She drank of Weary Well,
She moved beyond my lingering look,
  Ah, whither none can tell!

She came, she went. In other lands,
  Perchance in fairer skies,
Her hands shall cling with other hands,
  Her eyes to other eyes.

She vanished. In the sounding town,
  Will she remember too?
Will she recall the eyes of brown
  As I recall the blue?

VI

THE infinite shining heavens
  Rose and I saw in the night
Uncountable angel stars
  Showering sorrow and light.

I saw them distant as heaven,
  Dumb and shining and dead,
And the idle stars of the night
  Were dearer to me than bread.

Night after night in my sorrow
  The stars stood over the sea,
Till lo! I looked in the dusk
  And a star had come down to me.

VII

Madrigal

PLAIN as the glistering planets shine
    When winds have cleaned the skies,
Her love appeared, appealed for mine
    And wantoned in her eyes.

Clear as the shining tapers burned
    On Cytherea's shrine,
Those brimming, lustrous beauties turned,
    And called and conquered mine.

The beacon-lamp that Hero lit
    No fairer shone on sea,
No plainlier summoned will and wit,
    Than hers encouraged me.

I thrilled to feel her influence near,
    I struck my flag at sight.
Her starry silence smote my ear
    Like sudden drums at night.

I ran as, at the cannon's roar,
    The troops the ramparts man—
As in the holy house of yore
    The willing Eli ran.

Here, lady, lo! that servant stands
    You picked from passing men,
And should you need nor heart nor hands
    He bows and goes again.

[249]

VIII

To you, let snow and roses
    And golden locks belong:
These are the world's enslavers,
    Let these delight the throng.
But for her of duskier lustre,
    Whose favour still I wear,
The snow be in her kirtle,
    The rose be in her hair!

The hue of Highland rivers
    Careering, full and cool,
From sable on to golden,
    From rapid on to pool—
The hue of heather-honey,
    The hue of honey-bees,
Shall tinge her golden shoulder,
    Shall gild her tawny knees.

IX

LET Beauty awake in the morn from beautiful dreams,
    Beauty awake from rest!
    Let Beauty awake
    For Beauty's sake
In the hour when the birds awake in the brake
    And the stars are bright in the west!

Let Beauty awake in the eve from the slumber of day,
    Awake in the crimson eve!
    In the day's dusk end
    When the shades ascend,
Let her wake to the kiss of a tender friend
    To render again and receive!

X

I KNOW not how it is with you—
        I love the first and last,
The whole field of the present view,
        The whole flow of the past.

One tittle of the things that are,
        Nor you should change nor I—
One pebble in our path—one star
        In all our heaven of sky.

Our lives, and every day and hour,
        One symphony appear:
One road, one garden—every flower
        And every bramble dear.

XI

I WILL make you brooches and toys for your delight
Of bird-song at morning and star-shine at night.
I will make a palace fit for you and me
Of green days in forests and blue days at sea.

I will make my kitchen, and you shall keep your room,
Where white flows the river and bright blows the broom,
And you shall wash your linen and keep your body white
In rainfall at morning and dewfall at night.

And this shall be for music when no one else is near,
The fine song for singing, the rare song to hear!
That only I remember, that only you admire,
Of the broad road that stretches and the roadside fire.

XII

We Have Loved of Yore

To an air of Diabelli

BERRIED brake and reedy island,
   Heaven below, and only heaven above,
Through the sky's inverted azure
   Softly swam the boat that bore our love.
      Bright were your eyes as the day;
      Bright ran the stream,
      Bright hung the sky above.
Days of April, airs of Eden,
   How the glory died through golden hours,
And the shining moon arising,
   How the boat drew homeward filled with flowers!
      Bright were your eyes in the night:
      We have lived, my love—
      O, we have loved, my love.

Frost has bound our flowing river,
   Snow has whitened all our island brake,
And beside the winter faggot
   Joan and Darby doze and dream and wake.
      Still, in the river of dreams
      Swims the boat of love—
      Hark! chimes the falling oar!
And again in winter evens
   When on firelight dreaming fancy feeds,
In those ears of agèd lovers
   Love's own river warbles in the reeds.
      Love still the past, O, my love!
      We have lived of yore,
      O, we have loved of yore.

[252]

XIII

Ditty

To an air from Bach

THE cock shall crow
    In the morning grey,
The bugles blow
    At the break of day;
The cock shall sing and the merry bugles ring,
And all the little brown birds sing upon the spray.

The thorn shall blow
    In the month of May,
And my love shall go
    In her holiday array;
But I shall lie in the kirkyard nigh
While all the little brown birds sing upon the spray.

XIV

Mater Triumphans

SON of my woman's body, you go, to the drum and fife,
To taste the colour of love and the other side of life—
From out of the dainty the rude, the strong from out of
    the frail,
Eternally through the ages from the female comes the
    male.

The ten fingers and toes, and the shell-like nail on each,
The eyes blind as gems and the tongue attempting speech;

[253]

Impotent hands in my bosom, and yet they shall wield the
sword!
Drugged with slumber and milk, you wait the day of the
Lord.

Infant bridegroom, uncrowned king, unanointed priest,
Soldier, lover, explorer, I see you nuzzle the breast.
You that grope in my bosom shall load the ladies with rings,
You, that came forth through the doors, shall burst the
doors of kings.

XV

Bright is the ring of words
    When the right man rings them,
Fair the fall of songs
    When the singer sings them.
Still they are carolled and said—
    On wings they are carried—
After the singer is dead
    And the maker buried.

Low as the singer lies
    In the field of heather,
Songs of his fashion bring
    The swains together.
And when the west is red
    With the sunset embers,
The lover lingers and sings
    And the maid remembers.

XVI

In the highlands, in the country places,
Where the old plain men have rosy faces,
And the young fair maidens
Quiet eyes;
Where essential silence cheers and blesses,
And for ever in the hill-recesses
Her more lovely music
Broods and dies.

O to mount again where erst I haunted;
Where the old red hills are bird-enchanted,
And the low green meadows
Bright with sward;
And when even dies, the million-tinted,
And the night has come, and planets glinted,
Lo, the valley hollow
Lamp-bestarred!

O to dream, O to awake and wander
There, and with delight to take and render,
Through the trance of silence,
Quiet breath;
Lo! for there, among the flowers and grasses,
Only the mightier movement sounds and passes;
Only winds and rivers,
Life and death.

XVII

To the Tune of Wandering Willie

HOME no more home to me, whither must I wander?
   Hunger my driver, I go where I must.
Cold blows the winter wind over hill and heather;
   Thick drives the rain, and my roof is in the dust.
Loved of wise men was the shade of my roof-tree.
   The true word of welcome was spoken in the door—
Dear days of old, with the faces in the firelight,
   Kind folks of old, you come again no more.

Home was home then, my dear, full of kindly faces,
   Home was home then, my dear, happy for the child.
Fire and the windows bright glittered on the moorland;
   Song, tuneful song, built a palace in the wild.
Now, when day dawns on the brow of the moorland,
   Lone stands the house, and the chimney-stone is cold.
Lone let it stand, now the friends are all departed,
   The kind hearts, the true hearts, that loved the place of
      old.

Spring shall come, come again, calling up the moorfowl,
   Spring shall bring the sun and rain, bring the bees and
      flowers;
Red shall the heather bloom over hill and valley,
   Soft flow the stream through the even-flowing hours;
Fair the day shine as it shone on my childhood—
   Fair shine the day on the house with open door;
Birds come and cry there and twitter in the chimney—
   But I go for ever and come again no more.

XVIII

Winter

In rigorous hours, when down the iron lane
The redbreast looks in vain
For hips and haws,
Lo, shining flowers upon my window-pane
The silver pencil of the winter draws.

When all the snowy hill
And the bare woods are still;
When snipes are silent in the frozen bogs,
And all the garden garth is whelmed in mire,
Lo, by the hearth, the laughter of the logs—
More fair than roses, lo, the flowers of fire!

XIX

The stormy evening closes now in vain,
Loud wails the wind and beats the driving rain,
While here in sheltered house
With fire-ypainted walls,
I hear the wind abroad,
I hark the calling squalls—
'Blow, blow,' I cry, 'you burst your cheeks in vain!
Blow, blow,' I cry, 'my love is home again!'

Yon ship you chase perchance but yesternight
Bore still the precious freight of my delight,
That here in sheltered house
With fire-ypainted walls,
Now hears the wind abroad,
Now harks the calling squalls.
'Blow, blow,' I cry, 'in vain you rouse the sea,
My rescued sailor shares the fire with me!'

XX

To Dr Hake

On receiving a Copy of Verses

In the belovèd hour that ushers day,
In the pure dew, under the breaking grey,
One bird, ere yet the woodland quires awake,
With brief réveillé summons all the brake:
Chirp, chirp, it goes; nor waits an answer long;
And that small signal fills the grove with song.

Thus on my pipe I breathed a strain or two;
It scarce was music, but 'twas all I knew.
It was not music, for I lacked the art,
Yet what but frozen music filled my heart?
Chirp, chirp, I went, nor hoped a nobler strain;
But Heaven decreed I should not pipe in vain,
For, lo! not far from there, in secret dale,
All silent, sat an ancient nightingale.
My sparrow notes he heard; thereat awoke;
And with a tide of song his silence broke.

XXI

To Sidney Colvin

I KNEW thee strong and quiet like the hills;
I knew thee apt to pity, brave to endure,
In peace or war a Roman full equipt;
And just I knew thee, like the fabled kings
Who by the loud sea-shore gave judgment forth,
From dawn to eve, bearded and few of words.

What, what, was I to honour thee? A child;
A youth in ardour but a child in strength,
Who after virtue's golden chariot-wheels
Runs ever panting, nor attains the goal.
So thought I, and was sorrowful at heart.

Since then my steps have visited that flood
Along whose shore the numerous footfalls cease,
The voices and the tears of life expire.
Thither the prints go down, the hero's way
Trod large upon the sand, the trembling maid's:
Nimrod that wound his trumpet in the wood,
And the poor, dreaming child, hunter of flowers,
That here his hunting closes with the great:
So one and all go down, nor aught returns.

For thee, for us, the sacred river waits,
For me, the unworthy, thee, the perfect friend;
There Blame desists, there his unfaltering dogs
He from the chase recalls, and homeward rides;
Yet Praise and Love pass over and go in.
So when, beside that margin, I discard
My more than mortal weakness, and with thee
Through that still land unfearing I advance:
If then at all we keep the touch of joy
Thou shalt rejoice to find me altered—I,
O Felix, to behold thee still unchanged.

XXII

THE morning drum-call on my eager ear
Thrills unforgotten yet; the morning dew
Lies yet undried along my field of noon.

But now I pause at whiles in what I do,
And count the bell, and tremble lest I hear
(My work untrimmed) the sunset gun too soon.

XXIII

I HAVE trod the upward and the downward slope;
I have endured and done in days before;
I have longed for all, and bid farewell to hope;
And I have lived and loved, and closed the door.

XXIV

HE hears with gladdened heart the thunder
    Peal, and loves the falling dew;
He knows the earth above and under—
    Sits and is content to view.

He sits beside the dying ember,
    God for hope and man for friend,
Content to see, glad to remember,
    Expectant of the certain end.

XXV

FAREWELL, fair day and fading light!
The clay-born here, with westward sight,
Marks the huge sun now downward soar.
Farewell. We twain shall meet no more.

Farewell. I watch with bursting sigh
My late contemned occasion die.
I linger useless in my tent:
Farewell, fair day, so foully spent!

Farewell, fair day. If any God
At all consider this poor clod,
He who the fair occasion sent
Prepared and placed the impediment.

Let him diviner vengeance take—
Give me to sleep, give me to wake
Girded and shod, and bid me play
The hero in the coming day!

XXVI

If This Were Faith

GOD, if this were enough,
That I see things bare to the buff
And up to the buttocks in mire;
That I ask nor hope nor hire,
Nut in the husk,
Nor dawn beyond the dusk,
Nor life beyond death:
God, if this were faith?

Having felt thy wind in my face
Spit sorrow and disgrace,
Having seen thine evil doom
In Golgotha and Khartoum,
And the brutes, the work of thine hands,
Fill with injustice lands
And stain with blood the sea:
If still in my veins the glee
Of the black night and the sun
And the lost battle, run:
If, an adept,
The iniquitous lists I still accept

With joy, and joy to endure and be withstood,
And still to battle and perish for a dream of good:
God, if that were enough?

If to feel, in the ink of the slough,
And the sink of the mire,
Veins of glory and fire
Run through and transpierce and transpire,
And a secret purpose of glory in every part,
And the answering glory of battle fill my heart;
To thrill with the joy of girded men
To go on for ever and fail and go on again,
And be mauled to the earth and arise,
And contend for the shade of a word and a thing
    not seen with the eyes:
With the half of a broken hope for a pillow at night
That somehow the right is the right
And the smooth shall bloom from the rough:
Lord, if that were enough?

XXVII

My Wife

TRUSTY, dusky, vivid, true,
With eyes of gold and bramble-dew,
Steel-true and blade-straight,
The great artificer
Made my mate.

Honour, anger, valour, fire;
A love that life could never tire,
Death quench or evil stir,
The mighty master
Gave to her.

Teacher, tender comrade, wife,
A fellow-farer true through life,
Heart-whole and soul-free
The august father
Gave to me.

XXVIII

To the Muse

RESIGN the rhapsody, the dream,
  To men of larger reach;
Be ours the quest of a plain theme,
  The piety of speech.

As monkish scribes from morning break
  Toiled till the close of light,
Nor thought a day too long to make
  One line or letter bright:

We also with an ardent mind,
  Time, wealth, and fame forgot,
Our glory in our patience find
  And skim, and skim the pot:

Till last, when round the house we hear
  The evensong of birds,
One corner of blue heaven appear
  In our clear well of words.

Leave, leave it then, muse of my heart!
  Sans finish and sans frame,
Leave unadorned by needless art
  The picture as it came.

[263]

XXIX

To an Island Princess

SINCE long ago, a child at home,
I read and longed to rise and roam,
Where'er I went, whate'er I willed,
One promised land my fancy filled.
Hence the long roads my home I made;
Tossed much in ships; have often laid
Below the uncurtained sky my head,
Rain-deluged and wind-buffeted:
And many a thousand hills I crossed
And corners turned—Love's labour lost,
Till, Lady, to your isle of sun
I came, not hoping; and, like one
Snatched out of blindness, rubbed my eyes,
And hailed my promised land with cries.

Yes, Lady, here I was at last;
Here found I all I had forecast:
The long roll of the sapphire sea
That keeps the land's virginity;
The stalwart giants of the wood
Laden with toys and flowers and food;
The precious forest pouring out
To compass the whole town about;
The town itself with streets of lawn,
Loved of the moon, blessed by the dawn,
Where the brown children all the day
Keep up a ceaseless noise of play,
Play in the sun, play in the rain,
Nor ever quarrel or complain;
And late at night, in the woods of fruit,
Hark! do you hear the passing flute?

[264]

I threw one look to either hand,
And knew I was in Fairyland.
And yet one point of being so,
I lacked. For, Lady (as you know),
Whoever by his might of hand,
Won entrance into Fairyland,
Found always with admiring eyes
A Fairy princess kind and wise.
It was not long I waited; soon
Upon my threshold, in broad noon,
Gracious and helpful, wise and good,
The Fairy Princess Moë stood.

XXX

To Kalakaua

With a present of a Pearl

THE Silver Ship, my King—that was her name
In the bright islands whence your fathers came—
The Silver Ship, at rest from winds and tides,
Below your palace in your harbour rides:
And the seafarers, sitting safe on shore,
Like eager merchants count their treasures o'er.
One gift they find, one strange and lovely thing,
Now doubly precious since it pleased a king.

The right, my liege, is ancient as the lyre
For bards to give to kings what kings admire.
'Tis mine to offer for Apollo's sake;
And since the gift is fitting, yours to take.
To golden hands the golden pearl I bring:
The ocean jewel to the island king.

[265]

XXXI

To Princess Kaiulani

FORTH from her land to mine she goes,
The island maid, the island rose,
Light of heart and bright of face:
The daughter of a double race.

Her islands here, in Southern sun,
Shall mourn their Kaiulani gone,
And I, in her dear banyan shade,
Look vainly for my little maid.

But our Scots islands far away
Shall glitter with unwonted day,
And cast for once their tempests by
To smile in Kaiulani's eye.

XXXII

To Mother Maryanne

To see the infinite pity of this place,
The mangled limb, the devastated face,
The innocent sufferer smiling at the rod—
A fool were tempted to deny his God.
He sees, he shrinks. But if he gaze again,
Lo, beauty springing from the breast of pain!
He marks the sisters on the mournful shores;
And even a fool is silent and adores.

XXXIII

In Memoriam E. H.

I KNEW a silver head was bright beyond compare,
I knew a queen of toil with a crown of silver hair.
Garland of valour and sorrow, of beauty and renown,
Life, that honours the brave, crowned her himself with the
    crown.

The beauties of youth are frail, but this was a jewel of age.
Life, that delights in the brave, gave it himself for a gage.
Fair was the crown to behold, and beauty its poorest part—
At once the scar of the wound and the order pinned on the
    heart.

The beauties of man are frail, and the silver lies in the dust,
And the queen that we call to mind sleeps with the brave
    and the just;
Sleeps with the weary at length; but, honoured and ever
    fair,
Shines in the eye of the mind the crown of the silver hair.

XXXIV

To My Wife

A Fragment

LONG must elapse ere you behold again
Green forest frame the entry of the lane—
The wild lane with the bramble and the briar,
The year-old cart-tracks perfect in the mire,
The wayside smoke, perchance, the dwarfish huts,
And ramblers' donkey drinking from the ruts:
Long ere you trace how deviously it leads,

[267]

Back from man's chimneys and the bleating meads
To the woodland shadow, to the sylvan hush,
When but the brooklet chuckles in the brush—
Back from the sun and bustle of the vale
To where the great voice of the nightingale
Fills all the forest like a single room,
And all the banks smell of the golden broom;
So wander on until the eve descends,
And back returning to your firelit friends,
You see the rosy sun, despoiled of light,
Hung, caught in thickets, like a schoolboy's kite.

Here from the sea the unfruitful sun shall rise,
Bathe the bare deck and blind the unshielded eyes;
The allotted hours aloft shall wheel in vain
And in the unpregnant ocean plunge again.
Assault of squalls that mock the watchful guard,
And pluck the bursting canvas from the yard,
And senseless clamour of the calm, at night
Must mar your slumbers. By the plunging light,
In beetle-haunted, most unwomanly bower
Of the wild-swerving cabin, hour by hour . . .

XXXV

To My Old Familiars

Do you remember—can we e'er forget?—
How, in the coiled perplexities of youth,
In our wild climate, in our scowling town,
We gloomed and shivered, sorrowed, sobbed and
    feared?
The belching winter wind, the missile rain,
The rare and welcome silence of the snows,

The laggard morn, the haggard day, the night,
The grimy spell of the nocturnal town,
Do you remember?—Ah, could one forget!

As when the fevered sick that all night long
Listed the wind intone, and hear at last
The ever-welcome voice of chanticleer
Sing in the bitter hour before the dawn,
With sudden ardour, these desire the day:
So sang in the gloom of youth the bird of hope;
So we, exulting, hearkened and desired.
For lo! as in the palace porch of life
We huddled with chimeras, from within—
How sweet to hear!—the music swelled and fell,
And through the breach of the revolving doors
What dreams of splendour blinded us and fled!

I have since then contended and rejoiced;
Amid the glories of the house of life
Profoundly entered, and the shrine beheld:
Yet when the lamp from my expiring eyes
Shall dwindle and recede, the voice of love
Fall insignificant on my closing ears,
What sound shall come but the old cry of the wind
In our inclement city? what return
But the image of the emptiness of youth,
Filled with the sound of footsteps and that voice
Of discontent and rapture and despair?
So, as in darkness, from the magic lamp,
The momentary pictures gleam and fade
And perish, and the night resurges—these
Shall I remember, and then all forget.

XXXVI

THE tropics vanish, and meseems that I,
From Halkerside, from topmost Allermuir,
Or steep Caerketton, dreaming gaze again.
Far set in fields and woods, the town I see
Spring gallant from the shallows of her smoke,
Cragged, spired, and turreted, her virgin fort
Beflagged. About, on seaward-drooping hills,
New folds of city glitter. Last, the Forth
Wheels ample waters set with sacred isles,
And populous Fife smokes with a score of towns.

There, on the sunny frontage of a hill,
Hard by the house of kings, repose the dead,
My dead, the ready and the strong of word.
Their works, the salt-encrusted, still survive;
The sea bombards their founded towers; the night
Thrills pierced with their strong lamps. The artificers,
One after one, here in this grated cell,
Where the rain erases and the rust consumes,
Fell upon lasting silence. Continents
And continental oceans intervene;
A sea uncharted, on a lampless isle,
Environs and confines their wandering child
In vain. The voice of generations dead
Summons me, sitting distant, to arise,
My numerous footsteps nimbly to retrace,
And, all mutation over, stretch me down
In that devoted city of the dead.

XXXVII

To S. C.

I HEARD the pulse of the besieging sea
Throb far away all night. I heard the wind
Fly crying and convulse tumultuous palms.
I rose and strolled. The isle was all bright sand,
And flailing fans and shadows of the palm;
The heaven all moon and wind and the blind vault;
The keenest planet slain, for Venus slept.

The king, my neighbour, with his host of wives,
Slept in the precinct of the palisade;
Where single, in the wind, under the moon,
Among the slumbering cabins, blazed a fire,
Sole street-lamp and the only sentinel.

To other lands and nights my fancy turned—
To London first, and chiefly to your house,
The many-pillared and the well-beloved.
There yearning fancy lighted; there again
In the upper room I lay, and heard far off
The unsleeping city murmur like a shell;
The muffled tramp of the Museum guard
Once more went by me; I beheld again
Lamps vainly brighten the dispeopled street;
Again I longed for the returning morn,
The awaking traffic, the bestirring birds,
The consentaneous trill of tiny song
That weaves round monumental cornices
A passing charm of beauty. Most of all,
For your light foot I wearied, and your knock
That was the glad réveillé of my day.

Lo, now, when to your task in the great house
At morning through the portico you pass,

One moment glance, where by the pillared wall
Far-voyaging island gods, begrimed with smoke,
Sit now unworshipped, the rude monument
Of faiths forgot and races undivined:
Sit now disconsolate, remembering well
The priest, the victim, and the songful crowd,
The blaze of the blue noon, and the huge voice,
Incessant, of the breakers on the shore.
As far as these from their ancestral shrine,
So far, so foreign, your divided friends
Wander, estranged in body, not in mind.

XXXVIII

The House of Tembinoka

ENVOI

Let us, who part like brothers, part like bards;
And you in your tongue and measure, I in mine,
Our new division duly solemnise.
Unlike the strains, and yet the theme is one:
The strains unlike, and how unlike their fate!
You to the blinding palace-yard shall call
The prefect of the singers, and to him,
Listening devout, your valedictory verse
Deliver; he, his attribute fulfilled,
To the island chorus hand your measures on,
Wed now with harmony: so then, at last,
Night after night, in the open hall of dance,
Shall thirty matted men, to the clapped hand,
Intone and bray and bark. Unfortunate!
Paper and print alone shall honour mine.

THE SONG

LET now the King his ear arouse
And toss the bosky ringlets from his brows,
The while, our bond to implement,
My muse relates and praises his descent.

I

BRIDE of the shark, her valour first I sing
Who on the lone seas quickened of a King.
She, from the shore and puny homes of men,
Beyond the climber's sea-discerning ken,
Swam, led by omens; and devoid of fear,
Beheld her monstrous paramour draw near.
She gazed; all round her to the heavenly pale,
The simple sea was void of isle or sail—
Sole overhead the unsparing sun was reared—
When the deep bubbled and the brute appeared.
But she, secure in the decrees of fate,
Made strong her bosom and received the mate,
And, men declare, from that marine embrace
Conceived the virtues of a stronger race.

II

HER stern descendant next I praise,
Survivor of a thousand frays:
In the hall of tongues who ruled the throng;
Led and was trusted by the strong;
And when spears were in the wood,
Like a tower of vantage stood:
Whom, not till seventy years had sped,
Unscarred of breast, erect of head,
Still light of step, still bright of look,
The hunter, Death, had overtook.

[273]

III

His sons, the brothers twain, I sing,
Of whom the elder reigned a King.
No Childeric he, yet much declined
From his rude sire's imperious mind,
Until his day came when he died,
He lived, he reigned, he versified.
But chiefly him I celebrate
That was the pillar of the state,
Ruled, wise of word and bold of mien,
The peaceful and the warlike scene;
And played alike the leader's part
In lawful and unlawful art.
His soldiers with emboldened ears
Heard him laugh among the spears.
He could deduce from age to age
The web of island parentage;
Best lay the rhyme, best lead the dance,
For any festal circumstance:
And fitly fashion oar and boat,
A palace or an armour coat.
None more availed than he to raise
The strong, suffumigating blaze,
Or knot the wizard leaf: none more,
Upon the untrodden windward shore
Of the isle, beside the beating main,
To cure the sickly and constrain,
With muttered words and waving rods,
The gibbering and the whistling gods.
But he, though thus with hand and head
He ruled, commanded, charmed, and led,
And thus in virtue and in might
Towered to contemporary sight—

Still in fraternal faith and love,
Remained below to reach above,
Gave and obeyed the apt command,
Pilot and vassal of the land.

IV

My Tembinok' from men like these
Inherited his palaces,
His right to rule, his powers of mind,
His cocoa-islands sea-enshrined.
Stern bearer of the sword and whip,
A master passed in mastership,
He learned, without the spur of need,
To write, to cipher, and to read;
From all that touch on his prone shore
Augments his treasury of lore,
Eager in age as erst in youth
To catch an art, to learn a truth,
To paint on the internal page
A clearer picture of the age.
His age, you say? But ah, not so!
In his lone isle of long ago,
A royal Lady of Shalott,
Sea-sundered, he beholds it not;
He only hears it far away.
The stress of equatorial day
He suffers; he records the while
The vapid annals of the isle;
Slaves bring him praise of his renown,
Or cackle of the palm-tree town;
The rarer ship and the rare boat
He marks; and only hears remote,
Where thrones and fortunes rise and reel,
The thunder of the turning wheel.

V

For the unexpected tears he shed
At my departing, may his lion head
Not whiten, his revolving years
No fresh occasion minister of tears;
At book or cards, at work or sport,
Him may the breeze across the palace court
For ever fan; and swelling near
For ever the loud song divert his ear.

XXXIX

The Woodman

In all the grove, nor stream nor bird
Nor aught beside my blows was heard,
And the woods wore their noonday dress—
The glory of their silentness.
From the island summit to the seas,
Trees mounted, and trees drooped, and trees
Groped upward in the gaps. The green
Inarboured talus and ravine
By fathoms. By the multitude
The rugged columns of the wood
And bunches of the branches stood;
Thick as a mob, deep as a sea,
And silent as eternity.

With lowered axe, with backward head,
Late from this scene my labourer fled,
And with a ravelled tale to tell,
Returned. Some denizen of hell,
Dead man or disinvested god,
Had close behind him peered and trod,
And triumphed when he turned to flee.

[276]

How different fell the lines with me!
Whose eye explored the dim arcade
Impatient of the uncoming shade—
Shy elf, or dryad pale and cold,
Or mystic lingerer from of old:
Vainly. The fair and stately things,
Impassive as departed kings,
All still in the wood's stillness stood,
And dumb. The rooted multitude
Nodded and brooded, bloomed and dreamed,
Unmeaning, undivined. It seemed
No other art, no hope, they knew,
Than clutch the earth and seek the blue.
Mid vegetable king and priest
And stripling, I (the only beast)
Was at the beast's work, killing; hewed
The stubborn roots across, bestrewed
The glebe with the dislustred leaves,
And bade the saplings fall in sheaves;
Bursting across the tangled math
A ruin that I called a path,
A Golgotha that, later on,
When rains had watered, and suns shone,
And seeds enriched the place, should bear
And be called garden. Here and there,
I spied and plucked by the green hair
A foe more resolute to live,
The toothed and killing sensitive.
He, semi-conscious, fled the attack;
He shrank and tucked his branches back;
And straining by his anchor-strand,
Captured and scratched the rooting hand.
I saw him crouch, I felt him bite;
And straight my eyes were touched with sight.
I saw the wood for what it was:

[277]

The lost and the victorious cause,
The deadly battle pitched in line,
Saw silent weapons cross and shine:
Silent defeat, silent assault,
A battle and a burial vault.

Thick round me in the teeming mud
Briar and fern strove to the blood:
The hooked liana in his gin
Noosed his reluctant neighbours in:
There the green murderer throve and spread,
Upon his smothering victims fed,
And wantoned on his climbing coil.
Contending roots fought for the soil
Like frightened demons: with despair
Competing branches pushed for air.
Green conquerors from overhead
Bestrode the bodies of their dead:
The Caesars of the sylvan field,
Unused to fail, foredoomed to yield:
For in the groins of branches, lo!
The cancers of the orchid grow.
Silent as in the listed ring
Two chartered wrestlers strain and cling;
Dumb as by yellow Hooghly's side
The suffocating captives died;
So hushed the woodland warfare goes
Unceasing; and the silent foes
Grapple and smother, strain and clasp
Without a cry, without a gasp.
Here also sound thy fans, O God,
Here too thy banners move abroad:
Forest and city, sea and shore,
And the whole earth, thy threshing-floor!
The drums of war, the drums of peace,

Roll through our cities without cease,
And all the iron halls of life
Ring with the unremitting strife.

The common lot we scarce perceive.
Crowds perish, we nor mark nor grieve:
The bugle calls—we mourn a few!
What corporal's guard at Waterloo?
What scanty hundreds more or less
In the man-devouring Wilderness?
What handful bled on Delhi ridge?
—See, rather, London, on thy bridge
The pale battalions trample by,
Resolved to slay, resigned to die.
Count, rather, all the maimed and dead
In the unbrotherly war of bread.
See, rather, under sultrier skies
What vegetable Londons rise,
And teem, and suffer without sound:
Or in your tranquil garden ground,
Contented, in the falling gloom,
Saunter and see the roses bloom.
That these might live, what thousands died!
All day the cruel hoe was plied;
The ambulance barrow rolled all day;
Your wife, the tender, kind, and gay,
Donned her long gauntlets, caught the spud,
And bathed in vegetable blood;
And the long massacre now at end,
See! where the lazy coils ascend,
See, where the bonfire sputters red
At even, for the innocent dead.

Why prate of peace? when, warriors all,
We clank in harness into hall,

And ever bare upon the board
Lies the necessary sword.
In the green field or quiet street,
Besieged we sleep, beleaguered eat;
Labour by day and wake o' nights,
In war with rival appetites.
The rose on roses feeds; the lark
On larks. The sedentary clerk
All morning with a diligent pen
Murders the babes of other men;
And like the beasts of wood and park,
Protects his whelps, defends his den.

Unshamed the narrow aim I hold;
I feed my sheep, patrol my fold;
Breathe war on wolves and rival flocks,
A pious outlaw on the rocks
Of God and morning; and when time
Shall bow, or rivals break me, climb
Where no undubbed civilian dares,
In my war harness, the loud stairs
Of honour; and my conqueror
Hail me a warrior fallen in war.

XL

Tropic Rain

As the single pang of the blow, when the metal is mingled
    well,
Rings and lives and resounds in all the bounds of the bell,
So the thunder above spoke with a single tongue,
So in the heart of the mountain the sound of it rumbled
    and clung.

Sudden the thunder was drowned—quenched was the levin
    light—
And the angel-spirit of rain laughed out loud in the night.
Loud as the maddened river raves in the cloven glen,
Angel of rain! you laughed and leaped on the roofs of men;
And the sleepers sprang in their beds, and joyed and feared
    as you fell.
You struck, and my cabin quailed; the roof of it roared
    like a bell,
You spoke, and at once the mountain shouted and shook
    with brooks.
You ceased, and the day returned, rosy, with virgin looks.

And methought that beauty and terror are only one, not
    two;
And the world has room for love, and death, and thunder,
    and dew;
And all the sinews of hell slumber in summer air;
And the face of God is a rock, but the face of the rock is
    fair.
Beneficent streams of tears flow at the finger of pain;
And out of the cloud that smites, beneficent rivers of rain.

XLI

An End of Travel

Let now your soul in this substantial world
Some anchor strike. Be here the body moored;
This spectacle immutably from now
The picture in your eye; and when time strikes,
And the green scene goes on the instant blind—
The ultimate helpers, where your horse today
Conveyed you dreaming, bear your body dead.

[281]

XLII

WE uncommiserate pass into the night
From the loud banquet, and departing leave
A tremor in men's memories, faint and sweet
And frail as music. Features of our face,
The tones of the voice, the touch of the loved hand,
Perish and vanish, one by one, from earth:
Meanwhile, in the hall of song, the multitude
Applauds the new performer. One, perchance,
One ultimate survivor lingers on,
And smiles, and to his ancient heart recalls
The long forgotten. Ere the morrow die,
He too, returning, through the curtain comes,
And the new age forgets us and goes on.

XLIII

The Last Sight

ONCE more I saw him. In the lofty room,
Where oft with lights and company his tongue
Was trump to honest laughter, sate attired
A something in his likeness. 'Look!' said one,
Unkindly kind, 'look up, it is your boy!'
And the dread changeling gazed on me in vain.

XLIV

SING me a song of a lad that is gone,
    Say, could that lad be I?
Merry of soul he sailed on a day
    Over the sea to Skye.

[282]

Mull was astern, Rum on the port,
    Eigg on the starboard bow;
Glory of youth glowed in his soul:
    Where is that glory now?

Sing me a song of a lad that is gone,
    Say, could that lad be I?
Merry of soul he sailed on a day
    Over the sea to Skye.

Give me again all that was there,
    Give me the sun that shone!
Give me the eyes, give me the soul,
    Give me the lad that's gone!

Sing me a song of a lad that is gone,
    Say, could that lad be I?
Merry of soul he sailed on a day
    Over the sea to Skye.

Billow and breeze, islands and seas,
    Mountains of rain and sun,
All that was good, all that was fair,
    All that was me is gone.

XLV

To S. R. Crockett

On receiving a Dedication

BLOWS the wind today, and the sun and the rain are flying,
    Blows the wind on the moors today and now,
Where about the graves of the martyrs the whaups are
    crying,
    My heart remembers how!

Grey recumbent tombs of the dead in desert places,
   Standing-stones on the vacant wine-red moor,
Hills of sheep, and the howes of the silent vanished races,
   And winds, austere and pure:

Be it granted me to behold you again in dying,
   Hills of home! and to hear again the call;
Hear about the graves of the martyrs the peewees crying,
   And hear no more at all.

XLVI

Evensong

THE embers of the day are red
Beyond the murky hill.
The kitchen smokes: the bed
In the darkling house is spread:
The great sky darkens overhead,
And the great woods are shrill.
So far have I been led,
Lord, by Thy will:
So far I have followed, Lord, and
   wondered still.

The breeze from the embalmèd land
Blows sudden toward the shore,
And claps my cottage door.
I hear the signal, Lord—I understand.
The night at Thy command
Comes. I will eat and sleep and will not
   question more.

[284]

POEMS 1880–1894

POEMS 1880–1894

I

Alcaics to H. F. Brown

BRAVE lads in olden musical centuries
Sang, night by night, adorable choruses,
 Sat late by ale-house doors in April
Chaunting in joy as the moon was rising.

Moon-seen and merry, under the trellises,
Flush-faced they played with old polysyllables
 Spring scents inspired, old wine diluted,
Love and Apollo were there to chorus.

Now these, the songs, remain to eternity,
Those only, those, the bountiful choristers
 Gone—those are gone, those unremembered
Sleep and are silent in earth forever.

So man himself appears and evanishes,
So smiles and goes; as wanderers halting at
 Some green-embowered house, play their music,
Play and are gone on the windy highway;

Yet dwells the strain enshrined in the memory
Long after they departed eternally,
 Forth-faring toward far mountain summits
Cities of men or the sounding Ocean.

Youth sang the song in years immemorial
Brave chanticleer he sang and was beautiful;
   Bird-haunted, green tree-tops in April
Heard and were pleased by the voice of singing.

Youth goes and leaves behind him a prodigy—
Songs sent by thee afar from Venetian
   Sea-grey lagunes, sea-paven highways,
Dear to me here in my Alpine exile.

II

Tales of Arabia

YES, friend, I own these tales of Arabia
Smile not, as smiled their flawless originals
   Age-old but yet untamed, for ages
     Pass and the magic is undiminished.

Thus, friend, the tales of old Camaralzaman,
Ayoub, the Slave of Love, or the Calendars
   Blind-eyed and ill-starred royal scions,
     Charm us in age as they charmed in childhood.

Fair ones, beyond all numerability,
Beam from the palace, beam on humanity,
   Bright-eyed, in truth, yet soulless houries
     Offering pleasures and only pleasure.

Thus they, the venal Muses Arabian—
Unlike, indeed, to nobler divinities,
   Greek Gods or old time-honoured muses
     Easily proffer unloved caresses.

[288]

Lost, lost, the man who mindeth their minstrelsy;
Since still, in sandy, glittering pleasances,
    Cold, stony fruits, gem-like but quite in-
      Edible, flatter and wholly starve him.

III

STILL I love to rhyme, and still more, rhyming, to wander
    Far from the commoner way;
Old trills and falls by the brook-side still do I ponder,
    Dreaming tomorrow today.

Come here, come, revive me, Sun-God, teach me, Apollo,
    Measures descanted before;
Since I ancient verses seek, I emulous follow
    Prints in the marble of yore.

Still strange, strange, they sound in old-young raiment
      invested,
    Songs for the brain to beget—
Young song birds of late in grave old temples benested
    Piping and chirruping yet.

Thoughts? no thought has yet unskilled attempted to
      flutter
    Trammelled so vilely in verse;
He who writes but aims at fame and his bread and his
      butter,
    Won with a groan and a curse.

IV

FLOWER god, god of the spring, beautiful, bountiful,
Gold-dyed shield in the sky, lover of versicles,
    Here I wander in April,
      Cold, grey-headed; and still to my

Heart, Spring comes with a bound, Spring the deliverer,
Spring, song-leader in woods, chorally resonant,
    Spring, flower planter in meadows,
      Child conductor in willowy

Fields deep clotted with bloom, daisies and crocuses:
Here that child from his heart drinks of eternity:
    O child, happy are children!
      She still smiles on their innocence.

She, dear mother in God, fostering violets,
Fills earth full of her scents, voices and violins:
    Thus one cunning in music
      Wakes old chords in the memory:

Thus fair earth in the Spring leads her performances.
One more touch of the bow, smell of the virginal
    Green—one more, and my bosom
      Feels new life with an ecstasy.

V

Horace, Book II, Ode III

WHERE the pine and the shivering poplar
Love to join with their branches their shadow;
Where through glimmering valleys, the water,
Glass-clear, hurries in murmur, toward Ocean—
Thither command them carry the wine jars—
Wine jars full of the juice of Falernum—
Unguents, Roses to bind in our Chaplets,
Bid your slaves carry down to the margin.
Now, we glory in youth and in riches:
Now, the sisters are merciful toward us.

Soon, our Fortune shall turn from us coldly:
Soon, we leave our groves and our houses,
Soon, our gardens by yellow old Tiber;
While our gold that we hoarded so closely
Gladly seizes the joyful successor.

VI

Lines for H. F. Brown

Yes, I remember, still remember wailing
Wind in the shrouds and rainy sea horizon,
Empty and lit with low, nocturnal glimmer,
How in the strong, deep-plunging, transatlantic
Emigrant ship we sang our songs in chorus.
Piping, the gull flew by, the roaring billows
Yawned and resounded round the mighty vessel
Infinite uproar, endless contradiction ;
Yet over all our chorus rose reminding
Wanderers here at sea of unforgotten
Homes and undying, old, memorial loves.

Brown in his haste demanded this from me.
I in my leisure made the present verse.

VII

Translations from Martial

EPITAPHIUM EROTII

x. 61

Here lies Erotion, whom at six years old
Fate pilfered. Stranger (when I too am cold
Who shall succeed me in my rural field),
To this small spirit annual honours yield.
Bright be thy hearth, hale be thy babes, I crave,
And this, in thy green farm, the only grave.

v. 34

Mother and sire, to you do I commend
Tiny Erotion, who must now descend,
A child, among the shadows, and appear
Before hell's bandog and hell's gondolier.
Of six hoar winters she had felt the cold,
But lacked six days of being six years old.
Now she must come, all playful, to that place
Where the great ancients sit with reverend face;
Now lisping, as she used, of whence she came,
Perchance she names and stumbles at my name.
O'er these so fragile bones, let there be laid
A plaything for a turf; and for that maid
That swam light-footed as the thistle-burr
On thee. O Mother earth, be light on her.

TRANSLATIONS FROM MARTIAL

DE EROTIO PUELLA

V. 37

THIS girl was sweeter than the song of swans,
And daintier than the lamb upon the lawns
Or Lucrine oyster. She, the flower of girls,
Outshone the light of Erythræan pearls;
The teeth of India that with polish glow,
The untouched lilies or the morning snow.
Her tresses did gold-dust outshine
And fair hair of women of the Rhine.
Compared to her the peacock seemed not fair,
The squirrel lively, or the phoenix rare;
Her on whose pyre the smoke still hovering waits,
Her whom the greedy and unequal fates
On the sixth dawning of her natal day
My child-love and my playmate—snatcht away.

IN MAXIMUM

II. 53

WOULDST thou be free? I think it not, indeed
But if thou wouldst, attend this simple rede:
When quite contented thou canst dine at home
And drink a small wine of the march of Rome;
When thou canst see unmoved thy neighbour's plate,
And wear my threadbare toga in the gate;
When thou hast learned to love a small abode,
And not to choose a mistress à la mode:
When thus contained and bridled thou shalt be,
Then, Maximus, then first shalt thou be free.

DE CŒNATIONE MICÆ

II. 59

Look round: You see a little supper room;
But from my window, lo! great Cæsar's tomb!
And the great dead themselves, with jovial breath
Bid you be merry and remember death.

AD OLUM

II. 68

Call me not rebel, though in what I sing
If I no longer hail thee Lord and King
I have redeemed myself with all I had,
And now possess my fortunes poor but glad.
With all I had I have redeemed myself,
And escaped at once from slavery and pelf.
The unruly wishes must a ruler take,
Our high desires do our low fortunes make:
Those only who desire palatial things
Do bear the fetters and the frowns of Kings;
Set free thy slave; thou settest free thyself.

AD QUINTILIANUM

II. 90

O chief director of the growing race,
Of Rome the glory and of Rome the grace,
Me, O Quintilian, may you not forgive
Though, far from labour, I make haste to live?
Some burn to gather wealth, lay hands on rule,
Or with white statues fill the atrium full.

The talking hearth, the rafters swart with smoke,
Live fountains and rough grass, my love invokes:
A sturdy slave: a not too learned wife:
Nights filled with slumber, and a quiet life.

AD PISCATOREM

IV. 30

FOR these are sacred fishes all
Who know that lord who is lord of all;
Come to the brim and nose the friendly hand
That sways and can beshadow all the land.
Nor only so, but have their names, and come
When they are summoned by the Lord of Rome.
Here once his line an impious Libyan threw;
And as with tremulous reed his prey he drew,
Straight, the light failed him.
He groped, nor found the prey that he had ta'en.
Now as a warning to the fisher clan
Beside the lake he sits, a beggarman.
Thou, then, while still thine innocence is pure,
Flee swiftly, nor presume to set thy lure;
Respect these fishes, for their friends are great
And in the waters empty all thy bait.

DE HORTIS JULII MARTIALIS

IV. 64

MY Martial owns a garden, famed to please,
Beyond the glades of the Hesperides;
Along Janiculum lies the chosen block
Where the cool grottos trench the hanging rock.

The moderate summit, something plain and bare,
Tastes overhead of a serener air;
And while the clouds besiege the vales below,
Keeps the clear heaven and doth with sunshine glow.
To the June stars that circle in the skies
The dainty roofs of that tall villa rise.
Hence do the seven imperial hills appear;
And you may view the whole of Rome from here:
Beyond, the Alban and the Tuscan hills;
And the cool groves and the cool falling rills.
Rubre Fidenæ, and with virgin blood
Anointed once Perenna's orchard wood.
Thence the Flaminian, the Salarian way,
Stretch far abroad below the dome of day;
And lo! the traveller toiling toward his home;
And all unheard, the chariot speeds to Rome!
For here no whisper of the wheels; and tho'
The Mulvian Bridge, above the Tiber's flow,
Hangs all in sight, and down the sacred stream
The sliding barges vanish like a dream,
The seaman's shrilling pipe not enters here,
Nor the rude cries of porters on the pier.
And if so rare the house, how rarer far
The welcome and the weal that therein are!
So free the access, the doors so widely thrown
You half imagine all to be your own.

AD MARTIALEM

V. 20

God knows, my Martial, if we two could be
To enjoy our days set wholly free;
To the true life together bend our mind,
And take a furlough from the falser kind,

[296]

No rich saloon, nor palace of the great,
Nor suit at law should trouble our estate;
On no vainglorious statues should we look,
But of a walk, a talk, a little book,
Baths, wells, and meads and the verandah shade,
Let all our travels and our toils be made.
Now neither lives unto himself, alas!
And the good suns we see, that flash and pass
And perish; and the bell that knells them cries,
'Another gone: O when will ye arise?'

AN IMITATION, PUDORIS CAUSA

VI. 16

Lo, in thy green enclosure here,
Let not the ugly or the old appear,
Divine Priapus; but with leaping tread
The schoolboy, and the golden head
Of the slim filly twelve years old—
Let these to enter and to steal be bold!

AD NEPOTEM

VI. 27

O NEPOS, twice my neighbour (since at home
We're door by door by Flora's temple dome,
And in the country, still conjoined by fate,
Behold our villas, standing gate by gate!)
Thou hast a daughter, dearer far than life,
Thy image and the image of thy wife;
But why for her neglect the flowing can
And lose the prime of thy Falernian?

Hoard casks of money, if to hoard be thine;
But let the daughter drink a younger wine!
Let her go rich and wise, in silk and fur;
Lay down a bin that shall grow old with her;
But thou, meantime, the while the batch is sound,
With pleased companions pass the bowl around:
Nor let the childless only taste delights,
For Fathers also may enjoy their nights.

DE M. ANTONIO

x. 23

Now Antonius, in a smiling age,
Counts of his life the fifteenth finished stage.
The rounded days and the safe years he sees
Nor fears death's water mounting round his knees,
To him remembering not one day is sad,
Not one but that its memory makes him glad.
So good men lengthen life; and to recall
The past, is to have twice enjoyed it all.

IN LUPUM

xi. 18

Beyond the gates, you gave a farm to till:
I have a larger on my window-sill!
A farm, d'ye say? Is this a farm to you?—
Where for all woods I spy one tuft of rue,
And that so rusty, and so small a thing,
One shrill cicada hides it with a wing;
Where one cucumber covers all the plain;
And where one serpent rings himself in vain

To enter wholly; and a single snail
Eats all, and exit fasting—to the jail.
Here shall I wait in vain till figs be set,
Or till the spring disclose the violet.
Through all my wilds a tameless mouse careers,
And in that narrow boundary appears,
Huge as the stalking lion of Algiers,
Huge as the fabled boar of Calydon.
And all my hay is at one swoop impresst.
By one low-flying swallow for her nest.
Strip god Priapus of each attribute
Here finds he scarce a pedestal to foot.
The gathered harvest scarcely brims a spoon;
And all my vintage drips in a cocoon.
Generous are you, but I more generous still:
Take back your farm and hand me half a gill!

IN CHARIDEMUM

XI. 39

You, Charidemus, who my cradle swung
And watched me all the days that I was young—
You, at whose steps the laziest slaves awake
And both the bailiff and the butler quake—
The barber's suds now blacken with my beard
And my rough kisses make the maids afeard:
Still, in your eyes, before your judgement seat,
I am the baby that you used to beat.
You must do all things, unreproved; but I
If once to play or to my love I fly,
Big with reproach, I see your eyebrows twitch,
And for the accustomed cane your fingers itch.

If something daintily attired I go,
Straight you exclaim: 'Your father did not so!'
And, frowning, count the bottles on the board,
As though my cellar were your private hoard.
Enough, at last! I have borne all I can,
And your own mistress hails me for a man.

DE LIGURRA

XII. 61

You fear, Ligurra—above all, you long—
That I should smite you with a stinging song,
This dreadful honour you both fear and hope:
Both quite in vain: you fall below my scope.
The Libyan lion tears the roaring bull,
He does not harm the midge along the pool.
But if so close this stands in your regard,
From some blind tap fish forth a drunken bard,
Who shall, with charcoal, on the privy wall,
Immortalise your name for once and all.

VIII

As in their flight the birds of song
Halt here and there in sweet and sunny dales
But halt not overlong;
The time one rural song to sing
They pause; then following bounteous gales
Steer forward on the wing:
Sun-servers they, from first to last,
Upon the sun they await
To ride the sailing blast.

So he a while in our contested state,
A while abode, not longer—for his Sun—
Mother we say, no tenderer name we know—
With whose diviner glow
His early days had shone,
Now to withdraw her radiance had begun.
Or lest a wrong I say, not she withdrew,
But the loud stream of men day after day
And great dust columns of the common way
Between them grew and grew:
And he and she for evermore might yearn,
But to the spring the rivulets not return
Nor to the bosom comes the child again.

And he (O may we fancy so!),
He, feeling time for ever flow
And flowing bear him forth and far away
From that dear ingle where his life began
And all his treasure lay—
He, waxing into man,
And ever farther, ever closer wound
In this obstreperous world's ignoble round
From that poor prospect turned his face away.

IX

To Mrs MacMorland

Im Schnee der Alpen—so it runs
    To those divine accords—and here
We dwell in Alpine snows and suns
    A motley crew, for half the year:
A motley crew we dwell, to taste—
    A shivering band in hope and fear—
That sun upon the snowy waste,
    That Alpine ether cold and clear.

[301]

Up from the laboured plain, and up
   From low sea-levels, we arise
To drink of that diviner cup,
   The rarer air, the clearer skies;
For, as the great, old, godly King
   From mankind's turbid valley cries,
So all we mountain-lovers sing:
   I to the hills will lift mine eyes!

The bells that ring, the peaks that climb,
   The frozen snow's unbroken curd,
Might well revindicate in rhyme
   The pauseless stream, the absent bird:
In vain—for to the deeps of life
   You, lady, you, my heart have stirred;
And since you say you love my wife,
   Be sure I love you for the word.

Of kindness, here, I nothing say—
   Such loveless kindnesses there are
In that grimacing, common way,
   That old, unhonoured social war:
Love but my dog and love my love
   Adore with me a common star—
I value not the rest above
   The ashes of a bad cigar.

X

COME, my beloved, hear from me
Tales of the woods or open sea.
Let our aspiring fancy rise
A wren's flight higher toward the skies;
Or far from cities, brown and bare,
Play at the least in open air.

In all the tales we hear or tell
Still let the unfathomed ocean swell,
Or shallower forest sound abroad
Below the lonely stars of God;
In all, let something still be done,
Still in a corner shine the sun,
Slim-ankled maids be fleet of foot
Nor man disown the rural flute.
Still let the hero from the start
In honest sweat and beats of heart
Push on along the untrodden road
For some inviolate abode.
Still, O beloved, let me hear
The great bell beating far and near—
The odd, unknown, enchanted gong
That on the road hales men along,
That from the mountain calls afar,
That lures the vessel from a star,
And with a still, aërial sound
Makes all the earth enchanted ground.
Love and the love of life and act
Dance, live and sing through all our
        favoured tract;
Till the great God enamoured gives,
To him who reads, to him who lives,
That rare and fair romantic strain
That whoso hears must hear again.

XI

SINCE years ago for evermore
My cedar ship I drew to shore;
And to the road and river-bed
And the green, nodding reeds, I said

[303]

Mine ignorant and last farewell:
Now with content at home I dwell,
And now divide my sluggish life
Betwixt my verses and my wife:
In vain: for when the lamp is lit
And by the laughing fire I sit,
Still with the tattered atlas spread
Interminable roads I tread.

XII

FAR over seas an island is
    Whereon when day is done
A grove of tossing palms
    Are printed on the sun.
And all about the reefy shore
    Blue breakers flash and fall.
There shall I go, methinks,
    When I am done with all.

Have I no castle then in Spain,
    No island of the mind,
Where I can turn and go again
    When life shall prove unkind.
Up, sluggard soul! and far from here
    Our mountain forest seek;
Or nigh the enchanted island, steer
    Down the desirèd creek.

XIII

IF I could arise and travel away
Over the plains of the night and the day,
I should arrive at a land at last
Where all of our sins and sorrows are past
    And we're done with the ten commandments.

The name of the land I must not tell;
Green is the grass and cool the well;
Virtue is easy to find and to keep,
And the sinner may lie at his pleasure and sleep
 By the side of the ten commandments.

Income and honour, and glory and gold
Grow on the bushes all over the wold;
And if ever a man has a touch of remorse,
He eats of the flower of the golden gorse,
 And to hell with the ten commandments.

He goes to church in his Sunday's best;
He eats and drinks with perfect zest;
And whether he lives in heaven or hell
Is more than you or I can tell;
 But he's done with the ten commandments.

XIV

Now bare to the beholder's eye,
Your late denuded lendings lie,
Subsiding slowly where they fell,
A disinvested citadel;
The obdurate corset, cupid's foe,
The Dutchman's breeches frilled below.
Hose that the lover loves to note,
And white and crackling petticoat.

From these, that on the ground repose,
Their lady lately re-arose;
And laying by the lady's name
A living woman re-became.
Of her, that from the public eye
They do inclose and fortify,

Now, lying scattered as they fell
An indiscreeter tale they tell:
Of that more soft and secret her
Whose daylong fortresses they were,
By fading warmth, by lingering print,
These now discarded scabbards hint.

A twofold change the ladies know.
First, in the morn the bugles blow,
And they, with floral hues and scents,
Man their be-ribboned battlements.
But let the stars appear, and they
Shed inhumanities away;
And from the changeling fashion sees,
Through comic and through sweet degrees,
In nature's toilet unsurpassed,
Forth leaps the laughing girl at last.

XV

MEN are Heaven's piers; they evermore
Unwearying bear the skyey floor;
Man's theatre they bear with ease,
Unfrowning caryatides!
I, for my wife, the sun uphold
Or, dozing, strike the seasons cold.
She, on her side, in fairy-wise
Deals in diviner mysteries,
By spells to make the fuel burn
And keep the parlour warm, to turn
Water to wine and stones to bread
By her unconquered hero-head.
Sequestered in the seas of life,
A Crusoe couple, man and wife,

[306]

With all our good, with all our ill,
Our unfrequented isle we fill;
And victor in day's petty wars,
Each for the other lights the stars.
Come then, my Eve, and to and fro
Let us about our garden go;
And grateful-hearted, hand in hand,
Revisit all our tillage land
And marvel at our strange estate.
For hooded ruin at the gate
Sits watchful, and the angels fear
To see us tread so boldly here.
Meanwhile, my Eve, with flowers and grass,
Our perishable days we pass:
Far more the thorn observe—and see
How our enormous sins go free—
Nor less admire, beside the rose,
How far a little virtue goes.

XVI

FIXED is the doom; and to the last of years
Teacher and taught, friend, lover, parent, child,
Each walks, though near, yet separate; each beholds
His dear ones shine beyond him like the stars.
We also, love, for ever dwell apart;
With cries approach, with cries behold the gulph,
The Unvaulted: as two great eagles that do wheel
    in air
Above a mountain, and with screams confer,
Far heard athwart the cedars.

                Yet the years
Shall bring us ever nearer; day by day
Endearing, week by week; till death at last

Dissolve that long divorce. By faith we love,
Not knowledge; and by faith though far removed
Dwell as in perfect nearness, heart to heart.

                         We but excuse
Those things we merely are; and to our souls
A brave deception cherish.
So from unhappy war a man returns
Unfearing, or the seaman from the deep;
So from cool night and woodlands, to a feast
May some one enter, and still breathe of dews,
And in her eyes still wear the dusky night.

XVII

So live, so love, so use that fragile hour,
That when the dark hand of the shining power
Shall one from other, wife or husband, take,
The poor survivor may not weep and wake.

XVIII

To Mrs E. F. Strickland

THE freedom and the joy of days
When health was with us still,
The pleasure of green woods and ways
And of the breathing hill:
These that so dear a value set
Upon the times of yore,
We may remember, may forget—
We must enjoy no more.
As in strange lands, when exiles meet
And dream of long ago,
They with a nearer kindness greet

The sharers of their woe:
So, all unknown, from far away,
I, lady, turn to you—
Your fellow exile from the day,
The breezes and the dew.

XIX

For Richmond's Garden Wall

WHEN Thomas set this tablet here,
Time laughed at the vain chanticleer;
And ere the moss had dimmed the stone,
Time had defaced that garrison.
Now I in turn keep watch and ward
In my red house, in my walled yard
Of sunflowers, sitting here at ease
With friends and my bright canvasses.
But hark, and you may hear quite plain
Time's chuckled laughter in the lane.

XX

To Frederick Locker

NOT roses to the rose, I trow,
    The thistle sends, nor to the bee
Do wasps bring honey. Wherefore now
    Should Locker ask a verse from me?

Martial, perchance—but he is dead,
    And Herrick now must rhyme no more;
Still burning with the muse, they tread
    (And arm in arm) the shadowy shore.

[309]

They, if they lived, with dainty hand,
    To music as of mountain brooks,
Might bring you worthy words to stand
    Unshamed, dear Locker, in your books.

But tho' these fathers of your race
    Be gone before, yourself a sire,
Today you see before your face
    Your stalwart youngsters touch the lyre.

On these—on Lang, or Dobson—call,
    Long leaders of the songful feast.
They lend a verse your laughing fall—
    A verse they owe you at the least.

XXI

To Master Andrew Lang

On his re-editing of 'Cupid and Psyche'

You, that are much a fisher in the pool
Of things forgotten, and from thence bring up
Gold of old song and diamonds of dead speech,
The scholar, and the angler, and the friend
Restore and this dead author re-inspire;
And lo, oblivion the iniquitous
Remembers, and the stone is rolled away.
And he, the long asleep, sees once again
The busy bookshop; once again is read.

Brave as at first, in his new garb of print,
Shines forth the Elizabethan. But when death,
The unforgetful shepherd, shall have come

[310]

And numbered us with these, the numberless,
The inheritors of slumber and neglect—
O correspondent of the immortal dead,
Shall any pious hand re-edit us?

XXII

FAIR Isle at Sea—thy lovely name
Soft in my ear like music came.
That sea I loved, and once or twice
I touched at isles of Paradise.

XXIII

The Family

I

MOTHER AND DAUGHTER

High as my heart!—the quip be mine
That draws their stature to a line,
My pair of fairies plump and dark,
The dryads of my cattle park.
Here by my window close I sit
And watch (and my heart laughs at it)
How these my dragon-lilies are
Alike and yet dissimilar.
From European womankind
They are divided and defined
By the free limb and the plain mind,
The nobler gait, the naked foot,
The indiscreeter petticoat;

[311]

And show, by each endearing cause,
More like what Eve in Eden was:
Buxom and free, flowing and fine,
In every limb, in every line,
Inimitably feminine.
Like ripe fruit on the espaliers
Their sun-bepainted hue appears,
And the white lace (when lace they wear)
Shows on their golden breast more fair.
So far the same they seem, and yet
One apes the shrew, one the coquette:
A sybil or a truant child,
One runs—with a crop halo—wild;
And one, more sedulous to please,
Her long dark hair, deep as her knees
And thrid with living silver, sees.

What need have I of wealth or fame,
A club, an often-printed name?
It more contents my heart to know
Them going simply to and fro:
To see the dear pair pause and pass
Girded, among the drenching grass,
In the resplendent sun; or hear,
When the huge moon delays to appear,
Their kindred voices sounding near
In the verandah twilight.
                                    So
Sound ever; so, for ever go
And come upon your strong brown feet,
Twin honours, to my country seat
And its too happy master lent:
My solace and its ornament!

II

THE DAUGHTER
TEUILA—HER NATIVE NAME—THE ADORNER

Man, child or woman, none from her,
The insatiable embellisher,
Escapes! She leaves, where'er she goes,
A wreath, a ribbon, or a rose:
A bow or else a button changed,
Two hairs coquettishly deranged,
Some vital trifle, takes the eye
And shows the Adorner has been by.
Is fortune more obdurate grown?
And does she leave my dear alone
With none to adorn, none to caress?
Straight on her proper loveliness
She broods and lingers, cuts and carves,
With combs and brushes, rings and scarves.
The treasure of her hair she takes;
Therewith a new presentment makes.
Babe, goddess, naïad of the grot;
And weeps if any like it not!

    Her absent, she shall still be found,
A posse of native maids around
Her and her whirring instrument
Collected, and on learning bent.
Oft clustered by her tender knees
(Smiling himself) the gazer sees,
Compact as flowers in garden beds,
The smiling faces and shaved heads
Of the brown island babes: with whom
She exults to decorate her room,
To draw them, cheer them when they cry,
And still to pet and prettify.

[313]

Or see, as in a looking-glass,
Her pigmy, dimpled person pass,
Nought great therein but eyes and hair,
On her true business here and there:
Her huge, half-naked staff, intent,
See her review and regiment,
An ant with elephants! and how
A smiling mouth, a clouded brow,
Satire and turmoil, quips and tears,
She deals among her grenadiers!
Her pantry and her kitchen squad,
Six-footers all, hang on her nod,
Incline to her their martial chests,
With schoolboy laughter hail her jests,
And do her in her girded dress
Obsequious obeisances.

But rather to behold her when
She plies for me the unresting pen!
And while her crimson blood peeps out,
Hints a suggestion, halts a doubt,
Laughs at a jest; or with a shy
Glance of a particoloured eye
Half brown, half gold, approves, delights
And warms the slave for whom she writes!

So, dear, may you be never done
Your pretty, busy round to run,
And show, with changing frocks and scents,
Your ever-varying lineaments:
Your saucy step, your languid grace,
Your sullen and your smiling face,
Sound sense, true valour, baby fears,
And bright unreasonable tears:
The Hebe of our ageing tribe:
Matron and child, my friend and scribe!

III

About my fields, in the broad sun
And blaze of noon, there goeth one
Barefoot and robed in blue, to scan
With the hard eye of the husbandman
My harvests and my cattle. Her,
When even puts the birds astir
And day has set in the great woods,
We seek, among her garden roods,
With bells and cries in vain: the while
Lamps, plate and the decanter smile
On the forgotten board. But she,
Deaf, blind, and prone on face and knee,
Forgets time, family and feast
And digs like a demented beast.

IV

Tall as a guardsman, pale as the east at dawn,
Who strides in strange apparel on the lawn?
Rails for his breakfast? routs his vassals out
(Like boys escaped from school) with song and shout?
Kind and unkind, his Maker's final freak,
Part we deride the child, part dread the antique!
See where his gang, like frogs, among the dew
Crouch at their duty, an unquiet crew;
Adjust their staring kilts; and their swift eyes
Turn still to him who sits to supervise.
He in the midst, perched on a fallen tree,
Eyes them at labour; and, guitar on knee,
Now ministers alarm, now scatters joy,
Now twangs a halting chord—now tweaks a boy.

Thorough in all, my resolute vizier,
Plays both the despot and the volunteer,
Exacts with fines obedience to my laws,
—And for his music, too, exacts applause.

V

WHAT glory for a boy of ten,
Who now must three gigantic men,
And two enormous, dapple grey
New Zealand pack-horses, array
And lead, and wisely resolute
Our day-long business execute
In the far shore-side town. His soul
Glows in his bosom like a coal;
His innocent eyes glitter again,
And his hand trembles on the rein.
Once he reviews his whole command
And chivalrously planting hand
On hip—a borrowed attitude—
Rides off downhill into the wood.

VI

The old lady (so they say) but I
Admire your young vitality.
Still brisk of foot, still busy and keen
In and about and up and down.
I hear you pass with bustling feet
The long verandahs round, and beat
Your bell, and 'Lotu! Lotu!' cry;
Thus calling our queer company
At morning or at evening dim,
To prayers and the oft mangled hymn.

[316]

All day you watch across the sky
The silent, shining cloudlands ply,
That, huge as countries, swift as birds,
Beshade the isles by halves and thirds;
Till each, with battlemented crest,
Stands anchored in the ensanguined west,
An Alp enchanted. And all day
You hear the exuberant wind at play
Its vast, unbroken voice uplift
In roaring tree, round whistling clift.

VII

TUSITALA

I MEANWHILE, in the populous house apart,
Sit snugly chambered; and my silent art
Uninterrupted, unremitting ply,
Before the dawn by morning lamplight, by
The glow of sweltering noon, and when the sun
Dips past my westward peak and day is done;
So, bending still over my trade of words,
I hear the morning and the evening birds,
The morning and the evening stars behold.
So thus apart I sit, as once of old,
Napier in wizard Merchiston; and my
Brown innocent aides in house and husbandry
Wonder askance. *What ails the Boss?* they ask,
Him, richest of the rich, an endless task
Before the earliest birds or servants stir
Calls, and detains him daylong prisoner?
He, whose innumerable dollars hewed
This cleft in the boar- and devil-haunted wood,
And bade therein, far seen to seas and skies,
His many-windowed, painted palace rise,

Red-roofed, blue-walled, a rainbow on the hill,
A wonder in the wild-wood glade: he still

Unthinkable Aladdin, dawn and dark,
Scribbles and scribbles like a German clerk.
We see the fact, but tell, O tell us why?
My reverend washman and wise butler cry.
And from their lips the unanswered questions drop.
How can he live that does not keep a shop?
And why does he, being acclaimed so rich,
Not dwell with other gentry on the beach?
But harbour, impiously brave,
In the cold, uncanny wood, haunt of the fleeing slave?
The sun and the loud rain here alternate:
Here, in the unfathomable bush, the great
Voice of the wind makes a magnanimous sound.
Here, too, no doubt, the shouting doves abound
To be a dainty; here, in the twilight stream
That brawls adown the forest, frequent gleam
The jewel-eyes of crawfish. These be good:
Grant them! and can the thing be understood?
That this white chief, whom no distress compels,
Far from all compeers in the mountain dwells?
And finds a manner of living to his wish
Apart from high society—and sea fish?

VIII

THESE rings, O my beloved pair,
For me on your brown fingers wear:
Each, a perpetual caress,
To tell you of my tenderness.

Let—when at morning as ye rise
The golden topaz takes your eyes—
To each her emblem whisper sure
Love was awake an hour before.

Ah yes! an hour before ye woke
Low to my heart *my* emblem spoke,
And grave, as to renew an oath,
It I have kissed and blessed you both.

XXIV

LIGHT foot and tight foot
    And green grass spread,
Early in the morning—
    But hope is on ahead.

Stout foot and proud foot
    And gray dust spread,
Early in the evening—
    And hope lies dead.

Long life and short life,
    The last word said,
Early in the evening
    There lies the bed.

[319]

Brief day and bright day
And sunset red,
Early in the evening
The stars are overhead.

XXV

To the Stormy Petrel

To my Wife, on her Birthday

EVER perilous
And precious, like an ember from the fire
Or gem from a volcano, we today
When the drums of war reverberate in the land
And every face is for the battle blacked,
Nor less the sky that, over sodden woods,
Menaces now in the disconsolate calm
The hurly-burly of the hurricane,
Do now most fitly celebrate your day.

Yet amid turmoil keep for me, my dear,
The kind domestic faggot. Let the hearth
Shine ever as (I praise my honest gods)
In peace and tempest it has ever shone.

XXVI

I, WHOM Apollo sometime visited,
Or feigned to visit, now, my day being done,
Do slumber wholly; nor shall know at all
The weariness of changes, nor perceive
Immeasurable sands of centuries
Drink up the blanching ink, or the loud sound
Of generations beat the music down.

[320]

XXVII

As with heaped bees at hiving time
The boughs are clotted, as (ere prime)
Heaven swarms with stars, or the city street
Pullulates with faring feet;
So swarmed my senses once; that now
Repose behind my tranquil brow,
Unsealed, asleep, quiescent, clear;
Now only the vast shapes I hear
Hear—and my hearing slowly fills—
Rivers and winds among the twisting hills,
And hearken—and my face is lit—
Life pacing; death pursuing it.

DEDICATIONS
AND POEMS FROM BOOKS

I

To the Hesitating Purchaser

From 'Treasure Island'

IF sailor tales to sailor tunes,
    Storm and adventure, heat and cold,
If schooners, islands, and maroons
    And Buccaneers and buried Gold,
And all the old romance, retold
    Exactly in the ancient way,
Can please, as me they pleased of old,
    The wiser youngsters of today:

So be it, and fall on! If not,
　　If studious youth no longer crave,
His ancient appetites forgot,
　　Kingston, or Ballantyne the brave,
Or Cooper of the wood and wave:
　　So be it, also! And may I
And all my pirates share the grave
　　Where these and their creations lie!

II

Pirate Ditty

From 'Treasure Island'

FIFTEEN men on the Dead Man's Chest—
　　Yo-ho-ho, and a bottle of rum!
Drink and the devil had done for the rest—
　　Yo-ho-ho, and a bottle of rum!

III

The Song of the Sword of Alan

From 'Kidnapped'

THIS is the song of the sword of Alan:
The smith made it,
The fire set it;
Now it shines in the hand of Alan Breck.

Their eyes were many and bright,
Swift were they to behold,
Many the hands they guided:
The sword was alone.

[322]

The dun deer troop over the hill,
They are many, the hill is one:
The dun deer vanish,
The hill remains.

Come to me from the hills of heather,
Come from the isles of the sea.
O far-beholding eagles,
Here is your meat.

IV

To Virgil and Dora Williams

With a copy of 'The Silverado Squatters'

HERE, from the forelands of the tideless sea,
Behold and take my offering, unadorned
Or—shall we say? defaced, by Joseph's art.
In the Pacific air, it sprang; it grew
Among the silence of the Alpine air;
In Scottish heather blossomed; and at last
By that unshaken sapphire, in whose face
Spain, Italy, France, Algiers and Tunis view
Their introverted mountains, came to fruit.
Back now, my Booklet! on the diving ship
And posting on the rails, to home return—
Home, and the friends whose honouring name you
    bear.

V

To Nelly Sanchez

With a copy of 'Prince Otto'

Go, little book—the ancient phrase
And still the daintiest—go your ways,
My Otto, over sea and land,
Till you shall come to Nelly's hand.

How shall I your Nelly know?
By her blue eye and her black brow,
By her fierce and slender look,
And by her goodness, little book!

What shall I say when I come there?
You shall speak her soft and fair:
See—you shall say—the love they send
To greet their unforgotten friend!

Giant Adulpho you shall sing
The next, and then the cradled king:
And the four corners of the roof
Then kindly bless; and to your perch aloof,
Where Balzac all in yellow dressed
And the dear Webster of the west
Encircle the prepotent throne
Of Shakespeare and of Calderon,
Shall climb an upstart.

           There, with these,
You shall give ear to breaking seas
And windmills turning in the breeze,
A distant undetermined din
Without; and you shall hear within

The blazing and the bickering logs,
The crowing child, the yawning dogs,
And ever agile, high and low,
Our Nelly going to and fro.

There shall you all silent sit,
Till, when perchance the lamp is lit
And the day's labour done, she takes
Poor Otto down, and, warming for our sakes,
Perchance beholds, alive and near,
Our distant faces reappear.

VI

To H. C. Bunner

With a copy of 'A Child's Garden of Verses'

You know the way to Arcady
Where I was born;
You have been there, and fain
Would there return.
Some that go thither bring with them
Red rose or jewelled diadem
As secrets of the secret king:
I, only what a child would bring.
Yet I do think my song is true;
For this is how the children do;
This is the tune to which they go
In sunny pastures high and low;
The treble pipes not otherwise
Sing daily under sunny skies
In Arcady the dear;
And you who have been there before,
And love that country evermore,
May not disdain to hear.

VII

To Katharine de Mattos

With a copy of 'Dr Jekyll and Mr Hyde'

BELLS upon the city are ringing in the night;
High above the gardens are the houses full of light;
On the heathy Pentlands is the curlew flying free,
And the broom is blowing bonnie in the north countrie.

It's ill to break the bonds that God decreed to bind,
Still we'll be the children of the heather and the wind.
Far away from home, O, it's still for you and me
That the broom is blowing bonnie in the north countrie!

VIII

To My Wife

Found in the Manuscript of 'Weir of Hermiston'

I SAW rain falling and the rainbow drawn
On Lammermuir. Hearkening I heard again
In my precipitous city beaten bells
Winnow the keen sea wind. And here afar
Intent on my own race and place I wrote.

Take thou the writing: thine it is. For who
Burnished the sword, blew on the drowsy coal,
Held still the target higher, chary of praise
And prodigal of censure—who but thou?
So now, in the end, if this the least be good,
If any deed be done, if any fire
Burn in the imperfect page, the praise be thine.

LIGHT VERSE

LIGHT VERSE

I

For laughing I very much vote   give
   Yet was never opposed to the church,   a
So why do grave people agree,   dog
   To leave me alone in the lurch.   a
From my birth a desirable youth   bad
   In amenity ever I shone   name
Yet no merry andrew was I   and
   To be carelessly flouted upon.
High, angry and sour are the words   hang
   With which I have ever been curst,
And yet though impenitent now   him
   I was easily led at the first.

II

Here he comes, big with Statistics,
   Troubled and sharp about fac's.
He has heaps of the *Form* that is thinkable—
   The *stuff* that is feeling, he lacks.

Do you envy this whiskered absurdity,
   With *pince-nez* and clerical tie?
Poor fellow, he's blind of a sympathy!
   I'd rather be blind of an eye.

III

To Charles Baxter

BLAME me not that this epistle
  Is the first you have from me.
    Idleness has held me fettered;
    But at last the times are bettered
And once more I wet my whistle
  Here, in France, beside the sea.

All the green and idle weather
  I have had in sun and shower
    Such an easy, warm subsistence,
    Such an indolent existence
I should find it hard to sever
  Day from day and hour from hour.

Many a tract-provided ranter
  May upbraid me, dark and sour,
    Many a bland Utilitarian
    Or excited Millenarian,
—'Pereunt et imputantur
  You must speak to every hour.'

But (the very term's deceptive)
  You at least, my friend, will see
    That in sunny grassy meadows
    Trailed across by moving shadows
To be actively receptive
  Is as much as man can be.

He that all the winter grapples
   Difficulties—thrust and ward—
      Needs to cheer him thro' his duty
      Memories of sun and beauty,
Orchards with the russet apples
   Lying scattered on the sward.

Many such I keep in prison,
   Keep them here at heart unseen,
      Till my muse again rehearses
      Long years hence, and in my verses
You shall meet them re-arisen
   Ever comely, ever green.

You know how they never perish,
   How, in time of later art,
      Memories consecrate and sweeten
      These defaced and tempest-beaten
Flowers of former years we cherish,
   Half a life, against our heart.

Most, those love-fruits withered greenly,
   Those frail sickly amourettes,
      How they brighten with the distance
      Take new strength and new existence
Till we see them sitting queenly
   Crowned and courted by regrets!

All that loveliest and best is,
   Aureole-fashion round their head,
      They that looked in life but plainly,
      How they stir our spirits vainly
When they come to us Alcestis-
   Like, returning from the dead!

[331]

Not the old love but another,
 Bright she comes at Memory's call,
  Our forgotten vows reviving
  To a newer, livelier living,
As the dead child to the mother
 Seems the fairest child of all.

Thus our Goethe, sacred master,
 Travelling backward thro' his youth,
  Surely wandered wrong in trying
  To renew the old, undying
Loves that cling in memory faster
 Than they ever lived in truth.

IV

Ne Sit Ancillae Tibi Amor Pudori

THERE'S just a twinkle in your eye
That seems to say I *might*, if I
Were only bold enough to try
 An arm about your waist.

I hear, too, as you come and go,
That pretty nervous laugh, you know;
And then your cap is always so
 Coquettishly displaced.

Your cap! the word's profanely said,
That little topknot, white and red,
That quaintly crowns your graceful head,
 No bigger than a flower,

You set with such a witching art,
And so provocatively smart,
I'd like to wear it on my heart,
 An order for an hour!

[332]

O graceful housemaid, tall and fair,
I love your shy imperial air,
And always loiter on the stair,
    When you are going by.

A strict reserve the fates demand;
But, when to let you pass I stand,
Sometimes by chance I touch your hand
    And sometimes catch your eye.

V

Poem for a Class Re-union

WHETHER we like it, or don't,
    There's a sort of a bond in the fact
That we all by one master were taught,
    By one master were bullied and whackt.
And now all the more, when we see
    Our class in so shrunken a state
And we, who were seventy-two,
    Diminished to seven or eight.

One has been married; and one
    Has taken to letters for bread,
Several are over the seas;
    And some I imagine are dead.
And that is the reason, you see,
    Why, as I have the honour to state,
We, who were seventy-two,
    Are now only seven or eight.

One took to heretical views,
    And one, they inform me, to drink;
Some construct fortunes in trade,
    Some starve in professions, I think.

[333]

But one way or other alas!
　　Through the culpable action of Fate
We, who were seventy-two,
　　Are now shrunken to seven or eight.

So, whether we like it or not,
　　Let us own there's a bond in the past,
And, since we were playmates at school,
　　Continue good friends to the last.
The roll-book is closed in the room,
　　The clacken is gone with the slate,
We, who were seventy-two,
　　Are now only seven or eight.

We shall never, our books on our back,
　　Trudge off in the morning again,
To the slide at the Janitor's door,
　　By the ambush of cads in the lane!
We shall never be sent for the tawse,
　　Nor lose places for coming too late;
We shall never be seventy-two,
　　Who now are but seven or eight!

We shall never have peeries for luck,
　　We shall never be strapped by Maclean,
We shall never take Lothian down,
　　Nor ever be schoolboys again.
But still for the sake of the past,
　　For the love of the days of lang syne
The remnant of seventy-two
　　Shall rally together to dine.

VI

Browning

BROWNING made the verses,
Your servant the critique.
Browning couldn't sing at all—
I fancy I could speak.
Although his book was clever
(To give the deil his due)
I wasn't pleased with Browning's verse
Nor he with my review.

VII

On An Inland Voyage

WHO would think, herein to look,
That from these exiguous bounds,
I have dug a printed book
And a cheque for twenty pounds.
Thus do those who trust the Lord
Go rejoicing on their way
And receive a great reward
For having been so kind as play.

I had the fun of the voyage
I had the sport of the boats
Who could have hoped in addition
The pleasure of fing'ring the notes?

Yes, sir, I wrote the book, I own the fact,
It was perhaps, sir, an unworthy act.
Have you perused it, sir?—You have?—Indeed!
Then between you and me there no debate is.
I did a silly act, but I was fee'd;
You did a sillier, and you did it gratis!

VIII

Dedication

To her, for I must still regard her
As feminine in her degree,
Who has been my unkind bombarder
Year after year, in grief and glee,
Year after year, with oaken tree;
And yet between whiles my laudator
In terms astonishing to me:
To the Right Reverend THE SPECTATOR
I here, a humble dedicator,
Bring the last apples from my tree.

In tones of love, in tones of warning
She hailed me through my brief career;
And kiss and buffet, night and morning,
Told me my grandmamma was near;
Whether she praised me high and clear
Through her unrivalled circulation,
Or, sanctimonious insincere
She damned me with a misquotation—
A chequered but a sweet relation,
Say, was it not, my granny dear?

Believe me, granny, altogether
Yours, though perhaps to your surprise.
Oft have you spruced my wounded feather,
Oft brought a light into my eyes—
For notice still the writer cries.
In any civil age or nation,
The book that is not talked of dies.
So that shall be my termination:
Whether in praise or execration,
Still, if you love me, criticise!

IX

On Some Ghastly Companions at A Spa

THAT was an evil day when I
To Strathpeffer drew anigh,
For there I found no human soul
But Ogres occupied the whole.

They had at first a human air
In coats and flannel underwear.
They rose and walked upon their feet
And filled their bellies full of meat.
They wiped their lips when they had done,
But they were Ogres every one.

Each issuing from his secret bower,
I marked them in the morning hour.
By limp and totter, lisp and droop,
I singled each one from the group.
I knew them all as they went by—
I knew them by their blasted eye!

[337]

Detested Ogres, from my sight
Depart to your congenial night!
From these fair vales, from this fair day,
Fleet, spectres, on your downward way,
Like changing figures in a dream,
To Muttonhole or Pittenweem!
As, by some harmony divine
The devils quartered in the swine,
If any baser place exist
In God's great registration list—
Some den with wallow and a trough—
Find it, ye ogres, and be off!

X

Brasheanna

*Sonnets on Peter Brash, a publican, dedicated to Charles
Baxter*

I

We found him first as in the dells of May
   The dreaming damsel finds the earliest flower;
   Thoughtless we wandered in the evening hour;
Aimless and pleased we went our random way:
In the foot-haunted city in the night,
   Among the alternate lamps, we went and came
   Till, like a humourous thunderbolt, that name,
The hated name of Brash, assailed our sight.
We saw, we paused, we entered, seeking gin.
   His wrath, like a huge breaker on the beach,
     Broke instant forth. He on the counter beat
     In his infantile fury; and his feet
Danced impotent wrath upon the floor within.
   Still as we fled, we heard his idiot screech.

[338]

II

WE found him and we lost. The glorious BRASH
   Fell as the cedar on the mountain side
   When the resounding thunders far and wide
Redoubling grumble, and the instant flash
Divides the night a moment and is gone;
   He fell not unremembered nor unwept;
   And the dim shop where that great hero stept
Is sacred still. We, steering past the *Tron*,
And past the *College* southward, and thy square
   Fitz-Symon! reach at last that holier clime,
And do with tears behold that pot-house, where
     BRASH the divine once ministered in drink,
   Where BRASH, the *Beershop Hornet*, bowed by time,
     In futile anger grinned across the zinc.

III

THERE let us often wend our pensive way,
   There often pausing celebrate the past;
   For though indeed our BRASH be dead at last,
Perchance his spirit, in some minor way,
Nor pure immortal nor entirely dead,
   Contrives upon the farther shore of death
   To pick a rank subsistence, and for breath
Breathes ague, and drinks Acetate of Lead.
There, on the way to that infernal den,
   Where burst the flames forth thickly, and the sky
     Flares horrid through the murk, methinks he doles
     Damned liquors out to Hellward-faring souls,
   And as his impotent anger ranges high
Gibbers and gurgles at the shades of men.

IV

Alas! that while the beautiful and strong,
   The pious and the wise, the grave and gay,
   All journey downward by one common way,
Bewailed and honoured yet with flowers and song,
There must come crowding with that serious throng,
   Jostling the ranks of that discreet array,
   Infirm and scullion spirits of decay,
The dull, the droll, the random and the wrong.
An ape in church, an artificial limb
   Tacked to a marble god serene and blind—
   For such as Brash, high death was not designed,
That canonising rite was not for him;
   Nor where the Martyr and the Hero trod
   Should idiot Brash go hobbling up to God.

V

To Goodness or Greatness: to be good and die,
   Or to be great and live forever great:
   To be the unknown Smith that saves the state
And blooms unhonoured by the public eye:
To be the unknown Robinson or Brown
   Whose piping virtues perish in the mud
   Or triumphing in blasphemy and blood,
The imperial pirate, pickled in renown:
Unfaltering Brash the latter member chose
   Of this eterne antithesis: and still
The flower of his immortal memory blows
Where'er the spirits of the loathed repose
   Where'er the trophy of the gibbet hill
Dejects the traveller and collects the crows.

[340]

XI

To A. G. Dew-Smith

In return for a box of cigarettes

FIGURE me to yourself, I pray—
   A man of my peculiar cut—
Apart from dancing and deray,
   Into an Alpine valley shut:

Shut in a kind of damned Hotel
   Discountenanced by God and man:
The food?—Sir, you would do as well
   To cram your belly full of bran!

The company?—Alas, the day,
   That I should dwell with such a crew
With devil anything to say
   Nor any one to say it to!

The place?—Although they call it Platz,
   I will be bold and state my view:
It's not a place at all—and that's
   The bottom verity, my Dew.

There are, as I will not deny,
   Innumerable inns; a road;
Several Alps indifferent high,
   The snow's inviolable abode;

Eleven English parsons, all
   Entirely inoffensive; four
True human beings—what I call
   Human—the deuce a cipher more;

[341]

A climate of surprising worth;
  Innumerable dogs that bark;
Some air, some weather, and some earth;
  A native race—God save the mark!

A race that works yet cannot work,
  Yodels but cannot yodel right,
Such as, unhelpt, with rusty dirk,
  I vow that I could wholly smite;

A river that from morn to night
  Down all the valley plays the fool;
Nor once she pauses in her flight;
  Nor knows the comforts of a pool.

But still keeps up, by straight or bend,
  The self-same pace that she begun—
Still hurry, hurry, to the end—
  Good God, is that the way to run?

If I a river were, I hope
  That I should better realise
The opportunities and scope
  Of that romantic enterprise.

I should not ape the merely strange,
  But aim besides at the divine;
And continuity and change
  I still should labour to combine.

Here should I gallop down the race,
  Here charge the sterling like a bull;
There, as a man might wipe his face,
  Lie, pleased and panting, in a pool.

But what, my Dew, in idle mood,
  What prate I, minding not my debt?
What do I talk of bad or good?
  The best is still a cigarette.

Me, whether evil fate assault,
  Or smiling providences crown—
Whether on high the eternal vault
  Be blue, or crash with thunder down—

I judge the best, whate'er befal,
  Is still to sit on one's behind
And, having duly moistened all,
  Smoke with an unperturbèd mind.

So sitting, so engaged, I write;
  So puffing, so puffed up, I sing,
In modest climates of delight
  And from the islands of the spring:

My manner, even as I can:
  My matter—Frenchly—to agree
As from a much delighted man,
  A gift unspeakable to me.

XII

Long time I lay in little ease
  Where, paced by the Turanian,
Marseilles, the many-masted, sees
  The blue Mediterranean.

Now songful in the hour of sport,
  Now riotous for wages,
She camps around her ancient port
  An ancient of the ages.

[343]

Algerian airs through all the place
　　Unconquerably sally;
Incomparable women pace
　　The shadows of the alley.

And high o'er dock and graving yard
　　And where the sky is paler,
The golden virgin of the guard
　　Shines, beckoning the sailor.

She hears the city roar on high,
　　Thief, prostitute and banker;
She sees the masted vessels lie
　　Immovably at anchor.

She sees the snowy islets dot
　　The sea's immortal azure,
And If, that castellated spot,
　　Tower, turret and embrazure.

There Dantès pined; and here today
　　Behold me his successor:
For here imprisoned long I lay
　　In pledge for a professor.

XIII

My wife and I, in our romantic cot,
The world forgetting, by the world forgot,
High as the gods upon Olympus dwell,
Pleased with what things we have, and pleased as well
To wait in hope for those which we have not.

She burns in ardour for a horse to trot;
I stake my votive prayers upon a yacht;
Which shall be first remembered, who can tell,
  My wife or I?

Harvests of flowers o'er all our garden-plot,
She dreams; and I to enrich a darker spot
My unprovided cellar; both to swell
Our narrow cottage huge as a hotel,
Where portly friends may come and share the lot—
  Of wife and I.

XIV

 At morning on the garden seat
 I dearly love to drink and eat.
 To drink and eat, to drink and sing,
 At morning, in the time of Spring.
 In winter honest men retire
 And sup their possets by the fire,
 But when the Spring comes round, you see,
 The garden breakfast pleases me.
 The morning star that melts on high
 The fires that cleanse the changing sky,
 The air that smells so new and sweet,
 All put me in the cue to eat
 A pot at five, a crust at four,
 At half past six a pottle more.

XV

Last night we had a thunderstorm in style.
The wild lightning streaked the airs,
As though my God fell down a pair of stairs.
The thunder boomed and bounded all the while;
All cried and sat by water-side and stile—
To mop our brow had been our chief of cares.
I lay in bed with a Voltairean smile,
The terror of good, simple guilty pairs,
And made this rondeau in ironic style,
Last night we had a thunderstorm in style.
Our God the Father fell down-stairs,
The stark blue lightning went its flight, the while,
The very rain you might have heard a mile—
The strenuous faithful buckled to their prayers.

XVI

To Time

God of the business man, to thee,
O Time, I bow the suppliant knee,
And to thy dwarfish temple bring
My books as a peace-offering.
Thou cleaver of the crowded woods,
That drivest from green solitudes
The sylvan deer; and dost conspire,
Or for the shipyard or the fire,
The fall of woodland colonnades;
O time, that lovest in the glades
To cheer the ringing areas din
And let the untrammelled sunshine in:

[346]

Think but once more, nor let this be,
Thy servant should survive to see
His native country and his head
Lie both alike disforested.

XVII

Fragment

Thou strainest through the mountain fern,
A most exiguously thin
    Burn.
For all thy foam, for all thy din,
Thee shall the pallid lake inurn,
With well-a-day for Mr. Swin-
    Burne!
Take then this quarto in thy fin
And, O thou stoker huge and stern,
The whole affair, outside and in,
    Burn!
But save the true poetic kin,
The works of Mr. Robert Burn!
And William Wordsworth upon Tin-
    Tern!

XVIII

A Sonnet to Mr William Mackintosh

Maker of Matches

Thee, Mackintosh, artificer of light,
  Thee, the lone smoker hails; the student, thee;
  Thee, oft upon the ungovernable sea,
The seaman, conscious of approaching night:
Thou, with industrious fingers, hast outright
  Mastered that art, of other arts the key,
  That bids thick night before the morning flee,

And lingering day retains for mortal sight.
O Promethean workman, thee I hail,
  Thee hallowed, thee unparalleled, thee bold
   To affront the reign of sleep and darkness old—
     Thee William, thee Æneas, thee I sing;
Thee by the glimmering taper clear and pale,
     Of light, and light's purveyance, hail, the king.

XIX

Rhymes to Henley

I

O HENLEY, in my hours of ease
You may say anything you please,
But when I join the Muses' revel,
Begad, I wish *you* at the devil!
In vain my verse I plane and bevel,
Like Banville's rhyming devotees;
In vain by many an artful swivel
Lug in my meaning by degrees;
I'm sure to hear my Henley cavil;
And grovelling prostrate on my knees,
Devote his body to the seas,
His correspondence to the devil.

II

DEAR Henley, with a pig's snout on
I am starting for London,
Where I likely shall arrive,
On Saturday, if still alive:
Perhaps your pirate doctor might
See me on Sunday? If all's right,
I should then lunch with you and with she
Who's dearer to you than you are to me.

I shall remain but little time
In London, as a wretched clime,
But not so wretched (for none are)
As that of bloody old Braemar.
My doctor sends me skipping. I
Have many facts to meet your eye.
My pig's snout's now upon my face;
And I inhale with fishy grace,
My gills out-flapping right and left,
Ol. pin. sylvest. I am bereft
Of a great deal of charm by this—
Not quite the bull's eye for a kiss—
But like a gnome of olden time
Or bogey in a pantomime.
For ladies' love I once was fit;
But now am rather out of it.
Where'er I go, revolted curs
Snap round my military spurs;
The children all retire in fits
And scream their bellowses to bits.
Little I care: the worst's been done:
Now let the cold impoverished sun
Drop frozen from his orbit; let
Fury and fire, cold, wind and wet,
And cataclysmal mad reverses
Rage through the federate universes;
Let Lawson triumph, cakes and ale,
Whiskey and hock and claret fail;
Tobacco, love and letters perish,
With all that any man could cherish:
You it may touch, not me. I dwell
Too deep already—deep in hell;
And nothing can befall, O damn!
To make me uglier than I am.

III

My indefatigable pen
I here lay down forever. Men
Have used, and left me, and forgot;
Men are entirely off the spot;
Men are a *blague* and an abuse;
And I commit them to the deuce!

IV

I HAD companions, I had friends,
I had of whisky various blends.
The whisky was all drunk; and lo!
The friends were gone for evermo!

V

ALL men are rot: but there are two—
Sidney, the oblivious Slade, and you—
Who from that rabble stand confest
Ten million times the rottenest.

VI

WHEN I was sick and safe in gaol
I thought my friends would never fail.
One wrote me nothing; t'other bard
Sent me an insolent post card.

VII

My letters fail, I learn with grief, to please
Proud spirits that sit and read them at their ease
Not recking how, from an exhausted mind,
By wheel and pulley, tug and strain and grind,
These humble efforts are expressed, like cheese.

VIII

We dwell in these melodious days
When every author trolls his lays;
And all, except myself and you,
Must up and print the nonsense, too.
Why then, if this be so indeed,
If adamantine walls recede
And old Apollo's gardens gape
For Arry and the grinder's ape;
I too may enter in perchance
Where paralytic graces dance,
And cheering on each tottering set
Blow my falsetto flageolet.

IX. TRIOLETS

I

Si je l'aime, ce Montépin,
J'aime de cœur mais pas de tête!
J'en atteste le roi Pépin
Si je l'aime, ce Montépin!
Son meilleur roman, le Sapin,
Je n'y crois pas, mais je l'achète!
Si je l'aime, ce Montépin,
J'aime de cœur mais pas de tête.

2

Ce que j'adore chez Xavier
C'est l'absence de tout mérite.
Et vous rirez si vous saviez
Ce que j'adore chez Xavier!
Trois vieux sous dans un gravier
Où tout le monde est Marguerite!
Ce que j'adore chez Xavier
C'est l'absence de tout mérite.

3

Ses romans sont pas mal lichés.
Il n'y a que de la rengaine!
En fait de style, des clichés!
Ses romans sont pas mal lichés.
Nous nous en sommes tous fichés
Mais nous les préférons à Taine!
Ses romans sont pas mal lichés:
Il n'y a que de la rengaine!

X.   A LYTLE JAPE OF TUSHERIE

By A. Tusher

The pleasant river gushes
    Among the meadows green;
At home the author tushes;
    For him it flows unseen.

The Birds among the Bushes
    May wanton on the spray;
But vain for him who tushes,
    The brightness of the day!

The frog among the rushes
   Sits singing in the blue.
By 'r la'kin! but these tushes
   Are wearisome to do!

The task entirely crushes
   The spirit of the bard:
God pity him who tushes—
   His task is very hard.

The filthy gutter slushes,
   The clouds are full of rain,
But doomed is he who tushes
   To tush and tush again.

At morn with his hair-brushes,
   Still 'tush' he says, and weeps;
At night again he tushes
   And tushes till he sleeps.

And when at length he pŭshes
   Beyond the river dark—
'Las, to the man who tushes,
   'Tush' shall be God's remark!

XX

Epitaphs

I

HERE lies a man who never did
Anything but what he was bid;
Who lived his life in paltry ease,
And died of commonplace disease.

II

The angler rose, he took his rod,
He kneeled and made his prayers to God.
The living God sat overhead:
The angler tripped, the eels were fed.

III.   ON HIMSELF

He may have been this and that,
    A drunkard or a guttler;
He may have been bald and fat;
    At least he kept a butler.

He may have sprung from ill or well,
    From Emperor or sutler;
He may be burning now in Hell;
    On earth he kept a butler.

IV.   ON HIMSELF AT THE PIANO

Where is now the Père Martini?
Where is Bumptious Boccherini?
Where are Hertz and Crotch and Batch?
—Safe in bed in Colney Hatch?

XXI

The Fine Pacific Islands

Heard in a Public-house at Rotherhithe

THE jolly English Yellowboy
  Is a 'ansome coin when new,
The Yankee Double-eagle
  Is large enough for two.
O, these may do for seaport towns,
  For cities these may do;
But the dibbs that takes the Hislands
  Are the dollars of Peru:
      O, the fine Pacific Hislands,
      O, the dollars of Peru!

It's there we buy the cocoanuts
  Mast 'eaded in the blue;
It's there we trap the lasses
  All waiting for the crew;
It's there we buy the trader's rum
  What bores a seaman through . . .
In the fine Pacific Hislands
  With the dollars of Peru:
      In the fine Pacific Hislands
      With the dollars of Peru!

Now, messmates, when my watch is up,
  And I am quite broached to,
I'll give a tip to 'Evving
  Of the 'ansome thing to do:

[355]

Let 'em just refit this sailor-man
    And launch him off anew
To cruise among the Hislands
    With the dollars of Peru:
        . In the fine Pacific Hislands
        With the dollars of Peru!

XXII

To Henry James

ADELA, Adela, Adela Chart
What have you done to my elderly heart?
Of all the ladies of paper and ink
I count you the paragon, call you the pink.

The word of your brother depicts you in part:
'You raving maniac!' Adela Chart;
But in all the asylums that cumber the ground,
So delightful a maniac was ne'er to be found.

I pore on you, dote on you, clasp you to heart,
I laud, love, and laugh at you, Adela Chart,
And thank my dear maker the while I admire
That I can be neither your husband nor sire.

Your husband's, your sire's were a difficult part;
You're a byway to suicide, Adela Chart;
But to read of, depicted by exquisite James,
O, sure you're the flower and quintessence of dames.

Eructavit cor meum

My heart was inditing a goodly matter about Adela Chart

Though oft I've been touched by the volatile dart,
To none have I grovelled but Adela Chart,

There are passable ladies, no question, in art—
But where is the marrow of Adela Chart?
I dreamed that to Tyburn I passed in the cart—
I dreamed I was married to Adela Chart:
From the first I awoke with a palpable start,
The second dumbfoundered me, Adela Chart!

XXIII

Athole Brose

WILLIE an' I cam doun by Blair
    And in by Tullibardine,
The kye were at the waterside,
    An' bee-skeps in the garden.
I saw the reek of a private still—
    Says I, 'Gud Lord, I thank ye!'
As Willie and I cam in by Blair
    And out by Killiecrankie.

Ye hinny bees, ye smuggler lads,
    Thou, Muse, the bard's protector,
I never kent what kye were for
    Till I had drunk the nectar!
And shall I never drink it mair?
    Gud troth, I beg your pardon!
The neist time I come doun by Blair
    And in by Tullibardine.

XXIV

THE Gods are dead. Perhaps they are. God knows.
They dwell, at least, in Lemprière undeleted;
And I, lone wandering in a world of prose,
Prefer to think them gracefully retreated
In some still land of lilacs and the rose.

There let them rule some province of repose!
And yet I think I hear the words repeated,
Plangent and sad, on every wind that blows:
    The Gods are dead.

Once high they sat; and high o'er earthly shows,
At their good pleasure all mankind entreated:
Once . . . long ago; but now the story goes
That one and all, the awful, the jocose,
The fair, the brave, the liberal-conceited
    Gods are dead.

POEMS FOR CHILDREN

A CHILD'S GARDEN OF VERSES

TO
ALISON CUNNINGHAM

FROM HER BOY

For the long nights you lay awake
And watched for my unworthy sake:
For your most comfortable hand
That led me through the uneven land:
For all the story-books you read:
For all the pains you comforted:
For all you pitied, all you bore,
In sad and happy days of yore:
My second Mother, my first Wife,
The angel of my infant life—
From the sick child, now well and old,
Take, nurse, the little book you hold!

And grant it, Heaven, that all who read
May find as dear a nurse at need,
And every child who lists my rhyme,
In the bright, fireside, nursery clime,
May hear it in as kind a voice
As made my childish days rejoice!

R. L. S.

I

Bed in Summer

In winter I get up at night
And dress by yellow candle-light.
In summer, quite the other way,
I have to go to bed by day.

I have to go to bed and see
The birds still hopping on the tree,
Or hear the grown-up people's feet
Still going past me in the street.

And does it not seem hard to you,
When all the sky is clear and blue,
And I should like so much to play
To have to go to bed by day?

II

A Thought

It is very nice to think
The world is full of meat and drink,
With little children saying grace
In every Christian kind of place.

III

At the Sea-Side

When I was down beside the sea
A wooden spade they gave to me
    To dig the sandy shore.
My holes were empty like a cup,
In every hole the sea came up,
    Till it could come no more.

[362]

IV

Young Night Thought

ALL night long and every night,
When my mamma puts out the light,
I see the people marching by,
As plain as day, before my eye.

Armies and emperors and kings,
All carrying different kinds of things,
And marching in so grand a way,
You never saw the like by day.

So fine a show was never seen,
At the great circus on the green;
For every kind of beast and man
Is marching in that caravan.

At first they move a little slow,
But still the faster on they go,
And still beside them close I keep
Until we reach the town of Sleep.

V

Whole Duty of Children

A CHILD should always say what's true
And speak when he is spoken to,
And behave mannerly at table:
At least as far as he is able.

VI

Rain

THE rain is raining all around,
    It falls on field and tree,
It rains on the umbrellas here,
    And on the ships at sea.

VII

Pirate Story

THREE of us afloat in the meadow by the swing,
    Three of us aboard in the basket on the lea.
Winds are in the air, they are blowing in the spring,
    And waves are on the meadow like the waves there
        are at sea.

Where shall we adventure, to-day that we're afloat,
    Wary of the weather and steering by a star?
Shall it be to Africa, a-steering of the boat,
    To Providence, or Babylon, or off to Malabar?

Hi! but here's a squadron a-rowing on the sea—
    Cattle on the meadow a-charging with a roar!
Quick, and we'll escape them, they're as mad as they can
        be,
    The wicket is the harbour and the garden is the shore.

VIII

Foreign Lands

Up into the cherry tree
Who should climb but little me?
I held the trunk with both my hands
And looked abroad on foreign lands.

I saw the next door garden lie,
Adorned with flowers, before my eye,
And many pleasant places more
That I had never seen before.

I saw the dimpling river pass
And be the sky's blue looking-glass;
The dusty roads go up and down
With people tramping in to town.

If I could find a higher tree
Farther and farther I should see,
To where the grown-up river slips
Into the sea among the ships,

To where the roads on either hand
Lead onward into fairy land,
Where all the children dine at five,
And all the playthings come alive.

IX

Windy Nights

WHENEVER the moon and stars are set,
  Whenever the wind is high,
All night long in the dark and wet,
  A man goes riding by.
Late in the night when the fires are out,
Why does he gallop and gallop about?

Whenever the trees are crying aloud,
  And ships are tossed at sea,
By, on the highway, low and loud,
  By at the gallop goes he.
By at the gallop he goes, and then
By he comes back at the gallop again.

X

Travel

I SHOULD like to rise and go
Where the golden apples grow;
Where below another sky
Parrot islands anchored lie,
And, watched by cockatoos and goats,
Lonely Crusoes building boats;
Where in sunshine reaching out
Eastern cities, miles about,
Are with mosque and minaret
Among sandy gardens set,
And the rich goods from near and far
Hang for sale in the bazaar;

Where the Great Wall round China goes,
And on one side the desert blows,
And with bell and voice and drum,
Cities on the other hum;
Where are forests, hot as fire,
Wide as England, tall as a spire,
Full of apes and cocoa-nuts
And the negro hunters' huts;
Where the knotty crocodile
Lies and blinks in the Nile,
And the red flamingo flies
Hunting fish before his eyes;
Where in jungles, near and far,
Man-devouring tigers are,
Lying close and giving ear
Lest the hunt be drawing near,
Or a comer-by be seen
Swinging in a palanquin;
Where among the desert sands
Some deserted city stands,
All its children, sweep and prince,
Grown to manhood ages since,
Not a foot in street or house,
Not a stir of child or mouse,
And when kindly falls the night,
In all the town no spark of light.
There I'll come when I'm a man
With a camel caravan;
Light a fire in the gloom
Of some dusty dining-room;
See the pictures on the walls,
Heroes, fights and festivals;
And in a corner find the toys
Of the old Egyptian boys.

XI

Singing

Of speckled eggs the birdie sings
　　And nests among the trees;
The sailor sings of ropes and things
　　In ships upon the seas.

The children sing in far Japan,
　　The children sing in Spain;
The organ with the organ man
　　Is singing in the rain.

XII

Looking Forward

When I am grown to man's estate
I shall be very proud and great.
And tell the other girls and boys
Not to meddle with my toys.

XIII

A Good Play

We built a ship upon the stairs
All made of the back-bedroom chairs,
And filled it full of sofa pillows
To go a-sailing on the billows.

[368]

We took a saw and several nails,
And water in the nursery pails;
And Tom said, 'Let us also take
An apple and a slice of cake';
Which was enough for Tom and me
To go a-sailing on, till tea.

We sailed along for days and days,
And had the very best of plays;
But Tom fell out and hurt his knee,
So there was no one left but me.

XIV

Where Go the Boats?

Dark brown is the river,
    Golden is the sand.
It flows along for ever,
    With trees on either hand.

Green leaves a-floating,
    Castles of the foam,
Boats of mine a-boating—
    Where will all come home?

On goes the river
    And out past the mill,
Away down the valley,
    Away down the hill.

Away down the river,
    A hundred miles or more,
Other little children
    Shall bring my boats ashore.

XV

Auntie's Skirts

WHENEVER Auntie moves around,
Her dresses make a curious sound;
They trail behind her up the floor,
And trundle after through the door.

XVI

The Land of Counterpane

WHEN I was sick and lay a-bed,
I had two pillows at my head,
And all my toys beside me lay
To keep me happy all the day.

And sometimes for an hour or so
I watched my leaden soldiers go,
With different uniforms and drills,
Among the bed-clothes, through the hills;

And sometimes sent my ships in fleets
All up and down among the sheets;
Or brought my trees and houses out,
And planted cities all about.

I was the giant great and still
That sits upon the pillow-hill,
And sees before him, dale and plain,
The pleasant land of counterpane.

XVII

The Land of Nod

From breakfast on through all the day
At home among my friends I stay;
But every night I go abroad
Afar into the Land of Nod.

All by myself I have to go,
With none to tell me what to do—
All alone beside the streams
And up the mountain-sides of dreams.

The strangest things are there for me,
Both things to eat and things to see,
And many frightening sights abroad
Till morning in the Land of Nod.

Try as I like to find the way,
I never can get back by day,
Nor can remember plain and clear
The curious music that I hear.

XVIII

My Shadow

I have a little shadow that goes in and out with me,
And what can be the use of him is more than I can see.
He is very, very like me from the heels up to the head;
And I see him jump before me, when I jump into my bed.

The funniest thing about him is the way he likes to
    grow—
Not at all like proper children, which is always very slow;
For he sometimes shoots up taller like an india-rubber ball,
And he sometimes gets so little that there's none of him
    at all.

He hasn't got a notion of how children ought to play,
And can only make a fool of me in every sort of way.
He stays so close beside me, he's a coward you can see;
I'd think shame to stick to nursie as that shadow sticks
    to me!

One morning, very early, before the sun was up,
I rose and found the shining dew on every buttercup;
But my lazy little shadow, like an arrant sleepy-head,
Had stayed at home behind me and was fast asleep in bed.

XIX

System

EVERY night my prayers I say,
And get my dinner every day;
And every day that I've been good,
I get an orange after food.

The child that is not clean and neat,
With lots of toys and things to eat,
He is a naughty child, I'm sure—
Or else his dear papa is poor.

[372]

XX

A Good Boy

I woke before the morning, I was happy all the day,
I never said an ugly word, but smiled and stuck to play.

And now at last the sun is going down behind the wood,
And I am very happy, for I know that I've been good.

My bed is waiting cool and fresh, with linen smooth and
    fair,
And I must off to sleepsin-by, and not forget my prayer.

I know that, till to-morrow I shall see the sun arise,
No ugly dream shall fright my mind, no ugly sight my
    eyes,

But slumber hold me tightly till I waken in the dawn,
And hear the thrushes singing in the lilacs round the lawn.

XXI

Escape at Bedtime

The lights from the parlour and kitchen shone out
    Through the blinds and the windows and bars;
And high overhead and all moving about,
    There were thousands of millions of stars.

[373]

There ne'er were such thousands of leaves on a tree,
　　Nor of people in church or the Park,
As the crowds of the stars that looked down upon me,
　　And that glittered and winked in the dark.

The Dog, and the Plough, and the Hunter, and all,
　　And the star of the sailor, and Mars,
These shone in the sky, and the pail by the wall
　　Would be half full of water and stars.
They saw me at last, and they chased me with cries,
　　And they soon had me packed into bed;
But the glory kept shining and bright in my eyes,
　　And the stars going round in my head.

XXII

Marching Song

Bring the comb and play upon it!
　　Marching, here we come!
Willie cocks his highland bonnet,
　　Johnnie beats the drum.

Mary Jane commands the party,
　　Peter leads the rear;
Feet in time, alert and hearty,
　　Each a Grenadier!

All in the most martial manner
　　Marching double-quick;
While the napkin like a banner
　　Waves upon the stick!

[374]

Here's enough of fame and pillage,
   Great commander Jane!
Now that we've been round the village,
   Let's go home again.

XXIII

The Cow

THE friendly cow all red and white,
   I love with all my heart:
She gives me cream with all her might,
   To eat with apple-tart.

She wanders lowing here and there,
   And yet she cannot stray,
All in the pleasant open air,
   The pleasant light of day;

And blown by all the winds that pass
   And wet with all the showers,
She walks among the meadow grass
   And eats the meadow flowers.

XXIV

Happy Thought

THE world is so full of a number of things,
I'm sure we should all be as happy as kings.

XXV

The Wind

I saw you toss the kites on high
And blow the birds about the sky;
And all around I heard you pass,
Like ladies' skirts across the grass—
    O wind, a-blowing all day long,
    O wind, that sings so loud a song!

I saw the different things you did,
But always you yourself you hid.
I felt you push, I heard you call,
I could not see yourself at all—
    O wind, a-blowing all day long,
    O wind, that sings so loud a song!

O you that are so strong and cold,
O blower, are you young or old?
Are you a beast of field and tree,
Or just a stronger child than me?
    O wind, a-blowing all day long,
    O wind, that sings so loud a song!

XXVI

Keepsake Mill

Over the borders, a sin without pardon,
   Breaking the branches and crawling below,
Out through the breach in the wall of the garden,
   Down by the banks of the river, we go.

[376]

Here is the mill with the humming of thunder,
  Here is the weir with the wonder of foam,
Here is the sluice with the race running under—
  Marvellous places, though handy to home!

Sounds of the village grow stiller and stiller,
  Stiller the note of the birds on the hill;
Dusty and dim are the eyes of the miller,
  Deaf are his ears with the moil of the mill.

Years may go by, and the wheel in the river
  Wheel as it wheels for us, children, today,
Wheel and keep roaring and foaming for ever
  Long after all of the boys are away.

Home from the Indies and home from the ocean,
  Heroes and soldiers we all shall come home;
Still we shall find the old mill wheel in motion,
  Turning and churning that river to foam.

You with the bean that I gave when we quarrelled,
  I with your marble of Saturday last,
Honoured and old and all gaily apparelled,
  Here we shall meet and remember the past.

XXVII

Good and Bad Children

  CHILDREN, you are very little,
  And your bones are very brittle;
  If you would grow great and stately,
  You must try to walk sedately.

You must still be bright and quiet,
And content with simple diet;
And remain, through all bewild'ring,
Innocent and honest children.

Happy hearts and happy faces,
Happy play in grassy places—
That was how, in ancient ages,
Children grew to kings and sages.

But the unkind and the unruly,
And the sort who eat unduly,
They must never hope for glory—
Theirs is quite a different story!

Cruel children, crying babies,
All grow up as geese and gabies,
Hated, as their age increases,
By their nephews and their nieces.

XXVIII

Foreign Children

LITTLE Indian, Sioux or Crow,
Little frosty Eskimo,
Little Turk or Japanee,
O! don't you wish that you were me?

You have seen the scarlet trees
And the lions over seas;
You have eaten ostrich eggs,
And turned the turtles off their legs.

[378]

Such a life is very fine,
But it's not so nice as mine:
You must often, as you trod,
Have wearied *not* to be abroad.

You have curious things to eat,
I am fed on proper meat;
You must dwell beyond the foam,
But I am safe and live at home.

Little Indian, Sioux or Crow,
Little frosty Eskimo,
Little Turk or Japanee,
O! don't you wish that you were me?

XXIX

The Sun's Travels

The sun is not a-bed, when I
At night upon my pillow lie;
Still round the earth his way he takes,
And morning after morning makes.

While here at home, in shining day,
We round the sunny garden play,
Each little Indian sleepy-head
Is being kissed and put to bed.

And when at eve I rise from tea,
Day dawns beyond the Atlantic Sea,
And all the children in the West
Are getting up and being dressed.

XXX

The Lamplighter

My tea is nearly ready and the sun has left the sky;
It's time to take the window to see Leerie going by;
For every night at teatime and before you take your seat,
With lantern and with ladder he comes posting up the
    street.

Now Tom would be a driver and Maria go to sea,
And my papa's a banker and as rich as he can be;
But I, when I am stronger and can choose what I'm to
    do,
O Leerie, I'll go round at night and light the lamps with
    you!

For we are very lucky, with a lamp before the door,
And Leerie stops to light it as he lights so many more;
And O! before you hurry by with ladder and with light,
O Leerie, see a little child and nod to him to-night!

XXXI

My Bed is a Boat

My bed is like a little boat;
    Nurse helps me in when I embark;
She girds me in my sailor's coat
    And starts me in the dark.

[380]

At night, I go on board and say
   Good-night to all my friends on shore;
I shut my eyes and sail away
   And see and hear no more.

And sometimes things to bed I take,
   As prudent sailors have to do:
Perhaps a slice of wedding-cake,
   Perhaps a toy or two.

All night across the dark we steer:
   But when the day returns at last,
Safe in my room, beside the pier,
   I find my vessel fast.

XXXII

The Moon

THE moon has a face like the clock in the hall;
She shines on thieves on the garden wall,
On streets and fields and harbour quays,
And birdies asleep in the forks of the trees.

The squalling cat and the squeaking mouse,
The howling dog by the door of the house,
The bat that lies in bed at noon,
All love to be out by the light of the moon.

But all of the things that belong to the day
Cuddle to sleep to be out of her way;
And flowers and children close their eyes
Till up in the morning the sun shall arise.

XXXIII

The Swing

How do you like to go up in a swing,
    Up in the air so blue?
Oh, I do think it the pleasantest thing
    Ever a child can do!

Up in the air and over the wall,
    Till I can see so wide,
Rivers and trees and cattle and all
    Over the countryside—

Till I look down on the garden green,
    Down on the roof so brown—
Up in the air I go flying again,
    Up in the air and down!

XXXIV

Time to Rise

A BIRDIE with a yellow bill
Hopped upon the window sill,
Cocked his shining eye and said:
'Ain't you 'shamed, you sleepy-head?'

XXXV

Looking-Glass River

SMOOTH it slides upon its travel,
    Here a wimple, there a gleam—
        O the clean gravel!
        O the smooth stream!

[382]

Sailing blossoms, silver fishes,
   Paven pools as clear as air—
     How a child wishes
     To live down there!

We can see our coloured faces
   Floating on the shaken pool
     Down in cool places,
     Dim and very cool;

Till a wind or water wrinkle,
   Dipping marten, plumping trout,
     Spreads in a twinkle
     And blots all out.

See the rings pursue each other;
   All below grows black as night,
     Just as if mother
     Had blown out the light!

Patience, children, just a minute—
   See the spreading circles die;
     The stream and all in it
     Will clear by-and-by.

XXXVI

Fairy Bread

COME up here, O dusty feet!
   Here is fairy bread to eat.
Here in my retiring room,
   Children, you may dine
On the golden smell of broom
   And the shade of pine;
And when you have eaten well,
Fairy stories hear and tell.

[383]

XXXVII

From a Railway Carriage

FASTER than fairies, faster than witches,
Bridges and houses, hedges and ditches;
And charging along like troops in a battle,
All through the meadows the horses and cattle:
All of the sights of the hill and the plain
Fly as thick as driving rain;
And ever again, in the wink of an eye,
Painted stations whistle by.

Here is a child who clambers and scrambles,
All by himself and gathering brambles;
Here is a tramp who stands and gazes;
And there is the green for stringing the daisies!
Here is a cart run away in the road
Lumping along with man and load;
And here is a mill and there is a river:
Each a glimpse and gone for ever!

XXXVIII

Winter-Time

LATE lies the wintry sun a-bed,
A frosty, fiery sleepy-head;
Blinks but an hour or two; and then,
A blood-red orange, sets again.

Before the stars have left the skies,
At morning in the dark I rise;
And shivering in my nakedness,
By the cold candle, bathe and dress.

[384]

Close by the jolly fire I sit
To warm my frozen bones a bit;
Or with a reindeer-sled, explore
The colder countries round the door.

When to go out, my nurse doth wrap
Me in my comforter and cap:
The cold wind burns my face, and blows
Its frosty pepper up my nose.

Black are my steps on silver sod;
Thick blows my frosty breath abroad;
And tree and house, and hill and lake,
Are frosted like a wedding-cake.

XXXIX

The Hayloft

THROUGH all the pleasant meadow-side
    The grass grew shoulder-high,
Till the shining scythes went far and wide
    And cut it down to dry.

These green and sweetly smelling crops
    They led in waggons home;
And they piled them here in mountain tops
    For mountaineers to roam.

Here is Mount Clear, Mount Rusty-Nail,
    Mount Eagle and Mount High;
The mice that in these mountains dwell,
    No happier are than I!

O what a joy to clamber there,
    O what a place for play,
With the sweet, the dim, the dusty air,
    The happy hills of hay!

XL

Farewell to the Farm

THE coach is at the door at last;
The eager children, mounting fast
And kissing hands, in chorus sing:
Good-bye, good-bye, to everything!

To house and garden, field and lawn,
The meadow-gates we swang upon,
To pump and stable, tree and swing,
Good-bye, good-bye, to everything!

And fare you well for evermore,
O ladder at the hayloft door,
O hayloft where the cobwebs cling,
Good-bye, good-bye, to everything!

Crack goes the whip, and off we go;
The trees and houses smaller grow;
Last, round the woody turn we swing:
Good-bye, good-bye, to everything!

XLI

North-West Passage

I.   GOOD NIGHT

WHEN the bright lamp is carried in,
The sunless hours again begin;
O'er all without, in field and lane,
The haunted night returns again.

Now we behold the embers flee
About the firelit hearth; and see
Our faces painted as we pass,
Like pictures, on the window-glass.

Must we to bed indeed? Well then,
Let us arise and go like men,
And face with an undaunted tread
The long black passage up to bed.

Farewell, O brother, sister, sire!
O pleasant party round the fire!
The songs you sing, the tales you tell,
Till far to-morrow, fare ye well!

II.   SHADOW MARCH

ALL round the house is the jet-black night;
   It stares through the window-pane;
It crawls in the corners, hiding from the light,
   And it moves with the moving flame.

Now my little heart goes a-beating like a drum,
   With the breath of the Bogie in my hair;
And all round the candle the crooked shadows come
   And go marching along up the stair.

[387]

The shadow of the balusters, the shadow of the lamp,
  The shadow of the child that goes to bed—
All the wicked shadows coming, tramp, tramp, tramp,
  With the black night overhead.

III. IN PORT

LAST, to the chamber where I lie
My fearful footsteps patter nigh,
And come from out the cold and gloom
Into my warm and cheerful room.

There, safe arrived, we turn about
To keep the coming shadows out,
And close the happy door at last
On all the perils that we past.

Then, when mamma goes by to bed,
She shall come in with tip-toe tread,
And see me lying warm and fast
And in the Land of Nod at last.

THE CHILD ALONE

I

The Unseen Playmate

WHEN children are playing alone on the green,
In comes the playmate that never was seen.
When children are happy and lonely and good,
The Friend of the Children comes out of the wood.

Nobody heard him and nobody saw,
His is a picture you never could draw,
But he's sure to be present, abroad or at home,
When children are happy and playing alone.

He lies in the laurels, he runs on the grass,
He sings when you tinkle the musical glass;
Whene'er you are happy and cannot tell why,
The Friend of the Children is sure to be by!

He loves to be little, he hates to be big,
'Tis he that inhabits the caves that you dig;
'Tis he when you play with your soldiers of tin
That sides with the Frenchmen and never can win.

'Tis he, when at night you go off to your bed,
Bids you go to your sleep and not trouble your head;
For wherever they're lying, in cupboard or shelf,
'Tis he will take care of your playthings himself!

II

My Ship and I

O it's I that am the captain of a tidy little ship,
    Of a ship that goes a-sailing on the pond;
And my ship it keeps a-turning all around and all about;
But when I'm a little older, I shall find the secret out
    How to send my vessel sailing on beyond.

For I mean to grow as little as the dolly at the helm,
   And the dolly I intend to come alive;
And with him beside to help me, it's a-sailing I shall go,
It's a-sailing on the water, when the jolly breezes blow,
   And the vessel goes a divie-divie-dive.

O it's then you'll see me sailing through the rushes and the
    reeds,
   And you'll hear the water singing at the prow;
For beside the dolly sailor, I'm to voyage and explore,
    To land upon the island where no dolly was before,
   And to fire the penny cannon in the bow.

III

My Kingdom

Down by a shining water well
I found a very little dell,
   No higher than my head.
The heather and the gorse about
In summer bloom were coming out,
   Some yellow and some red.

I called the little pool a sea;
The little hills were big to me;
   For I am very small.
I made a boat, I made a town,
I searched the caverns up and down,
   And named them one and all.

And all about was mine, I said,
The little sparrows overhead,
    The little minnows too.
This was the world and I was king;
For me the bees came by to sing,
    For me the swallows flew.

I played there were no deeper seas,
Nor any wider plains than these,
    Nor other kings than me.
At last I heard my mother call
Out from the house at evenfall,
    To call me home to tea.

And I must rise and leave my dell,
And leave my dimpled water well,
    And leave my heather blooms.
Alas! and as my home I neared,
How very big my nurse appeared,
    How great and cool the rooms!

IV

Picture-Books in Winter

SUMMER fading, winter comes—
Frosty mornings, tingling thumbs,
Window robins, winter rooks,
And the picture story-books.

Water now is turned to stone
Nurse and I can walk upon;
Still we find the flowing brooks
In the picture story-books.

[391]

All the pretty things put by,
Wait upon the children's eye,
Sheep and shepherds, trees and crooks,
In the picture story-books.

We may see how all things are,
Seas and cities, near and far,
And the flying fairies' looks,
In the picture story-books.

How am I to sing your praise,
Happy chimney-corner days,
Sitting safe in nursery nooks,
Reading picture story-books?

V

My Treasures

These nuts, that I keep in the back of the nest
Where all my lead soldiers are lying at rest,
Were gathered in autumn by nursie and me
In a wood with a well by the side of the sea.

This whistle we made (and how clearly it sounds!)
By the side of a field at the end of the grounds,
Of a branch of a plane, with a knife of my own,
It was nursie who made it, and nursie alone!

The stone, with the white and the yellow and grey,
We discovered I cannot tell *how* far away;
And I carried it back although weary and cold,
For though father denies it, I'm sure it is gold.

But of all of my treasures the last is the king,
For there's very few children possess such a thing;
And that is a chisel, both handle and blade,
Which a man who was really a carpenter made.

VI

Block City

WHAT are you able to build with your blocks?
Castles and palaces, temples and docks.
Rain may keep raining, and others go roam,
But I can be happy and building at home.

Let the sofa be mountains, the carpet be sea,
There I'll establish a city for me:
A kirk and a mill and a palace beside,
And a harbour as well where my vessels may ride.

Great is the palace with pillar and wall,
A sort of a tower on the top of it all,
And steps coming down in an orderly way
To where my toy vessels lie safe in the bay.

This one is sailing and that one is moored:
Hark to the song of the sailors on board!
And see on the steps of my palace, the kings
Coming and going with presents and things!

Now I have done with it, down let it go!
All in a moment the town is laid low.
Block upon block lying scattered and free,
What is there left of my town by the sea?

Yet as I saw it, I see it again,
The kirk and the palace, the ships and the men,
And as long as I live and where'er I may be,
I'll always remember my town by the sea.

VII

The Land of Story-Books

At evening, when the lamp is lit,
Around the fire my parents sit;
They sit at home and talk and sing,
And do not play at anything.

Now, with my little gun, I crawl
All in the dark along the wall,
And follow round the forest track
Away behind the sofa back.

There, in the night, where none can spy,
All in my hunter's camp I lie,
And play at books that I have read
Till it is time to go to bed.

These are the hills, these are the woods,
These are my starry solitudes;
And there the river by whose brink
The roaring lions come to drink.

I see the others far away
As if in firelit camp they lay,
And I, like to an Indian scout,
Around their party prowled about.

So, when my nurse comes in for me,
Home I return across the sea,
And go to bed with backward looks
At my dear land of Story-books.

VIII

Armies in the Fire

THE lamps now glitter down the street;
Faintly sound the falling feet;
And the blue even slowly falls
About the garden trees and walls.

Now in the falling of the gloom
The red fire paints the empty room:
And warmly on the roof it looks,
And flickers on the backs of books.

Armies march by tower and spire
Of cities blazing, in the fire;
Till as I gaze with staring eyes,
The armies fade, the lustre dies.

Then once again the glow returns;
Again the phantom city burns;
And down the red-hot valley, lo!
The phantom armies marching go!

Blinking embers, tell me true
Where are those armies marching to,
And what the burning city is
That crumbles in your furnaces!

IX

The Little Land

WHEN at home alone I sit
And am very tired of it,
I have just to shut my eyes
To go sailing through the skies—
To go sailing far away
To the pleasant Land of Play;
To the fairy land afar
Where the Little People are;
Where the clover-tops are trees,
And the rain-pools are the seas,
And the leaves like little ships
Sail about on tiny trips;
And above the daisy tree
    Through the grasses,
High o'erhead the Bumble Bee
    Hums and passes.

In that forest to and fro
I can wander, I can go;
See the spider and the fly,
And the ants go marching by
Carrying parcels with their feet
Down the green and grassy street.
I can in the sorrel sit
Where the ladybird alit.
I can climb the jointed grass;
    And on high
See the greater swallows pass
    In the sky,
And the round sun rolling by
Heeding no such things as I.

Through that forest I can pass
Till, as in a looking-glass,
Humming fly and daisy tree
And my tiny self I see,
Painted very clear and neat
On the rain-pool at my feet.
Should a leaflet come to land
Drifting near to where I stand,
Straight I'll board that tiny boat
Round the rain-pool sea to float.

Little thoughtful creatures sit
On the grassy coasts of it;
Little things with lovely eyes
See me sailing with surprise.
Some are clad in armour green—
(These have sure to battle been!)—
Some are pied with ev'ry hue,
Black and crimson, gold and blue;
Some have wings and swift are gone;
But they all look kindly on.

When my eyes I once again
Open, and see all things plain:
High bare walls, great bare floor;
Great big knobs on drawer and door;
Great big people perched on chairs,
Stitching tucks and mending tears,
Each a hill that I could climb,
And talking nonsense all the time—
    O dear me,
     That I could be
A sailor on the rain-pool sea,
A climber in the clover tree,
And just come back, a sleepy head.
Late at night to go to bed.

GARDEN DAYS
I
Night and Day

WHEN the golden day is done,
 Through the closing portal,
Child and garden, flower and sun,
 Vanish all things mortal.

As the blinding shadows fall,
 As the rays diminish,
Under evening's cloak, they all
 Roll away and vanish.

Garden darkened, daisy shut,
 Child in bed, they slumber—
Glow-worm in the highway rut,
 Mice among the lumber.

In the darkness houses shine,
 Parents move with candles;
Till on all, the night divine
 Turns the bedroom handles.

Till at last the day begins
 In the east a-breaking,
In the hedges and the whins
 Sleeping birds a-waking.

In the darkness shapes of things,
 Houses, trees, and hedges,
Clearer grow; and sparrow's wings
 Beat on window ledges.

[398]

These shall wake the yawning maid;
  She the door shall open—
Finding dew on garden glade
  And the morning broken.

There my garden grows again
  Green and rosy painted,
As at eve behind the pane
  From my eyes it fainted.

Just as it was shut away,
  Toy-like, in the even,
Here I see it glow with day
  Under glowing heaven.

Every path and every plot,
  Every bush of roses,
Every blue forget-me-not
  Where the dew reposes,

'Up!' they cry, 'the day is come
  On the smiling valleys:
We have beat the morning drum;
  Playmate, join your allies!'

II

Nest Eggs

BIRDS all the sunny day
  Flutter and quarrel
Here in the arbour-like
  Tent of the laurel.

[399]

Here in the fork
  The brown nest is seated;
Four little blue eggs
  The mother keeps heated.

While we stand watching her,
  Staring like gabies,
Safe in each egg are the
  Bird's little babies.

Soon the frail eggs they shall
  Chip, and upspringing
Make all the April woods
  Merry with singing.

Younger than we are,
  O children, and frailer,
Soon in blue air they'll be.
  Singer and sailor.

We, so much older,
  Taller and stronger,
We shall look down on the
  Birdies no longer.

They shall go flying
  With musical speeches
High overhead in the
  Tops of the beeches.

In spite of our wisdom
  And sensible talking,
We on our feet must go
  Plodding and walking.

III

The Flowers

ALL the names I know from nurse:
Gardener's garters, Shepherd's purse,
Bachelor's buttons, Lady's smock,
And the Lady Hollyhock.

Fairy places, fairy things,
Fairy woods where the wild bee wings,
Tiny trees for tiny dames—
These must all be fairy names!

Tiny woods below whose boughs
Shady fairies weave a house;
Tiny tree tops, rose or thyme,
Where the braver fairies climb!

Fair are grown-up people's trees,
But the fairest woods are these;
Where if I were not so tall,
I should live for good and all.

IV

Summer Sun

GREAT is the sun, and wide he goes
Through empty heaven without repose;
And in the blue and glowing days
More thick than rain he showers his rays.

Though closer still the blinds we pull
To keep the shady parlour cool,
Yet he will find a chink or two
To slip his golden fingers through.

The dusty attic spider-clad
He, through the keyhole, maketh glad;
And through the broken edge of tiles,
Into the laddered hayloft smiles.

Meantime his golden face around
He bares to all the garden ground,
And sheds a warm and glittering look
Among the ivy's inmost nook.

Above the hills, along the blue,
Round the bright air with footing true,
To please the child, to paint the rose,
The gardener of the World, he goes.

V

The Dumb Soldier

WHEN the grass was closely mown,
Walking on the lawn alone,
In the turf a hole I found
And hid a soldier underground.

Spring and daisies came apace;
Grasses hide my hiding place;
Grasses run like a green sea
O'er the lawn up to my knee.

[402]

GARDEN DAYS

Under grass alone he lies,
Looking up with leaden eyes,
Scarlet coat and pointed gun,
To the stars and to the sun.

When the grass is ripe like grain,
When the scythe is stoned again,
When the lawn is shaven clear,
Then my hole shall reappear.

I shall find him, never fear,
I shall find my grenadier;
But for all that's gone and come,
I shall find my soldier dumb.

He has lived, a little thing,
In the grassy woods of spring;
Done, if he could tell me true,
Just as I should like to do.

He has seen the starry hours
And the springing of the flowers;
And the fairy things that pass
In the forests of the grass.

In the silence he has heard
Talking bee and ladybird,
And the butterfly has flown
O'er him as he lay alone.

Not a word will he disclose,
Not a word of all he knows.
I must lay him on the shelf,
And make up the tale myself.

VI

Autumn Fires

In the other gardens
    And all up the vale,
From the autumn bonfires
    See the smoke trail!

Pleasant summer over
    And all the summer flowers,
The red fire blazes,
    The grey smoke towers.

Sing a song of seasons!
    Something bright in all!
Flowers in the summer,
    Fires in the fall!

VII

The Gardener

The gardener does not love to talk,
He makes me keep the gravel walk;
And when he puts his tools away,
He locks the door and takes the key.

Away behind the currant row
Where no one else but cook may go,
Far in the plots, I see him dig
Old and serious, brown and big.

He digs the flowers, green, red and blue,
Nor wishes to be spoken to.
He digs the flowers and cuts the hay,
And never seems to want to play.

Silly gardener! summer goes,
And winter comes with pinching toes,
When in the garden bare and brown
You must lay your barrow down.

Well now, and while the summer stays
To profit by these garden days
O how much wiser you would be
To play at Indian wars with me!

VIII

Historical Associations

DEAR Uncle Jim, this garden ground
That now you smoke your pipe around,
Has seen immortal actions done
And valiant battles lost and won.

Here we had best on tip-toe tread,
While I for safety march ahead,
For this is that enchanted ground
Where all who loiter slumber sound.

Here is the sea, here is the sand,
Here is simple Shepherd's Land,
Here are the fairy hollyhocks,
And there are Ali Baba's rocks.

But yonder, see! apart and high,
Frozen Siberia lies; where I,
With Robert Bruce and William Tell,
Was bound by an enchanter's spell.

There, then, awhile in chains we lay,
In wintry dungeons, far from day;
But ris'n at length, with might and main,
Our iron fetters burst in twain.

Then all the horns were blown in town;
And to the ramparts clanging down,
All the giants leaped to horse
And charged behind us through the gorse.

On we rode, the others and I,
Over the mountains blue, and by
The Silver River, the sounding sea
And the robber woods of Tartary.

A thousand miles we galloped fast,
And down the witches' lane we passed,
And rode amain, with brandished sword,
Up to the middle, through the ford.

Last we drew rein—a weary three—
Upon the lawn, in time for tea,
And from our steeds alighted down
Before the gates of Babylon.

ENVOYS

I

To Willie and Henrietta

If two may read aright
These rhymes of old delight
And house and garden play,
You two, my cousins, and you only, may.

You in a garden green
With me were king and queen,
Were hunter, soldier, tar,
And all the thousand things that children are.

Now in the elders' seat
We rest with quiet feet,
And from the window-bay
We watch the children, our successors, play.

'Time was,' the golden head
Irrevocably said;
But time which none can bind,
While flowing fast away, leaves love behind.

II

To My Mother

You too, my mother, read my rhymes
For love of unforgotten times,
And you may chance to hear once more
The little feet along the floor.

[407]

III

To Auntie

Chief of our aunts—not only I,
But all your dozen of nurslings cry—
What did the other children do ?
And what were childhood, wanting you?

IV

To Minnie

THE red room with the giant bed
Where none but elders laid their head;
The little room where you and I
Did for awhile together lie
And, simple suitor, I your hand
In decent marriage did demand;
The great day nursery, best of all,
With pictures pasted on the wall
And leaves upon the blind—
A pleasant room wherein to wake
And hear the leafy garden shake
And rustle in the wind—
And pleasant there to lie in bed
And see the pictures overhead—
The wars about Sebastopol,
The grinning guns along the wall,
The daring escalade,
The plunging ships, the bleating sheep,
The happy children ankle-deep
And laughing as they wade:
All these are vanished clean away,
And the old manse is changed today;

[408]

It wears an altered face
And shields a stranger race.

The river, on from mill to mill,
Flows past our childhood's garden still;
But ah! we children never more
Shall watch it from the water-door!
Below the yew—it still is there—
Our phantom voices haunt the air
As we were still at play,
And I can hear them call and say:
'*How far is it to Babylon?*'

Ah, far enough, my dear,
Far, far enough from here—
Yet you have farther gone!
'*Can I get there by candlelight?*'
So goes the old refrain.
I do not know—perchance you might—
But only, children, hear it right,
Ah, never to return again!
The eternal dawn, beyond a doubt,
Shall break on hill and plain,
And put all stars and candles out,
Ere we be young again.

To you in distant India, these
I send across the seas,
Nor count it far across.
For which of us forgets
The Indian cabinets,
The bones of antelope, the wings of albatross,
The pied and painted birds and beans,
The junks and bangles, beads and screens,
The gods and sacred bells,
And the loud-humming, twisted shells?

[409]

The level of the parlour floor
Was honest, homely, Scottish shore;
But when we climbed upon a chair,
Behold the gorgeous East was there!
Be this a fable; and behold
Me in the parlour as of old,
And Minnie just above me set
In the quaint Indian cabinet!
Smiling and kind, you grace a shelf
Too high for me to reach myself.
Reach down a hand, my dear, and take
These rhymes for old acquaintance' sake.

V

To My Name-Child

I

SOME day soon this rhyming volume, if you learn with
        proper speed,
Little Louis Sanchez, will be given you to read.
Then shall you discover that your name was printed down
By the English printers, long before, in London town.

In the great and busy city where the East and West are
        met,
All the little letters did the English printer set;
While you thought of nothing, and were still too young
        to play,
Foreign people thought of you in places far away.

Ay, and while you slept, a baby, over all the English
        lands
Other little children took the volume in their hands;
Other children questioned, in their homes across the seas:
Who was little Louis, won't you tell us, mother, please?

II

Now that you have spelt your lesson, lay it down and go
    and play,
Seeking shells and seaweed on the sands of Monterey,
Watching all the mighty whalebones, lying buried by the
    breeze,
Tiny sandy-pipers, and the huge Pacific seas.

And remember in your playing, as the sea-fog rolls to
    you,
Long ere you could read it, how I told you what to do;
And that while you thought of no one, nearly half the
    world away
Some one thought of Louis on the beach of Monterey!

VI

To Any Reader

As from the house your mother sees
You playing round the garden trees,
So you may see, if you will look
Through the windows of this book,
Another child, far, far away,
And in another garden, play.
But do not think you can at all,
By knocking on the window, call
That child to hear you.   He intent
Is all on his play-business bent.
He does not hear; he will not look,
Nor yet be lured out of this book.
For, long ago, the truth to say,
He has grown up and gone away,
And it is but a child of air
That lingers in the garden there.

NOT I

AND OTHER POEMS

I

Not I

Some like drink
In a pint pot,
Some like to think;
     Some not.

Strong Dutch Cheese,
Old Kentucky Rye,
Some like these;
     Not I.

Some like Poe
And others like Scott,
Some like Mrs Stowe;
     Some not.

Some like to laugh,
Some like to cry.
Some like chaff;
     Not I.

II

HERE, perfect to a wish,
We offer, not a dish,
    But just the platter:
A book that's not a book,
A pamphlet in the look
    But not the matter.

I own in disarray;
As to the flowers of May
    The frosts of Winter,
To my poetic rage,
The smallness of the page
    And of the printer.

III

As seamen on the seas
With song and dance descry
Adown the morning breeze
An islet in the sky:
In Araby the dry,
As o'er the sandy plain
The panting camels cry
To smell the coming rain.

So all things over earth
A common law obey
And rarity and worth
Pass, arm in arm, away;
And even so, today,
The printer and the bard,
In pressless Davos, pray
Their sixpenny reward.

IV

THE pamphlet here presented
Was planned and printed by
A printer unindented,
A bard whom all decry.

The author and the printer,
With various kinds of skill,
Concocted it in Winter
At Davos on the Hill.

They burned the nightly taper
But now the work is ripe
Observe the costly paper,
Remark the perfect type!

MORAL EMBLEMS I

I

SEE how the children in the print
Bound on the book to see what's in 't!
O, like these pretty babes, may you
Seize and *apply* this volume too!
And while your eye upon the cuts
With harmless ardour opes and shuts,
Reader, may your immortal mind
To their sage lessons not be blind.

II

READER, your soul upraise to see,
In yon fair cut designed by me,
The pauper by the highwayside
Vainly soliciting from pride.
Mark how the Beau with easy air
Contemns the anxious rustic's prayer,
And casting a disdainful eye,
Goes gaily gallivanting by.
He from the poor averts his head . . .
He will regret it when he's dead.

III

A Peak in Darien

Broad-gazing on untrodden lands,
See where adventurous Cortez stands;
While in the heavens above his head,
The Eagle seeks its daily bread.
How aptly fact to fact replies:
Heroes and Eagles, hills and skies.
Ye, who contemn the fatted slave,
Look on this emblem and be brave.

IV

See in the print, how moved by whim
Trumpeting Jumbo, great and grim,
Adjusts his trunk, like a cravat,
To noose that individual's hat.
The sacred Ibis in the distance
Joys to observe his bold resistance.

V

MARK, printed on the opposing page,
The unfortunate effects of rage.
A man (who might be you or me)
Hurls another into the sea.
Poor soul, his unreflecting act
His future joys will much contract;
And he will spoil his evening toddy
By dwelling on that mangled body.

MORAL EMBLEMS II

I

WITH storms a-weather, rocks a-lee,
The dancing skiff puts forth to sea.
The lone dissenter in the blast
Recoils before the sight aghast.
But she, although the heavens be black,
Holds on upon the starboard tack.
For why? although today she sink
Still safe she sails in printers' ink,
And though today the seamen drown,
My cut shall hand their memory down.

II

THE careful angler chose his nook
At morning by the lilied brook,
And all the noon his rod he plied
By that romantic riverside.
Soon as the evening hours decline
Tranquilly he'll return to dine,
And breathing forth a pious wish,
Will cram his belly full of fish.

III

THE Abbot for a walk went out
A wealthy cleric, very stout,
And Robin has that Abbot stuck
As the red hunter spears the buck.
The djavel or the javelin
Has, you observe, gone bravely in,
And you may hear that weapon whack
Bang through the middle of his back.
*Hence we may learn that abbots should
Never go walking in a wood.*

IV

THE frozen peaks he once explored,
But now he's dead and by the board.
How better far at home to have stayed
Attended by the parlour maid,
And warmed his knees before the fire
Until the hour when folks retire!
So, if you would be spared to friends,
Do nothing but for business ends.

V

INDUSTRIOUS pirate! see him sweep
The lonely bosom of the deep,
And daily the horizon scan
From Hatteras or Matapan.
Be sure, before that pirate's old,
He will have made a pot of gold,
And will retire from all his labours
And be respected by his neighbours.
You also scan your life's horizon
For all that you can clap your eyes on.

A MARTIAL ELEGY

FOR SOME LEAD SOLDIERS

For certain soldiers lately dead
Our reverent dirge shall here be said.
Them, when their martial leader called,
No dread preparative appalled;
But leaden-hearted, leaden-heeled,
I marked them steadfast in the field.
Death grimly sided with the foe,
And smote each leaden hero low.
Proudly they perished one by one:
The dread Pea-cannon's work was done!
O not for them the tears we shed,
Consigned to their congenial lead;
But while unmoved their sleep they take,
We mourn for their dear Captain's sake,
For their dear Captain, who shall smart
Both in his pocket and his heart,
Who saw his heroes shed their gore
And lacked a shilling to buy more!

THE GRAVER AND THE PEN:

OR, SCENES FROM NATURE
WITH APPROPRIATE VERSES

Proem

UNLIKE the common run of men,
   I wield a double power to please,
And use the GRAVER and the PEN
   With equal aptitude and ease.

I move with that illustrious crew,
   The ambidextrous Kings of Art;
And every mortal thing I do
   Brings ringing money in the mart.

Hence, in the morning hour, the mead,
   The forest and the stream perceive
Me wandering as the muses lead—
   Or back returning in the eve.

Two muses like two maiden aunts,
   The engraving and the singing muse,
Follow, through all my favourite haunts,
   My devious traces in the dews.

To guide and cheer me, each attends;
   Each speeds my rapid task along;
One to my cuts her ardour lends,
   One breathes her magic in my song.

The Precarious Mill

ALONE above the stream it stands,
  Above the iron hill,
The topsy-turvy, tumble-down,
  Yet habitable mill.

Still as the ringing saws advance
  To slice the humming deal,
All day the pallid miller hears
  The thunder of the wheel.

He hears the river plunge and roar
  As roars the angry mob,
He feels the solid building quake,
  The trusty timbers throb.

All night beside the fire he cowers:
  He hears the rafters jar:
O why is he not in a proper house
  As decent people are!

The floors are all aslant, he sees,
  The doors are all a-jam;
And from the hook above his head
  All crooked swings the ham.

'Alas,' he cries and shakes his head,
  'I see by every sign,
There soon will be the deuce to pay,
  With this estate of mine.'

The Disputatious Pines

The first pine to the second said
'My leaves are black, my branches red;
I stand upon this moor of mine,
A hoar, unconquerable pine.'

The second sniffed and answered: 'Pooh,
I am as good a pine as you.'

'Discourteous tree,' the first replied,
'The tempest in my boughs had cried,
The hunter slumbered in my shade,
A hundred years ere you were made.'

The second smiled as he returned:
'I shall be here when you are burned.'

So far dissension ruled the pair,
Each turned on each a frowning air,
When flickering from the bank anigh,
A flight of martins met their eye.
Sometime their course they watched; and then
They nodded off to sleep again.

The Tramps

Now long enough has day endured,
Or King Apollo Palinured,
Seaward he steers his panting team,
And casts on earth his latest gleam.

But see! the Tramps with jaded eye
Their destined provinces espy.
Long through the hills their way they took,
Long camped beside the mountain brook ;
'Tis over; now with rising hope
They pause upon the downward slope.
And as their aching bones they rest,
Their anxious captain scans the west.

So paused Alaric on the Alps
And ciphered up the Roman scalps.

The Foolhardy Geographer

THE howling desert miles around,
The tinkling brook the only sound—
Wearied with all his toils and feats,
The traveller dines on potted meats;
On potted meats and princely wines,
Not wisely but too well he dines.

The brindled Tiger loud may roar,
High may the hovering Vulture soar,
Alas! regardless of them all,
Soon shall the empurpled glutton sprawl—

[432]

Soon, in the desert's hushed repose,
Shall trumpet tidings through his nose!
Alack, unwise! that nasal song
Shall be the Ounce's dinner-gong!

A blemish in the cut appears;
Alas! it cost both blood and tears.
The glancing graver swerved aside,
Fast flowed the artist's vital tide!
And now the apologetic bard
Demands indulgence for his pard!

The Angler & the Clown

THE echoing bridge you here may see,
The pouring lynn, the waving tree,
The eager angler fresh from town—
Above, the contumelious clown.
The angler plies his line and rod,
The clodpole stands with many a nod—
With many a nod and many a grin,
He sees him cast his engine in.

'What have you caught?' the peasant cries.

'Nothing as yet,' the Fool replies.

[435]

MORAL TALES

I

Robin and Ben : or, the Pirate and the Apothecary

Come lend me an attentive ear
A startling moral tale to hear,
Of Pirate Rob and Chemist Ben,
And different destinies of men.

Deep in the greenest of the vales
That nestle near the coast of Wales,
The heaving main but just in view,
Robin and Ben together grew,
Together worked and played the fool,
Together shunned the Sunday school,
And pulled each other's youthful noses
Around the cots, among the roses.

Together but unlike they grew;
Robin was rough, and through and through,
Bold, inconsiderate, and manly,
Like some historic Bruce or Stanley.
Ben had a mean and servile soul,
He robbed not, though he often stole.
He sang on Sunday in the choir,
And tamely capped the passing Squire.

At length, intolerant of trammels—
Wild as the wild Bithynian camels,
Wild as the wild sea-eagles—Bob
His widowed dam contrives to rob,

[436]

And thus with great originality
Effectuates his personality.
Thenceforth his terror-haunted flight
He follows through the starry night;
And with the early morning breeze,
Behold him on the azure seas.
The master of a trading dandy
Hires Robin for a go of brandy;
And all the happy hills of home
Vanish beyond the fields of foam.

Ben, meanwhile, like a tin reflector,
Attended on the worthy rector;
Opened his eyes and held his breath,
And flattered to the point of death;
And was at last, by that good fairy,
Apprenticed to the Apothecary.

So Ben, while Robin chose to roam,
A rising chemist was at home,

Tended his shop with learnèd air,
Watered his drugs and oiled his hair,
And gave advice to the unwary,
Like any sleek apothecary.

Meanwhile upon the deep afar
Robin the brave was waging war,
With other tarry desperadoes
About the latitude of Barbadoes.
He knew no touch of craven fear;
His voice was thunder in the cheer;
First, from the main-to'-gallan' high,
The skulking merchantman to spy—
The first to bound upon the deck,
The last to leave the sinking wreck.
His hand was steel, his word was law,
His mates regarded him with awe.
No pirate in the whole profession
Held a more honourable position.

At length, from years of anxious toil,
Bold Robin seeks his native soil;
Wisely arranges his affairs,
And to his native dale repairs.
The Bristol *Swallow* sets him down
Beside the well-remembered town.
He sighs, he spits, he marks the scene,
Proudly he treads the village green;
And free from pettiness and rancour,
Takes lodgings at the 'Crown and Anchor.'

Strange, when a man so great and good,
Once more in his home-country stood,
Strange that the sordid clowns should show
A dull desire to have him go.

[438]

His clinging breeks, his tarry hat,
The way he swore, the way he spat,
A certain quality of manner,
Alarming like the pirate's banner—
Something that did not seem to suit all—
Something, O call it bluff, not brutal—
Something at least, howe'er it's called,
Made Robin generally black-balled.

His soul was wounded; proud and glum,
Alone he sat and swigged his rum,
And took a great distaste to men
Till he encountered Chemist Ben.
Bright was the hour and bright the day,
That threw them in each other's way;
Glad were their mutual salutations,
Long their respective revelations.
Before the inn in sultry weather
They talked of this and that together;

[439]

Ben told the tale of his indentures,
And Rob narrated his adventures.
Last, as the point of greatest weight,
The pair contrasted their estate,
And Robin, like a boastful sailor,
Despised the other for a tailor.

'See,' he remarked, 'with envy, see
A man with such a fist as me!
Bearded and ringed, and big, and brown,
I sit and toss the stingo down.
Hear the gold jingle in my bag—
All won beneath the Jolly Flag!'

Ben moralised and shook his head:
'You wanderers earn and eat your bread.
The foe is found, beats or is beaten,
And either how, the wage is eaten.
And after all your pully-hauly
Your proceeds look uncommon small-ly.
You had done better here to tarry
Apprentice to the Apothecary.
The silent pirates of the shore
Eat and sleep soft, and pocket more
Than any red, robustious ranger
Who picks his farthings hot from danger.
You clank your guineas on the board;
Mine are with several bankers stored.
You reckon riches on your digits,
You dash in chase of Sals and Bridgets,
You drink and risk delirium tremens,
Your whole estate a common seaman's!
Regard your friend and school companion,
Soon to be wed to Miss Trevanion
(Smooth, honourable, fat and flowery,

[440]

With Heaven knows how much land in dowry).
Look at me—am I in good case?
Look at my hands, look at my face;
Look at the cloth of my apparel;
Try me and test me, lock and barrel;
And own, to give the devil his due,
I have made more of life than you.
Yet I nor sought nor risked a life;
I shudder at an open knife;
The perilous seas I still avoided
And stuck to land whate'er betided.
I had no gold, no marble quarry,
I was a poor apothecary,
Yet here I stand, at thirty-eight,
A man of an assured estate.'

'Well,' answered Robin—'well, and how?'

The smiling chemist tapped his brow.
'Rob,' he replied, 'this throbbing brain
Still worked and hankered after gain.
By day and night, to work my will,
It pounded like a powder mill;
And marking how the world went round
A theory of theft it found.
Here is the key to right and wrong:
Steal little, but steal all day long;
And this invaluable plan
Marks what is called the Honest Man.
When first I served with Doctor Pill,
My hand was ever in the till.
Now that I am myself a master
My gains come softer still and faster.
As thus: on Wednesday, a maid

[441]

Came to me in the way of trade.
Her mother, an old farmer's wife,
Required a drug to save her life.
'At once, my dear, at once,' I said,
Patted the child upon the head,
Bade her be still a loving daughter,
And filled the bottle up with water.'

'Well, and the mother?' Robin cried.

'O she!' said Ben, 'I think she died.'

'Battle and blood, death and disease,
Upon the tainted Tropic seas—
The attendant sharks that chew the cud—
The abhorred scuppers spouting blood—
The untended dead, the Tropic sun—
The thunder of the murderous gun—
The cut-throat crew—the Captain's curse—
The tempest blustering worse and worse—

[442]

These have I known and these can stand,
But you, I settle out of hand!'

Out flashed the cutlass, down went Ben
Dead and rotten, there and then.

II

The Builder's Doom

In eighteen-twenty Deacon Thin
Feu'd the land and fenced it in,
And laid his broad foundations down
About a furlong out of town.

Early and late the work went on.
The carts were toiling ere the dawn;
The mason whistled, the hodman sang;
Early and late the trowels rang;
And Thin himself came day by day
To push the work in every way.
An artful builder, patent king
Of all the local building ring,
Who was there like him in the quarter
For mortifying brick and mortar,
Or pocketing the odd piastre
By substituting lath and plaster?
With plan and two-foot rule in hand,
He by the foreman took his stand,
With boisterous voice, with eagle glance
To stamp upon extravagance.

For thrift of bricks and greed of guilders,
He was the Buonaparte of Builders.
The foreman, a desponding creature,
Demurred to here and there a feature:
'For surely, sir—with your permeesion—
Bricks here, sir, in the main parteetion. . . .'
The builder goggled, gulped and stared,
The foreman's services were spared.
Thin would not count among his minions
A man of Wesleyan opinions.

'Money is money,' so he said.
'Crescents are crescents, trade is trade.
Pharaohs and emperors in their seasons
Built, I believe, for different reasons—
Charity, glory, piety, pride—
To pay the men, to please a bride,
To use their stone, to spite their neighbours,
Not for a profit on their labours.
They built to edify or bewilder;
I build because I am a builder.
Crescent and street and square I build,
Plaster and paint and carve and gild.
Around the city see them stand,
These triumphs of my shaping hand,
With bulging walls, with sinking floors,
With shut, impracticable doors,
Fickle and frail in every part,
And rotten to their inmost heart.
There shall the simple tenant find
Death in the falling window-blind,
Death in the pipe, death in the faucet,
Death in the deadly water-closet!
A day is set for all to die:
Caveat emptor! what care I ?'

[444]

As to Amphion's tuneful kit
Thebes rose, with towers encircling it;
As to the Mage's brandished wand
A spiry palace clove the sand;
To Thin's indomitable financing,
That phantom crescent kept advancing.
When first the brazen bells of churches
Called clerk and parson to their perches,
The worshippers of every sect
Already viewed it with respect;
A second Sunday had not gone
Before the roof was rattled on:
And when the fourth was there, behold
The crescent finished, painted, sold!

The stars proceeded in their courses,
Nature with her subversive forces,
Time, too, the iron-toothed and sinewed,
And the edacious years continued.
Thrones rose and fell; and still the crescent,
Unsanative and now senescent,
A plastered skeleton of lath,
Looked forward to a day of wrath.
In the dead night, the groaning timber
Would jar upon the ear of slumber,
And, like Dodona's talking oak,
Of oracles and judgments spoke.
When to the music fingered well
The feet of children lightly fell,
The sire, who dozed by the decanters,
Started, and dreamed of misadventures.
The rotten brick decayed to dust;
The iron was consumed by rust;
Each tabid and perverted mansion
Hung in the article of declension.

So forty, fifty, sixty passed;
Until, when seventy came at last,
The occupant of number three
Called friends to hold a jubilee.
Wild was the night; the charging rack
Had forced the moon upon her back;
The wind piped up a naval ditty;
And the lamps winked through all the city.
Before that house, where lights were
      shining,
Corpulent feeders, grossly dining,
And jolly clamour, hum and rattle,
Fairly outvoiced the tempest's battle.
As still his moistened lip he fingered,
The envious policeman lingered;
While far the infernal tempest sped,
And shook the country folks in bed,
And tore the trees and tossed the ships,
He lingered and he licked his lips.
Lo, from within, a hush! the host
Briefly expressed the evening's toast;
And lo, before the lips were dry,
The Deacon rising to reply!
'Here in this house which once I built,
Papered and painted, carved and gilt,
And out of which, to my content,
I netted seventy-five per cent.;
Here at this board of jolly neighbours,
I reap the credit of my labours.
These were the days—I will say more—
These were the grand old days of yore!
The builder laboured day and night;
He watched that every brick was right:
The decent men their utmost did;
And the house rose—a pyramid!

[446]

These were the days, our provost knows,
When forty streets and crescents rose,
The fruits of my creative noddle,
All more or less upon a model,
Neat and commodious, cheap and dry,
A perfect pleasure to the eye!
I found this quite a country quarter;
I leave it solid lath and mortar.
In all, I was the single actor—
And am this city's benefactor!
Since then, alas! both thing and name,
Shoddy across the ocean came—
Shoddy that can the eye bewilder
And makes me blush to meet a builder!
Had this good house, in frame or fixture,
Been tempered by the least admixture
Of that discreditable shoddy,
Should we today compound our toddy,
Or gaily marry song and laughter
Below its sempiternal rafter?
Not so!' the Deacon cried.

            The mansion
Had marked his fatuous expansion.
The years were full, the house was fated,
The rotten structure crepitated!

A moment, and the silent guests
Sat pallid as their dinner vests.
A moment more, and root and branch,
That mansion fell in avalanche,
Story on story, floor on floor,
Roof, wall and window, joist and door,

Dead weight of damnable disaster,
A cataclysm of lath and plaster.

Siloam did not choose a sinner—
All were not builders at the dinner.

III

Lord Nelson and the Tar

'FAIR is the sea', Lord Nelson said,
'And fair yon vessel shears ahead.
But yet from all that I can learn
Tis best to leave the sea astern.
If you and I, sea-faring Robin,
Were with yon harbour-buoy a bobbin;
The thing is beyond reach of question,
All would be up with our digestion,
And I, your Admiral of the Blue,
Should have to strike my flag and spew.'
Thus spake Old England's naval glory,
And the old salt confirmed his story.

Hence we may learn that all is vanity
Sea, shore and sky, and poor humanity.

NOTES

The purpose of these Notes is not to explain every allusion in the poems, but to put them, where necessary, in their context: by supplying the circumstances in which they were written, describing the persons to whom they were addressed or the occasions which inspired them, and giving cross-references to Stevenson's other writings—especially the *Letters*. For the poems not published in Stevenson's lifetime, or prepared by him for the press, I have given the details of first publication. The manuscripts are fair copies in ink, and the dates are Stevenson's own, unless otherwise stated. The following abbreviations have been used in these notes:

Edinburgh: *The Works of Robert Louis Stevenson*, Edinburgh Edition, Vol. XIV (*A Child's Garden, Underwoods, Ballads, Songs of Travel*), 1895, and Vol. XXVIII (*Miscellanea, Moral Emblems, &c.*), 1898.

R. L. S. Teuila: *R. L. S. Teuila*, privately printed, 1899. 'Being fugitive verses and lines by Robert Louis Stevenson now first collected' by Isobel Strong.

Thistle: *Works of Robert Louis Stevenson*, Thistle Edition, New York, 1895, Vol. XVI (*A Child's Garden of Verses, Underwoods*—including *Songs of Travel* as *Underwoods III, Ballads*).

Pentland: *Works of Robert Louis Stevenson*, Pentland Edition, with Bibliographical Notes by Edmund Gosse, Vol. XIII (*Poetical Works*), 1907.

Gosse: *Biographical Notes on the Writings of Robert Louis Stevenson*, privately printed, 1908. A collection of the biographical and bibliographical notes to the Pentland Edition.

B.B.S. I and II: *Poems by Robert Louis Stevenson: Hitherto Unpublished.* With Introduction and Notes by George S. Hellman. The Bibliophile Society, Boston, 1916. 2 vols. Printed for members only.

New Poems: New Poems and Variant Readings by Robert Louis Stevenson. London, 1918. Containing substantially the same poems as the above.

B.B.S. III: Poems by Robert Louis Stevenson: Hitherto Unpublished. With Introduction and Notes by George S. Hellman and William P. Trent. The Bibliophile Society, Boston, 1921. Printed for members only.

Stevenson's Workshop: Stevenson's Workshop with 29 ms. facsimiles. Edited by William P. Trent. The Bibliophile Society, Boston, 1921. Printed for members only.

Vailima: Works of Robert Louis Stevenson, Vailima Edition, New York and London, 1922; edition limited to 1000 copies for the United States and 1000 copies for Great Britain. Vol. VIII (*A Child's Garden of Verses, Underwoods*—including *Songs of Travel* as *Underwoods III—Ballads, New Poems*; with prefatory notes by Mrs Stevenson to *A Child's Garden* and *Underwoods,* and by Lloyd Osbourne to *Moral Emblems*), and Vol. XXVI (*Miscellanea,* containing some additional poems). For editorship, see p. 38.

Scribner: Complete Poems of Robert Louis Stevenson, New York, November, 1923.

Tusitala I and II: The Works of Robert Louis Stevenson, Tusitala Edition, Vols. XXII (Poems I) and XXIII (Poems II) with prefatory notes by Mrs Stevenson to *A Child's Garden* and *Underwoods,* and by Lloyd Osbourne to *Moral Emblems,* London, 1923.

Letters 1899: Letters of Robert Louis Stevenson to his Family and Friends, selected and edited with Notes and Introductions by Sidney Colvin, London, 1899.

Letters 1911: Letters of Robert Louis Stevenson, edited by Sidney Colvin, with 150 new letters, London, 1911.

Balfour: Life of Robert Louis Stevenson by Graham Balfour, 1901. Page references are to the twenty-first edition.

Memories of Vailima: Memories of Vailima by Isobel Strong and Lloyd Osbourne, 1902.

Widener: Catalogue of the Books and Manuscripts of Robert Louis Stevenson in the Library of the late Harry Elkins Widener by A. S. W. Rosenbach. Privately printed, Philadelphia, 1913.

Sotheby: Catalogues of sales on 9 and 10 May, 1949, and 14 and

15 November, 1949. Most of these manuscripts are now in
the Beinecke Collection at Yale, and are listed in Vol. V of
the Catalogue; but to save re-setting of type I have kept the
references to the Sotheby Catalogues.

Anderson Galleries I, II, and III : Catalogues of the Stevenson
sales on 23–25 November, 1914, 25–27 January, 1915, and
16–17 February, 1916.

*Beinecke: A Stevenson Library: Catalogue of a Collection of
Writings by and about Robert Louis Stevenson formed by
Edwin J. Beinecke,* compiled by George L. McKay.
Vols. I–VI, New Haven, 1951–1964. I have given
Beinecke references (by item number, not page number) for
poems and letters whose manuscripts, now at Yale, were
not available for checking in 1950.

Baxter Letters: Stevenson's Letters to Charles Baxter, edited by
De Lancey Ferguson and Marshall Waingrow. New Haven,
1956.

The manuscripts formerly in the Stevenson Museum, Howard
Place, Edinburgh, are now in Lady Stair's House Museum,
Edinburgh.

POEMS 1869–1879

In 1869 Stevenson was an engineering student at Edinburgh,
living at home, and often in rebellion against the conventions
and restrictions of his life. In 1879 he was beginning to be
recognised as an author, though he was making no kind of a
living from his writings. In that year he went out to California
to marry Fanny Van de Grift Osbourne, whom he had first met
at Grez-sur-Loing in 1876. In the years between he had trans-
ferred his formal studies from engineering to law; had decided to
make writing his career; had explored the underworld of Edin-
burgh; had met Sidney Colvin and Mrs Sitwell and, through
them, other dons, writers and intellectual persons in London;
had spent a winter in the South of France for his health, and
several summers with the artist colony at Fontainebleau; had
made the canoe journey of *An Inland Voyage* and the walking
tour of *Travels with a Donkey.*

The poems in this section reflect the preoccupations of a sensi-
tive young man growing up in an environment that he both
loved and hated—his love affairs, his crises of faith, his disagree-
ments with his elders, his affection for his contemporaries,

especially Charles Baxter and Bob Stevenson, his frequent
loneliness and his horror of Edinburgh's climate, his reading of
Arnold and Whitman, his interest in early French verse forms
and in traditional Scottish measures, his resolution to be a writer.
Many of the poems written during these years were chosen by
Stevenson for *Underwoods*, 1887; many more will be found in the
Tusitala Edition (see Introduction, p. 52). Those in this section
are a selection only of what remained after Stevenson's own
selection for *Underwoods* had been made.

I. *Dedication*

Checked with manuscript *Sotheby*, November, 1949, 406;
first published *B.B.S. I*, 1916. 'This fascicle of songs' is an
exercise-book with fifteen poems numbered and dated 1870–
1872. They are:

I. *Lo! in thine honest eyes* (October, 1870); II. *My heart, when
first the blackbird* (February, 1871); III. (1) *I dreamed of forest
alleys fair*, (2) *I am as one that keeps awake*, (3) *Last night I
lingered*, (4) *Once more upon the same old seat*, (5) *St. Martin's
Summer*, (6) This *Dedication* (February to October, 1871);
IV. *About the sheltered garden ground*; V. *After reading 'Antony
and Cleopatra'*; VI. *I know not how, but as I count*; (There is no
VII); VIII. *Spring-Song*; IX. *The summer sun shone round me*;
X. *You looked so tempting*; XI. *As Love and Hope*; XII. *Dud-
dingston*—(1) *With caws and chirrupings*, (2) *Now fancy paints*,
(Autumn, 1871), (3) *Apologetic postscript of a year later*; XIII.
Prelude: By sunny market-place (Spring, 1871); XIV. *The
Vanquished Knight* (Spring, 1871); XV. *Away with funeral
music* (Autumn, 1872).

II. *Last night, I lingered long without*

Checked with manuscript *Sotheby*, November, 1949, 348 and
406; first published *B.B.S. I*, 1916.

III. *After Reading 'Antony and Cleopatra'*

Checked with manuscript *Sotheby*, November, 1949, 382 and
406; first published *B.B.S. I*, 1916. The manuscript is dated by
Stevenson 'Sept. 1871' and he adds a comment, '*Pas mal.*'

In *B.B S. I* the poem appears with the following note—a fair
example of the commentaries in the Bibliophile Society volumes:

Stevenson's mind is here still in a chaotic state. He is

aware of desires and of stirrings yet unformulated. His restive spirit reacts to 'the sea's roar,' 'the white moon-shine' and 'the reddening of the fire.' In such a mood, reason is a thing of little worth. He has read *Antony and Cleopatra* and under the magic sway of Shakespeare's colossal poem he becomes imbued with the conviction of the predominant influence of passionate love. 'To have died in Cleopatra's arms' seems to him for the moment—as it has seemed in many moments to many poets, and to others than poets—the greatest fulfilment that life could bring.

IV. *Spring-Song*

Checked with manuscripts *Sotheby*, May, 1949, 51 and November, 1949, 382 and 406; first published *B.B.S. I*, 1916. No date on manuscripts; *B.B.S. I* assigns it to 1871.

V. *As Love and Hope together*

Checked with manuscripts *Sotheby*, May, 1949, 83 and November, 1949, 406; first published *B.B.S. I*, 1916. One manu-script has Stevenson's comment, '*Bon.*' In the first manuscript, it is headed XII and the page numbered 17; the page appears to have been torn from a manuscript-book which also contained *The relic taken*, p. 63, dated 1871, and *To Sydney*, p. 72, dated Spring, 1872. This poem may well belong to those years. A facsimile of a manuscript is reproduced in *B.B.S. I*, facing page 76.

VI. *Duddingston*

Checked with manuscripts *Sotheby*, November, 1949, 406; first published *B.B.S. I*, 1916. From the same manuscript note-book as *Dedication*, p. 59, where it is numbered XII, and dated Autumn, 1871.

An afternoon at Duddingston Loch three years later is described in a letter to Mrs Sitwell, 23 December, 1874:

> Then I went to Duddingston and skated all afternoon. If you had seen the moon rising, a perfect sphere of smoky gold, in the dark air above the trees, and the white loch thick with skaters, and the great hill, snow-sprinkled over-head! It was a sight for a king.

Flora Masson, in *I Can Remember Robert Louis Stevenson*, has another picture of Duddingston:

> Louis Stevenson came and went about them, skating alone; a slender, dark figure with a muffler about his neck; darting

in and out among the crowd, and disappearing and re-
appearing like a melancholy minnow among the tall reeds
that fringe the Loch.

VII. *The relic taken, what avails the shrine?*

Checked with manuscripts *Sotheby*, May, 1949, 74 and 88;
first published *B.B.S. I*, 1916. The first of these manuscripts is
on a page taken from the same exercise-book as *As Love and Hope
together*, p. 61. The second manuscript is in an exercise-book
containing several poems entitled *Little Odes*. The contents are:
I. *To Sydney: Not thine where marble-still*; II. *Though deep
indifference*; III. *The relic taken*; IV. *O South, South*; V. *Though
he, that ever kind*; VI. *This gloomy northern day*; VII. *To
Minnie with a hand-glass*; (published as *Underwoods, I*, VIII);
VIII. *To Walt Whitman*. Only two lines of this poem appear,
at the foot of a page; there may have been more on the next
page, but the note-book has been dismembered.

The poem is dated Swanston, July, 1871, and the comment is
'*Pas mal*'.

Both manuscripts have *weathergaw* in l. 9, but in the second it
has been cancelled and *weather-gleam* inserted. According to
Jamieson's *Dictionary of the Scottish Language*, *weathergaw*
means a partial or secondary rainbow, *weather-gleam* 'clear sky
near the horizon; spoken of objects seen in the twilight or dusk.'
The two words therefore suggest two different scenes; I have
preferred the *weather-gleam* as best suiting the rest of the poem.

VIII. *All things on earth and sea*

Checked with Beinecke 3271; sent in a letter to Mrs Sitwell
(?1874). First published in *Three Short Poems*, 1898, in *Three
Letters*, 1902, then in the Household edition, New York, 1906.

IX. *I sit up here at midnight*

Checked with manuscript *Sotheby*, November, 1949, 361;
first published *B.B.S. III*, 1921. The manuscript is dated 'Dec.
1871, Edinburgh' and annotated '*miscel.*' In tone and feeling
it resembles *Underwoods, I*, VI. *A Visit from the Sea*, and both
may owe something to Heine.

X. *I am a hunchback, yellow faced*

Checked with Beinecke 6326. First published in *B.B.S. III*,
1921.

Stevenson to Mrs Sitwell, 6 September, 1873:

I was out this evening to call on a friend, and, coming back through the wet, crowded, lamp-lit streets, was singing after my own fashion, '*Du hast Diamanten und Perlen*,' when I heard a poor cripple man in the gutter wailing over a pitiful Scotch air, his club-foot supported on the other knee, and his whole woebegone body propped sideways against a crutch. . . . My own false notes stuck in my chest. How well off I am! is the burthen of my songs all day long— '*Drum ist so wohl mir in der Welt!*' and the ugly reality of the cripple man was an intrusion on the beautiful world in which I was walking.

XI. *Death*

Checked with manuscript *Sotheby*, November, 1949, 367; first published *B.B.S. III*, 1921. Dated Paris, 1 September, 1872.

XII. *A little before me, and hark!*

Published here for the first time, from a manuscript sold at Sotheby's, November, 1949, 355. Undated.

Stevenson to Henley, 11 December, 1879:

How old are all truths, and yet how far from commonplace; old, strange, and inexplicable, like the Sphinx. So I learn day by day the value and high doctrinality of suffering. Let me suffer always; not more than I am able to bear, for that makes a man mad, as hunger drives the wolf to sally from the forest; but still to suffer some, and never to sink up to my eyes in comfort and grow dead in virtues and respectability.

XIII. *Epistle to Charles Baxter*

Published here for the first time, from a manuscript sold at Sotheby's, May, 1949, 63. The second part, beginning O *South, South, South!* appears as a poem by itself in another manuscript (*Sotheby*, May, 1949, 88)—No. IV of the *Little Odes* (see note to *The relic taken*, p. 455) dated 'Edinburgh, Feb. 1872.'

In the first manuscript, this poem is the last in a sequence of poems, all in the same manuscript-book, called *Recruiting Songs*, and dedicated '*Ad Dilectos Tres Amicos Stevenson Wilson et Baxter.*' The other poems are: *By Sunny Market-Place*; *The old world moans and tosses*; *Take not my hand*; *The whole day through*; *The old Chimaeras*; *Here he comes big with Statistics*; *All influences were in vain*; *The moon is sinking*; *The Vanquished*

Knight; *Link your arm in mine.*

Charles Baxter was one of Stevenson's Edinburgh cronies, who became his lawyer and man of affairs, handling all Stevenson's business after he left Scotland. *Kidnapped* and *Catriona* are dedicated to him, and he was the model for Michael Finsbury in *The Wrong Box*. See notes to *Brasheanna*, p. 542.

XIV. *Consolation*

Checked with manuscripts *Sotheby*, May, 1949, 88, where it appears as No. V of *Little Odes* under the title of *Toward the South* (see note to *The relic taken*, p. 455); and November, 1949, 367, where it is given the title *Consolation*, dated 'Feb. 1872' and headed 'Inscribed to Sydney' (see note to following poem). Also checked with a facsimile of a manuscript in the Parrish Collection of the Princeton University Library.

Gosse prints it in his *Biographical Notes* under the title of *To a Mourner*, with this comment:

> The following stanzas, written in Edinburgh at the time when it was decided that Stevenson should give up the profession of civil engineer, and should read for the Bar, have never, it is believed, been printed until now.

In fact, they had appeared under the heading *A Fragment— In Memoriam* in *R.L.S. Teuila*, 1899, and were there dated 27 June, 1872.

XV. *To Sydney*

Checked with manuscripts *Sotheby*, May, 1949, 88, and November, 1949, 358; first published *B.B.S. I*, 1916. The first of these manuscripts is in the exercise-book containing the *Little Odes* (see note to *The relic taken*, p. 455).

To Sydney is dated 'Edinburgh, Spring 72'; 'Sydney' is a pseudonym for Stevenson's cousin R. A. M. Stevenson (see note to *Underwoods*, *I*, XV, p. 475); in the same series of poems 'Marcus' stands for Charles Baxter.

XVI. *O dull, cold northern sky*

Checked with manuscript *Sotheby*, November, 1949, 366; first published *B.B.S. I*, 1916. I have also seen the manuscript of a draft of the poem, in a note-book belonging to Mr E. J. Beinecke (No. 309 in the Isobel Strong sale, Anderson Galleries, New York, 1915). Dated Spring, 1872.

> Indeed, there are not many uproars in this world more dismal than that of the Sabbath bells in Edinburgh.

To none but those who have themselves suffered the thing in the body, can the gloom and depression of our Edinburgh winter be brought home. For some constitutions there is something almost physically disgusting in the bleak ugliness of easterly weather; the wind wearies, the sickly sky depresses them; and they turn back from their walk to avoid the aspect of the unrefulgent sun going down among perturbed and pallid mists.

Edinburgh: Picturesque Notes, IV and IX.

XVII. *Swallows travel to and fro*

Checked with manuscript *Sotheby*, November, 1949, 366; first published *B.B.S. I*, 1916. At the top of the manuscript is written *Claire*: it is dated 'Mentone, Dec. 7th'—the year would be 1873 when Stevenson was ordered south for his health and spent five months at Mentone. Claire was a name Stevenson had for Mrs Sitwell; see footnote to p. 52. This was the poem which led Hellman astray.

XVIII. *Let Love go, if go she will*

Checked with manuscript *Sotheby*, November, 1949, 366; first published *B.B.S. I*, 1916. Dated May, 1874.

XIX. *I am like one that for long days had sate*

Checked with manuscript *Sotheby*, November, 1949, 366. Dated 16 June, 1874. In *Fragments by Robert Louis Stevenson*, collected by Clement Shorter, 1915—a privately printed edition limited to twenty-five copies—an eleven-line version of the second sonnet only appears. First published complete in *B.B.S. I*, 1916.

This is Stevenson sonneteering in high serious mood. A lighter-hearted sonnet can be found in *Sonnets of this Century*, edited by William Sharp (1886)—*The Touch of Life.*

> I saw a circle in a garden sit
> Of dainty dames and solemn cavaliers,
> Whereof some shuddered at the burrowing nit,
> And at the carrion worm some burst in tears:
> And all, as envying the abhorred estate
> Of empty shades and disembodied elves,
> Under the laughing stars, early and late,

> Sat shamefast at their birth and at themselves.
> The keeper of the house of life is fear;
> In the rent lion is the honey found
> By him that rent it; out of stony ground
> The toiler, in the morning of the year,
> Beholds the harvest of his grief abound
> And the green corn put forth the tender ear.

Another sonnet by Stevenson, *The Arabesque*, also appeared in this anthology.

XX. *The roadside lined with ragweed, the sharp hills*

Checked with Beinecke 6794; dated 'Monday 15th August 1870, Ross of Mull'. This sonnet, with three others—*To the Sea*; *To My Pipe*; *Sir Alan M'Lean's Effigy, on Inch Kenneth*—first appeared in print in Vol. XXVI of the Vailima Edition, along with two others—*So shall this book*; *I have a hoard of treasure* —which had already appeared in a series of eight in *B.B.S. II*, and been reprinted in Vol. VIII of the Vailima Edition.

A manuscript-book with the sonnets mentioned above was sold at the Anderson Sale in January, 1915, lot 323; on the last page was written:

> Those are very clever men,
> Who can write with current pen
> Those fourteen convoluted lines,
> That experts call a sonnet.

XXI. *Not undelightful, friend, our rustic ease*

Checked with Beinecke 6637 and 6638; dated 'Between B of Allan and Dunblane 1872'; first published in *B.B.S. II*, 1916. The 'small cottage' is the Stevensons' summer cottage at Swanston, under the eastern slopes of the Pentlands.

XXII. *As Daniel, burd-alone, in that far land*

Checked with Beinecke 5976; dated 'Above Dunblane, by the riverside, 1872'. There is another version in a letter to Charles Baxter dated 9 April, 1872, headed 'To the members of the L.J.R.' (*Baxter Letters*, 1956, p. 11). First published in *B.B.S. II*, 1916. 'Burd-alone' is a Scots word for the only child left in a family, hence 'all alone'—see also *Underwoods*, *II*, X, verse 5, 'Aft whan I laboured burd-alane.'

XXIII. *The Light-Keeper*

Part I checked from manuscript *Sotheby*, May, 1949, 56. First published in Vol. XXVIII of the Edinburgh Edition.

> The sets of Lighthouse verses were recovered by Mr Sidney Colvin from note-books of 1869 and 1870.
>
> GOSSE

Stevenson belonged to a family of lighthouse-builders (see notes to *Underwoods I*, XXVIII, XXXIV and XXXVIII) and when he wrote these verses was training to become one himself. In 1869 he made a cruise with his father on the *Pharos*, the steamer for the Commissioners of Northern Lights, and in 1870 spent some weeks on Earraid, off Mull, the headquarters for the building of the deep-sea lighthouse of Dhu Heartach.

XXIV. *My brain swims empty and light*

Not checked; first published in the Vailima Edition, 1922.

This poem, and some lines in the four following poems, reflect Stevenson's early enthusiam for Whitman. In or about 1871 he had written, or at least begun, an *Ode to Whitman* (see note to *The relic taken*, p. 455); in 1873–1874 he was busy with the article on Whitman that finally appeared in *The New Quarterly Magazine*, October, 1878. In the fragment of biography written at San Francisco in 1880 (quoted by Graham Balfour, p. 86) he says, talking of his youth in Edinburgh:

> I date my new departure from three circumstances: natural growth, the coming of friends, and the study of Walt Whitman.

And in his essay *Books which have influenced me*, published in *The British Weekly*, 13 May, 1887 (reprinted in *The Art of Writing*) he speaks of *Leaves of Grass* as

> a book of singular service, a book which tumbled the world upside down for me, blew into space a thousand cobwebs of genteel and ethical illusion.

Stevenson discusses Whitman's verse style at some length in section V of the essay on Whitman mentioned above.

XXV. *The Cruel Mistress*

Not checked; first published in the Vailima Edition, 1922. The scene in the poem is also described in two of Stevenson's essays: briefly in 'The Education of an Engineer' (1888), and more fully in 'On the Enjoyment of Unpleasant Places' (1874), which is largely about his experiences at Wick in the autumn of 1868, when the Stevenson firm was engaged on engineering work in the harbour. The poem seems to owe a good deal to the Matthew Arnold of *The Strayed Reveller* as well as to Whitman: and the reference to Obermann reinforces the point.

> Upon the average book a writer may be silent; he may set it down to his ill-hap that when his own youth was in the acrid fermentation, he should have fallen and fed upon the cheerless fields of Obermann. Yet to Mr Arnold, who led him to these pastures, he still bears a grudge.

Old Mortality, 1884, in *Memories and Portraits*.

XXVI. *Storm*

Not checked; first published in the Vailima Edition, 1922. With its references to the sea, the bay and a room in a hotel, this poem may reflect memories of the storms at Wick in 1868.

XXVII. *Stormy Nights*

Not checked; first published in the Vailima Edition, 1922. Stevenson to Mrs Sitwell, from Swanston, Autumn, 1874:

> Last night it blew a fearful gale; I was kept awake about a couple of hours, and could not get to sleep for the horror of the wind's noise; the whole house shook; and, mind you, our house *is* a house, a great castle of jointed stone that would weigh up a street of English houses; so that when it quakes, as it did last night, it means something. But the quaking was not what put me about; it was the horrible howl of the wind round the corner; the audible haunting of an incarnate anger about the house; the evil spirit that was abroad; and, above all, the shuddering silent pauses when the storm's heart stands dreadfully still for a moment. O how I hate a storm at night! They have been a great influence in my life, I am sure; for I can remember them so far back—long before I was six at least, for we left the house in which I remember listening to them times without number when I was six. And in those days the storm had for me a perfect impersonation, as durable and unvarying as any heathen deity. I always heard it, as a horseman riding past with his cloak about his head, and somehow always carried away, and riding past again, and being baffled yet once more, *ad infinitum*, all night long. I think I wanted him to get past, but I am not sure; I know only that I had

> some interest either for or against in the matter; and I
> used to lie and hold my breath, not quite frightened, but in a
> state of miserable exaltation.

And again, from a fragment of autobiography printed in
Balfour's *Life*, p. 32:

> I had an extreme terror of Hell, implanted in me, I
> suppose, by my good nurse, which used to haunt me terribly
> on stormy nights, when the wind had broken loose and was
> going about the town like a bedlamite. I remember that
> the noises on such occasions always grouped themselves
> for me into the sound of a horseman, or rather a succession
> of horsemen, riding furiously past the bottom of the street
> and away up the hill into town; I think even now that I
> hear the terrible *howl* of his passage, and the clinking that I
> used to attribute to his bit and stirrups. On such nights I
> would lie awake and pray and cry, until I prayed and cried
> myself asleep.

The same image of the storm as a galloping horseman occurs
in *Windy Nights,* in *A Child's Garden of Verses* (p. 366).

XXVIII. *Song at Dawn*

Not checked; first published in the Vailima Edition, 1922.

XXIX. *Nous n'irons plus aux bois*

Checked with Beinecke 3275; sent in a letter to Mrs Sitwell
from Château Renard, August, 1875; first published in *Letters*,
1899. Stevenson to Mrs Sitwell:

> I send you here two rondeaux; I don't suppose they will
> amuse anybody but me; but this measure, short and yet
> intricate, is just what I desire; and I have had some good
> times walking along the glaring roads, or down the poplar
> alley of the great canal, pitting my own humour to this old
> verse.

The rondeau is a paraphrase of Banville's poem, *Nous n'irons
plus aux bois,* itself based on an earlier nursery rhyme. See also
Housman's variation on Banville's theme in his introductory lines
to *Last Poems*: 'We'll to the woods no more.'

The other rondeau referred to was *Far have you come, my lady,
from the town, Tusitala,* II, p. 144.

Between 1875 and 1879 Stevenson wrote a number of rondeaux,
ballades and triolets: his interest in these French forms had been

aroused by his study of Charles d'Orléans and Villon (on whom he wrote essays in 1875 and 1876); there was much discussion of them among the writers he met in London. Henley, Austin Dobson, Andrew Lang and Robert Bridges also practised them. See also *Rhymes to Henley*, pp. 348 and 351.

XXX. *In Autumn when the woods are red*

Checked with Beinecke 6405 (very poor manuscript); on the back of the manuscript is 'A French Legend', which is part of 'Forest Notes', so the poem can be dated 1875–1876. First published in *B.B.S. III*, 1921.

XXXI. *Love is the very heart of Spring*

Checked with manuscript *Sotheby*, November, 1949, 384. Pencil manuscript, very rough draft. First published *B.B.S. III*, 1921, which dates it 1876.

XXXII. *I who all the winter through*

Checked with manuscript *Sotheby*, May, 1949, 61; dated 'last of Feby. 1876.' First published *B.B.S. I*, 1916.

The last line in each stanza, 'And my old love comes to meet me in the dawning and the dew,' is echoed very closely in a poem of Henley's dated 1878, *To S. C.*

> For the old love comes to meet us
> In the dawning and the dew.

Perhaps this is the place to draw attention to two other very close resemblances between Stevenson's poems and Henley's. Stevenson's poem (not in this collection, but in *Tusitala II*, p. 138):

> The look of Death is both severe and mild
> And all the words of Death are grave and sweet.

can be dated approximately 1875. Henley, in the poem *I.M.— R.C.G.B.*, 1878, has:

> The ways of Death are soothing and serene,
> And all the words of Death are grave and sweet.

In Henley's poem, *To R. L. S.* 1876, he uses an image of a child running to its mother, which also appears in this poem. Mr Hellmann pointed out this similarity on p. 154 of *The True Stevenson*, 1925.

XXXIII. *Here you rest among the vallies*

Checked with manuscript *Sotheby*, May, 1949, 61, where it is dated 'Feb. 79' and written out on the same page as *Underwoods*, *I*, II, *A Song of the Road*. A facsimile is given in *B.B.S. I*, facing page 40. First printed privately in *Three Short Poems*, 1898, and then in the Vailima Edition, 1922.

XXXIV. *Grown about by fragrant bushes*

Checked with Beinecke 6968 where the first line 'There where the land of love', as printed in 1950 and earlier, is deleted. The manuscript is beneath XXXI, so probably of the same date; first published *B.B.S. III*, 1921.

XXXV. *Love—what is love? A great and aching heart*

Checked with manuscript *Sotheby*, May, 1949, 61; dated 'March 1876'; first published *B.B.S. I*, 1916.

XXXVI. *Death, to the dead for evermore*

Checked, as far as possible, with a manuscript, a very rough pencil draft, *Sotheby*, November, 1949, 396. A manuscript in the Huntington Library has a draft of verses 3 and 1, in that order. First published *B.B.S. I*, 1916, which dates it 1875.

Stevenson to John Addington Symonds, Spring, 1886:

> Death is a great and gentle solvent; it has never had justice done it, no, not by Whitman.

XXXVII. *I saw red evening through the rain*

Checked *Sotheby*, November, 1949, 392; first published in *B.B.S. III*, which dates it 1875.

XXXVIII. *The Daughter of Herodias*

Not checked; first published in the Vailima Edition, 1922. I cannot find any reference of Stevenson's to this poem, nor any other poem of his in this metre, and it is by style and feeling that I place it among these earlier poems.

XXXIX. *As one who having wandered all night long*

Checked with manuscript *Sotheby*, May, 1949, 61; dated April, 1878. First published *B.B.S. I*, 1916.

XL. *Praise and Prayer*

Checked with a facsimile of a manuscript in the New York Public Library; first published in W. H. Arnold's 'My

Stevensons' in *Scribner's Magazine*, January 1922. Then in his book *Ventures in Book Collecting*, 1923, then in *Scribner*, 1923 (though not in *Vailima* or *Tusitala*). It is dated from Monastier, which Stevenson visited in 1878, before his tour in the Cevennes. See note to *John Cavalier*.

XLI. *John Cavalier*

Unchecked; there is a rough, incomplete and cancelled draft in Beinecke 6087; published the same way as *Praise and Prayer* above. Catalogue of Sale at Anderson Gallery, 23–25 November, 1914, No. 316:

> Note-book containing 83 pages in the handwriting of Stevenson, being, for the most part, material for his book *Travels with a Donkey*. . . . At the back are three finished poems, one of which, *The Gauger's Flute*, is published in *Underwoods* . . . The other two appear to be unpublished. Their titles are—*John Cavalier* and *Praise and Prayer*.

As the latter poem was written in 1878 (see previous note), *John Cavalier* almost certainly belongs to the same year.

Jean Cavalier (1681–1740) was a leader of the Protestants in the Cevennes—the Camisards—in their stand against the French king. Stevenson, who became very interested in Cavalier during his tour in the Cevennes (there are several references to him in *Travels with a Donkey*), had an idea of writing at length on him:

> A baker's apprentice with a genius for war, elected brigadier of Camisards at seventeen, to die at fifty-five the English governor of Jersey.

Cavalier's *Memoirs of the Wars of the Cevennes* were translated and published in Dublin in 1726.

Stevenson to Gosse, Pitlochry, 6 June, 1881:

> I am a beggar: ask Dobson, Saintsbury, yourself, and any other of these cheeses who know something of the eighteenth century, what became of Jean Cavalier between his coming to England and his death in 1740. Is anything interesting known about him?

XLII. *The Iron Steed*

Checked with facsimile of manuscript, in *English Poetical Autographs*, selected and edited by Desmond Flower and A. N. L. Munby, 1938. First published in that collection, though a facsimile of a very rough draft had appeared in *Stevenson's Work-*

shop, 1921, No. 15, with a transcript; never hitherto included
in any collection of Stevenson's verse.

The manuscript is not dated but in *Stevenson's Workshop* it is
linked with a note in a notebook dated May 12th 1881.

XLIII. *Of where or how, I nothing know*

Checked with manuscript *Sotheby*, May, 1949, 61, first
published in *Letters*, 1899.

Sent with a letter to Colvin from 'the cars between Pitts-
burgh and Chicago, just now bowling through Ohio,' of the
emigrant train on which Stevenson crossed the States in August,
1879. His prose account of the scene is to be found in the
essay *Across the Plains*, written in the same year:

> Our American sunrise had ushered in a noble summer's
> day . . . I stood on the platform by the hour . . . And
> when I had asked the name of a river from the brakesman,
> and heard that it was called the Susquehanna, the beauty
> of the name seemed to be part and parcel of the beauty
> of the land. As when Adam with divine fitness named the
> creatures, so this word Susquehanna was at once accepted
> by the fancy. That was the name, as no other could be,
> for that shining river and desirable valley.

PIECES IN LALLAN

Stevenson assembled and wrote out several of his Scots poems
in a manuscript book headed *Pieces in Lallan*. This book was
dismembered in due course (see Introduction, p. 45), and the
sheets bound up in eight separate volumes which were sold at
Sotheby's in May and November, 1949. As the poems were
numbered, it is now possible, with the help of the Beinecke
Catalogue, to reconstruct the order of the original note-
book. I. *To the Commissioners of Northern Lights*; II. *To Mes-
dames Zassetsky and Garschine*; III. *To W. E. Henley*: 'It's
rainin'; IV. *To Charles Baxter*: 'Noo lyart leaves'; V. *To the
Same, on the death of their common friend, Mr John Adam*;
VI. *Ille Terrarum*; VII. 'When aince Aprile'; VIII. *Embro Hie
Kirk*; IX. *A Mile an' a Bittock*; X. *The Spaewife*; XII. *Their
Laureate to an Academy Class Dinner Club*; XIII. 'It's an ower
come sooth'; XIV. *The Counterblast—1886*; XV. *The Counter-
blast Ironical*; XVI. *A Lowden Sabbath Morn*. There seems to

have been no XI. The four poems, I, II, IV, V, not chosen for
Underwoods, are printed here.

See general note to *Underwoods II* (p. 488) for Burns stanza.

I. *To The Commissioners of Northern Lights*

Checked with manuscript *Sotheby*, May, 1949, 71; dated
Swanston, 1871; first published *B.B.S. I*, 1916. The 'paper'
referred to was *On a New Form of Intermittent Light for Light-
houses* which Stevenson read before the Royal Scottish Society
of Arts in March, 1871. On 8 April he told his father he wished
to be a writer, not an engineer. Thomas Stevenson, his wife
recorded in her diary, was 'wonderfully resigned'; and as a com-
promise, it was decided he should study law. And lawyers, as he
remembered in his last verse, had (like Scott) sometimes been
Commissioners of Northern Lights.

II. *To Mesdames Zassetsky and Garschine*

Checked with manuscript *Sotheby*, May, 1949, 71; dated
Mentone, February, 1874. First published *B.B.S. I*, 1916.

Mesdames Zassetsky and Garschine were two Russian ladies
with whom Stevenson became very friendly during his months
at Mentone, after he had been ordered south for his health in
the Autumn of 1873.

III. *To Charles Baxter*

Checked with manuscript *Sotheby*, May, 1949, 60. Sent in a
letter, dated Edinburgh, October, 1875; first published in *Letters*,
1899. 'The Court' is Parliament House, in Edinburgh, where
young members of the Scottish Bar, like Stevenson and Baxter,
paced up and down while waiting to be briefed.

IV. *To the same*

Checked with manuscript *Sotheby*, May, 1949, 60; dated
Edinburgh, October, 1875; first published in *B.B.S. I*, 1916.
Like the previous poem, it celebrates Parliament House. For
some observations on the text, as printed in *New Poems*, see
Introduction, pp. 43, 46. The phrase 'writer lads' (v. 6)
appears in v. 9 of Allan Ramsay's *Elegy on Lucky Wood*, an early
eighteenth-century example of the Scots *genre* of mock-elegy in
the Burns stanza which started a century earlier with Sir Robert
Sempill's *Epitaph of Habbie Simson, Piper of Kilbarchan*.

UNDERWOODS

Underwoods was first published by Chatto and Windus in 1887.

This name he borrowed from Ben Jonson, who had . . . explained the title as signifying a miscellany of 'lesser poems of later growth,' springing up between the more massive timber of his plays. Stevenson, in his turn, modestly suggested by his adoption of the same title that his little poems were not to prejudice any welcome the world of readers might be prepared to give to his more serious and laboured prose.   GOSSE

Letter to Henry James from Bournemouth, January, 1887:

I am also considering a volume of verse, much of which will be cast in my native speech, that very dark oracular medium: I suppose this is a folly, but what then? As the nurse says in Marryat, 'It was only a little one.'

Stevenson's Dedication to *Underwoods* ran as follows:

There are men and classes of men that stand above the common herd: the soldier, the sailor, and the shepherd not unfrequently; the artist rarely; rarelier still, the clergyman; the physician almost as a rule. He is the flower (such as it is) of our civilisation; and when that stage of man is done with, and only remembered to be marvelled at in history, he will be thought to have shared as little as any in the defects of the period, and most notably exhibited the virtues of the race. Generosity he has, such as is possible to those who practise an art, never to those who drive a trade; discretion, tested by a hundred secrets; tact, tried in a thousand embarrassments; and, what are more important, Heraclean cheerfulness and courage. So it is that he brings air and cheer into the sick-room, and often enough, though not so often as he wishes, brings healing.

Gratitude is but a lame sentiment; thanks, when they are expressed, are often more embarrassing than welcome; and yet I must set forth mine to a few out of many doctors who have brought me comfort and help: to Dr Willey of San Francisco, whose kindness to a stranger it must be as grateful to him, as it is touching to me, to remember; to Dr Karl Ruedi of Davos, the good genius of the English in his frosty mountains; to Dr Herbert of Paris, whom I knew only for a week, and to Dr Caissot of Montpellier,

[469]

whom I knew only for ten days, and who have yet written their names deeply in my memory; to Dr Brandt of Royat; to Dr Wakefield of Nice; to Dr Chepmell, whose visits make it a pleasure to be ill; to Dr Horace Dobell, so wise in counsel; to Sir Andrew Clark, so unwearied in kindness; and to that wise youth, my uncle, Dr Balfour.

I forget as many as I remember; and I ask both to pardon me, these for silence, those for inadequate speech. But one name I have kept on purpose to the last, because it is a household word with me, and because if I had not received favours from so many hands and in so many quarters of the world, it should have stood upon this page alone: that of my friend Thomas Bodley Scott of Bournemouth. Will he accept this, although shared among so many, for a dedication to himself? and when next my ill-fortune (which has thus its pleasant side) brings him hurrying to me when he would fain sit down to meat or lie down to rest, will he care to remember that he takes this trouble for one who is not fool enough to be ungrateful?

BOOK I: IN ENGLISH

I. *Envoy*

One manuscript (according to *B.B.S. II*, 139) has an extra couplet between lines 2 and 3:

> An active conscience, honoured life,
> A tender and a laughing wife.

According to Will H. Low's *A Chronicle of Friendships*, 1908, the Lows' house on the river-bank at Montigny-sur-Loing, where they spent the summer of 1875, suggested this Envoy to Stevenson. See note to *To Will H. Low*, p. 473.

II. *A Song of the Road*

A manuscript, with some minor variations in punctuation, was sold at Sotheby's, May, 1949, 61. Throughout, Stevenson wrote *Guager*. A *gauger* is an exciseman: Burns was a gauger. There is a prose version of this tale in Chapter X of *Edinburgh: Picturesque Notes*, 1878.

The poem is dated Forest of Montargis, 1878.

III. *The Canoe Speaks*

Sent with a letter to W. H. Low from Hyères, April, 1884:

> Herewith are a set of verses which I thought pretty enough to send to press. Then I thought of the *Manhattan*, towards

whom I have guilty and compunctious feelings. Last, I
had the best thought of all—to send them to you in case
you might think them suitable for illustration. It seemed to
me quite in your vein. If so, good; if not, hand them on to
Manhattan, Century, or *Lippincott,* at your pleasure, as all
three desire my work, or pretend to. But I trust the lines
will not go unattended. Some river-side will haunt you;
and O! be tender to my bathing girls.

The poem does not appear to have been published in any of
the magazines named. A manuscript with several variants from
the published version is described in *B.B.S. II,* 140. After the
line 'To loose their girdles on the grass' follow three lines not in
the *Underwoods* version:

> And stepping free, each breathing lass
> From her discarded ring of clothes
> Into the crystal coolness goes.

See also note to *Now bare to the beholder's eye,* p. 527.

IV. *It is the season now to go*

This would be a good poem to set for an examination question
on A. E. Housman's debt to Stevenson, and the differences
between them. The echoes of Stevenson in Housman have been
pointed out by a number of writers, among them Alfred Noyes,
H. W. Garrod, John Sparrow and Doris N. Dalglish. *Balfour*
dates it 1884.

VI. *A Visit from the Sea*

Balfour dates it 1884.

VII. *To a Gardener*

Stevenson to Edmund Gosse from La Solitude, Hyères,
where the poem was written, 20 May, 1883:

> This spot our garden and our view, are sub-celestial. I
> sing daily with my Bunyan, that great bard,
>
> > I dwell already the next door to Heaven!
>
> If you could see my roses, and my aloes, and my fig-mari-
> golds, and my olives, and my view over a plain, and my
> view of certain mountains as graceful as Apollo, as severe as
> Zeus, you would not think the phrase exaggerated.

See also *Flower god,* p. 289, and *My wife and I,* p. 344.

VIII. *To Minnie*

Minnie was a Balfour cousin who went to India. See *A Child's Garden of Verses, Envoys,* IV, p. 408.

A manuscript version of this poem, with several variations, was sold at Sotheby's, May, 1949, 88. It was part of an exercise book with other poems which Stevenson had entitled *Little Odes.* See note to *The relic taken,* p. 455. Of these *Little Odes,* dated between 1869 and 1872, *To Minnie,* written in 1869, was probably the earliest, and the only one Stevenson chose to include in *Underwoods.*

IX. *To K. de M.*

Mrs Katharine de Mattos, sister to R. A. M. Stevenson, was one of Stevenson's favourite cousins. See note to *To Katharine de Mattos,* p. 537. A manuscript of this poem with eight additional lines is described in *B.B.S. II,* 142. The lines are:

> More human grown, yet more divine
> You now outsavour, now outshine,
> The golden lamps that rare and far
> Along the blue embankments are,
> The salty smell of running tides,
> The rowan wild on mountain sides,
> The silver and the saffron dawn
> Across the arched orient drawn.

They are said to come between the fifteenth and sixteenth lines of the published version, but as the verse goes in couplets this is rather difficult to understand.

The note goes on to mention that in the margin of the manuscript are eight more unpublished lines, beginning:

> We see you as we see a face
> That trembles in a forest place . . .

and comments:

> One might wish that Stevenson had not eliminated the lines in which he describes the subtle loveliness of the face that hovered between 'smiles and tears.'

Far from eliminating them, Stevenson published them as a separate poem of *Underwoods, I,* XIX, *Katharine.*

There is a poem *To K. de M.* by Henley, dated 1878, in *A Book of Verses,* 1888.

X. *To N. V. de G. S.*

Nelly Van de Grift Sanchez, Mrs R. L. Stevenson's sister and biographer, who acted as Stevenson's amanuensis when he was working on the first draft of *Prince Otto* at Oakland, California, in 1880. She married Adulpho Sanchez, saloon-keeper at Monterey, whom Stevenson had met there a few months before and found 'delightful.' See notes to *To Nelly Sanchez*, p. 535, and to *A Child's Garden of Verses*, Envoys, V, p. 556.

XI. *To Will H. Low*

Stevenson first met this American painter (1853–1932), in Paris in April, 1875. Low and R. A. M. Stevenson belonged to the colony of artists that went every summer to Barbizon and Grez-sur-Loing, and R. L. Stevenson joined them there in 1875 and subsequent summers. There is a pleasant record of Stevenson in Paris and at Fontainebleau in Will H. Low's *A Chronicle of Friendships*, 1908. In 1885 Low dedicated his illustrated edition of Keats's *Lamia* to Stevenson; in his letter of thanks of 2 January, 1886, Stevenson wrote:

> I have copied out on the other sheet some bad verses, which somehow your picture suggested; as a kind of image of things that I pursue and cannot reach, and that you seem —no, not to have reached—but to have come a thought nearer to than I. This is the life we have chosen: well, the choice was mad, but I should make it again.

Under the heading, *To Will H. Low*, Stevenson wrote, *Damned bad lines in return for a beautiful book.* There are minor variations of punctuation between the version sent with the letter and that printed in *Underwoods*.

The poem was published in *The Century Magazine*, May, 1886, through the good offices of Edmund Gosse, for on receiving five pounds payment in advance, Stevenson wrote to Gosse from Bournemouth, February 17, 1886:

> *Non, c'est honteux!* for a set of shambling lines that don't know whether they're trochees or what they are, that you or any of the crafty ones would blush all over if you had so much as thought upon, all by yourselves, in the w.c.

XII. *To Mrs Will H. Low*

See note to previous poem. Written at 12 Rue Vernier, Paris, where Stevenson visited the Lows in 1886. Mrs Low, a Frenchwoman, translated *Jekyll and Hyde* into French (1889).

XIII. *To H. F. Brown*

Horatio Forbes Brown (1854–1926—a grandson of Colcnel Ranald Macdonell of Glengarry) was the lifelong friend, literary executor and biographer of John Addington Symonds. He spent most of his life between Venice and Davos, where Stevenson met him in 1880 or 1881. Brown wrote books on Venice, on which he was an authority, and a book of poetry, *Drift*, 1900, which includes, *To R. L. S.*, a poem in answer to this epistle (quoted on p. 520).

W. G. Lockett, *Robert Louis Stevenson at Davos* (1934):

> During a dangerous illness Stevenson read what is perhaps Brown's most widely known book, *Life on the Lagoons*, and as a thank-offering for the pleasure it had given him, he wrote the noteworthy verses, 'To H. F. Brown' . . . which are included in *Underwoods*. In this poem Brown's *Life on the Lagoons* is called 'Your fire-surviving roll' because the original was burnt in a fire at his publishers, Messrs Kegan, Paul, Trench and Co's. Brown seems to have had a sort of pride in having been the victim of the extraordinary and surely unparalleled coincidence that the original manuscripts of no fewer than four of his books were destroyed at different times and places by fire: two in publishers' warehouses, one in a mail van in Switzerland, and the other in Cecil Rhodes's house at Rondebosch.

XIV. *To Andrew Lang*

Written in 1886. Andrew Lang (1844–1912), poet, literary journalist, expert on folk-lore and editor of fairy-tales, whom Stevenson first met at Mentone in 1874 and described as 'good-looking, delicate, Oxfordish, etc.' Lang was one of Stevenson's sponsors for the Savile Club; he suggested various ideas for essays and stories and remained a very good friend all his life. He wrote the Introduction to the Swanston Edition of Stevenson's works (1911). See also *To Master Andrew Lang*, p. 310, and note to *The Fine Pacific Islands*, p. 548.

Lang replied to Stevenson's poem in verses which began:

> Dear Louis of the awful cheek!
> Who told you it was right to speak,
> Where all the world might hear and stare,
> Of other fellows' 'brindled hair'?

Rosaline Masson, in her *Life* of Stevenson, quotes some other lines on Lang which Stevenson sent in a letter to Henley from Davos:

> My name is Andrew Lang
> 　　Andrew Lang
> 　　That's my name,
> And criticism and cricket is my game.
> With my eyeglass in my eye
> 　　Am not *I*
> 　　Am *I* not
> A lady-dady Oxford kind of Scot
> 　　Am I not?

XV. *Et Tu in Arcadia Vixisti*

R. A. M. S. was R. L. Stevenson's cousin R. A. M. Stevenson (1847–1900), the painter and art-critic. He was a consistently stimulating influence in Stevenson's life, supported him in his troubles with his father, and introduced him to artist life in Paris and Fontainebleau. Stevenson described him as Spring-Heel'd Jack in his essay on *Talk and Talkers* (*Memories and Portraits*), and modelled Prince Otto, and Somerset (of *More New Arabian Nights*) on him. 'My daily life is one repression from beginning to end, and my letters to you are the only safety valve' wrote Stevenson to Bob in an unpublished letter of 17 November, 1868 (printed in *The Times*, 17 June, 1922). Henley had a poem to R. A. M. S. in *A Book of Verses*, 1888.

Balfour dates it 1881. *Tusitala* has *planets* for *plants* in l. 22.

XVI. *To W. E. Henley*

Henley (1849–1903), poet and literary journalist. In 1875, Leslie Stephen, the critic and editor of the *Cornhill*, who had printed stories by Stevenson, took Stevenson to the infirmary at Edinburgh to visit

> a poor fellow, a sort of poet who writes for him, and who has been eighteen months in our infirmary . . . Stephen and I sat on a couple of chairs, and the poor fellow sat up in his bed with his hair and beard all tangled, and talked as cheerfully as if he had been in a King's palace.

Henley became, till Stevenson's marriage, one of his closest friends; he was the model of Long John Silver in *Treasure Island*. The two collaborated in writing four plays: *Deacon Brodie*,

Beau Austin, *Admiral Guinea* and *Macaire*. Henley's sonnet on Stevenson, *Apparition*, published in *A Book of Verses* (1888), begins: 'Thin-legged, thin-chested, slight unspeakably.'

XVII. *Henry James*

Henry James (1843–1916) the novelist. The names in italics are those of the heroines of James's stories: *Madame de Mauves*, *Georgina's Reasons*, *Daisy Miller*, *Lady Barberina*, and *The Bostonians*.

Stevenson and Henry James first met at Bournemouth in 1885, when an acquaintance that had begun with letters quickly developed into a warm and lasting friendship. It is amusing to contrast these verses, written after Stevenson knew James, with the following doggerel written to Henley from Davos, 1882, when Stevenson only knew James through his works. The manuscript is in the National Library of Scotland.

H. James

Not clad in transatlantic furs
    But clinking English pence
The young republic claims me hers
    In no parochial sense.

A bland colossus, mark me stride
    From land to land, the sea
And patronise on every side
    Far better men than me.

My books, that models are of wit
    And masterworks of art
From occident to orient flit
    And please in every part.

Yet I'm a sentimental lot
    And fairly weep to see
Poor Hawthorne and the rest who've not
    To Europe been like me.

XVIII. *The Mirror Speaks*

Facsimile in *Henry James and R. L. Stevenson*, edited by Janet Adam Smith, 1948, p. 113, shows minor variations from the *Underwoods* version.

Henry James, a regular evening visitor at Skerryvore, the Stevensons' house in Bournemouth, had sent them a mirror which they hung in the drawing-room. Mrs Stevenson wrote to James on 25 February, 1886:

A magic mirror has come to us which seems to reflect
not only our own plain faces, but the kindly one of a friend
entwined in the midst of all sorts of pleasant memories.
Louis felt that verse alone would fitly convey his sentiments
concerning this beautiful present, but his muse, I believe,
has not as yet responded to his call!

Ten days later, on 7 March, Stevenson sent this poem, intro-
duced by, 'This is what the glass says.'

XIX. *Katharine*

Katharine de Mattos. See note to *To K. de M.*, p. 472.

XX. *To F. J. S.*

Mrs Frances Sitwell, who, with Sidney Colvin, met Stevenson
in 1873, and gave him the sympathy, and the introductions, which
were so to help him as a writer. It is from his long letters to her
that we know so much about Stevenson's feelings and ambitions
during the years 1873–1876. Mrs Sitwell married Colvin in 1903.
A manuscript described in *B.B.S. II,* 144, and now Beinecke
6998, is reproduced in facsimile in *Beinecke* V, facing page 2013:
the words 'To Claire' at the head have been deleted. Dated
'Mentone, Novr. 15th 1873'. Another copy was sent in a letter
to Mrs Sitwell, Beinecke 3274 (published in *Three Letters,* 1902)
where it is prefaced by the words

> Here is what I have often said in good prose, put into
> bad verse.

Four stanzas not printed in *Underwoods* follow:

> And thorns! But did the sculptor spare
> Sharp steel upon the marble ere
> Thro' cruel discipline of blows,
> From the dead stone, the statue rose?
>
> Think you I grudge the seed, who see,
> Wide armed, the consummated tree?
> Or would go back, if it might be,
> To some old geologic time
> With Saurians wallowing in the slime,
>
> Before the rivers and the rains
> Had fashioned, and made fair with plains
> And shadowy places fresh with flowers,
> This green and quiet world of ours,

> Where, as the grass in springtime heals
> The furrows of the winter's wheels,
> Serene maturity conceals
> All memory, on the perfect earth
> Of the bygone tempestuous birth.

XXI. *Requiem*

Although the poem is dated 'Hyères, May, 1884', the first draft, of which there is a facsimile in *Beinecke* V facing p. 1954, is dated 'Train August 79', when Stevenson was on his way to California to marry Fanny Osbourne and feeling very ill. It runs:

> Now when the number of my years
> Is all fulfilled, and I
> From sedentary life
> Shall rouse me up to die,
> > Bury me low and let me lie
> > Under the wide and starry sky,
> > Joying to live, I joyed to die.
> > Bury me low and let me lie.
>
> Clear was my soul, my deeds were free,
> > Honour was called my name,
> > I fell not back from fear
> > Nor followed after fame.
> > Bury me low and let me lie
> > Under the wide and starry sky, etc.
>
> Bury me low in vallies green
> > And where the milder breeze
> > Blows fresh along the stream,
> > Sings roundly in the trees—
> > > Bury me low, etc.

Stevenson to Colvin, San Francisco, February, 1880:

Sketch of my tomb follows:

ROBERT LOUIS STEVENSON

BORN 1850, OF A FAMILY OF ENGINEERS,

DIED ....

'NITOR AQUIS'

HOME IS THE SAILOR, HOME FROM SEA,
AND THE HUNTER HOME FROM THE HILL.

. . . I may perhaps try to write it better some day; but that is what I want in sense. The verses are from a beayootiful poem by me. [They were in fact engraved on his tomb on Mount Vaea.]

To Gosse, 8 December, 1879:

Nitor aquis said a certain Eton boy, translating for his sins a part of the *Inland Voyage* into Latin elegiacs; and from the hour I saw it, or rather a friend of mine, the admirable Jenkin, saw and recognised its absurd appropriateness, I took it for my device in life.

A facsimile of the manuscript of another version is reproduced in *Beinecke* V, facing page 1995. It is dated '1880 Jan. S.F.' and has three verses; the first and third are the first and second of the *Underwoods* version, and the second runs:

Here may the winds about me blow;
Here the clouds may come and go;
Here shall be rest for evermo,
    And the heart for aye shall be still.

Stevenson died suddenly in Samoa on 3 December, 1894; on 22 December the following verses by A. E. Housman appeared in the *Academy*:

R. L. S.

Home is the sailor, home from sea:
    Her far-borne canvas furled
The ship pours shining on the quay
    The plunder of the world.

Home is the hunter from the hill:
    Fast in the boundless snare
All flesh lies taken at his will
    And every fowl of air.

'Tis evening on the moorland free,
    The starlit wave is still:
Home is the sailor from the sea,
    The hunter from the hill.

(Other verses were written on Stevenson's death by John Davidson, Richard Garnett, Richard Le Gallienne, and J. M. Barrie.)

XXII. *The Celestial Surgeon*

Balfour dates it 1882.

XXIII. *Our Lady of the Snows*

Stevenson visited the Trappist Monastery of Our Lady of the Snows, among the hills of Vivarais, during his walking tour in the Cevennes in 1878. See *Travels with a Donkey*. *Balfour* dates it 1878.

Stevenson to Henley, Edinburgh, April, 1879, in answer to some criticism of *Our Lady of the Snows*:

> Heavens! have I done the like? 'Clarify and strain,' indeed? 'Make it like Marvell,' no less. I'll tell you what— you may go to the devil; that's what I think. 'Be eloquent' is another of your pregnant suggestions. I cannot sufficiently thank you for that one. Portrait of a person about to be eloquent at the request of a literary friend. You seem to forget, sir, that rhyme is rhyme, sir, and—go to the devil.
>
> I'll try to improve it, but I shan't be able to—O go to the devil.
>
> Seriously, you're a cool hand. And then you have the brass to ask me *why* 'my steps went one by one'? Why? Powers of man! to rhyme with *sun*, to be sure. Why else could it be? And you yourself have been a poet! G-r-r-r-r! I'll never be a poet any more. Men are so d—d ungrateful and captious, I declare I could weep.

Then follow the lines printed on p. 348, beginning 'O Henley, in my hours of ease.'

> . . . I see I must write some more to you about my Monastery. I am a weak brother in verse. You ask me to re-write things that I have already managed just to write with the skin of my teeth. If I don't re-write them, it's because I don't see how to write them better, not because I don't think they should be. But, curiously enough, you condemn two of my favourite passages, one of which is J. W. Ferrier's favourite of the whole. Here I shall think it's you who are wrong. You see, I did not try to make good verse, but to say what I wanted as well as verse would let me. I don't like the rhyme 'ear' and 'hear.' But the couplet, 'My undissuaded heart I hear Whisper courage in my ear,' is exactly what I want for the thought, and to me seems very energetic as speech, if not as verse. Would 'daring' be better than courage? *Je me le demande*. No, it would be ambiguous, as though I had used it licentiously for 'daringly,' and that would cloak the sense.
>
> In short, your suggestions have broken the heart of the

scald. He doesn't agree with them all; and those he does agree with, the spirit indeed is willing, but the damned flesh cannot, cannot, cannot see its way to profit by. I think I'll lay it by for nine years, like Horace. I think the well of Castaly's run out. No more the Muses round my pillow haunt. I am fallen once more to the mere proser. God bless you.

Professor Garrod has pointed out (in *Essays presented to Sir Humphrey Milford*, 1948) the similarity of theme between this poem and Matthew Arnold's *Stanzas from the Grande Chartreuse*.

A. E. Housman, who so often has echoes from Stevenson, may have had two lines from this poem:

> And bear the falling sky with ease,
> Unfrowning caryatides—

in mind when writing his *Epitaph on an Army of Mercenaries*:

> These, in the day when heaven was falling . . .
> Their shoulders held the sky suspended.

See also note to *Men are Heaven's piers*, p. 528.

In the first edition of *Underwoods*, *bell* in l. 11 was printed as *hell*.

XXIV. *Not yet, my soul, these friendly fields desert*

Written at the same time as a letter from Stevenson to Gosse, San Francisco, 16 April, 1880:

You have not answered my last; and I know you will repent when you hear how near I have been to another world. For about six weeks I have been in utter doubt; it was a toss-up for life or death all that time; but I won the toss, sir, and Hades went off once more discomfited. This is not the first time, nor will it be the last, that I have a friendly game with that gentleman. I know he will end by cleaning me out; but the rogue is insidious, and the habit of that sort of gambling seems to be a part of my nature; it was, I suspect, too much indulged in youth; break your children of this tendency, my dear Gosse, from the first. It is, when once formed, a habit more fatal than opium—I speak, as St. Paul says, like a fool. I have been very very sick; on the verge of a galloping consumption, cold sweats, prostrating attacks of cough, sinking fits in which I lost the power of speech, fever, and all the ugliest circumstances of the disease; and I have cause to bless God, my wife that is to be, and one Dr Bamford (a name the Muse repels), that I have come out of all this, and got my feet once more upon a little hilltop, with a fair prospect of life and some new desire of living. Yet I did not wish to die, neither; only I felt unable to go on farther with that rough horseplay of human life: a man must be pretty well to take the business in good part. Yet I felt all the time that I had done nothing to entitle me to an honourable discharge; that I had taken up many obligations and begun many friendships which I had no right to put away from me; and that for me to die was to play the cur and slinking sybarite, and desert the colours on the eve of the decisive fight. Of course I have done no work for I do not know how long; and here you can triumph. I have been reduced to writing verses for amusement. A fact. The whirligig of time brings in its revenges, after all. But I'll have them buried with me, I think, for I have not the heart to burn them while I live.

XXV. *It is not yours, O mother, to complain*
Balfour dates it 1880.

XXVI. *The Sick Child*

The poem was first published in the first number of *The State*, 10 April, 1886, a short-lived magazine edited by A. Egmont Hake. This version has two extra stanzas:

> So in the dream-beleaguered night,
> 　While the other children lie
> 　Quiet, and the stars are high,
> The poor, unused and playful mite
> Lies strangling in the grasp of fright.

> O, when all golden comes the day,
> 　And the other children leap
> 　Singing from the doors of sleep,
> Lord, take Thy heavy hand away!
> Lord, in Thy mercy heal or slay!

Stevenson to Mrs Sitwell, 24 September, 1873:

. . . Most of the lamps had been extinguished but not all, and there were two or three lit windows in the opposite façade that showed where sick people and watchers had been awake all night and knew not yet of the new, cool day. This appealed to me with a special sadness: how often in the old times my nurse and I had looked across at these, and sympathised.

XXVII. *In Memoriam F. A. S.*

F. A. S. was Mrs Sitwell's son Bertie. Stevenson had gone to Davos for the winter of 1880–1881, for the sake of his lungs; and, early in 1881, Mrs Sitwell arrived there with her son of eighteen, already very ill, who died a few days after.

Stevenson to Colvin, Davos, January, 1881:

> As to F. A. S., I believe I am no sound authority; I alternate between a stiff disregard and a kind of horror. In neither mood can a man judge at all. I know the thing to be terribly perilous, I fear it to be now altogether hopeless. Luck has failed; the weather has not been favourable; and in her true heart, the mother hopes no more. But—well, I feel a great deal, that I either cannot or will not say, as you well know. It has helped to make me more conscious of the wolverine on my own shoulders, and that also makes me a poor judge and poor adviser.

Balfour dates it 1881; a facsimile of an early draft of this poem, in blank verse, appears in *Stevenson's Workshop*, 1921, Nos. 10 and 11.

XXVIII. *To My Father*

Thomas Stevenson (1818–1887) was, like his father, grandfather, and two of his brothers, Engineer to the Board of Northern Lights.

> Thomas Stevenson did much valuable work in lighthouse building and in the improvement of rivers and harbours, but it is in connection with the illumination of lighthouses that his name will be remembered. He brought to perfection the revolving light, and himself invented 'the azimuthal condensing system.' More familiar to the world at large, if less remarkable, are the louvre-boarded screens which he applied to the protection of meteorological instruments.   BALFOUR

Stevenson also wrote of his father in an essay *Thomas Stevenson, Civil Engineer*, which was included in *Memories and Portraits*, and in a fragment, *Memoirs of Himself*, which appears in the Tusitala Edition volume of *Memories and Portraits*. See also *The Last Sight*, p. 282, and note, p. 516.

XXIX. *In the States*

Stevenson arrived in San Francisco in August, 1879, having crossed the States on an emigrant train. After spending the autumn in the Coast-line Mountains and at Monterey, he returned to San Francisco in December, where this poem was written. There is another poem in much the same key, and possibly written at the same time, which was not included in *Underwoods*, and was published first in *B.B.S. III*, 1921:

> I look across the ocean,
>   And kneel upon the shore,
> I look out seaward—westward,
>   My heart swells more and more.
>
> I see the great new nation,
>   New spirit and new scope
> Rise there from the sea's round shoulder—
>   A splendid sun of hope!
>
> I see it and I tremble—
>   My voice is full of tears—
> America tread softly,
>   You bear the fruit of years.
>
> Tread softly—you are pregnant
>   And growing near your time.

XXX. *A Portrait*

The verses entitled *A Portrait* have puzzled many readers and have been often, but always erroneously, explained. They were the outcome of a strong, improvised distaste for a certain writer who was much before the public in the seventies, and whom Stevenson met in the flesh but once. I happen to have been present on that solitary occasion, and I was the witness of a certain clash of temperaments, very unfortunate and rather inexplicable, in the course of which the fault lay not on Stevenson's side. *A Portrait*—as it was afterwards called—was written that afternoon, in what was certainly a ruffled mood of high spirits; and I possess the MS. of another epigram, directed, at the same time, against the same author, which, if it were printed (but it shall not be printed), would end in a moment all discussion as to who was portrayed as 'a kind of farthing dip.' There is no good to be done by speculating as to the identity of the object of Stevenson's satire, about whom there is indeed no doubt, but shall be as much discretion as possible.

                                                          GOSSE

Stevenson's original title, on a manuscript sold at Sotheby's in November, 1949, 364, saves us from speculating: it is *Mallock loquitur.* W. H. Mallock (1849–1923) was the author of *The New Republic.*

This manuscript, now in the Beinecke Collection 6733, has four additional verses. A copy of the poem written out by Henley and given to Gosse in 1882 is now in the Huntington Library and is printed in Elsie Caldwell's *Last Witness for Robert Louis Stevenson*, 1960, pp. 308–309. It contains one of the additional verses, also the epigram mentioned by Gosse in the passage quoted above.

XXXII. *A Camp*

Lines, ascribed to an *Old Play*, which preface the chapters on *Upper Gévaudan (continued)* in *Travels with A Donkey* (1879).

XXXIII. *The Country of the Camisards*

Lines, ascribed to W. P. Bannatyne, which appear at the head of the section with the same title in *Travels with a Donkey*. See note to *John Cavalier*, p. 466.

XXXIV and XXXV. *Skerryvore* and *Skerryvore: The Parallel*

When the Stevensons moved into a house of their own at Bournemouth in 1885—given to Mrs Stevenson by her father-in-law—R. L. Stevenson gave it the name of Skerryvore, the lighthouse ten miles S.W. of Tiree built by his father and his uncle Alan Stevenson, 'the noblest of all extant deep-sea lights.'

Stevenson to Miss Monroe, June, 1886:

> We are all very proud of the family achievements, and the name of my house here in Bournemouth is stolen from one of the sea-towers of the Hebrides which are our pyramids and monuments.

An exchange of verses between Stevenson and Dr Dobell of Bournemouth (brother of Sydney Dobell) occasioned by the name Skerryvore and the model of the lighthouse in the hall, was printed in *The Times Literary Supplement* of 4 December, 1919.

Two other inscriptions for Skerryvore will be found in the Tusitala Edition, II, 178.

XXXVI. *My house, I say. But hark to the sunny doves*

A manuscript with eight additional lines is described in *B.B.S. II*, 149.

XXXVIII. *Say not of me that weakly I declined*

But in a letter to Will H. Low many years later (15 January, 1894), within a year of his death, Stevenson burst out with: 'I ought to have been able to build lighthouses and write *David Balfours* too.'

BOOK II: IN SCOTS

Stevenson's own note to the poems in Scots:

The human conscience has fled of late the troublesome
domain of conduct for what I should have supposed to be
the less congenial field of art: there she may now be said to
rage, and with special severity in all that touches dialect; so
that in every novel the letters of the alphabet are tortured,
and the reader wearied, to commemorate shades of mis-
pronunciation. Now spelling is an art of great difficulty in
my eyes, and I am inclined to lean upon the printer, even
in common practice, rather than to venture abroad upon
new quests. And the Scots tongue has an orthography of
its own, lacking neither 'authority nor author.' Yet the
temptation is great to lend a little guidance to the be-
wildered Englishman. Some simple phonetic artifice might
defend your verses from barbarous mishandling, and yet
not injure any vested interest. So it seems at first; but
there are rocks ahead. Thus, if I wish the diphthong *ou* to
have its proper value, I may write *oor* instead of *our*; many
have done so and lived, and the pillars of the universe
remained unshaken. But if I did so, and came presently to
doun, which is the classical Scots spelling of the English
down, I should begin to feel uneasy; and if I went on a little
farther, and came to a classical Scots word, like *stour* or *dour*
or *clour*, I should know precisely where I was—that is to
say, that I was out of sight of land on those high seas of
spelling reform in which so many strong swimmers have
toiled vainly. To some the situation is exhilarating; as for
me, I give one bubbling cry and sink. The compromise at
which I have arrived is indefensible, and I have no thought
of trying to defend it. As I have stuck for the most part to
the proper spelling, I append a table of some common vowel
sounds which no one need consult; and just to prove that
I belong to my age and have in me the stuff of a reformer,
I have used modification marks throughout. Thus I can tell
myself, not without pride, that I have added a fresh
stumbling-block for English readers, and to a page of print
in my native tongue, have lent a new uncouthness. *Sed non
nobis.*

I note again, that among our new dialecticians, the local
habitat of every dialect is given to the square mile. I could
not emulate this nicety if I desired; for I simply wrote my

Scots as well I was able, not caring if it hailed from Lauder-
dale or Angus, from the Mearns or Galloway; if I had ever
heard a good word, I used it without shame; and when
Scots was lacking, or the rhyme jibbed, I was glad (like my
betters) to fall back on English. For all that, I own to a
friendly feeling for the tongue of Fergusson and of Sir
Walter, both Edinburgh men; and I confess that Burns
has always sounded in my ear like something partly foreign.
And indeed I am from the Lothians myself; it is there I
heard the language spoken about my childhood; and it is in
the drawling Lothian voice that I repeat it to myself. Let
the precisians call my speech that of the Lothians. And if it
be not pure, alas! what matters it? The day draws near
when this illustrious and malleable tongue shall be quite
forgotten: and Burns's Ayrshire, and Dr Macdonald's
Aberdeen-awa', and Scott's brave, metropolitan utterance
will be all equally the ghosts of speech. Till then I would
love to have my hour as a native Maker, and be read by my
own countryfolk in our own dying language: an ambition
surely rather of the heart than of the head, so restricted as it
is in prospect of endurance, so parochial in bounds of space.

TABLE OF COMMON SCOTTISH VOWEL SOUNDS

ae ⎫
ai ⎬ = open A as in rare.

a' ⎫
au ⎬ = AW as in law.
aw ⎭

ea = open E as in mere, but this with exceptions, as
  heather = heather, wean = wain, lear = lair.

ee ⎫
ei ⎬ = open E as in mere.
ie ⎭

oa = open O as in more.
ou = double O as in poor.
ow = OW as in bower.
u = double O as in poor.
ui or ü before R = (say roughly) open A as in rare.
ui or ü before any other consonant = (say roughly) close I
  as in grin.
y = open I as in kite.

[487]

i = pretty nearly what you please, much as in English. Heaven guide the reader through that labyrinth! But in Scots it dodges usually from the short I, as in grin, to the open E, as in mere. Find and blind, I may remark, are pronounced to rhyme with the preterite of grin.

Poems I, II, III, V, VII, VIII, X, XI, XIII, XIV, XV (and the *Pieces in Lallan* on pp. 101–108) are written in the 'Burns stanza,' which was in fact used long before Burns. It was a troubadour measure which had been popular in Scotland since the fifteenth century: Sir Robert Sempill's *Epitaph of Habbie Simson, Piper of Kilbarchan* (early seventeenth century) is the best known of the early examples, and Ramsay, Fergusson and Burns established it as the distinctively Scottish measure.

II. *Ille Terrarum*

Written 1875. In the Stevenson Museum at 8 Howard Place, Edinburgh, is a manuscript which contains seven of the twelve verses of this poem, under the heading *Swanston*.

Letter to Alison Cunningham from Bournemouth, 16 April, 1887:

> . . . as I write, there is a blackbird singing in our garden trees, as it were at Swanston. I would like fine to go up the burnside a bit, and sit by the pool and be young again— or no, be what I am still, only there instead of here, for just a little.

III. *When aince Aprile has fairly come*

The manuscript note-book of Stevenson's (*Sotheby*, May, 1949, 79) headed *Pieces in Lallan*, includes this as No. VII, and gives a variant version of lines 2 and 3.

> An' winter turned his icy bum
>   Wi' pleasand days to a' and some—

See note to *Pieces in Lallan*, p. 467.

IV. *A mile an' a bittock, a mile or twa*
    Balfour dates it 1884.

V. *A Lowden Sabbath Morn*

Stevenson's own note:

> It may be guessed by some that I had a certain parish in my eye, and this makes it proper I should add a word of disclamation. In my time there have been two ministers

in that parish. Of the first I have a special reason to speak well, even had there been any to think ill. The second I have often met in private and long (in the due phrase) 'sat under' in his church, and neither here nor there have I heard an unkind or ugly word upon his lips. The preacher of the text had thus no original in that particular parish; but when I was a boy, he might have been observed in many others; he was then (like the schoolmaster) abroad; and by recent advices it would seem he has not yet entirely disappeared.

There are some additional stanzas in a manuscript described in *B.B.S. II*, p. 152.

Between stanzas 1 and 2:

> A' legs an' airms, the dand'rin men
> Hing round the doors and doun the glen—
> They're naethin', wantin' work, ye ken,
>   Tho' blythe to want it—
> While weemin folk are hit an' hen
>   An' gey fu' handit.

Between stanzas 5 and 6:

> Again the bells begin to jowl,
> And as their airn summons rowl,
> Gudeman, just clappin' hat on pow
>   Taks first the gate;
> An' the hale clan comes on in tow
>   Wi' face sedate.

> Noo under rowth o' hawthorn bloom
> Whaur simmer flees may swarf and soom,
> The thrangin' gate shune lacks for room
>   As friens foregaither.
> —The day, the kirk'll no be toom
>   Says ain to ither.

The same manuscript has a variant for the first two lines of stanza 10:

> But here we are, we've no been lang
> The mill-door sings its sabbath sang.

Stevenson's Workshop prints a facsimile, No. 21, of a much corrected draft of verses 6, 9 and 10.

VI. *The Spaewife*

Mrs Stevenson, in her Prefatory Note to *Underwoods* in the Tusitala Edition, Vol. I, p. 59, prints a Scottish tune, sent to her

by 'a Scotsman, Mr George St. J. Bremner, of San Francisco
. . . that perfectly corresponds with the peculiar movement of
the poem.'

VII. *The Blast—1875*

Cf. Housman, *Last Poems*, IX: *The Chestnut casts his Flam-
beaux.*

X. *Their Laureate to an Academy Class Dinner Club*

Stevenson went in 1861 to Edinburgh Academy and spent
a year and a half in the class of 'my own Academy master, the
delightful D'Arcy Thompson.' Class and master moved up
the school together, so they were always the 'Thamson class.'
This poem was written for the 1885 dinner, and privately
printed and distributed in a leaflet of four pages, *To The Thompson
Class Club: The Laureat Ste'enson to the Thamson Class.* A set
of verses for the 1883 dinner, *Friends that here together met*, is
printed in *Widener* 73; the verses for 1875 are printed in this
volume, *Light Verse: Poem for a Class Re-union*, p. 333.

XI. *Embro Hie Kirk*

The tradition of engaging in ecclesiastical controversy in the
'Burns stanza' goes back at least as far as Burns's *Holy Willie*
and *Twa Herds.* The current question was the installation of an
organ ('The rumlin' kist o' whustles') in the High Kirk of St.
Giles.

XII. *The Scotsman's Return from Abroad*

Written, says Mrs Stevenson, in 1880, after his own return
from California, 'to amuse his father when we were stopping
with his family in Strathpeffer, a dreary "hydropathic" in the
Highlands.' (See *On Some Ghastly Companions at a Spa*, p. 337.)
'Thomson' and 'Johnstone' were roles invented for themselves
in their student days by Stevenson and his friend and lawyer
Charles Baxter. They wrote letters to each other in character:
Stevenson described Thomson (letter to Baxter of 13 November,
1884) as:

> A plain, auld ex-elder that, tak him the way he taks
> himsel', 's just aboot as honest as he can weel afford, an'
> but for a wheen auld scandals, near forgotten noo, is a
> pairfec'ly respectable and thoroughly decent man.

See also letter of 12 January, 1883.

Several of the Scots poems in *Underwoods* might be spoken in the character of Thomson. In the Preface to *The Master of Ballantrae* in Vol. XXVIII of the Edinburgh Edition, mention is made of the discovery of papers in the office of Mr Johnstone Thomson, W.S.

XV. *To Doctor John Brown*

Dr John Brown (1810–1882) doctor and essayist, was the author of *Horae Subsecivae*.

Stevenson to his parents, Davos, 21 December, 1880:

> About John Brown, I have been breaking my heart to finish a Scotch poem to him. Some of it is not really bad, but the rest will not come, and I mean to get it right before I do anything else.

Neil is Niel Gow, a fiddler of almost legendary excellence and fame who lived in Atholl at the end of the eighteenth century: he was painted by Raeburn.

BALLADS

Stevenson wrote the greater part of the first two ballads during his two months in Tahiti in 1888 as the guest of Princess Moë and Ori, the sub-chief of the village of Tautira where they stayed. He originally planned a volume to consist entirely of South Sea Ballads: but his plans for others were not fulfilled, so he put in *Ticonderoga*, written in 1887, *Heather Ale*, *Christmas at Sea* and some shorter poems, including *The House of Tembinoka*, which were ultimately left out of the volume and published later in *Songs of Travel*, 1895.

Stevenson to E. L. Burlingame of Scribner's, Sydney, August 1890, on receiving proofs:

> The deuce is in this volume. It has cost me more bothera-tion and dubiety than any other I ever took in hand. On one thing my mind is made up: the verses at the end have no business there, and throw them down. Many of them are bad, many of the rest want nine years' keeping, and the re-mainder are not relevant—throw them down; some I never want to hear of more, others will grow in time towards decent items in a second *Underwoods*—and in the meanwhile, down with them! At the same time, I have a sneaking idea the ballads are not altogether without merit—I don't

> know if they're poetry, but they're good narrative, or I'm
> deceived.

When the *Ballads* were published in 1890 their reception was
not very encouraging. Stevenson to H. B. Baildon, Spring 1891:

> Glad the *Ballads* amused you. They failed to entertain a
> coy public, at which I wondered; not that I set much
> account by my verses, which are the verses of Prosator; but
> I do know how to tell a yarn, and two of the yarns are great.

And to Gosse, April, 1891:

> By the by, my *Ballads* seem to have been dam bad; all
> the crickets sing so in their crickety papers; and I have no
> ghost of an idea on the point myself: verse is always to me
> the unknowable.

The Song of Rahéro

Dedication: Ori a Ori was the sub-chief of Tautira, in whose
house the Stevensons stayed during November and December,
1888. Stevenson to Colvin, 14 January, 1889:

> But the best fortune of our stay at Tautira was my
> knowledge of Ori himself, one of the finest creatures extant.
> The day of our parting was a sad one. We deduced from it a
> rule for travellers: not to stay two months in one place—
> which is to cultivate regrets.

Mrs Stevenson to Colvin, 4 December, 1888:

> Ori is the very finest specimen of a native we have seen
> yet; he is several inches over six feet, of perfect though
> almost gigantic proportions, and looks more like a Roman
> Emperor in bronze than words can express. One day, when
> Moë gave a feast, it being the correct thing to do, we all
> wore wreaths of golden yellow leaves on our heads; when
> Ori walked in and sat down at the table, as with one voice
> we all cried out in admiration. His manners and I might
> say his habit of thought are English. In some ways, he is so
> like a Colonel of the Guards that we often call him Colonel.
> It was either the day before, or the morning of our public
> feast, that Louis asked the Princess if she thought Ori would
> accept his name. She was sure of it, and much pleased at the
> idea. I wish you could have seen Louis, blushing like a school-
> girl, when Ori came in, and the brotherhood was offered.
> So now if you please, Louis is no more Louis, having given
> that name away in the Tahitian form of Rui, but is known

as Terii-Tera (pronounced Ter*ee*terah) that being Ori's Christian name. 'Ori of Ori' is his clan name.

The feeling was not one-sided. The day after the Stevensons finally sailed from Tahiti, Ori wrote them the following words:

> I make you to know my great affection. At the hour when you left us, I was filled with tears; my wife, Rui Tehini, also, and all of my household. When you embarked I felt a great sorrow. It is for this that I went upon the road, and you looked from that ship, and I looked at you on the ship with great grief until you had raised the anchor and hoisted the sails. When the ship started, I ran along the beach to see you still; and when you were on the open sea I cried out to you, 'farewell Louis': and when I was coming back to my house I seemed to hear your voice crying 'Rui, farewell.' Afterwards I watched the ship as long as I could until the night fell; and when it was dark I said to myself, 'if I had wings I should fly to the ship to meet you, and to sleep amongst you, so that I might be able to come back to shore and to tell Rui Tehini, 'I have slept upon the ship of Teriitera.'

Extract from Stevenson's Will:

> I leave to Ori a Ori, sub-chief of Tautira, Island of Tahiti, a gold watch and chain with a suitable inscription, on the purchase of which I pray my executors to spare no reasonable expense.

Stevenson heard the legend of Rahéro from the beautiful Tahitian Princess Moë, his hostess at Tautira. Half was written before he left Tahiti, in 1888, the rough draft finished later, on board the yacht *Casco*. Stevenson to H. B. Baildon, Vailima, Spring, 1891:

> *Rahéro* is for its length a perfect folk-tale: savage and yet fine, full of tailforemost morality, ancient as the granite rocks; if the historian, not to say the politician, could get that yarn into his head, he would have learned some of his A.B.C. But the average man at home cannot understand antiquity; he is sunk over the ears in Roman civilisation; and a tale like that of *Rahéro* falls on his ears inarticulate.

Stevenson's own notes to the ballad run:

INTRODUCTION.—This tale, of which I have not consciously changed a single feature, I received from tradition. It is highly popular through all the country of the eight Tevas, the clan to which Rahéro belonged; and particularly in Taiárapu, the windward peninsula of Tahiti, where he lived. I have heard from end to end two versions; and as many as five different persons have helped me with details. There seems no reason why the tale should not be true.

P. 182, l. 14. 'The aito,' *quasi* champion, or brave. One skilled in the use of some weapon, who wandered the country challenging distinguished rivals and taking part in local quarrels. It was in the natural course of his advancement to be at last employed by a chief, or king; and it would then be a part of his duties to purvey the victim for sacrifice. One of the doomed families was indicated; the aito took his weapon and went forth alone; a little behind him bearers followed with the sacrificial basket. Sometimes the victim showed fight, sometimes prevailed; more often, without doubt, he fell. But whatever body was found, the bearers indifferently took up.

P. 183, l. 19. 'Pai,' 'Honoura,' and 'Ahupu.' Legendary persons of Tahiti, all natives of Taiárapu. Of the first two, I have collected singular although imperfect legends, which I hope soon to lay before the public in another place. Of Ahupu, except in snatches of song, little memory appears to linger. She dwelt at least about Tepari—'the sea-cliffs'—the eastern fastness of the isle; walked by paths known only to herself upon the mountains; was courted by dangerous suitors who came swimming from adjacent islands, and defended and rescued (as I gather) by the loyalty of native fish. My anxiety to learn more of 'Ahupu Vehine' became (during my stay in Taiárapua) cause of some diversion to that mirthful people, the inhabitants.

P. 185, l. 10. 'Covered an oven.' The cooking fire is made in a hole in the ground, and is then buried.

P. 185, l. 15. 'Flies.' This is perhaps an anachronism. Even speaking of today in Tahiti, the phrase would have to be understood as referring mainly to mosquitoes, and these only in watered valleys with close woods, such as I suppose to form the surroundings of Rahéro's homestead. A quarter of a mile away where the air moves freely, you shall look in vain for one.

P. 187, l. 7. 'Hook' of mother-of-pearl. Bright-hook fishing, and that with the spear, appear to be the favourite native methods.

P. 188, l. 7. 'Leaves,' the plates of Tahiti.

P. 188, l. 18. 'Yottowas,' so spelt for convenience of pronunciation, *quasi* Tacksmen in the Scottish Highlands. The organisation of eight subdistricts and eight yottowas to a division, which was in use (until yesterday) among the Tevas, I have attributed without authority to the next clan: see page 198.

P. 189, l. 16. 'Ómare,' pronounced as a dactyl. A loaded quarter-staff, one of the two favourite weapons of the Tahitian brave; the javelin, or casting spear, was the other.

P. 191, l. 16. 'The ribbon of light.' Still to be seen—and heard—spinning from one marae to another on Tahiti; or so I have it upon evidence that would rejoice the Psychical Society.

P. 192, l. 13. 'Námunu-úra.' The complete name is Námunu-úra te aropa. Why it should be pronounced Námunu, dactyllically, I cannot see, but so I have always heard it. This was the clan immediately beyond the Tevas on the south coast of the island. At the date of the tale the clan organisation must have been very weak. There is no particular mention of Támatéa's mother going to Papara, to the head chief of her own clan, which would appear her natural recourse. On the other hand, she seems to have visited various lesser chiefs among the Tevas, and these to have excused themselves solely on the danger of the enterprise. The broad distinction here drawn between Nateva and Námunu-úra is therefore not impossibly anachronistic.

P. 192, l. 15. 'Hiopa the king.' Hiopa was really the name of the king (chief) of Vaiau; but I could never learn that of the king of Paea—pronounce to rhyme with the Indian *ayah*—and I gave the name where it was most needed. This note must appear otiose indeed to readers who have never heard of either of these two gentlemen; and perhaps there is only one person in the world capable at once of reading my verses and spying the inaccuracy. For him, for Mr Tati Salmon, hereditary high chief of the Tevas, the note is solely written: a small attention from a clansman to his chief.

P. 193, l. 11. 'Let the pigs be tapu.' It is impossible to explain 'tapu' in a note; we have it as an English word, taboo. Suffice it, that a thing which was 'tapu' must not be touched, nor a place that was 'tapu' visited.

P. 199, l. 1. 'Fish, the food of desire.' There is a special word in the Tahitian language to signify 'hungering after fish.' I may remark that here is one of my chief difficulties about the whole story. How did king, commons, women and all come to eat together at this feast? But it troubled none of my numerous authorities; so there must certainly be some natural explanation.

P. 202, l. 14. 'The mustering word of the clan.'

> Teva te ua,
> Teva te matai!
>
> Teva the wind,
> Teva the rain!

P. 208, ll. 4 and 6. 'The star of the dead.' Venus as a morning star. I have collected much curious evidence as to this belief. The dead retain their taste for a fish diet, enter into copartnery with living fishers, and haunt the reef and the lagoon. The conclusion attributed to the nameless lady of the legend would be reached today, under the like circumstances, by ninety per cent of Polynesians: and here I probably understate by one-tenth.

The Feast of Famine

Written in the Autumn of 1888, in Tahiti, and sent to Colvin at the same time as a letter dated 16 October:

> I can imagine how you will wag your pow over it; and how ragged you will find it, etc., but has it not spirit all the same? and though the verse is not all your fancy painted it, has it not some life? And surely, as narrative, the thing has considerable merit! Read it, get a typewritten copy taken, and send me that and your opinion to the Sandwiches . . .
>
> > O, how my spirit languishes
> > To step ashore on the Sanguishes;
> > For there my letters wait,
> > There I shall know my fate
> > O, how my spirit languidges
> > To step ashore on the Sanguidges.

Colvin prefaces this letter with a note saying,

> I never very much admired his South Sea Ballads for any quality except their narrative vigour, thinking them unequal and uncertain both in metre and style.

Professor Garrod, in his essay, *The Poetry of R. L. Stevenson* (*Essays Presented to Sir Humphrey Milford*, 1948), suggests that Rua's four-line song in Part II:

> Night, night it is, night upon the palms.
> Night, night it is, the land wind has blown.
> Starry, starry night, over deep and height;
> Love, love in the valley, love all alone.

may have been written for some undefined context at Hyères, where Stevenson first read Meredith's *Love in the Valley* in October 1883, and 'it got me, I wept.'

Stevenson's own notes run:

> In this ballad, I have strung together some of the more striking particularities of the Marquesas. It rests upon no authority; it is in no sense, like *Rahéro*, a native story; but a patchwork of details of manners and the impressions of a traveller. It may seem strange, when the scene is laid upon these profligate islands, to make the story hinge on love. But love is not less known in the Marquesas than elsewhere; nor is there any cause of suicide more common in the islands.
>
> P. 209, l. 2. 'Pit of popoi.' Where the breadfruit was stored for preservation.
>
> P. 210, l. 9. 'Ruby-red.' The priest's eyes were probably red from the abuse of kava. His beard—*ib.*—is said to be worth an estate; for the beards of old men are the favourite head adornment of the Marquesans, as the hair of women formed their most costly girdle. The former, among this generally beardless and short-lived people, fetch today considerable sums.
>
> P. 210, l. 14. 'Tikis.' The tiki is an ugly image hewn out of wood or stone.
>
> P. 212, l. 18. 'The one-stringed harp.' Usually employed for serenades.
>
> P. 214, l. 5. 'The sacred cabin of palm.' Which, however, no woman could approach. I do not know where women were tattooed; probably in the common house, or in the bush, for a woman was a creature of small account. I must guard the reader against supposing Taheia was at all disfigured; the art of the Marquesan tattooer is extreme; and she would appear to be clothed in a web of lace, inimitably delicate, exquisite in pattern, and of a bluish hue that at once contrasts and harmonises with the warm pigment of

[497]

the native skin. It would be hard to find a woman more becomingly adorned than 'a well-tattooed' Marquesan.

P. 215, l. 23. 'The horror of night.' The Polynesian fear of ghosts and of the dark has been already referred to. Their life is beleaguered by the dead.

P. 216, l. 13. 'The quiet passage of souls.' So, I am told, the natives explain the sound of a little wind passing overhead unfelt.

P. 218, l. 8. 'The first of the victims fell.' Without doubt this whole scene is untrue to fact. The victims were disposed of privately and some time before. And indeed I am far from claiming the credit of any high degree of accuracy for this ballad. Even in a time of famine, it is probable that Marquesan life went far more gaily than is here represented. But the melancholy of today lies on the writer's mind.

Ticonderoga

Ticonderoga was written during Stevenson's last visit to Edinburgh in May 1887 in the days following his father's death and funeral. The manuscript in the Ashley Library in the British Museum is partly written on the verso of some of the pages of a draft of his essay on his father published in the *Contemporary Review* for June, 1887 and reprinted in *Memories and Portraits*. In a letter to Colvin Stevenson described it as a 'damn fine ballad'. It first appeared in *Scribner's Magazine* for December, 1887; what was long regarded as a privately printed edition of 50 copies published for Christmas, 1887 is now known to be a forgery by T. J. Wise.

Before its publication in the *Ballads* in 1890 *Ticonderoga* was set up in type by the De Vinne Press of New York, at Stevenson's request. Two copies only were printed, one of which was forwarded to Stevenson in the South Seas, and presented by him to King Kalakaua: this presentation issue, of which the other copy is in the Widener Library and described in the Widener Catalogue, has several variations from the ordinary edition.

Stevenson's own notes run:

> INTRODUCTION.—I first heard this legend of my own country from that friend of men of letters, Mr Alfred Nutt, 'there in roaring London's central stream,' and since the ballad first saw the light of day in *Scribner's Magazine* Mr Nutt and Lord Archibald Campbell have been in public

controversy on the facts. Two clans, the Camerons and the Campbells, lay claim to this bracing story; and they do well: the man who preferred his plighted troth to the commands and menaces of the dead is an ancestor worth disputing. But the Campbells must rest content: they have the broad lands and the broad page of history; this appanage must be denied them; for between the name of 'Cameron' and that of 'Campbell,' the muse will never hesitate.

P. 229, l. 16. Mr Nutt reminds me it was 'by my sword and Ben Cruachan' the Cameron swore.

P. 232, l. 9. 'A periwig'd lord of London'. The first Pitt.

P. 233, l. 24. 'Cathay.' There must be some omission in General Stewart's charming *History of the Highland Regiments*, a book that might well be republished and continued; or it scarce appears how our friend could have got to China.

In his Introduction to the Swanston Edition Andrew Lang rebukes Stevenson ' for giving to a Cameron the part of the generous hero . . . The tale is a tale of the Campbells, of Clan Diarmaid, and the Muse must adhere to the historic truth.'

Heather Ale

Stevenson's own note runs:

Among the curiosities of human nature, this legend claims a high place. It is needless to remind the reader that the Picts were never exterminated, and form to this day a large proportion of the folk of Scotland: occupying the eastern and the central parts, from the Firth of Forth, or perhaps the Lammermoors, upon the south, to the Ord of Caithness on the north. That the blundering guess of a dull chronicler should have inspired men with imaginary loathing for their own ancestors is already strange: that it should have begotten this wild legend seems incredible. Is it possible the chronicler's error was merely nominal? that what he told, and what the people proved themselves so ready to receive, about the Picts, was true or partly true of some anterior and perhaps Lappish savages, small of stature, black of hue, dwelling underground—possibly also the distillers of some forgotten spirit? See Mr Campbell's *Tales of the West Highlands*.

Christmas at Sea

I can find no clue as to when, or in what circumstances this ballad was written, beyond the fact that it was first published in the *Scots Observer* for 22 December, 1888. In fact Stevenson himself spent Christmas Day of that year at sea, in the yacht *Casco*, between Tahiti and Hawaii.

SONGS OF TRAVEL

Published in December, 1895, in Vol. XIV of the Edinburgh Edition of Stevenson's *Works*, and as a separate volume by Chatto and Windus in September, 1896.

When Charles Baxter wrote outlining the plan of the Edinburgh Edition, Stevenson answered (from Vailima, 1 January, 1894): 'In the verse business I can do just what I like better than anything else, and extend *Underwoods* with a lot of unpublished stuff.' And on 18 May, in a letter to Colvin about the edition, 'I am sending you a lot of verses, which had best, I think, be called *Underwoods* Book III, but in what order are they to go?' A set of first rough proofs was printed in October, 1895; these proofs, bound in green leather and entitled *Posthumous Poems*, with Edmund Gosse's bookplate, were sold at Sotheby's in May, 1949, 39. A pencil note by Gosse runs:

> The poems are here printed in the order in which R. L. S. sent them to me. In the published edition they appear re-arranged by Sidney Colvin. Two pieces, and a portion of a third, which are found here, are not in the published volume. [The 'portion of a third' are the extra lines to XXVI, *If This Were Faith*. See note to that poem, p. 508.] Several minor differences will be discovered.

Bound up in this volume of proofs also are two letters from Colvin to Gosse. In the first (14 November, 1895) he writes:

> Some of your criticisms confirmed my own views: with others I am less in accord: no. 16 for instance, *Bright is the ring of words*, I like, and cannot bring myself to discard: indeed I have only discarded two, the *Ditty* and *The Last Sight*, thinking it best to let the rest stand with all their technical imperfections, especially as it was his expressed wish to me that the lot should be printed.

[500]

In the second letter (15 November, 1895) acknowledging one from Gosse which had crossed his first, Colvin goes on:

> It is one of the curiosities of literature that L's hand, so unerring in prose, should have been so wavering in verse. And yet in these often halting verses he has put so much of himself that they cannot be let drop. As usual he is his own best critic:
>
>> It was not music, for I lacked the art,
>> Yet what [but] frozen music filled my heart.

In his Bibliographical Note to *Songs of Travel* in Vol. XIV of the Edinburgh Edition, Colvin wrote:

> The following verses are here collected for the first time. The author had tried them in several different orders and under several different titles, as *Songs and Notes of Travel*, *Vailima*, *Posthumous Poems*, etc.: finally, leaving their naming and arrangement to the present editor, with the suggestion that they should be added, as Book III, to future editions of *Underwoods*.

Why Stevenson should have thought of the title *Posthumous Poems* Colvin does not make clear.

Songs of Travel remained the title in all subsequent editions—though the half-title in Vol. XVI of the Thistle Edition of Stevenson's *Works*, where these poems follow directly on *Underwoods* Book I and Book II, runs 'Book III Being Songs of Travel and Other Verses written Principally in the South Seas 1888–1894.'

E. V. Lucas, in *The Colvins and their Friends*, 1928, quotes a letter written by Mrs Stevenson to Colvin on these poems:

> I have just received your letter asking about adding the poem addressed to me, 'Dusky, trusty,' etc., to the new edition. Do just what you think well to do. It is a very beautiful thing, and I do not think it would be bad taste to publish it. As to the other, 'Oh, God, if that were all,' I agree that this should be kept for the Life. But there was another that Louis rather liked—I *think* it was called 'In praise of dark women'; what do you think of adding that? I only suggest the looking at it. I shall, as I have always done, feel sure that you have done right, whatever your views may be . . .

In printing the poems here, I have kept the title of *Songs of Travel* (though Stevenson always referred to the collection as

Underwoods III), and to Colvin's order, as both have become so familiar to readers of Stevenson's poetry. But I have restored the two poems left out by Colvin, *Ditty* and *The Last Sight*, and placed them where Stevenson had placed them.

I. *The Vagabond*

Robert Graves, in his lecture on *What is Bad Poetry?* (delivered in 1922, reprinted in *Poetic Unreason*, 1925), comments on this poem:

> Stevenson has a famous ballad in praise of the Open Road, saying that all he asks is Heaven above and the road before him, and that bread dipped in running water is enough for him to subsist on for ever. One would at first sight, picking up that poem without knowing who Stevenson was, say that a tramp was the only fit person to judge whether that poem was good or bad. But a tramp called in to bear witness would say in his own way that it was the most malicious and wicked poem ever written, countenancing with a shoddy idealism the miseries of a life of which Stevenson can have had no experience. He would speak with horror of the condition called Breadsickness; after two or three months of unrelieved bread-diet the stomach revolts and even the smell of a baker's shop is enough to make the man vomit. A cup of hot tea to a tramp after innumerable cups of cold water—the Gospel emblem loses its force here—is the greatest gift that can be given. But the poem is not written for tramps, it is written by an invalid with an overpowering desire for freedom and a hatred of the dietary delicacies that his condition demands, to be read by invalids in a similar case. It is a good poem but with evident limitations.

II and III. *Youth and Love* I and II

A manuscript was sold at Sotheby's, November, 1949, 355, with these two poems, but in reverse order, and a third, *A little before me, and hark!*, printed here in *Poems 1869–1879*, p. 67. This manuscript gives *onward road* for *open road* in l. 11 of I, *weal* for *well* in l. 13.

In I, the phrase 'the bright eyes of danger' recalls a passage in *The Lantern Bearers*, 1888 (*Across the Plains*, 1892): 'Not only love, and the fields, and the bright face of danger, but sacrifice and death and unmerited suffering humbly supported, touch in us the vein of the poetic.'

IV and V. *In dreams, unhappy* and *She rested by the Broken Brook*

An earlier draft of these poems, entitled *The Unforgotten* I and II, is described in *B.B.S. II*, p. 154. *Tusitala* uses this title.

VII. *Madrigal*

The title *Madrigal* appears in the set of proofs referred to in the Introductory Note to *Songs of Travel*, p. 500, but was omitted from that book.

VIII. *To you, let snow and roses*

In its first form the lyric entitled *For* (sic) *you let snow and roses* consisted of six, instead of, as now, two stanzas. The original stood as follows:

I

I must not cease from singing,
    And leave their praise unsung,
The praise of swarthy women,
    I've loved since I was young;
They shine like coloured pictures
    In the pale book of my life,
The gem of meditation,
    The clear reward of strife.

2

To you, let snow and roses, etc.

3

The hue of Highland rivers, etc.

4

There shines in her glowing favour
    A gem of darker look,
The eye of coal and topaz,
    The pool of the mountain brook;
And strands of brown and sunshine,
    And threads of silver and snow,
In her dusky treasure of tresses
    Twinkle and shine and glow.

5

I have been young and am old;
    I have trodden various ways;
Now I behold from a window
    The wonder of by-gone days;

[503]

The mingling of many colours,
    The crossing of many threads,
The dear and smiling faces,
    The dark and graceful heads.

6

The defeats and the successes,
    The strife, the race, the goal,
And the touch of a dusky woman
    Was fairly worth the whole;
And sun and moon and morning
    With glory I recall,
But the clasp of a dusky woman
    Outweighs them one and all.

GOSSE

On this occasion at least one can only be thankful to Colvin for his omissions.

A facsimile of a manuscript of this poem in six verses is given in G. S. Hellman's *The True Stevenson*, facing p. 224. It suggests various emendations to Gosse's text—*e.g.*, line 8, '*dear* reward' instead of '*clear* reward'; and to the text of the two verses as published in *Songs of Travel*. Another version was printed by Mrs Strong in *R. L. S. Teuila*: she gives, for instance, in line 27, 'The eye of *coral* and topaz' instead of '*coal* and topaz.' Another manuscript in the possession of Mr E. J. Beinecke has still further variations; and shows a cancelled line 6 in verse 1 (2 in the longer version)—*For her that I call fair.*

XI. *I will make you brooches and toys for your delight*

An earlier draft, with two additional lines to each stanza and some variants in the last stanza, is described in *B.B.S. II*, p. 155.

XII. *We Have Loved of Yore*

Written out by Stevenson to the accompaniment of an 'Air after Diabelli—op. 168, No. 1' (printed in Mrs Stevenson's Prefatory Note to *Underwoods*, Tusitala Edition, I, p. 57).

A very rough draft of this poem is printed in *B.B.S. II*, with explanatory comments; in the Vailima and Tusitala editions it appears among the 'New Poems' with no indication that it is only a draft of an already published poem.

XIII. *Ditty*

Written at Vailima. It was sent, and set up in print, with the other poems in *Songs of Travel*, but finally omitted by Colvin. First published in *Thistle*, 1895.

XV. *Bright is the ring of words*

An earlier draft, with additions and variants, is described in *B.B.S. II*, p. 157.

XVI. *In the highlands, in the country places*

A facsimile of the original manuscript accompanied the printed text when the poem was published in *The Pall Mall Gazette*, 21 December, 1894.

A variant of the first stanza appears in *B.B.S. III*, 135, where it is tacked on without explanation to the incomplete draft of another poem, *On the gorgeous hills of morning*.

XVII. *To the Tune of Wandering Willie*

The original song of Wandering Willie is printed in Herd's *Ancient and Modern Scots Songs* (1761); Burns also wrote a set of words to the tune (Henley and Henderson Edition, III, 208).

Stevenson to Charles Baxter, from Tautira, 10 November, 1888:

> Our mainmast is dry-rotten, and we are all to the devil; I shall lie in a debtor's jail. Never mind, Tautira is first chop. I am so besotted that I shall put on the back of this my attempt at words to Wandering Willie; if you can conceive at all the difficulty, you will also conceive the vanity with which I regard any kind of result; and whatever mine is like, it has some sense and Burns's has none.

Then follow the first two verses of the poem. During these weeks sailing in the Pacific in the yacht *Casco* Stevenson was writing the last chapters of *The Master of Ballantrae*, and he used a handful of the lines in Chapter IX.

> The chaise came to the door in a strong drenching mist. We took our leave in silence: the house of Durrisdeer standing with dropping gutters and windows closed, like a place dedicate to melancholy. I observed the Master kept his head out, looking back on these splashed walls and glimmering roofs, till they were suddenly swallowed in the mist; and I must suppose some natural sadness fell upon the man at this

departure; or was it some pre-vision of the end? At least, upon our mounting the long brae from Durrisdeer, as we walked side by side in the wet, he began first to whistle and then to sing the saddest of our country tunes, which sets folk weeping in a tavern, *Wandering Willie.* The set of words he used with it I have not heard elsewhere, and could never come by any copy; but some of them which were the most appropriate to our departure linger in my memory. One verse began—

> Home was home then, my dear, full of kindly faces;
> Home was home then, my dear, happy for the child.

And ended somewhat thus—

> Now, when day dawns on the brow of the moorland,
> Lone stands the house, and the chimney-stone is cold.
> Lone let it stand, now the folks are all departed,
> The kind hearts, the true hearts, that loved the place of old.

I could never be a judge of the merit of these verses; they were so hallowed by the melancholy of the air, and were sung (or rather 'soothed') to me by a master-singer at a time so fitting. He looked in my face when he had done, and saw that my eyes watered.

XVIII. *Winter*

Written at Saranac Lake, 1887.

XIX. *The stormy evening closes now in vain*

These lines were written out by Stevenson with their musical accompaniment, entitled *Air after Oldfield*: the music will be found in Mrs Stevenson's prefatory note to *Underwoods*, Tusitala Edition, I, p. 56.

XX. *To Dr Hake*

Thomas Gordon Hake (1809–1895), physician and poet, friend of Rossetti and Henley, had sent Stevenson some of his own verses in 1887, to which these are a reply. Rosaline Masson in her *Life* records that Dr Hake gave Stevenson the autograph despatch of General Gordon's which hung at Vailima.

XXI. *To Sidney Colvin*

Sidney Colvin (1845–1927), who was then Slade Professor of Fine Arts at Cambridge, met Stevenson first in 1873, at once recognised his talent, encouraged him to write and introduced him to literary circles in London. Later when Colvin was at the British Museum, Stevenson often stayed with him at his house in the East Wing of the Museum, which he called the Monument.

In *Songs of Travel* the poem appeared as *To ——*. One manuscript with several variations, was sold at Sotheby's, November, 1949 (393). Another, with some cancelled lines, is reproduced in facsimile in *B.B.S. II*, p. 101.

Stevenson had first thought of including this poem in *Underwoods*, then wrote to Colvin (from Bournemouth, April, 1886):

> I want to tell you also that I have suppressed your poem. I shall send it you for yourself, and I hope you will agree with me that it was not good enough in point of view of merit, and a little too intimate as between you and me. I would not say less of you, my friend, but I scarce care to say so much in public while we live. A man may stand on his own head; it is not fair to set his friend on a pedestal.

In a letter to Gosse (14 November, 1895) about the publication of *Songs of Travel* (bound up into Gosse's set of proofs of that volume) Colvin wrote:

> You ask to whom the piece 'I knew thee strong and quiet etc.' is addressed. It is an old thing of Bournemouth days to me, which I would not let him print in the first *Underwoods*. Of course it would be fatuous of me to print it at all if people knew: but 'Felix' is only a name used for me by the smallest circle of intimates (originally Slade (=Slade Professor), then Felix, the founders' name having been Felix Slade), and quite unknown outside. Do you agree with me in thinking the verses have too much beauty to be lost?

XXIV. *He hears with gladdened heart the thunder*

A draft, in three stanzas of six lines each, is printed in *B.B.S. II*, p. 159.

XXVI. *If This Were Faith*

Graham Balfour, as heading to his Chapter XVI, *The End—1894*, prints the following lines of Stevenson's as an Envoy to this poem, which he dates 1893.

> *Wanted Volunteers*
> *To do their best for twoscore years!*
> A ready soldier, here I stand,
> Primed for thy command,
> With burnished sword.
> If this be faith, O Lord,
> Help Thou mine unbelief
> And be my battle brief.

These lines are the 'portion of a third' poem mentioned by Gosse in his note on *Songs of Travel* quoted on p. 500.

XXVII. *My Wife*

Colvin, in a letter to Gosse on 14 November, 1895 (bound up by Gosse with his proofs of *Songs of Travel*):

> You made no remark on the one to his wife 'Dusky, trusty, etc.' which I wanted for its strong personal note, but which I feared might strike you as ill-written and even a little ridiculous in its first line.

I have followed these proofs in eliminating the comma which usually appears between *tender* and *comrade*.

XXIX. *To an Island Princess*

Dated Tautira, Tahiti, 5 November, 1888.
Original note in *Songs of Travel*:

> This is the same Princess Moë whose charms of person and disposition have been recorded by the late Lord Pembroke in *South Sea Bubbles*, and by M. Pierre Loti in the *Mariage de Loti*.

Princess Moë heard there was a white man ill at Tautira, came to see him and found Stevenson in a burning fever. As soon as he was well enough she insisted they should move to the house of Ori, sub-chief of the village, and stay there as her guests.
Mrs Stevenson to Colvin, Tautira, 4 December, 1888:

> I write you from fairyland, where we are living in a fairy-story, the guests of a beautiful brown princess. . . . Moë has gone to Papeete by the command of the king, whose letter was addressed 'To the great Princess at Tautira.

P.V.' P.V. stands for Pomaré 5th. Every evening, before she went, we played Van John lying in a circle on pillows in the middle of the floor with our heads together: and hardly an evening passed but it struck us afresh how very much you would like Moë, and we told her of you again.

Stevenson to John Addington Symonds, Tautira, 11 November, 1888:

We are *in heaven here.*

XXX. *To Kalakaua*

Dated Honolulu, 3 February, 1889.
Original note in *Songs of Travel* to 'the Silver Ship':

The yacht *Casco* had been so called by the people of Fakarava in the Paumotus.

Kalakaua was King of the Hawaiian Islands where Stevenson went when the *Casco* reached Honolulu after her cruise to the Marquesas, the Paumolus, and Tahiti.
Stevenson to E. L. Burlingame, January, 1889:

H.M. (who is a gentleman of a courtly order and much tinctured with letters) is very polite; I may possibly ask for the position of palace doorkeeper.

To Charles Baxter, 8 February, 1889:

. . . His Majesty here, who is a very fine intelligent fellow, but O, Charles! what a crop for the drink! He carries it, too, like a mountain with a sparrow on its shoulders. We calculated five bottles of champagne in three hours and a half (afternoon), and the sovereign quite presentable, although perceptibly more dignified at the end.

To Baxter again, 8 March, 1889:

Kalakaua is a terrible companion; a bottle of fizz is like a glass of sherry to him; he thinks nothing of five or six in an afternoon as a whet for dinner. You should see a photograph of our party after an afternoon with H.H.M.: My! what a crew!

XXXI. *To Princess Kaiulani*

Stevenson's own note runs:

Written in April to Kaiulani in the April of her age; and at Waikiki, within easy walk of Kaiulani's banyan! When

she comes to my land and her father's, and the rain beats
upon the window (as I fear it will) let her look at this page;
it will be like a weed gathered and pressed at home; and she
will remember her own islands, and the shadow of the mighty
tree; and she will hear the peacocks screaming in the dusk
and the wind blowing in the palms; and she will think of her
father sitting there alone.

Kaiulani's mother was sister to King Kalakaua, her father
was Alexander Cleghorn. From Honolulu Stevenson wrote to
Bain the bookseller in the Haymarket to get copies of *Treasure
Island*, *Kidnapped*, the *New Arabian Nights*, and *The Merry
Men* specially bound, 'elegantly imprimpted' with 'H.R.H.
Kaiulani from R. L. S.,' and posted to her at Liverpool.

Stevenson to W. H. Low, Honolulu, 20 May, 1889:

If you want to cease to be a republican, see my little
Kaiulani, as she goes through—but she is gone already.
You will die a red: I wear the colours of that little royal
maiden, *Nous allons chanter à la ronde, si vous voulez !* only
she is not blonde by several chalks, though she is but a half-
blood, and the wrong half Edinburgh Scots like mysel'.

XXXII. *To Mother Maryanne*

During his six months' stay at Honolulu in 1889 Stevenson
made a twelve-day journey to Molokai and spent a week in the
leper settlement of which Father Damien, but recently dead,
had been the director. Mother Maryanne was in charge of the
Sisters' home at Kalawao, where this poem was written:

I went there most days to play croquet with the poor
patients—think of a game of croquet with seven little lepers,
and the thermometer sometimes ninety in the shade!

Stevenson to his mother, June, 1889.

To his wife he wrote of the trip to the settlement that

I do not know how it would have been with me had the
sisters not been there. My horror of the horrible is about my
weakest point; but the moral loveliness at my elbow blotted
all else out.

In February 1890 Stevenson wrote *Father Damien : An Open
Letter to the Reverend Dr. Hyde of Honolulu*, who had made
public criticisms of Father Damien.

The original version of this poem as given to Mother Mary-
anne and dated 'Kalawao, May 22nd, 1889', is printed in
Sister Martha Mary McGaw's *Stevenson in Hawaii*, 1950. The

manuscript, in the archives of the Franciscan Sisters, Syracuse, New York, shows some variations from the text as printed in *Songs of Travel*: l. 3, *sufferers* for *sufferer*; l. 5, *and shrinks* for *he shrinks*, *look* for *gaze*; l. 7 *painful* for *mournful*.

XXXIII. *In Memoriam E. H.*

Written in Honolulu.

I found it hard to discover who E. H. was. At first I was tempted to make her Emma, the widowed Queen of Honolulu who modelled her behaviour on that of Queen Victoria. Isobel Strong had met her in Honolulu (she later described her in *This Life I've Loved*). But Queen Emma was discovered to have died in 1885, four years before Stevenson arrived at Honolulu. The real E. H. was another Emma, W. E. Henley's mother, who had brought up a family of six after her husband died penniless. She died on 25 October, 1888; the news reached the Stevensons in Honolulu. See *Baxter Letters*, p. 243. Stevenson's poem was published in *The Scots Observer*, which Henley then edited, for 11 May, 1889. 'God bless your mother' Stevenson had written to Henley from California in October, 1879.

XXXIV. *To My Wife*

In June, 1889, the Stevensons left Honolulu in the trading schooner *Equator* in which they visited the Gilbert Islands, where they stayed for several weeks on Butaritari and Apemama, and on which they then proceeded to Samoa, where they arrived for the first time in December. This poem was written on the *Equator*.

The first eighteen lines possibly describe Grez-sur-Loing, near Fontainebleau, where the Stevensons first met in 1876. Stevenson supplies a comment on the last three lines in a letter to his mother, 'Schooner *Equator*, at sea 240 miles from Samoa, 1 December, 1889':

> We were sixteen souls in this small schooner, eleven in the cabin; our confinement and overcrowding in the wet weather was excessive; we lost our foretopmast in a squall; the sails were continually being patched (we had but the one suit) and with all attention we lost the jibtopsail almost entirely and the staysail and mainsail are far through.

XXXV. *To my Old Familiars*

Sent to Charles Baxter in a letter dated February, 1890, from the steamer *Lübeck* between Apia and Sydney.

> . . . Sad and fine were the old days: when I was away in

Apemama, I wrote two copies of verse about Edinburgh and the past, so ink black, so golden bright. I will send them, if I can find them, for they will say something to you, and indeed one is more than half addressed to you. This is it—

(Then follows the poem, under the title *To my Old Comrades* with, between lines 14 and 15, the words 'Here a squall sends all flying.') Stevenson then goes on, 'They're pretty second-rate but felt. I can't be bothered to copy the other.'

A manuscript (*Sotheby*, November, 1949, 365) shows many variations in punctuation, and has an extra line between the present ll. 24 and 25. 'Kindlier it glows and brighter than we dreamed!'

XXXVI. *The tropics vanish, and meseems that I*

The second poem mentioned in the letter to Baxter quoted in the note to XXXV. A manuscript (*Sotheby*, November, 1949, 365) shows many variations of punctuation, and gives four extra lines between the present lines 10 and 11.

> There, in the silence of remembered time
> Sounds yet the innocent laughter of a child,
> Sound yet the unresting footsteps of a youth
> Now dead forever, and whose grave I am.

In the last line I have printed *devoted*, from the manuscript, for the *denoted* of previous editions.

XXXVII. *To S. C.*

Sent to Sidney Colvin with a letter from the schooner *Equator* 'at sea 190 miles off Samoa,' 2 December, 1889, in which Stevenson writes:

> My dear fellow, now that my father is done with his troubles, and 17 Heriot Row no more than a mere shell, you and that gaunt old Monument in Bloomsbury are all that I have in view when I use the word home; some passing thoughts there may be of the rooms at Skerryvore, and the blackbirds in the chine on a May morning; but the essence is S. C. and the Museum.

Colvin, in his note to this letter says, 'The allusion is to the two colossal images from Easter Island which used to stand under the portico to the right hand of the visitor entering the Museum, were for some years removed, and later restored to their old place.'

In a manuscript (*Sotheby*, November, 1949, 393) which shows minor variations in punctuation the poem is dated 'October 1889'; written at Apemama.

XXXVIII. *The House of Tembinoka*

Written on the schooner *Equator*, November or December, 1889.

Stevenson to E. L. Burlingame, editor of *Scribner's Magazine*, who had written to ask him for fresh contributions, from S.S. *Lübeck*, between Apia and Sydney, February, 1890:

> The only thing I have ready is the enclosed barbaric piece. As soon as I have arrived in Sydney I shall send you some photographs, a portrait of Tembinoka, perhaps a view of the palace or of the 'matted men' at their singing; also T's flag, which my wife designed for him: in a word, what I can do best for you. It will be thus a foretaste of my book of travels. I shall ask you to let me have, if I wish it, the use of the plates made, and to make up a little tract of the verses and illustrations of which you might send six copies to H.M. Tembinoka, King of Apemama, *via* Butaritari, Gilbert Islands. It might be best to send it by Crawford and Co., S.F. There is no postal service; and schooners must take it, how they may and when. Perhaps some such note as this might be prefixed:
>
> 'At my departure from the island of Apemama, for which you will look in vain in most atlases, the king and I agreed, since we both set up to be in the poetical way, that we should celebrate our separation in verse. Whether or not his majesty has been true to his bargain, the laggard posts of the Pacific may perhaps inform me in six months, perhaps not before a year. The following lines represent my part of the contract, and it is hoped, by their pictures of strange manners, they may entertain a civilised audience. Nothing throughout has been invented or exaggerated; the lady herein referred to as the author's Muse, has confined herself to stringing into rhyme facts and legends that I saw or heard during two months residence upon the island.
>
> R. L. S.'

[This note was prefixed to the poem, in *Scribner's Magazine*, July, 1890, and in *Songs of Travel*.]

> ... I am sending you *Tembinoka* as he stands; but there are parts of him that I hope to better, particularly in stanzas iii and ii. I scarce feel intelligent enough to try just now;

and I thought at any rate you had better see it, set it up if you think well, and let me have a proof; so, at least, we shall get the bulk of it straight. I have spared you Teñkoruti, Tembaitake, Tembinatake, and other barbarous names, because I thought the dentists in the States had work enough without my assistance; but my chief's name is TEMBINOKA, pronounced, according to the present quite modern habit in the Gilberts, Tembinok'.

XXXIX. *The Woodman*

Written in 1890 during the clearing of the jungle to make a home and settlement at Vailima. One of the jobs that Stevenson set himself was the making of a path up the gorge of a stream above the house.

Stevenson to Colvin, 'In the Mountain, Apia, Samoa, 2 November, 1890':

> A strange business it was, and infinitely solitary; away above, the sun was in the high tree-tops; the lianas noosed and sought to hang me; the saplings struggled and came up with that sob of death that one gets to know so well; great, soft, sappy trees fell at a lick of the cutlass, little tough switches laughed at and dared my best endeavour. . . . Right in the wild lime hedge which cuts athwart us just homeward of the garden, I found a great bed of kuikui—sensitive plant—our deadliest enemy. A fool brought it to this island in a pot, and used to lecture and sentimentalise over the tender thing. The tender thing has now taken charge of this island, and men fight it, with torn hands, for bread and life. A singular, insidious thing, shrinking and biting like a weasel; clutching by its roots as a limpet clutches to a rock. As I fought him, I bettered some verses in my poem, *The Woodman*; the only thought I gave to letters. Though the kuikui was thick, there was but a small patch of it, and when I was done I attacked the wild lime, and had a hand-to-hand skirmish with its spines and elastic suckers.
>
> . . . My long silent contests in the forests have had a strange effect on me. The unconcealed vitality of these vegetables, their exuberant number and strength, the attempts—I can use no other word—of lianas to enwrap and capture the intruder, the awful silence, the knowledge that all my efforts are only like the performance of an actor, the thing of a moment, and the wood will silently and swiftly heal

them up with fresh effervescence; the cunning sense of the tuitui, suffering itself to be touched with wind-swayed grasses and not minding—but let the grass be moved by a man, and it shuts up; the whole silent battle, murder, and slow death of the contending forest; weigh upon the imagination. My poem *The Woodman* stands; but I have taken refuge in a new story, which just shot through me like a bullet in one of my moments of awe, alone in that tragic jungle: *The High Woods of Ulufanua* [which Stevenson later wrote and published as *The Beach of Falesá*].

In *Presbyterian Pirate* (1937) Miss Doris N. Dalglish draws attention to certain similarities between Stevenson in this poem and Marvell:

> Within the space of a few lines it offers us 'the iron halls of life' and 'vegetable Londons' to compare with Marvell's 'iron gates' and 'vegetable lives.'

and she quotes from *The Woodman* to demonstrate Stevenson's even more skilful management of the sustained period and paragraph in this familiar metre.

XL. *Tropic Rain*

A manuscript, with fourteen extra lines, is described in *B.B.S. II*, p. 164. Stevenson to Colvin, Christmas Eve, 1890, from their temporary hut at Vailima:

> Yesterday, who could write? My wife near crazy with ear-ache; the rain descending in white crystal rods and playing hell's tattoo, like a *tutti* of battering rams, on our sheet-iron roof; the wind passing high overhead with a strange dumb mutter, or striking us full, so that all the huge trees in the paddock cried aloud, and wrung their hands, and brandished their vast arms. The horses stood in the shed like things stupid. The sea and the flagship lying on the jaws of the bay vanished in sheer rain. All day it lasted; I locked up my papers in the iron box, in case it was a hurricane, and the house might go. We went to bed with mighty uncertain feelings; far more than on shipboard, where you have only drowning ahead—whereas here you have a smash of beams, a shower of sheet iron, and a blind race in the dark and through a whirlwind for the shelter of an unfinished stable—and my wife with ear-ache! Well, well, this morning, we had word from Apia; a hurricane was

looked for, the ships were to leave the bay by 10 a.m.;
it is now 3.30, and the flagship is still a fixture, and the wind
round in the blessed east, so I suppose the danger is over.
But heaven is still laden; the day dim, with frequent rattling
bucketfuls of rain; and just this moment (as I write) a
squall went overhead, scarce striking us, with that singular,
solemn noise of its passage, which is to me dreadful. I
have always feared the sound of wind beyond everything.
In my hell it would always blow a gale.

XLI. *An End of Travel*

After their two and a half years' wandering in the Pacific
the Stevensons decided to make a home on Samoa. When
Stevenson died in 1894 his body was borne by helpers up to the
top of Mount Vaea. Written at Vailima.

XLIII. *The Last Sight*

Sent, and set up in print, with the other poems in *Songs of
Travel*, but finally omitted by Colvin. First published in *Thistle*,
1895.

The poem is about Stevenson's last sight of his father in May,
1887; it is part of a much longer poem, which exists in unfinished
form (Beinecke 6281 and 6282) of which this 'fragment' is the
last six lines. Gosse prints it in his *Biographical Notes* with the
last two words of line 3, and the first five words of line 4,
omitted.

Stevenson to Colvin, Edinburgh, June, 1887:

About the death, I have long hesitated, I was long before
I could tell my mind; and now I know it, and can but say
that I am glad. If we could have had my father, that would
have been a different thing. But to keep that changeling—
suffering changeling—any longer, could better none and
nothing. Now he rests; it is more significant, it is more
like himself. He will begin to return to us in the course of
time, as he was and as we loved him.

My favourite words in literature, my favourite scene—
'O let him pass,' Kent and Lear—was played for me here
in the first moment of my return. I believe Shakespeare
saw it with his own father. I had no words; but it was
shocking to see. He died on his feet, you know; was on
his feet the last day, knowing nobody—still he would be up.

This was his constant wish; also that he might smoke a pipe on his last day.

But seven years later Stevenson could write (to Adelaide Boodle, 14 July, 1894):

> You remember, perhaps, when my father died, you told me those ugly images of sickness, decline and impaired reason, which then haunted me day and night, would pass away and be succeeded by things more happily character-istic. I have found it so. He now haunts me, strangely enough, in two guises: as a man of fifty, lying on a hillside and carving mottoes on a stick, strong and well; and as a younger man, running down the sands into the sea near North Berwick, myself—*aetat.* 11—somewhat horrified at finding him so beautiful when stripped!

XLIV. *Sing me a song of a lad that is gone*

Balfour dates it 1887. Mrs Stevenson, in her Prefatory Note to *Underwoods*, records that:

> The writing of *Over the Sea to Skye* grew out of a visit from one of the last of the old school of Scots Gentlewomen, Miss Ferrier, a granddaughter of Professor Wilson (Christopher North). Her singing was a great delight to my husband, who would beg for song after song, especially the Jacobite airs, which had always to be repeated several times. The words to one of these seemed unworthy, so he made a new set of verses more in harmony with the plaintive tune.

According to the *Oxford Companion to Music*

> One half of the tune is a sea-shanty heard in 1879 by Miss Annie MacLeod (later Lady Wilson) when going by boat from Toran to Loch Coruisk; the other half is by Miss MacLeod herself. The words, by Sir Harold Boulton, Bart., [*Speed bonnie boat, like a bird on the wing*] date from 1884. Later some other words were written to the tune by Robert Louis Stevenson, who apparently believed the tune to be a pure folk tune and in the public domain.

XLV. *To S. R. Crockett*

Crockett (1860–1914), novelist, and minister of Penicuik, in the Pentlands, dedicated his *The Stickit Minister* to Stevenson in the following terms:

To Robert Louis Stevenson of Scotland and Samoa I
dedicate these stories of that Grey Galloway land where
About the Graves of the Martyrs The Whaups are crying—
his heart remembers how.

Stevenson to Colvin, Vailima, 23 August, 1893:

And then you could actually see Vailima, which I *would*
like you to, for it's beautiful and my home and tomb that
is to be; though it's a wrench not to be planted in Scotland
—that I never can deny—if I could only be buried in the
hills, under the heather and a table tombstone like the
martyrs, where the whaups and plovers are crying! Did you
see a man who wrote *The Stickit Minister*, and dedicated it
to me, in words that brought the tears to my eyes every
time I looked at them. 'Where about the graves of the
martyrs the whaups are crying. *His* heart remembers how.'
Ah, my God, it does! Singular that I should fulfil the Scots
destiny throughout, and live a voluntary exile and have my
head filled with the blessed, beastly place all the time!

Stevenson to Lord Rosebery, Vailima, 5 November, 1893
(unpublished letter in the National Library of Scotland;
Rosebery had acknowledged a copy of *Catriona*):

... And what you say of the Lothians has pleased me
beyond measure. I had always designed to make a book that
should travel over and illustrate that beloved piece of
country; beloved—and yet to me, in retrospect, almost
hateful also. I have been vigorously unhappy there in old
days—more unhappy than in the death of all my friends, and
a dose of leprosy, could make me now; my father is dead;
many of my friends are 'lapped in lead'; and to return
would be to me superlatively painful. Only I wish I could
be buried there—among the hills, say, on the head of
Allermuir—with a table tombstone like a Cameronian.

Stevenson may also have had in mind the tale of the Covenanter
whose grave on the Pentlands above Dolphinton is inscribed:
'Sacred to the memory of a Covenanter who fought and was
wounded at Rullion Green, November 28, 1666, and who died
at Oakenbush the day after the Battle and was buried here by
Adam Sanderson of Blackhill'. The dying Covenanter asked to
be buried in sight of his homeland, so Adam Sanderson took him

up to a point where he would face the distant Ayrshire hills. See article on the tercentenary of Rullion Green and the centenary of Stevenson's *The Pentland Rising*, in the *Glasgow Herald*, 26 and 29 November, 1966. In this youthful paper on the Rising, Stevenson speaks of the Covenanters after their defeat lifting their dying heads from the bloodstained heather to 'behold' the distant hills.

> (Cf. *The Scot Abroad* in *The Silverado Squatters*:
>
> There is no special loveliness in that gray country, with its rainy, sea-beat archipelago; its fields of dark mountains; its unsightly places, black with coal; its treeless, sour, unfriendly looking cornlands; its quaint, gray, castled city, where the bells clash of a Sunday, and the wind squalls, and the salt showers fly and beat. I do not even know if I desire to live there; but let me hear, in some far land, a kindred voice sing out, 'Oh, why left I my hame?' and it seems at once as if no beauty under the kind heavens, and no society of the wise and good, can repay me for my absence from my country. And though I think I would rather die elsewhere, yet in my heart of hearts I long to be buried among good Scots clods.)

The poem was printed as a prefatory poem, and reproduced in facsimile, in the eighth, limited, edition of *The Stickit Minister*, 1894, and in subsequent editions: it was also published in the *Pall Mall Gazette*, 12 December, 1894, under the title *Home Thoughts from Samoa*. *Howes*, in line 7, is often printed as *homes*. *Howes* are valleys or glens.

The Tusitala Edition prints *vanquished* for *vanished* in line 7.

XLVI. *Evensong*

Written at Vailima.

A manuscript is described in *B.B.S. II*, p. 168, with an additional second stanza of seven lines:

> So in the furthest camp of man—
>   Where he deems himself alone,
> Left without sign or plan,
>   At random in a desert thrown—
> For ears that hear, for running feet,
> There daily is the tattoo beat,
>   There the reveille blown.

POEMS 1880–1894

In 1880 Stevenson came back to Scotland from California with his wife. Then followed years of travel in search of health—Davos, with summers in the Highlands; from 1882 to 1884 the Mediterranean, where at Hyères he spent what was perhaps the happiest period of his life; Bournemouth; and finally, after the death of his father in 1887, across the Atlantic to the Adirondacks and, next summer, to the Pacific for two years of wandering among the South Sea islands before finally settling at Samoa in 1890. Stevenson never came back to Scotland after 1887; and the only big towns he saw after sailing from San Francisco in 1888 were Honolulu, Auckland, and Sydney.

Many of the poems Stevenson wrote between 1880 and 1887 were chosen by him for *Underwoods*, 1887; many of those he wrote from 1887 onwards were chosen for *Songs of Travel* (or *Underwoods III*), which he was preparing for the press when he died in 1894, and which were published at the end of the following year. Those printed in this section are (as with *Poems 1869–1879*) a selection only of what remained after Stevenson's own selections had been made.

I. *Alcaics to H. F. Brown*

Checked with manuscript *Sotheby*, November, 1949, 357. In an exercise-book of poems, among which are *Tales of Arabia* (see p. 288), *Still I love to rhyme* (p. 289), *Flower god, god of the spring* (p. 289). First published in *Letters*, 1899.

For H. F. Brown, see note to *To H. F. Brown*, p. 473. Brown, Symonds and Stevenson held long sessions at Davos discussing classical measures. These Horatian Alcaics were written in April, 1881, after Brown, on returning to Venice in the spring of 1881, had sent Stevenson some of his translations of old Venetian boat songs. Brown's interest in classical metres may have determined his choice of hexameters for his own long pcem, *A Railway Medley*, in *Drift*, 1900

W. G. Lockett, in *Robert Louis Stevenson at Davos*, 1934, quotes Brown as saying of Stevenson:

> I have vivid recollections of long talks with him all through snowy afternoons, when we drank old Valtelline wine and smoked, and eventually I got the impression that there was nothing of him in the room but his bright eyes moving about, and his voice.

Brown addressed these lines to Stevenson:

> Come then! the Istrian wine shall flow,
> Expressed from grapes that only grow
> Where old Poseidon once did dwell,
> Parenzo, deep in asphodel.

II. *Tales of Arabia*

Checked with manuscript *Sotheby*, November, 1949, 357—
see note to *Alcaics*, p. 519. First published *B.B.S. I*, 1916.
Horatian Alcaics, possibly sent with a copy of *New Arabian
Nights* (published August, 1882) to H. F. Brown or John
Addington Symonds.

III. *Still I love to rhyme, and still more, rhyming, to wander*

Checked with manuscript *Sotheby*, November, 1949, 357—
see note to *Alcaics*, p. 520. First published *B.B.S. I*, 1916.
Probably written in 1881, 1882 or 1883. The metre is the first
Archilochian, used by Horace in Book IV, Ode VII.

IV. *Flower god, god of the spring, beautiful, bountiful*

Checked with manuscript *Sotheby*, November, 1949, 357—
see note to *Alcaics*, p. 520. First published *B.B.S. I*, 1916.
Written in the Horatian fifth Asclepiad, probably in 1881, 1882
or 1883. *B.B.S.* dates it April, 1883, at Hyères, and thinks it refers
to Stevenson's garden at Hyères.

V. *Horace, Book II, Ode III*

Checked with facsimile in the privately printed pamphlet,
*An Ode of Horace Book II Ode III Translated by Robert Louis
Stevenson*, with a foreword by Clement Shorter, 1916; generally
published here for the first time. The pamphlet gives a facsimile
and a transcript of the manuscript, which contains three versions
of the Ode (*Ad Q. Dellium*), omitting, in each case, the first
two stanzas. The first version, of nine lines, is headed by Steven-
son 'Ordinary ten syllable blank verse'; the second, 'Iambic
feet: 8 syllable rhymed verse' ends abruptly after eight lines,
with Stevenson's comment—'Too poor to go on with. I was so
hampered with the rhyme.' The third, and most successful,
which is printed here, is headed '– ⌣ / – ∪ ∪ / – ∪ ∪ / – ⌣'.

Sent with a letter to Bob Stevenson, March or April 1868.
In 1950 I did not know of this letter, in the Widener Collection
at Harvard, and suggested 1880–1881 as a possible date of com-

position—a time when Stevenson, Symonds and H. F. Brown used to hold long discussions on classical metres at Davos. The poem therefore belongs to Poems 1869–1879 (which should then rightly be Poems 1868–1879), but to avoid re-setting, it remains among Poems 1880–1894.

Among Stevenson's books sold at the Anderson Galleries in 1914 were a copy of the Odes given him by Colvin in 1879, and an English translation of the Odes, Satires and Epistles which had belonged to his grandfather, Robert Stevenson.

VI. *Lines for H. F. Brown*

Checked with facsimile in *B.B.S. III*, p. 120, where it was first published. Not dated, but in all probability written at Davos along with the other poems in classical metres; see notes *To H. F. Brown* (p. 473), *Alcaics* (p. 519). Professor Garrod describes the metre as 'iambic trimeter catalectic, with substitution of choriamb for diiambus in the first metron. The scansion is $-\smile\smile- / \smile-\smile- / \smile-\smile-\smile\smile- / \smile-\smile- / \smile--\smile$.' The manuscript prints some rhyming alternatives for the last eight lines:

> Here in the strong, deep-plunging transatlantic
> Emigrant ship the waves arose gigantic,
> Piping the gull flew by, the roaring billows
> Rose and appeared before the eye like pillows.
> Piping the gull flew by, the roaring waves
> Rose and appeared, from subter-ocean caves,
> And as across the smoothing sea we roam,
> Still and anon we sang our songs of home.

The first four lines are in the same metre as the first version; 'in the last four Stevenson lapses into the familiar English iambic decasyllable, but with choriamb still for diiambus in the first metron (a substitution found often enough in our decasyllabic blank verse, e.g. Milton's Wōn frŏm thĕ vōid/ănd fōrmlĕs̃s īn/fīnĭte').

The voyage was Stevenson's crossing of the Atlantic in an emigrant ship in 1879 on his way out to California to get married.

VII. *Translations from Martial*

A manuscript with some remarks of Stevenson's on translating Martial (a very rough draft, considerably corrected) is reproduced in facsimile opposite p. 176 of *B.B.S. II*.

Stevenson apologises for his shortcomings as a translator, explains that he has forgotten what little Latin he once knew, and owns that he depended upon a French crib 'of which, to those who know French cribs, it may be enough to say I never saw a worse.' He expects criticism from 'the scholars, who understand the meaning of the original, and the poets, who are critical of verse.' His justification is that 'in this age, when we all lean to the reading of light verses, Martial, the neatest of versifiers, the wittiest of men, is passed over with contempt; and either no one reads, or everyone considers it decent to dissemble having read him.'

Martial (A.D. 43 to *c.* 102) left a collection of 1,500 short poems and epigrams, 'witty but frequently coarse, which throw a valuable light on Roman life and manners.' English translators of Martial have included Sir Charles Sedley, Abraham Cowley, and Leigh Hunt.

In an essay on *Books which have Influenced Me* contributed to the *British Weekly* of 13 May, 1887 (reprinted in the *Essays in the Art of Writing*, 1920) Stevenson writes:

> Martial is a poet of no good repute, and it gives a man new thoughts to read his works dispassionately, and find in this unseemly jester's serious passages the image of a kind, wise, and self-respecting gentleman. It is customary, I suppose, in reading Martial, to leave out these pleasant verses; I never heard of them, at least, until I found them for myself; and this partiality is one among a thousand things that help to build up our distorted and hysterical conception of the great Roman Empire.

Stevenson to John Addington Symonds, 21 November, 1887, talking of *Underwoods*:

> But I believe the very fact that it was only speech served the book with the public. Horace is much a speaker, and see how popular! Most of Martial is only speech, and I cannot conceive a person who does not love his Martial.

Stevenson thrice quotes Martial's phrase *pereunt et imputantur* (v. 20): in the rhyming letter to Baxter, *Blame me not that this epistle* (p. 330) dated September, 1872, in a letter to Charles Guthrie from Bournemouth, 18 January, 1886, and in 'A Christmas Sermon' (1888), included in *Across the Plains*.

These versions were all first published in *B.B.S. II*, 1916, except for *Mother and sire* and *An Imitation*, which first ap-

peared in *B.B.S. III*, 1921. The manuscripts I have examined
have no date; nor can I find any reference in the *Letters* to
fix the year of composition. I think it likely—in view of the
'French crib' and of his reawakened interest in classical poetry
after hobnobbing with J. A. Symonds and H. F. Brown in Davos
—that Stevenson wrote these at Hyères, where he and his wife
stayed from March, 1883, to July, 1884. A note-book in the
Anderson Sale, December, 1914, I, 343, which is described as
including a first draft of *A Child's Garden*, an unpublished
preface to *The Merry Men* (1882) and translations from Martial,
would seem to confirm this date. A Bohn's Library *Martial*
which had belonged to Stevenson was sold at the Anderson
Galleries in January, 1915; the 'French crib' is now at Yale
(Beinecke 2558).

x. 61. *Epitaphium Erotii*

Checked with manuscript *Sotheby*, May, 1949, 68. Erotion
was a little slave. Leigh Hunt's version runs:

> Underneath this greedy stone
> Lies little sweet Erotion;
> Whom the Fates, with hearts so cold,
> Nipp'd away at six years old.
> Thou, whoe'er thou mayest be,
> That hast this small field after me,
> Let the yearly rites be paid
> To her slender little shade;
> So shall no disease or jar
> Hurt thy house, or chill thy Lar,
> But this tomb be here alone
> The only melancholy stone.

v. 34. *Mother and sire*

Checked with manuscript *Sotheby*, May, 1949, 68.
'Light lie the turf!' wrote Stevenson, possibly with Martial
in his head, when John Addington Symonds died. Letter to
Gosse, 10 June, 1893.

v. 37. *De Erotio Puella*
Not checked with manuscript.

II. 53. *In Maximum*

Checked with manuscript *Sotheby*, May, 1949, 68.

II. 59. *De Cœnatione Micæ*

Not checked with manuscript.
The tomb was that of Domitian, who had also built the small banqueting hall overlooking it.

II. 68. *Ad Olum*

Some variant lines are given in *B.B.S. II*, p. 203.

II. 90. *Ad Quintilianum*

Checked with manuscript *Sotheby*, May, 1949, 68.
Quintilian was a great Roman practitioner and teacher of rhetoric.

IV. 30. *Ad Piscatorem*

Not checked with manuscript.

IV. 64. *De Hortis Julii Martialis*

Not checked with manuscript.

V. 20. *Ad Martialem*

Variants of the last two lines are given in *B.B.S. II*, p. 200.

VI. 16. *An Imitation*

Checked with manuscript *Sotheby*, May, 1949, 68.

VI. 27. *Ad Nepotem*

Checked with manuscript *Sotheby*, May, 1949, 68.

X. 23. *De M. Antonio*

Not checked with manuscript.

XI. 18. *In Lupum*

Checked with an incomplete manuscript *Sotheby*, May, 1949, 68, which ends at *Through*, line 13. Variant lines are given in *B.B.S. II*, p. 193.

XI. 39. *In Charidemum*

Checked with manuscript *Sotheby*, May, 1949, 68. Some variant lines are given in *B.B.S. II*, p. 187. Lines 7–12 are omitted in Tusitala Edition, II, p. 247.

XII. 61. *De Ligurra*

Checked with manuscript *Sotheby*, May, 1949, 68.

VIII. *As in their flight the birds of song*

Not checked with manuscript; first published in *B.B.S. I*, which dates it 1880. This poem, which so strongly shows the influence of Coventry Patmore, may have been inspired by the death of Mrs Sitwell's son (see note to *Underwoods*, *I*, XXVII, p. 482); in that case, the date would be 1881, or after.

IX. *To Mrs MacMorland*

Checked with manuscripts, in Lady Stair's House Museum, and *Sotheby*, November, 1949, 395. First published in *B.B.S. I*, 1916, where the lady's name is spelt MacMarland and where the first words are *In Schnee*. It was quite as much a wish to see the poem at last correctly titled and started, as the intrinsic merits of the verse, that decided me to include it. (Stevenson uses the same phrase, *im Schnee der Alpen*, in his essay on *Alpine Diversions* published in the *Pall Mall Gazette*, 26 February, 1881).

Mrs MacMorland was the wife of a Church of Scotland minister who had been at Davos for nearly ten years when Stevenson went there in 1880: she became a close friend of Fanny Stevenson. The verses are dated 2 February, 1881, Davos.

Stevenson to E. L. Burlingame, 2 November, 1892 :

> From a congenital defect, I must suppose, I am unable to write the word OR—whenever I write it the printer unerringly prints AS.

X. *Come, my beloved, hear from me*

Checked with manuscript *Sotheby*, November, 1949, 357; first published *B.B.S. I*, 1916. Not dated, but in the same manuscript-book are poems dated 1881–1884. I incline to think it and the two following poems, and *The Canoe Speaks* (*Underwoods I*, III), which also appears in the same manuscript-book, may have been some of the verses referred to in a letter to Henley from Hyères, in May or June, 1883 :

> Really, I have begun to learn some of the rudiments of that trade [verse], and have written three or four pretty enough pieces of octosyllabic nonsense, semi-serious, semi-smiling.

The Vailima and Tusitala editions print *cods* for *woods* in line 2.

XI. *Since years ago for evermore*

Checked with manuscript, *Sotheby*, November, 1949, 357; first published *B.B.S. I*, 1916. Not dated, but from the same manuscript book as poems dated 1881–1884. See note on previous poem, *Come, my beloved*. From the manuscript, it looks as if it might be a fragment of a longer poem.

XII. *Far over seas an island is*

Checked *Sotheby*, May, 1949, 67. After the two stanzas are written the following lines:

> There, where I never was,
> There, are no moral laws,
> Pleasures as thick as haws
>   Bloom on the bush!
> Incomes and honours grow
>   Thick on the hills.

Perhaps they provided the germ of the following poem, *If I could arise and travel away*.

The two poems (both first published in *B.B.S. III*, 1921) are written out in the same manuscript note-book, along with a list of the contents of *The Black Arrow*, which was begun in May, 1883. In reading them, it is perhaps relevant to recall Stevenson's account to Mrs Sitwell of the visit to Edinburgh, in spring, 1875, of the Hon. J. Seed, formerly Secretary to the Customs and Marine Department of New Zealand:

> Awfully nice man here to-night. Public servant—New Zealand. Telling us all about the South Sea Islands till I was sick with desire to go there; beautiful places, green for ever; perfect climate; perfect shapes of men and women, with red flowers in their hair; and nothing to do but to study oratory and etiquette, sit in the sun, and pick up the fruits as they fall. Navigator's Island is the place; absolute balm for the weary.

Navigator's Island is another name for Samoa.

XIII. *If I could arise and travel away*

Checked with manuscript *Sotheby*, May, 1949, 67. A facsimile appears in *B.B.S. III*, facing p. 112.

See notes to previous poem, *Far over seas an island is*.

XIV. *Now bare to the beholder's eye*

Checked with manuscript *Sotheby*, November, 1949, 349; first published *B.B.S. II*, 1916. Not dated, but from the same manuscript book as four poems published in 1887 in *Underwoods*: *A Mile and a Bittock*, *The Spaewife*, *The Canoe Speaks* and *Their Laureate to an Academy Class Dinner Club*. The last of these was privately printed and distributed for Christmas, 1883; so I think this poem can reasonably be assigned to 1882 or 1883. The note to this poem in *B.B.S. II*, p. 90, runs:

> If the reader should consult the third poem in *Underwoods*, he would find that *The Canoe Speaks* has a series of dots following the last line as there printed. In the present verses (written assuredly, previous to 1887) these dots are explained, for here we have the portion which Stevenson decided to omit when preparing *Underwoods* for the press.

The Bibliophile Society editor may have had further evidence for this supposition; but on the evidence available I disagree. The poem was written out in a manuscript book in which *The Canoe Speaks* also appears. But the lines *Now bare to the beholder's eye* are written first, not after *The Canoe Speaks*, as would seem natural if indeed they were a continuation. Further, though the metre is the same, and the theme feminine undressing, yet I find the tone of the two poems dissimilar. In *The Canoe Speaks* it is several girls undressing by the river in the day-time—a sort of Courbet scene; in *Now bare* it is one particular woman undressing, at night, and not necessarily out-of-doors.

XV. *Men are Heaven's piers*

Checked with manuscript *Sotheby*, November, 1949, 349; first published *B.B.S. II*, 1916. Not dated, but, for the same reasons as the previous poem, *Now bare to the beholder's eye*, assigned to 1883. The manuscript, in ink, is corrected in pencil; two lines after 'By her unconquered hero-head' deleted, but still legible, appear in the *B.B.S.* and later editions.

> A naked Adam, naked Eve,
> Alone the primal bower we weave.

The first four lines are very close to four lines in *Our Lady of the Snows*:

> For those he loves that underprop
> With daily virtues Heaven's top,
> And bear the falling sky with ease,
> Unfrowning caryatides.

See note to that poem, p. 480.

XVI. *Fixed is the doom; and to the last of years*

Checked with manuscript *Sotheby*, May, 1949, 58; first published in *B.B.S. II*, 1916.

XVII. *So live, so love, so use that fragile hour*

Checked with manuscript *Sotheby*, May, 1949, 76; first published *B.B.S. II*, 1916. Not dated, but the manuscript is very similar, as to writing, ink, and paper, with that of another poem sold in lot 76, a proposed inscription for Skerryvore (see *Underwoods, I*, XXXIV–XXXVI): this would date it about 1885, when the Stevensons moved in.

XVIII. *To Mrs E. F. Strickland*

Hitherto unpublished; transcribed from a facsimile of the manuscript in the New York Public Library. Dated 2 April, 1886.

I have been unable to find out anything about Mrs Strickland: perhaps she was a Davos acquaintance.

XIX. *For Richmond's Garden Wall*

Checked with manuscript *Sotheby*, May, 1949, 72; first published in *B.B.S. I*, 1916. Sir W. B. Richmond, whose painting of Stevenson is in the National Portrait Gallery, lived in Beavor Lodge, Upper Mall, Hammersmith, where he painted his portrait of Stevenson at one sitting in August, 1886.

XX. *To Frederick Locker*

Not checked with manuscript. First published as introductory poem to *Rowfant Rhymes*, by Frederick Locker, with an introduction by Austin Dobson, Cleveland, The Rowfant Club, 1895 (127 copies only printed); reprinted in 1899. Sent in a letter dated Skerryvore, 4 September, 1886.

Frederick Locker (1821–1895), who later changed his name to Locker-Lampson, author of *London Lyrics*, 1857, and compiler of *Lyra Elegantiarum*, 1867, had requested Andrew Lang to ask Stevenson for a set of verses.

XXI. *To Master Andrew Lang*

Not checked with manuscript; first published in the limited edition of *The most pleasant and delectable tale of the marriage of Cupid and Psyche. Done into English by W. Adlington. With a discourse on the Fable by Andrew Lang* in 1887. Stevenson's lines were printed in only a few of the sixty copies of the large paper edition, 'as they were rigidly suppressed before the book was published,' according to Prideaux's *Bibliography*. There is a facsimile of the rare printed version in *Beinecke* II, p. 430. See also note to *Underwoods*, *I*, XIV, p. 474.

XXII. *Fair Isle at Sea*

Checked with Beinecke 6207; first published in *B.B.S. II*, where the Fair Isle is said to be Samoa; the footnotes to the poem in the Vailima and Tusitala editions follow suit. But a passage in *Random Memories: The Coast of Fife* (published in *Scribner's Magazine*, October, 1888, and later collected in *Across the Plains*, 1892) shows that Stevenson had always been fascinated by the name itself.

> Half-way between Orkney and Shetland, there lies a certain isle; on the one hand the Atlantic, on the other the North Sea, bombard its pillared cliffs; sore-eyed, short-living, inbred fishers and their families herd in its few huts; in the graveyard pieces of wreckwood stand for monuments; there is nowhere a more inhospitable spot. *Belle-Isle-en-mer*—Fair-Isle-at-Sea—that is a name that has always rung in my mind's ear like music; but the only 'Fair Isle' on which I ever set my foot, was this unhomely, rugged turret-top of submarine sierras.

The similarity of phrasing makes it possible that the poem also belongs to 1888. A note in *B.B.S. II* explains that on the reverse side of the manuscript with the quatrain is the Envoi to the *House of Tembinoka*.

XXIII. *The Family*

Checked with Beinecke 6595 (for I), 6140 (II), 5930 (III), 6883 (IV), 7134 (V), 6673 (VI), 6566 (VII), 7085 (VIII). 6673 and 7134 are rough drafts, the others fair copies. Some of the variations from the manuscript in earlier printed versions, that I have now been able to correct, appear to have been due to simple misreadings: e.g. *smelting* for *sweltering* in VII, l. 5; others, to personal reasons, e.g. *graceful* for *pigmy* in II, l. 32. I, II, IV, VII and VIII were first printed in *R.L.S. Teuila*, 1899; III, V and VI were first printed in *B.B.S. II*, 1916. In the manuscript of II lines 47–54 are crossed out, then stetted.

The sequence celebrates the household at Vailima: Fanny Stevenson, and her daughter Isobel Strong (I, II, III), her son

Lloyd Osbourne (IV), her grandson, Austin Strong (V), Steven-
son's mother (VI) and Stevenson himself (VII). Stevenson in a
letter to Charles Baxter, 1 January, 1894:

> If I were to get printed off a very few poems which
> are somewhat too intimate for the public, could you get
> them run up in some luxurious manner, so that fools might
> be induced to buy them in just a sufficient quantity to pay
> expenses and the thing remain still in a manner private?
> We could supply photographs of the illustrations—and the
> poems are of Vailima and the family—I should much like to
> get this done as a surprise for Fanny.

I and II. Written in January, 1893, when he was convalescing
after a bad bout of influenza and two hæmorrhages. Isobel
Strong noted in her journal for 22 January (quoted in *Memories
of Vailima*) 'He generally fills in his convalescence with poetry;
today he read us some beautiful verses about Aolele and me.'
Teuila was the native name of Isobel Strong. What is clearly
an unfinished draft of this section is printed separately as Section
V in the Vailima Edition and there, and in the first impression of
the *Tusitala*, annotated as 'Mrs Strong's daughter, Mrs Steven-
son's granddaughter.'

Stevenson, in a letter to Barrie (April, 1893, quoted in G. E.
Brown's *A Book of R.L.S.*, 1919), describes his wife and step-
daughter:

> She [his wife] runs the show. Infinitely little, extra-
> ordinary wig of grey curls, handsome waxen face like
> Napoleon's, insane black eyes, boy's hands, tiny bare feet, a
> cigarette, wild blue native dress, usually spotted with garden
> mould . . . Hellish energy; relieved by fortnights of entire
> hibernation. . . . [Mrs Strong] runs me like a baby in a
> perambulator, sees I'm properly dressed, bought me silk
> socks, and made me wear them, takes care of me when I'm
> well, from writing my books to trimming my nails. Has a
> growing conviction that she is the author of my works,
> manages the house and the houseboys, who are very fond of
> her.

III. Stevenson to Miss Taylor, 7 October, 1892:

> Nor is Fanny any less active. Ill or well, rain or shine,
> a little blue indefatigable figure is to be observed howking
> about certain patches of garden. She comes in heated and
> bemired up to the eyebrows, late for every meal. She has

reached a sort of tragic placidity. Whenever she plants anything new, the boys weed it up. Whenever she tries to keep anything for seed, the house boys throw it away. And she has reached that pitch of a kind of noble dejection that she would almost say, she did not mind.

iv. In the same letter to Barrie quoted above, Lloyd Osbourne is described as

> Six foot, blond, eye-glasses—British eye-glasses, too. Address varying from an elaborate civility to a freezing haughtiness. Decidedly witty. Has seen an enormous amount of the world. Keeps nothing of youth, but some of its intolerance. Unexpected soft streak for the forlorn. When he is good he is very, very good, but when he is cross he is horrid. . . . Rather stiff with his equals, but apt to be very kindly with his inferiors—the only undemonstrative member of the family, which otherwise wears its heart upon both sleeves.

v. Stevenson describes Austin Strong's responsible activities in a letter to Adelaide Boodle (14 August, 1892) intended to be read to English children.

> . . . Setting off on horseback with his hand on his hip and his pockets full of letters and orders, at the head of quite a procession of huge white cart-horses with pack saddles, and big brown native men with nothing on but gaudy kilts. Mighty well he managed all his commissions; and those who saw him ordering and eating his single-handed luncheon in the queer little Chinese restaurant on the beach declare he looked as if the place, and the town, and the whole archipelago belonged to him.

Austin's Vailima nickname was 'The Overseer.'

vi. Although the last ten lines of this poem appear out of character with the first ten—and with Mrs Stevenson's mother—and may well be a rough draft for another poem, they are written out roughly on the same manuscript page, then again on the following page.

vii. I have now removed the final nine lines as printed in every edition up to 1950 (though not in *R.L.S. Teuila*); they appear only in a rough draft, Beinecke 6565, and then not at the end—and even so are incorrectly transcribed in *Tusitala*. The fair copy, Beinecke 6566, ends with the line '*Apart from high society—and sea fish?*', though there are six further lines in the manuscript which have been deleted. The Samoans' view of

Stevenson as the 'richest of the rich' is elaborated in *Memories of Vailima*, where it is recorded that

> to the Samoan mind he was inordinately rich, and many of them believe in the bottom of their hearts that the story of the bottle-imp was no fiction, but a tangible fact.

VIII. In spring of 1893 Stevenson went to Sydney, partly to recuperate from his illness earlier in the year, accompanied by his wife and stepdaughter. Isobel Strong, in her journal for 3 March, 1893 (quoted in *Memories of Vailima*) records:

> He has had three topaz rings made, for topaz is the stone of his birth month, November. Inside two of them are his initials, and these he has presented, with a memorial poem, to my mother and myself. On his own we engraved the first letters of our names.

XXIV. *Light foot and tight foot*

Checked with facsimile of a manuscript in the New York Public Library. First published in *Scribner's Magazine*, May, 1893, under the heading *Early in the Spring*: the first verse and the fourth are used as headings to Chapters V and XVI of *Balfour*; the same two stanzas only are printed in the Pentland edition, 1907.

XXV. *To the Stormy Petrel*

Checked with Beinecke 7045; dated 'March 10th, 1894, 'and inscribed at foot 'to Mrs F.V. de G.S.' First published in *Memories of Vailima*, 1902 (the Vailima edition, 1922, was the first edition of poems it appeared in) with an extract from Isobel Strong's journal for 10 March, 1894:

> Today is my mother's birthday, and she says the best of her presents is the piece of paper she found pinned on her mosquito-netting in the morning.

The 'drums of war' refer to a rising against the King of Samoa by young Tamasese, son of a high chief who had been displaced as a result of the Berlin Treaty of 1889 (*Balfour*, p. 422). Of some disturbances the previous summer, Isobel Strong wrote:

> These Samoan fighting men look very terrible in their battle array with blackened faces and a long 'head-knife' in their hands. But on close inspection their eyes are always kind and their smile sweet.

Of the other rhymes **Stevenson** made for his wife's birthday, the manuscript of the one for 1887 is in the National Library of Scotland: it was originally sold at Sotheby's in a sale of Lloyd Osbourne's property.

> What can I wish, what can I promise, dear,
> To make you gladder in the coming year?
> I wish you—ah, if I could promise too!—
> A kinder husband than you ever knew.

XXVI. *I, whom Apollo sometime visited*

Checked with manuscript in the National Library of Scotland, where it appears on the same sheet of paper as *An End of Travel*, p. 281. That poem is dated Vailima, so this, too, probably belongs to the years 1891–1894. First published *B.B.S. II*, 1916.

XXVII. *As with heaped bees at hiving time*

Checked with manuscript in the National Library of Scotland; first published *B.B.S. III*, 1921. Not dated, but bound up in a collector's volume (sold at Sotheby's, May, 1949, 54) with the previous poem and *An End of Travel*, p. 281; so possibly 1891–1894.

In the manuscript, which is in ink but looks like a draft rather than a fair copy, four lines appear at the top of the page:

> Rivers and winds among the twisted hills,
> Hears, and his hearing slowly fills,
> And hearkens, and his face is lit,
> Life pacing, death pursuing it—

with marks showing that the first two lines should be transposed. Then, after a space, follow the twelve lines of the poem. In *B.B.S. III*, these four lines are printed as part of the poem; after considerable reflection I have decided to omit them, as being probably only a first draft of the last four lines of the poem.

DEDICATIONS, AND POEMS FROM BOOKS

I. *To the Hesitating Purchaser*

First printed in *Treasure Island*, 1883, on a page facing the Contents. The version printed in the Vailima and Tusitala editions consists of twenty-six lines, of which ll. 8–10 are a version of the first three lines of the second stanza, ll. 11–18, and ll. 19–26 are versions of the whole second stanza (both differing from the final version published in the story). There is no note in these editions to explain that the manuscript they printed from was clearly a draft, and that a finished version could be found in any copy of *Treasure Island*.

When outlining his book on the South Seas to Colvin (in a letter from the schooner *Equator*, 2 December, 1890) Stevenson headed Part I: 'General, "Of schooners, islands, and maroons ".'

II. *Pirate Ditty*

From *Treasure Island*, 1883. Stevenson got the name of Dead Man's Chest, an island in the Caribbean much infested with pirates, from Kingsley's *At Last*: it chimed in with Billy Bones's sea-chest, which he had taken from Washington Irving's *Tales of a Traveller* (see essay on *My First Book*, 1894, included in *The Art of Writing*), to produce the unforgettable buccaneer's jingle which echoes through the story.

III. *The Song of the Sword of Alan*

From *Kidnapped*, 1886, Chapter X, *The Siege of the Round-House*:

> Thereupon he turned to the four enemies, passed his sword clean through each of them, and tumbled them out of doors one after the other. As he did so, he kept humming and singing and whistling to himself, like a man trying to recall an air; only what *he* was trying was to make one. All the while, the flush was in his face, and his eyes were as bright as a five-year-old child's with a new toy. And presently he sat down upon the table, sword in hand; the air that he was making all the time began to run a little clearer, and then clearer still; and then out he burst with a great voice into a Gaelic song.
>
> I have translated it here, not in verse (of which I have no skill) but at least in the King's English. He sang it often afterwards, and the thing became popular; so that I have heard it, and had it explained to me, many's the time.

David Balfour's comment, it should be noted, was:

> Now this song which he made (both words and music) in the hour of victory, is something less than just to me, who stood beside him in the tussle.

These verses have something of the same style as the translations from Gaelic songs and rhymes included in Campbell's *Popular Tales of the West Highlands*, 1860–1862, a book which Stevenson knew. See note to *Heather Ale*, p. 499.

[535]

IV. *To Virgil and Dora Williams*

Checked with Beinecke 7050; first published in *The Lark* (San Francisco), June, 1895; then in the Pentland Edition, 1907, where the lines are dated 'Hyères, 1883.' The poem was written inside a copy of *The Silverado Squatters*, 1883, and sent to Virgil and Dora Williams (to whom the book is also dedicated in print), two artists who made Stevenson welcome in their home in San Francisco in the winter of 1879–1880—'the Williamses— you know they were the parties who stuck up for us about our marriage, and Mrs W. was my guardian angel, and our Best Man and Bridesmaid rolled in one, and the only third of the wedding party,' wrote Stevenson to Henley from Davos in April, 1882.

The poem was printed in Katharine Osbourne's *Robert Louis Stevenson in California*, 1911, with the additional line between lines 2 and 3:

> Or, shall we say, defaced by Joseph's art

—Joseph Strong, Isobel Osbourne's husband, designed the frontispiece for *The Silverado Squatters*.

V. *To Nelly Sanchez*

Checked with manuscript *Sotheby*, May, 1949, 82. From an exercise-book of poems of Bournemouth days. *So live, so love*, p. 308, comes from the same book. First published *B.B.S. II*, 1916.

The lines went with a copy of *Prince Otto*, 1885, which was dedicated to his wife's sister (and later biographer) Nelly Van de Grift Sanchez. The first draft of *Prince Otto* was written in Mrs Sanchez' house near San Francisco. 'Giant Adulpho' was Mr Sanchez, and 'the king' Stevenson's name-child, Louis Sanchez. See notes to *To N. V. de G. S.*, p. 473, and to *A Child's Garden of Verses*, Envoys, V, p. 556.

VI. *To H. C. Bunner*

Checked with Beinecke 7003; dated 'Skerryvore, Bournemouth Oct. 21 1885'. First published in *Scribner's Magazine*, December, 1909, then in *Poems and Ballads* (Scribner, 1913). Written inside a copy of *A Child's Garden of Verses*. H. C. Bunner was an American who had written a paper on Stevenson in the *Century Magazine* in 1883 (see letter to W. H. Low, 23 October, 1883) and who was known as author of *The Way to Arcady* in a volume of poems *Airs from Arcady and*

Elsewhere, 1884. In a letter to Low of 22 October, 1885, Stevenson writes:

> I will send you with this a copy of the English edition of the *Child's Garden*. I have heard there is some vile rule of the post-office in the States against inscriptions; so I send herewith a piece of doggerel which Mr Bunner may, if he thinks fit, copy on the fly-leaf.

It was a practice of Stevenson's to write a verse inscription in the copies of his books he gave to friends. A set of those he wrote for Dr Trudeau of Saranac is described in the Grolier Club *First Editions of the Works of Robert Louis Stevenson*, 1915. The one in *Underwoods* goes:

> Some day or other ('tis a general curse)
> The wisest author stumbles into verse—

and the one in *Travels with a Donkey*:

> It blew, it rained, it thawed, it snowed, it thundered—
> Which was the Donkey? I have often wondered.

VII. *To Katharine de Mattos*

Checked with manuscript *Sotheby*, May, 1949, 48. First published in *Letters*, 1899; not hitherto published in any edition of the Poems.

Letter to Katharine de Mattos, his cousin (see note to *To K. de M.*, p. 472), from Bournemouth 1 January, 1886:

> Dearest Katharine,—Here, on a very little book and accompanied with lame verses, I have put your name. Our kindness is now getting well on in years; it must be nearly of age; and it gets more valuable to me with every time I see you. It is not possible to express any sentiment, and it is not necessary to try, at least between us. You know very well that I love you dearly, and that I always will. I only wish the verses were better, but at least you like the story; and it is sent to you by the one that loves you—Jekyll, and not Hyde.

Then follow under the heading *Ave*, the two verses of the poem. The book was *The Strange Case of Dr Jekyll and Mr Hyde*; the published dedication is to Katharine de Mattos, followed by the second verse only of this poem.

VIII. *To my Wife*

Checked with Beinecke 7114; the manuscript page is headed 'The Justice-Clerk', Stevenson's original title for *Weir of Hermiston*. First published as dedication to that novel in 1896. A note in the Vailima and Tusitala editions runs: 'These lines are found in the manuscript of *Weir of Hermiston*. They suggest a projected dedication of the book to Mrs Stevenson'—in fact, they had been printed with the book for over twenty-five years. Mrs Stevenson's version, in a letter to Colvin of 17 July, 1895 (quoted in E. V. Lucas's *The Colvins and their Friends*, p. 258), is:

> In looking over further papers to give Mr Balfour to carry to you, I found the dedication to me as Louis first [wrote] it for *Hermiston*. Please put it in as he meant it to be. He pinned it to my bed curtains when I was asleep, with other explanatory verses.

There are three drafts of the poem in the Beinecke Collection; there is also an early version in a letter to Baxter of *c.* 18 May, 1894 (*Baxter Letters*, pp. 355–356). At that time Stevenson was considering whether to use these verses, although designed for *Weir*, as a general dedication to the Edinburgh Edition. The Vailima and Tusitala editions print an early version which has two lines more than that published in the novel. It begins:

> The indefeasible impulse of my blood
> Surround [*sic*] me sleeping in this isle; and I
> Behold rain falling and the rainbow drawn, *etc.*

and has several other minor variations. I have used the *censure* of this version instead of the *counsel* of l. 9 of the version printed in *Weir*, as making much better sense.

The Vailima Edition and the first impression of the Tusitala Edition, print *indefensible* in l. 1, and *rainbow dawn* in l. 3.

LIGHT VERSE

I. *For laughing I very much vote*

From a facsimile in *Stevenson's Workshop*, 1921, No. 14, which also prints a text; not included in any collection of Stevenson's poems. In a note to the facsimile, Professor W. P. Trent writes:

> We may assume that the following uncouth poem was suggested by Stevenson's own stormy and somewhat unpromising youth in Edinburgh.

[538]

II. *Here he comes, big with Statistics*

Checked with manuscript *Sotheby*, May, 1949, 63. First published *B.B.S. III*, 1921. Stevenson's pencilled comment at the foot of the manuscript '*Pas mal, je crois.*' No. V of the *Recruiting Songs* (see note to *Epistle to Charles Baxter*, p. 457) some of which are dated 1871 and 1872. The verses probably describe one of the professors at Edinburgh University.

III. *To Charles Baxter*

Checked with manuscript in Ashley Library, British Museum. Printed for private distribution in 1896, in a very small issue, by T. J. Wise, to whom the manuscript belonged (*Gosse*). First general publication in *Letters*, 1911. Sent with a letter dated 'Boulogne sur Mer, Wednesday 3rd or 4th September, 1872'; Stevenson was then on his way home from a trip to Germany with Walter Simpson. After the verses, he goes on:

> So; *en voilà assez de mauvais vers.* Let us finish with a word or two in honest prose, tho' indeed I shall so soon be back again, and, if you be in town as I hope, so soon get linked again down the Lothian road by a cigar or two and a liquor, that it is perhaps scarce worth the postage to send my letter on before me.

IV. *Ne sit Ancillae Tibi Amor Pudori*

Checked with Beinecke 6623 and 6624; first published *B.B.S. II*, 1916. Beinecke 6624 is dated (18)72. So Mr Hellman's identification (in *The True Stevenson*) of the pretty housemaid with Valentine Roch, the French maid of Hyères and Bournemouth days, is disproved.

V. *Poem for a Class Re-union*

Checked with manuscript *Sotheby*, November, 1949, 392. First published *B.B.S. III*, 1921, which prints the first line of the last stanza as—'We shall never have *pennies* for *lunch*.' The reunion was in 1875, and the 'master' referred to was D'Arcy Wentworth Thompson, whose class Stevenson attended at Edinburgh Academy in 1861–1863. See *Underwoods, II, X, Their Laureate to an Academy Class Dinner Club*, p. 162, and note, p. 489. Stevenson to Mrs Sitwell, January, 1875:

> Well, I was at the annual dinner of my old Academy schoolfellows last night. We sat down ten, out of seventy-

two! The others are scattered all over the places of the earth, some in San Francisco, some in New Zealand, some in India, one in the backwoods—it gave one a wide look over the world to hear them talk so. I read them some verses. It is great fun; I always read verses, and in the vinous enthusiasm of the moment they always propose to have them printed; Ce qui n'arrive jamais du reste: in the morning, they are more calm.

A *clacken*, a purely local word, is a wooden hand-bat or racket still used in playing *Hailes* by the boys of the Edinburgh Academy. *Peeries* are marbles.

VI. *Browning*

Checked with Beinecke 6601; written on the verso of a photograph of Browning. First published in *Poetical Fragments by Robert Louis Stevenson*, edited by Clement Shorter, 1915, under the title *My Book*; not published in any edition of Stevenson's poems. The verse probably refers to a review by Stevenson of Browning's *Inn Album* in *Vanity Fair*, 11 December, 1875.

Stevenson to Mrs Sitwell, Edinburgh, December, 1875:

I have done rather an amusing paragraph or two for *Vanity Fair* on the *Inn Album*. I have slated R. B. pretty handsomely.

Colvin's note to this letter says 'The matter of the poem is praised; the "slating" is only for the form and metres.'

VII. *On An Inland Voyage*

Checked with Beinecke 7157; first published in *B.B.S. Hitherto Unpublished Prose Writings*, 1921. Written on one page of a note-book containing 106 pages of *An Inland Voyage*, 1878 (No. 315 in Anderson Sale, Part I and 346 in *Sotheby*, November, 1949).

VIII. *Dedication*

Checked with manuscript *Sotheby*, November, 1949, 379. First published in *B.B.S. II*, 1916, where a facsimile of the first two stanzas appears facing p. 22. The manuscript is undated; *B.B.S.* dates it 1886, on the grounds, possibly, that their editor took it to be a projected Dedication to *Underwoods*, published in 1887: and the Vailima and Tusitala editions print it at

the end of Book I of *Underwoods*, numbering it XXXIX (the
original Book I of *Underwoods* stopped at XXXVIII). But the
following extracts from letters suggest a much earlier date, and
no special connection with *Underwoods*. Stevenson to Henley
from California, October, 1879:

> O, and look here, why did you not send me the *Spectator*
> which slanged me? Rogues and rascals, is that all you are
> worth?

Stevenson to Professor Meiklejohn from California, 1 February,
1880:

> I have not seen the *Spectator* article; nobody sent it to
> me. If you had an old copy lying by you, you would be
> very good to despatch it to me. A little abuse from my
> grandmamma would do me good in health, if not in morals.

Stevenson to Colvin, from Strathpeffer, August, 1880:

> I enclose two poems of, I think, a high order. One is my
> dedication for my essays; it was occasioned by that delicious
> article in the *Spectator*.

The essays to which he projected these verses as a Dedication
were *Virginibus Puerisque*, published in April, 1881.

Praise and blame had been doled out to Stevenson by *The
Spectator* in reviews of *An Inland Voyage* on 20 July, 1878;
and *Travels with a Donkey* on 27 September, 1879 (referred to
in the letter to Professor Meiklejohn):

> No doubt donkeys are exasperating animals, but Mr
> Stevenson, though young, might have known that before
> undertaking such an expedition some technical knowledge
> of driving a donkey would have been advisable. . . . These
> little threads of sentiment are very pretty and evidently
> genuine, and give a charm to travels that are otherwise
> exceedingly thin. Seldom has any book of the kind been
> woven out of slighter material. . . . Throughout the
> volume we have felt that the charms of a solitary journey in
> the company of a donkey would not have been so attractive
> to the author, if he had not desired to write a book. It was
> a pardonable and in the main a successful ambition.

Ten years later, Stevenson referred to a criticism in the
Spectator of *The Song of Rahéro* (letter to H. B. Baildon from
Vailima, Spring, 1891):

> *The Spectator* said there was no psychology in it; that
> interested me much: my grandmother (as I used to call that

able paper, and an able paper it is, and a fair one) cannot so much as observe the existence of savage psychology when it is put before it.

IX. *On Some Ghastly Companions at a Spa*

Checked with manuscript *Sotheby*, November, 1949, 372; first published in *Letters*, 1911. Sent with a letter to Charles Baxter in August, 1880, from Strathpeffer, where Stevenson, after his return from California, spent some weeks with his wife and his parents: 'This is a heathenish place near delightful places, but inhabited, alas! by a wholly bestial crowd.'

X. *Brasheanna*

Checked with manuscripts in the Widener Library, Harvard. The sonnets, with the exception of 1, were first published in *Widener*, 1913, but have not hitherto appeared in any edition of Stevenson's poems. No. 1 was first printed in the *Outlook* for 26 February, 1898, under the heading of *A Literary Enigma*. Peter Brash was an Edinburgh publican well known to Stevenson and Baxter in their student days. These sonnets were written at Davos (as was another series, *Casparides*, on the shortcomings of certain local tradesmen, which I was unable to trace in 1950 but which are now in the Beinecke Collection 6414–6417) and were sent to Baxter early in 1882. Stevenson wished to make a pamphlet of them: Charles Baxter had the first two set up in old-face type, and sent proofs to Stevenson, who wrote from Nice, 12 January, 1883:

> It is true, man, God's trüth, what ye say about the body Stevison. The deil himsel, it's my belief, couldnae get the soul harled oot o' the creature's wame, or he had seen the hinder end o' they proofs. Ye crack o' Mæcenas, he's naebody by you! He gied the lad Horace a rax forrit by all accounts; but he never gied him proofs like yon. Horace may hae been a better hand at the clink than Stevison— mind, I'm no sayin' 't—but onyway he was never sae weel prentit. Damned, but it's bonny! Hoo mony pages will there be, think ye? Stevison maun hae sent ye the feck o' twenty sangs—fifteen I'se warrant. Weel, that'll can make thretty pages, gin ye were to prent on ae side only, whilk wad be perhaps what a man o' your *great* idees would be ettlin' at, may Johnson. Then there wad be the Pre-face, an' prose ye ken prents oot langer than po'try at the hinder

end, for ye hae to say things in't. An' then there'll be a
title-page and a dedication and an index wi' the first lines
like, and the deil an' a'. Man, it'll be grand. Nae copies to
be given to the Liberys.

There is no record of proofs for the others: and these proofs
of I and II (reproduced in *Widener*, pp. 71–72) are extremely rare
Stevensoniana. On the back of those in the Widener Collection
is this note by Baxter:

> Words by Stevenson, printing paid by me. Imitation from
> 4to Subscription Edition (original) of Gay's Poems. C. B.

There are now known to be many more Brash poems than was
thought in 1950. Sixteen, and the first lines of two more, are
listed in Beinecke (6024–6048); two of these are published in
Baxter Letters, pp. 96–97.

XI. *To A. G. Dew-Smith*

Checked *Sotheby*, November, 1949, 388. First published,
without the last two verses, in *Letters*, 1899, where it has a foot-
note referring to line 3, 'dancing and deray':

> 'The whole front of the house was lighted, and there
> were pipes and fiddles, and as much dancing and deray
> within as used to be in Sir Robert's house at Pace and Yule,
> and such high seasons'—see *Wandering Willie's Tale* in
> *Redgauntlet*.

Sterling (verse 13) is an architectural term for a series of
piles defending the pier of a bridge.

> 'The *Epistle to Albert Dew-Smith*, dated from Davos in
> November, 1880, is almost the only record of a friendship
> which Stevenson greatly valued. Mr Dew-Smith, long a
> resident, although not a Fellow of Trinity College, Cam-
> bridge, was a man of delicate culture and of refined and
> caustic wit. His manners were singularly finished and their
> elaboration and dignity made a lasting effect upon Stevenson,
> who was little more than a boy when he was presented to
> him. The figure of Attwater, in *The Ebb-Tide*, presents us
> with a close and even minute portrait of Dew-Smith, whom
> it pleased R. L. S. to conceive as transplanted from the
> solitude of his college rooms to the sovereignty of an
> unknown island in the Pacific.   GOSSE

A photograph of Stevenson aged thirty-five by A. G. Dew-Smith appears as the frontispiece of Vol. II of the four-volume *Letters*, 1911.

XII. *Long time I lay in little ease*

Checked with manuscript *Sotheby*, November, 1949, 357. First published *B.B.S. I*, 1916, where the last verse, which gives the poem its point, is omitted, as it is in *New Poems*, 1918: it appeared in the Vailima Edition, which also corrects various misprints pointed out by Colvin on p. 140 of *Memories and Notes*, 1921. The poem was the result of a meeting with Colvin in 1884; he had asked the Stevensons to join him for a day or two at Marseilles on his way home from Italy. He ran short of cash, Stevenson lent him his fare home, but left himself penniless till Colvin could repay him from Paris. Dantès and Château d'If are references to Dumas' *Count of Monte Cristo*.

Stevenson to Colvin, 2 December, 1889:

> Marseilles the many-masted (copyright epithet).

XIII. *My wife and I, in our romantic cot*

Checked with facsimile of manuscript in *B.B.S. III*: several variations in Tusitala version. First published in *B.B.S. III*, 1921 (or possibly in Sidney Colvin's *Memories and Notes*, 1921; I cannot discover which appeared the first). In the right-hand corner of the manuscript some rhyming words have been jotted down: mell, knell, bell, dell, hell, yell, sell, spell. *B.B.S. III* takes it to refer to the shack at Silverado where the Stevensons spent their honeymoon; I think there is no doubt it was written at the Châlet La Solitude, Hyères, on the slope of the hill above the town, where the Stevensons lived from March, 1883, to July, 1884. See notes to *To a Gardener*, p. 472, and *Flower-god, god of the spring*, p. 521.

XIV. *At morning on the garden seat*

Checked with facsimile, *B.B.S. III*, p. 110, in which it was first published, 1921. Not dated; *B.B.S.* assigns it to 1880, and places it in Silverado. Hyères, at the Châlet La Solitude 1883–1884, seems far more likely.

XV. *Last night we had a thunderstorm in style*

Checked with manuscript, a very rough pencil draft, *Sotheby*, November, 1949, 369. A facsimile appears in *B.B.S. III*, p. 94, where it was first published. Not dated; but like the other verses in traditional French forms it may belong to the years 1875–1879. *B.B.S. III* suggests 1875.

XVI. *To Time*

Taken from manuscript *Sotheby*, May, 1949, 58; no indication of date. Printed here for the first time. There is another and shorter version at Yale, Beinecke 7049.

XVII. *Fragment*

Checked with manuscript *Sotheby*, May, 1949, 73; first published *B.B.S. I*, 1916. Not dated; on the back of the manuscript are some draft lines for *The Canoe Speaks*, and that poem can be dated 1884.

XVIII. *A Sonnet to Mr William Mackintosh*

Checked with manuscript of an undated letter to Mackintosh at Columbia University; the sonnet is on the third page. First published in *The Bibliographer* (New York), October, 1902, and then in the Pentland Edition, 1907. William Aeneas Mackintosh (1870–1940) was the son of William Mackintosh, raised to the Bench as Lord Kyllachy, and Stevenson's cousin Jane, daughter of David Stevenson.

XIX. *Rhymes to Henley*

See note *To W. E. Henley*, p. 475.

i. Checked with manuscript in National Library of Scotland. First published in *Letters*, 1899. Included in a letter dated Edinburgh, April, 1879, in answer to one from Henley containing some criticism of *Our Lady of the Snows*. See also note to that poem, p. 480.

ii. Checked with manuscript of letter in National Library of Scotland. A rough draft of this poem, with many more lines, is reproduced in facsimile in *Stevenson's Workshop*, 1921, nos. 16–18. First published in *Letters*, 1911. Sent to Henley from Braemar, summer, 1881, when Stevenson was laid up with a particularly bad cold: hence the respirator, prescribed by his uncle Dr George Balfour.

'Let Lawson triumph': Sir Wilfrid Lawson was a temperance advocate who was a great subject for jokes between Henley and Stevenson. Kennedy Williamson in his *W. E. Henley*, 1930, quotes from an article of Henley's in *London*:

> The day that shall witness the divorce of cakes and ale
> has not yet arrived. When it does come, Sir Wilfrid will be
> a great man. Bands of Hope will escort him to and from his
> club with a noise of brass instruments and a glory of banners
> and blue sashes. Reclaimed drunkards will testify their
> gratitude to him by the presentation of beautifully bound
> sets of the *British Workman*. The discontented soaker will
> fuddle himself in the vile privacy of his *chez-lui*. Delirium
> Tremens will disappear from the files of mortality, and Mr
> Bass will bury Mr Allsopp and then die of a broken heart.
> The sun and solar systems will sing together an enormous
> temperance part-song; and the Immensities and Infinities
> (by special permission of Mr Carlyle) will wheel in mighty
> and mystic measure about the Apotheosis of the Tea-pot.

III, IV, V, VI. Checked with the manuscripts in Lady Stair's
House Museum. First published in *Letters*, 1911. Sent in a
letter to Henley from Hyères, February or March, 1884, which
is thus annotated by Colvin:

> Early in January, Stevenson, after a week's visit at Hyères
> from his friends Charles Baxter and W. E. Henley, accom-
> panied them as far as Nice, and there suddenly went down
> with an attack of acute congestion, first of the lungs, and
> then of the kidneys. At one moment there seemed no hope,
> but he recovered slowly and returned to Hyères. His friends
> had not written during his illness, fearing him to be too far
> gone to care for letters. As he got better he began to chafe
> at their silence.

The letter concludes:

IF NOBODY WRITES TO ME I
SHALL DIE

I now write no more.

Richard Lefanu Stevenson
Duke of Indignation

Mark Tacebo	Isaac Blood	
Secretary	John Blind	
	Vain-hope-Go-to-bed	witnesses
	Israel Sciatica	

The finger on the mouth.

vii. From manuscript in Lady Stair's House Museum; published here for the first time. The verses are on an undated scrap of paper.

viii. From facsimile of manuscript in *Stevenson's Workshop*, no. 22, where it was first published. The first draft of the last four lines, deleted in manuscript, runs:

> I too may enter in perchance
> And where the aged graces dance
> Behind the tenor and soprano
> Grind my mechanical piano.

The verses may refer to Stevenson's project of a book of *Penny Whistles* that later became *A Child's Garden of Verses*.

ix. *Triolets*

From manuscript in Lady Stair's House Museum; published here for the first time. The triolets appear in three columns, side by side, on p. 2 of a letter to Henley from Nice (written early January, 1883) which goes critically through the contents of a recent number of the *Magazine of Art*. In the manuscript there is a footnote to *Le Sapin—Le Fiacre* No. 16.

Stevenson had always been addicted to this kind of light French novel. His letter says:

> All Xavier's women are called Marguerite: *La Fille de Marguerite*, by the way, runs the *Sapin* hard. It is the romance of the time-table; everything turns on trains; very ingenious and exciting. I think the first Triolet is a great success.

x. *A Lytle Jape of Tusherie*

Checked with manuscript in National Library of Scotland. Sent in a letter to Henley from Hyères, May, 1883, and first published in *Letters*, 1899. 'Tushery' was Stevenson's and Henley's word for historical romances of the Wardour Street type. In an earlier letter that month he had confessed that the editor of *Young Folks* had begged him for another serial to follow *Treasure Island*, so

> I turned me to—what thinkest 'ou?—to Tushery, by the mass! Ay, friend, a whole tale of tushery. And every tusher tushes me so free, that may I be tushed if the whole thing is worth a tush. *The Black Arrow: a Tale of Tunstall Forest* is his name: tush! a poor thing!

The increasing tedium of tushing (and the 'strain and anxiety' of 'trying to support myself') provoked the 'Lytle Jape.'

XX. *Epitaphs*

1. Not checked with manuscript. First published in *Letters*, 1899—sent in a letter to Cosmo Monkhouse from Hyères, 16 March, 1884:

> After all boyhood's aspirations and youth's immoral day-dreams, you are condemned to sit down, grossly draw in your chair to the fat board, and be a beastly Burgess till you die. Can it be? Is there not some escape, some furlough from the Moral Law, some holiday jaunt contrivable into a Better Land? Shall we never shed blood? This prospect is too grey.

II. Checked with manuscript *Sotheby*, May, 1949, 67. First published *B.B.S. II*, 1916.

III. Not checked with manuscript. First published in *Letters*, 1911. Sent in a letter to Colvin which can be dated early June, 1887 (the date given in the *Letters*, April, 1886, is wrong):

> We have a butler! He doesn't buttle, but the point of the thing is the style. When Fanny gardens, he stands over her and looks genteel. He opens the door, and I am told waits at table. Well, what's the odds; I shall have it on my tomb— 'He ran a butler.'

IV. Checked with Beinecke 3093; first published in Colvin's 'Robert Louis Stevenson and Henry James', *Scribner's Magazine*, March 1924. Sent in a letter to Colvin, Bournemouth, Summer 1886.

> I have turned my bottom on Bloudy-Jackerie, and am now gay, free, and obnoxious. Je ne vis que pour le piano ; on the which I labour like an idiot as I am. You should hear me labouring away at Martini's celebrated, beroomed gavotte or Boccherini's beroomed, famous minuet. I have 'beroomed' on the brain, and sign myself,
>
> Sir,
The Beroomed Stevenson.

XXI. *The Fine Pacific Islands*

Not checked with manuscript; first published in Andrew Lang's causerie, *At the Sign of the Ship*, in *Longman's Magazine*, January, 1889, with this introduction:

The next sea-song came to us from the sea in an envelope with the postmark 'Taiohae Taiti, 21 Août, '88.' The hand-writing of the address appears to be that of the redoubted Viking who sailed in John Silver's crew, who winged *The Black Arrow*, and who wandered in the heather with Alan Breck. *Aut Robertus Ludovicus aut Diabolus* sent the song, I presume, but whether he really heard it sung at Rother-hithe, or whether he is the builder of the lofty rhyme, is between himself and his conscience.

First book publication in *R. L. S. Teuila*, 1899, which prints a version with several variations of words and punctuation, then the Pentland Edition, 1907.

XXII. *To Henry James*

Not checked with manuscript. First published in *Letters*, 1899. Adela Chart is the heroine of James's story *The Marriages* (published in *The Atlantic Monthly*, August, 1891) who carries tactlessness to a fine frenzy. The verses were sent in a letter to James from Vailima, October 1891, which began:

> From this perturbed and hunted being expect but a line, and that line shall be but a whoop for Adela. O she's delicious, delicious; I could live and die with Adela—die, rather the better of the two; you never did a straighter thing, and never will.

XXIII. *Athole Brose*

Not checked with manuscript. First published in Vol. XXVI of the Vailima Edition, in *Stevenson's Companion to the Cook Book, Adorned with a Century of Authentic Anecdotes* (the manu-script of which, in the hand of Stevenson, Mrs Stevenson and Lloyd Osbourne, was in the Anderson Sale, II, 394). This is a collection of humorous sham anecdotes, dating from Vailima, and *Athole Brose* comes in Anecdote III, about Robert Burns.

> On the way, Burns and Nichol were overtaken by a storm of rain, took refuge in a wayside inn beside the Blair, and passed some hours of the afternoon in drinking Athole Brose. It was the first time the poet had tasted the con-fection; he enquired exactly as to its constituents and going to the window, looked out with an abstracted countenance into the falling rain.... In less than twenty minutes, the

poet returned to the table, called for pen and ink, and wrote
the following ingenious trifle.

In 1950 I made some emendations to the text of the Vailima
Edition, and printed *reek* for Vailima *reck* (l. 5), *Killiecrankie* for
Killikrankie (l. 8), *neist* for *neiest* (l. 15). I have now emended
the Vailima *Rye* (ll. 3, 11) to *kye* (cows). (Stevenson's *k*, lower or
upper case, is very like *R*; I have corrected another *R* to *K* on
p. 557, 'Or Gerda following little *K*ay'—1950, *R*ay.)

In Chapter 25 of *Kidnapped*, Stevenson describes the constit-
uents of Athole Brose:

old whisky, strained honey, and sweet cream, slowly beaten
together in the right order and proportion.

So in the still, the bee-skeps and the *kye* of the poem he is
celebrating the source of the three ingredients. Nor would a
Scottish poet associate *Rye* with whisky, though American
editors might. I thank Lord Balerno for first suggesting *kye*.

XXIV. *The Gods are Dead*

These lines are published here for the first time from the
manuscript now in the National Library of Scotland. The manu-
script, together with four letters from Stevenson to Henley, was
originally given by Mrs Henley to Mr W. K. Dickson. The
lines must have been sent to Henley in July, 1877: a revised
version of them appears in Henley's magazine *London* for 28 July,
1877 (Vol. I, No. 26). It seems likely that Henley, always short
of copy for *London*, re-arranged and partly rewrote Stevenson's
poem and printed it (like his own) with no signature. When
Gleeson White published his anthology *Ballades and Rondeaus* in
the Canterbury Poets series in 1887, Henley allowed him to re-
print a number of the unsigned poems from *London* and acknow-
ledged them as his. Among this number *The Gods are Dead*
appears under Henley's signature on page 172.

Line 14 is crossed out in the manuscript, but I have restored it
on grounds of sense and because the rondeau form requires it.
For another rondeau written in the 1880s see *My Wife and I*
(p. 344) and note (p. 544). Below the poem Stevenson has
written: 'There! you see I'm not dead. I'm all right, and quite
the poet. R.L.S.'

POEMS FOR CHILDREN

A CHILD'S GARDEN OF VERSES

A Child's Garden of Verses was first published in 1885 by Messrs Longmans Green and Co. Stevenson began writing these verses at Braemar in 1881, when his mother showed him Kate Greenaway's *Birthday Book for Children*, with text by Mrs Sale Barker. He said, 'These are rather nice rhymes and I don't think such verses would be difficult to do' and almost immediately composed fourteen poems. The next considerable batch was written at Nice in the early spring of 1883. Many were composed during his illnesses, when he could not work on prose; several were written in the dark, with the left hand, at Hyères in 1884, when he was laid up with a hæmorrhage, sciatica and Egyptian ophthalmia. Stevenson, in a letter to Henley from Nice, March, 1883:

> As for the title, I think *Nursery Verses* the best. Poetry is not the strong point of the text, and I shrink from any title that might seem to claim that quality; otherwise we might have *Nursery Muses* or *New Songs of Innocence* (but that were a blasphemy), or *Rimes of Innocence*: the last not bad, or—an idea—*The Jew's Harp*, or—now I have it— *The Penny Whistle* . . . Fool! this is all wrong, here is the true name: *Penny Whistles for Small Whistlers*. The second title is queried, it is perhaps better as simply *Penny Whistles*.

And *Penny Whistles* it was till within a few weeks of publication. The poems were first set up, under this title, at Cambridge at the University Press, in 1883, and proofs sent to various of Stevenson's artist friends, who, he thought, might like to illustrate them. None was very keen to do so, and no illustrated edition appeared till 1896.

Stevenson to Henley from Hyères, October, 1883:

> I shall try to do the Whistle as suggested; but I can usually do whistles only by giving my whole mind to it: to produce even such limping verse demanding the whole forces of my untuneful soul.

Stevenson to Gosse, from Bournemouth, 12 March, 1885:

> They look ghastly in the cold light of print, but there is something nice in the little ragged regiment after all;

the blackguards seem to me to smile, to have a kind of
childish treble note that sounds in my ears freshly; not song,
if you will, but a child's voice.

Stevenson to William Archer, 27 March, 1894:

Marjorie Fleming I have known, as you surmise, for long.
She was possibly—no, I take back possibly—she was one of
the greatest works of God. Your note about the resemblance
of her verses to mine gave me great joy, though it only
proved me a plagiarist.

When finally published, *A Child's Garden of Verses* added six
Envoys, but omitted nine of the poems set up in the trial volume
of *Penny Whistles*. A set of *Penny Whistles* is in the H. E. Widener
Library at Harvard and the rejected poems appear in the privately
printed *Widener Catalogue*, 1913. They had also been privately
printed in 1912 by Luther S. Livingston in an edition of 100
copies for presentation. The titles are: *The Bull Hunt, The Hunt
Interrupted, The Garden Door, A Song of Days, A Proper Pride,
Birthday Party, Little Boy Blue, Good News,* and *Lesson on the
Sea,* reproduced below.

> The sea is the largest of waters I hear,
>   And behold! it is full to the brim,
> For the sun to go down in when evening draws near
>   And the birds and the boaties to skim.
>
> The ships may go sailing before them for days,
>   And the birds may go flying at will,
> But they never arrive at the end of their ways,
>   For the sea is in front of them still.
>
> It tosses the seaweed and shells on the sand
>   For the children to play with on shore;
> And it tumbles and roars at the edge of the land
>   As the beasts in menageries roar.
>
> The rain of the sky and the rivers that haste,
>   All run to the sea without halt;
> But the rain and the rivers are sweet to the taste,
>   And the sea is unpleasantly salt.

Most wonderful things are observed on the land,
　　Like the wind and the Chinaman's wall,
There are thousands of things that we can't
　　　　understand,
　　But the sea is the greatest of all!

The background of most of the verses in *A Child's Garden*
is Colinton Manse, where Stevenson spent many holidays with
his grandfather, Dr Lewis Balfour, his aunt Jane, and some
of his fifty first cousins (forty of them Balfours). The house
stood in a hollow, close by the Water of Leith, with mills above
and below.

That was my golden age: *et ego in Arcadia vixi.* There
is something so fresh and wholesome about all that went
on at Colinton, compared with what I recollect of the town,
that I can hardly, even in my own mind, knit the two
diaries of reminiscences together.

Fragment of Autobiography, quoted in *Balfour*, p. 40.

See the essay *The Manse* in *Memories and Portraits*.

Dedication: To Alison Cunningham from her Boy

Alison Cunningham—'Cummy'—was Stevenson's nurse, who
came to the family when he was eighteen months old.

Stevenson to Alison Cunningham, February, 1883:

But the real reason why you have been more in my mind
than usual is because of some little verses that I have been
writing, and that I mean to make a book of; and the real
reason of this letter (although I ought to have written to
you anyway) is that I have just seen that the book in
question must be dedicated to

ALISON CUNNINGHAM,

the only person who will really understand it. I don't
know when it may be ready, for it has to be illustrated,
but I hope in the meantime you may like the idea of what
is to be; and when the time comes, I shall try to make the
dedication as pretty as I can make it. . . . This little book,
which is all about my childhood, should indeed go to no
other person but you, who did so much to make that child-
hood happy.

[553]

Stevenson to Henley, March, 1883:

> I forgot to mention that I shall have a dedication; I am
> going to dedicate 'em to Cummy; it will please her, and
> lighten a little my burthen of ingratitude.

In an unpublished letter to his mother, quoted in the Anderson
Catalogue III, 222, he wrote:

> I stick to what I said about Cummy: which was that she
> was the person entitled to the dedication; if I said she was
> the only person who would understand it was a fashion of
> speaking; but to Cummy the dedication is due because she
> has had the most trouble and the least thanks. Ecco! as for
> Auntie, she is my aunt, and she is a lady, and I am often
> decently civil to her, and I don't think I ever insulted her:
> four advantages that could not be alleged for Cummy. That
> was why, out of the three of you, I chose Cummy; and that
> is why I think I chose right.

II. *A Thought*

The version in *Penny Whistles* begins,

> It is *so* very nice to think

VII. *Pirate Story*

Letter to Mrs Milne (his cousin, Henrietta Traquair) from
Hyères, November, 1883: she had seen the proofs and recognised
some allusions.

> Certainly; who else would they be? More by token, on
> that particular occasion, you were sailing under the title
> of Princess Royal; I, after a furious contest, under that of
> Prince Alfred; and Willie, still a little sulky, as the Prince
> of Wales. We were all in a buck basket about halfway.
> between the swing and the gate; and I can still see the Pirate
> Squadron heave in sight upon the weather bow.

See notes to *A Good Boy*, p. 555, and *Envoys*, I, p. 556.

IX. *Windy Nights*

See note to *Stormy Nights*, p. 462.

XIV. *Where Go the Boats?*

In *The Manse* (*Memories and Portraits*) Stevenson writes:

> I have named, among many rivers that make music in
> my memory, that dirty Water of Leith. Often and often

I desire to look upon it again; and the choice of a point of view is easy to me. It should be at a certain water-door, embowered in shrubbery. The river is there dammed back for the service of the flour-mill just below, so that it lies deep and darkling, and the sand slopes into brown obscurity with a glint of gold; and it has but newly been recruited by the borrowings of the snuff-mill just above, and these, tumbling merrily in, shake the pool to its black heart, fill it with drowsy eddies, and set the curded froth of many other mills solemnly steering to and fro upon the surface.

XX. *A Good Boy*

Stevenson to his cousin Henrietta Milne, from Hyères, November, 1883:

> I shall never forget some of the days at Bridge of Allan; they were one golden dream. See *A Good Boy* in the *Penny Whistles*, much of the sentiment of which is taken direct from one evening at B. of A. when we had had a great play with the little Glasgow girl.

See also notes to *Pirate Story*, p. 554, and *Envoys*, I, p. 556.

XXIV. *Happy Thought*

A version in *Stevenson's Workshop* runs:

> The world is so great, and I am so small
> I do not like it at all at all.

XXVI. *Keepsake Mill*

In 1868 Stevenson wrote a long poem in rhymed couplets, called *The Mill-house*, printed in the Tusitala *Poems*, Vol. II, p. 91. There was a mill at Colinton.

XXVII. *Good and Bad Children*

Letter to Colvin, from Hyères, October, 1883:

> Bewildering and childering are good enough for me. These are rhymes, jingles; I don't go for eternity and the three unities.

XXXIX. *The Hayloft* and XL. *Farewell to the Farm*

His mother's diary for 1856, printed in Vol. XXVI of the Vailima Edition, records that

> We spent June and July at Colinton this year; we lived in Mr Macfarlane's house . . . Two families of cousins were

home from India and then he had his cousins Henrietta and Willie Traquair at the Farm so he had a very happy time.

THE CHILD ALONE

IX. *The Little Land*

Letter to Sidney Colvin from Marseilles, June, 1884:

> You see how this damned poeshie flows from me in sickness: Are they good or bad? Wha kens? But I like *The Little Land*, I think, as well as any. As time goes on I get more fancy in.

ENVOYS

I. *To Willie and Henrietta*

His favourite cousins, Willie and Henrietta Traquair, the children of his mother's sister, with whom he played a great deal in their grandfather's house at Colinton. 'Willie Traquair was David Balfour'—Stevenson to Lloyd Osbourne, in a letter sold at Sothebys, June, 1914, and quoted in *The Times*, 30 June, 1914. See notes to *Pirate Story*, p. 554, and *A Good Boy*, p. 555.

III. *To Auntie*

Miss Jane Whyte Balfour, who kept house for her father at Colinton Manse; she was almost blind and deaf as the result of a riding accident.

> There were thirteen of the Balfours as (oddly enough) there were of the Stevensons also, and the children of the family came home to her to be nursed, to be educated, to be mothered, from the infanticidal climate of India. There must sometimes have been half a score of us children about the manse; and all were born a second time from Aunt Jane's tenderness.

> Fragment of autobiography,
> quoted in *Balfour*, pp. 44–45.

It is the same aunt in *Auntie's Skirts*, p. 370.

IV. *To Minnie*

Minnie was another Balfour cousin who stayed at Colinton Manse. See also *To Minnie, with a hand-glass*, p. 118.

V. *To My Name-Child*

Louis Sanchez was the son of Nelly and Adulpho Sanchez, of Monterey, California, where Stevenson lived from October to December, 1879. See notes to *To N. V. de G. S.*, p.473, and to *To Nelly Sanchez*, p. 536.

VI. *To Any Reader*

B.B.S. I, 1916, followed by later editions, prints a version of forty-four lines: the first twenty-eight run:

> Whether upon the garden seat
> You lounge with your uplifted feet
> Under the May's whole Heaven of blue;
> Or whether on the sofa, you,
> No grown up person being by,
> Do some soft corner occupy:
> Take you this volume in your hands
> And enter into other lands,
> For lo! (as children feign) suppose
> You, hunting in the garden rows,
> Or in the lumbered attic, or
> The cellar—a nail-studded door
> And dark, descending stairway found
> That led to kingdoms underground:
> There standing, you should hear with ease
> Strange birds a-singing, or the trees
> Swing in big robber woods, or bells
> On many fairy citadels:
> There passing through (a step or so
> Neither mamma nor nurse need know!)
> From your nice nurseries you would pass
> Like Alice through the Looking-Glass
> Or Gerda following Little Kay,
> To wondrous countries far away.
> Well, and just this volume can
> Transport each little maid or man,
> Presto, from where they live away
> Where other children used to play.

A manuscript of the Envoy in its longer form, with a slightly different version of ll. 15–20, was sold at Sotheby's, November, 1949, 405.

NOT I, MORAL EMBLEMS, &c.

Lloyd Osbourne operated a toy printing-press in 1880 when he, then a boy of eleven, and his mother and Stevenson were all living in California; a few copies of a paper called *The Surprise* survive (Beinecke 62–64). In the issue of 6 March (1880), Locust Grove, Sonoma, Vol. I, No. 1, the first two verses of *Not I* are printed. There is a facsimile in the frontispiece to the McCutcheon Sale Catalogue, American Art Association, April, 1926. Lloyd Osbourne continued with his printing at Davos in the winters of 1880-1881 and 1881–1882.

From concert-programmes, invitations, and lottery tickets he graduated to poetry: his stepfather's *Martial Elegy for some Lead Soldiers* was printed as a broadsheet, and sold for one penny. Then followed his own *Black Canyon, or Wild Adventures in the Far West*, for which he used up all the woodcuts acquired with his type. At sixpence, it had a ready sale, which stimulated his stepfather to submit the manuscript of *Not I, and Other Poems*: it was an instantaneous hit, Lloyd Osbourne recorded (in his prefatory note to *Moral Emblems*—in the Chatto and Windus edition of 1921 and the Vailima Edition of 1922), 'selling out an entire edition of fifty copies.' Then followed, also in 1882, *Moral Emblems* (containing the first five rhymes) and *Moral Emblems: Second Collection* (with the next five) with the new author launching out as artist too. Stevenson made his first cut on 'fretwood' which was then mounted on a wooden block: more blocks were ordered 'in a wood without any grain' from a dying Swiss woodcarver at Davos. In the summer of 1882 the Stevenson family spent some weeks at Kingussie, in Speyside: printing was resumed, but the press broke down, and the printer and his author had to ask 'an amiable old man . . . who had a press of his own behind a microscopic general shop' to come to their help. *The Graver and the Pen* was issued there in 1882. The *Moral Tales* were planned, and three woodcuts made; but the poems never got beyond a typescript in Stevenson's lifetime. A set of the Davos booklets, the leaflets announcing them, a printer's device designed by Stevenson and other relics of this partnership, all from Lloyd Osbourne's collection, were sold at Sotheby's in February, 1923. Facsimiles of these booklets, most ingeniously bound into the containing volume, were published in the Appendix to the Edinburgh Edition (issued as a bonus to subscribers in 1898), and again, in *A Stevenson Medley* by Chatto and Windus in 1899 in an edition of 300 copies. _A Stevenson Medley_ also includes various 'cuts without text'—'Map,' 'The Botanist,' 'The Smuggler's Cave' and 'Lord Nelson and the Tar' and the printer's device reproduced on p. 448 of this volume.

Since 1950, the text of _Lord Nelson and the Tar_ has been discovered, in a copy made by Graham Balfour, among the Balfour Papers in the National Library of Scotland. For the text and cut see p. 449.

NOT I, AND OTHER POEMS

An eight-page 24mo pamphlet: '_Not I, and other Poems_, by Robert Louis Stevenson, Author of _The Blue Scalper, Travels with a Donkey_ etc. Price 6_d_. Dedicated to Messrs R. & R. Clarke (_sic_) by S. L. Osbourne, Davos, 1881.' No illustrations, but the pages are decorated with cuts acquired with the press: a shield with the Scottish lion rampant at the end of the first and third rhymes. At the end of the fourth is a cut of a handclasp; beneath 'Begun Feb. ended Oct. 1881.'

The first two verses of the title-poem appeared in _The Surprise_ (see note on previous page), 6 March, 1880; a longer version appears in a letter to Lloyd Osbourne written about March, 1880 (see Beinecke 8058 and 6635).

MORAL EMBLEMS

The first five appeared in a twelve-page 24mo pamphlet, 'by Robert Louis Stevenson. Author of _The Blue Scalper, Travels with a Donkey, Treasure Island, Not I_ etc.' The poems are printed on the right hand page with the appropriate woodcut on the left. On the back page is printed :

Works recently issued by Samuel Osbourne & Co. Davos.

NOT I and other poems, by Robert Louis Stevenson.

A volume of enchanting poetry.

BLACK CANYON or wild adventures in the Far West, by S. Osbourne.

A beautiful gift-book.

To be obtained from the Publishers and all respectable Book-sellers.

No price is printed, but Lloyd Osbourne says sixpence in his Prefatory Note. There was also an Edition de Luxe at ninepence.

The above speciman (*sic*) cut, illustrates a new departure in the business of Osbourne & Co. Wood engraving, designed and executed by Mr and Mrs Stevenson and printed under the Personal supervision of Mr Osbourne, now form a branch ot (*sic*) their business.

Stevenson to Gosse from Davos, 23 March, 1882:

I now send (for Mrs Gosse)

BLACK CANYON

Also an advertisement of my new appearance as poet (bard, rather) and hartis on wood. The cut represents the Hero and the Eagle, and is emblematic of Cortez first viewing the Pacific Ocean, which (according to the bard Keats) it took place in Darien. The cut is much admired for the sentiment of discovery, the manly proportions of the voyager, and the fine impression of tropical scenes and the untrodden WASTE, so aptly rendered by the hartis.

I would send you the book; but I declare I'm ruined. I got a penny a cut and a halfpenny a set of verses from the flint-hearted publisher, and only one specimen copy, as I'm a sinner. Kegan Paul was apostolic alongside of Osbourne.

Stevenson to Colvin, March, 1882:

Herewith *Moral Emblems*. The elephant by Fanny—the rest by me.

Stevenson to R. A. M. Stevenson, Davos, April, 1882:

I enclose all my artistic works; they are woodcuts—I cut them with a knife out of blocks of wood: I am a wood-engraver; I aaaam a wooooood engraaaaver. Lloyd then prints 'em: are they not fun? I doat on them; in my next venture I am going to have colour printing; it will be very laborious, six blocks to cut for each picter, but the result would be pyramidal.

The remaining five rhymes were published in *Moral Emblems: A Second Collection of Cuts and Verses*, also printed 1882, in the same format as the first seven. The advertisements on the last page are the same as in the first series, with the addition of

MORAL EMBLEMS (first Series) by Robert Louis Stevenson. *Has only to be seen to be admired.*

Again there was an

Edition de Luxe, tall paper, (extra fine) first impression. Price 10 pence.

Popular Edition, for the Million, Small paper, cuts slightly worn, a great bargain, 8 pence.

Among the books of Stevenson's childhood, now at the Stevenson Museum, Edinburgh, is a copy of *Songs Divine and Moral for the Use of Children* by the Rev Isaac Watts, D.D., whose style was clearly in Stevenson's mind when he compiled his moral verses.

A MARTIAL ELEGY FOR SOME LEAD SOLDIERS

According to Lloyd Osbourne, the first-fruit of the Davos partnership in 1880. Printed on one side of a duodecimo leaflet sold for one penny. A copy presented by Stevenson to Edmund Gosse was inscribed:

> The verse is mine, the printing done by Sam,
>   The Boss of printing Bosses;
> This copy, of the first edition last,
>   I testify is Gosse's.

Stevenson and Lloyd Osbourne played elaborate games with toy soldiers at Davos.

THE GRAVER AND THE PEN

A twenty-four page 16mo pamphlet, issued in French-grey wrappers:

> *The Graver and the Pen*, or *Scenes from Nature with Appropriate Verses* by Robert Louis Stevenson author of *The New Arabian Nights, Moral Emblems, Not I, Treasure Island*, etc. Illustrated. Edinburgh S. L. Osbourne & Company No. 17 Heriot Row. (It was only by the kindness of Mr Crerar of Kingussie that we are able to issue this little work—having allowed us to print with his own press when ours was broken.)

The work had been announced in a leaflet, which ran:

> To-day is published by Samuel Osbourne & Co. *The Graver and the Pen* or *Scenes from Nature with Appropriate Verses* by Robert Louis Stevenson author of the *Emblems*. *The Graver and the Pen* is a most strikingly illustrated little work and the poetry so pleasing that when it is taken

title on the cover in red letters. Small 8vo. Granite paper
cover with coloured title Price Ninepence per Copy.
Splendid chance for an energetic publisher!!! For Sale.
Copyright of *Black Canyon* price 1/¾ Autograph of Mr
R. L. Stevenson price -/3, ditto of Mr S. L. Osbourne
price 1/- each. If copies of the *Graver*, *Emblems*, or *Black
Canyon*, are wanted apply to the publisher, 17 Heriot Row,
Edinburgh.

MORAL TALES

The woodcuts for *Robin and Ben, or The Pirate and the
Apothecary*, were made in 1882, but the first appearance of the
poems in print was the Appendix to the Edinburgh Edition,
1898. No illustrations had been drawn or engraved for *The
Builder's Doom*, which also never got beyond a typescript in
Stevenson's lifetime, and was first printed in the above Appendix
(though Lloyd Osbourne, in his Prefatory Note to the *Moral
Emblems* in the 1921 Chatto edition, says '*The Builder's Doom*
has remained in manuscript until the present time'). Facsimiles
of two manuscripts of *Robin and Ben* are reproduced in *A
Stevenson Medley* (they are not in the Edinburgh Edition):
they illustrate Stevenson's two styles of handwriting; it is loose
and sloping in the earlier draft, close, upright and smaller in the
fair copy.

A manuscript at Yale (Beinecke 6591) lists four titles for
Moral Tales; in addition to the two printed here there are *A
Perfect Cure; or the man of habit*, and *The Expressman's Tragedy*.
There is an unfinished manuscript of *A Perfect Cure* at Yale
(Beinecke 6713).

In the Edinburgh Edition and *A Stevenson Medley*, l. 56 of
The Builder's Doom runs:

Troy rose, with towers encircling it

—but in the 1921 Chatto edition *Troy* has been corrected to
Thebes. In the manuscript of *Moral Tales* (Anderson I, 339)
there is a marginal note by Stevenson referring to this mistake.
'I am informed that there has been some error; but I have a
kindness for the line and would rather do injustice to Amphion
than to my own poetical talents.'

INDEX TO FIRST LINES

INDEX TO FIRST LINES

INDEX TO FIRST LINES

INDEX TO FIRST LINES

INDEX TO FIRST LINES